S0-BIH-371

To George

Many thanks for your skills and willingness to assist us in our assessment plans! You are a true Community Citizen!

Lillian Elsinga

Thanks for your work
@ UND

Alan Allery

Thanks George - for making a great idea! (not just good)
Deb #Heiser

Thank you George for your knowledge & expertise. Very useful + enjoyable!
Rhandi Clow

Thanks for taking the time to share with us!
Me. Dropp

George -
We appreciate you sharing your knowledge & skills on assessment! Thank you for your great presentation to our campus.
Jessie Bopp

Dr. McClellan
Just a huge thank you for this professional development opportunity. I look forward to working with you in the future.
Leigh D.
Jeanette

George,
It's great to have you on our campus. You are an appreciated colleague!
Jerry Bulin

THANKS FOR A GREAT SESSION. I REALLY BENEFITED FROM IT + ENJOYED MEETING YOU. UNTIL NEXT TIME...
Tony

George -
Thank you for the excellent presentation on assessments! Your company was very much enjoyed by all!
Jennifer Kane

Prairie Peddlers

The Syrian-Lebanese in North Dakota

William C. Sherman
Paul L. Whitney
John Guerrero

Cataloging-in-Publication by University of North Dakota

Sherman, William C. (William Charles), 1927 -
      Prairie Peddlers: The Syrian-Lebanese in North Dakota/William
Sherman, Paul Whitney, John Guerrero.—Bismarck, N.D. : University of
Mary Press, 2002.
                          p. : maps;   cm.
              Includes bibliographical references.
              ISBN: 0-9652880-0-5

       The appendix includes the name of every person of Arab back-
ground found to be living in the state in U.S. Census data for 1900, 1910,
and 1920. It also includes naturalization records, land acquisitions records;
list of veterans, name changes, and a list of WPA interviewees.

       1. Lebanese—Social life and customs. 2. Lebanese Americans—
North Dakota—History. 3. Syrian-Americans—North Dakota—History.
4. Lebanese Americans—Cultural assimilation—North Dakota. 5. North
Dakota—History. I. Whitney, Paul. II. Guerrero, John. III. Title: Syrian
Lebanese in North Dakota.

F645.L34 S48 2002

Printed in Canada

Contents

Introduction

Iorth Dakota, a land of severe winters, virtually empty of mountains, sheltered valleys, and visual highlights, spills out across the prairie at least 1,000 miles from any sea. What less likely place for people of the Eastern Mediterranean to settle? From Lebanon, no less; from what has been called the "Riviera of the Middle East." Yet, by the hundreds they came during the homesteading days, taking land alongside the tens of thousands who arrived from more northerly climates: Scandinavians and Germans. By the hundreds they traversed the state as solitary peddlers, walking from farm to farm selling their wares. As the generations ensued, their sons and daughters, like the offspring of other national groups, left the state to become part of a larger American life. Yet it can be said that today, a century after the first arrivals, a thousand of their descendants are still part of the North Dakota scene.

In this book, the authors intend to tell the story of this unique portion of North Dakota's early-day settlers. We hope to present the reader with the times and conditions of their arrival and their dispersal throughout the state. We hope to show the special difficulties these Mediterranean people faced as they adjusted to the America of the Great Plains. Further, the story of those who constituted Dakota's second and third generation Lebanese will be sketched in some detail. Some note will be made concerning those who left the state and are now part of the large cities of America's East and West.

Terminology is a difficult thing. This book will deal with men and women who by birth or ancestry trace their roots to Lebanon. But what is Lebanon? Historical boundaries and political jurisdictions in that far eastern edge of the Mediterranean seem to have been in a continual state of fluidity. To put the matter in the kindest terms, the American reader is confused. The people we will see in the following pages have, at various times, been called Syrians, Assyrians, Mount Lebanese, Syrian-Lebanese,

Turks, Arabians, and Ottomans. In this volume where possible we will try to follow the precedent of Alixa Naff who in discussing the American Lebanese experience in *The Lebanese in the World* said, "For the sake of simplicity—I refer to them as Lebanese and when it makes better sense, as Syrian-Lebanese. They did not refer to themselves as Arabs. Yet Christians, Muslims and Druzes clung proudly to their Arabness. ..."

The Appendix of this volume contains the name of every person of Arab background who was found to be living in the state during the years in which census manuscripts are available for analysis: 1900, 1910, and 1920. Also in the Appendix are three sections that show the remarkable dispersion of the early settlers: naturalization lists, land acquisition records, and First World War veterans' accounts.

Scholars have divided Syrian-Lebanese migration to the Americas into various time periods. The latest of these, often called simply "late migrations," consists of those who came from 1940 to the present decade. These will not be discussed for in North Dakota they often represent individuals of professional or academic backgrounds, men and women who move frequently as their careers demand.

Instead, this volume will concern itself with the Arabic-speaking peoples who came starting in the 1890s and who continued moving to the prairies until World War I. Some few late arrivals in the 1920s and 30s will be mentioned. These "late comers" were often family members who joined immigrants who had already occupied a permanent place in the North Dakota landscape.

The reader will notice that the authors frequently use a series of interviews done sometime in the mid-1930s, but especially from 1939-1940. On these pages, immigrants who came at the turn of the century describe in their own words "the way it was." The interviews, now in the archives of the State Historical Society of North Dakota, were subsidized by federal funds in the midst of the Depression. Called the Federal Writers Project, through the Works Progress Administration, the program sent remarkably insightful individuals throughout North Dakota where they very successfully recorded the memories of pioneer settlers of a variety of ethnic backgrounds. This research survey came about as a part of the Roosevelt Administration's attempt to employ people in the more "white collar" job categories. Several names appear frequently at the introduction to the "Syrian" interviews used in this book. As a kind of posthumous tribute we salute Everal J. McKinnon, Frederick Anderson, and Leona A. Gauthier.

The Federal Writers Project interviews presented in the following chapters will usually be identified by the abbreviation "WPA." The location of the interview and the name of the informant will be included in the text. The reader is reminded that unless indicated otherwise, all these interviews took place between November 1939 and August 1940. The Appendix contains a complete list of the men and women whose accounts were recorded plus the location and precise date of the interview.

Of great help in determining the distribution and date-of-arrival of the early-day Lebanese are the Federal Land Office Tract Book entries. Now on microfilm, these books recorded the land claims in various parts of the state; names, exact locations, dates, and eventual dispositions are, thus, available to the patient researcher.

To the library staff at the State Historical Society of North Dakota we give special thanks. So, too, our gratitude goes to Sandy Slater of the Special Collections of the Chester Fritz Library at The University of North Dakota and to John Bye of the Institute for Regional Studies at North Dakota State University. Beth Postema, J. Stephan Hubbard and Greg Gilstrop of the Fargo Public Library were most helpful. Fr. Sharbel Maroun of the St. Maron's Church in Minneapolis assisted in many ways. Members of the mosque in Cedar Rapids, Iowa (The Cedar Rapids Islamic Center), were generous hosts and insightful "advisers" at the North American Islamic Conference in 1997.

We are especially grateful to a number of knowledgeable individuals who reviewed this volume in its almost-complete stages. First we thank Nicholas V. Samra, former archivist for the American Melkite Catholics and now Auxiliary Bishop of the Diocese of Newton. Bishop Samra has for almost a dozen years taken a special interest in our research. Our thanks go also to Albert Albert of Wilkes-Barre, PA. Mr. Albert, a longtime student of American Maronite history, gave us both good advice and encouragement. We are in debt also to Dr. Fariba Kabiry Roughead and Debbie Absey Kauffman for their help in the discussion of both Muslims and Christians on the prairies. For reviewing and assisting in the study of the North Dakota settlement experience, we thank Charles (Chuck) and Vicky Joseph of Williston, and Richard Omar of Stanley. Needless to say, the authors take full blame for any errors, and certainly part of the credit for accuracy must go to the people we acknowledge in this introduction.

To more than one hundred individuals throughout North Dakota and Minnesota we say "Thanks" for the hours they gave us as we plied them with questions and sought the loan of photographs and documents. We can number only a few, but coming to mind especially are Rosie Juma Chamley, Charlie Juma Sr., Richard Omar, Hassin Abdallah, and Omar Hamdan of Ross and Stanley, ND; Ed Absey, Phil and Al Srur, Phil and Art Deraney, Floyd Fayette, and Charlie Barkie of Grand Forks; John and

Mary Noah, Lyle Swor, Sam Eli, Sam Skaff, Delayne Nassif, James Kallod Jr., the Sam Aggie family, Don Nicholas, Hazel Starr, and Bob Leslie of Fargo; Robert and Pat Freije of Edmore and John Freije of Mayville; Chuck and Vicky Joseph, Vernon and Karma Deane Owan, Ray Atol, Wilber and Charles Kalil, of Williston; Paulette Brown Streitz of Stanley; Floyd Boutrous, Bill Shalhoob, and Eli and Florence Nemer and Helen Azar Youness of Bismarck; Joe and Gene Nicholas of Cando; and Katherine Harris, Ron and Freida Hasen, Shirley Hasen, and Kade and Evelyn Albert of Belcourt; also Diane (Shalala) Fritel of Wolford. In Winnipeg, Manitoba, Albert el Tassie and family. In Crookston, MN, Fr. Dan Noah, Bud Salem, and Lateefe Joseph were most helpful; so also in Cedar Rapids, IA, Mary Nassif, Bill Aossey Jr., David Omar, Joe and Laila Aossey, and Imam Taha Tawil; in Minneapolis, Fr. Sharbel Maroun; in Hutchinson, MN, Lori Kennedy; and of great help in Sioux Falls, SD, James Abourezk (former U.S. Senator). To all, our gratitude.

The authors, often anonymous, of several dozen county histories deserve our gratitude. We are grateful to Edward Wakin and the Our Sunday Visitor Press for permission to use a number of paragraphs from the book *The Immigrant Experience.* So also, we thank Gerald Newborg, Director of Archives, and Delores Vyzralek of The State Historical Society of North Dakota, for allowing us to use the compilation of naturalization records and also the Federal Land Office Tract Book entries found in the Appendix of this volume.

Our thanks go also to Joe Zsedeny and Joy Fisher whose labors made the Federal Land Office List of Acquisitions available through Roots Web (rootsweb.com). Joy Fisher, in particular, searched the Land Office books and compiled the North Dakota list. Joe Zsedeny is the Web File Manager. For permission to use the material in our Appendix we are grateful.

A search of immigrant passenger manifests provided little of value for this North Dakota study.

We appreciate especially the many hours that Blanche Abdallah and Margaret "Peg" O'Leary spent in reviewing the manuscript, not just in terms of factual data, but also literary accuracy.

We are grateful to the typists: Michele Delmore, Ethel Mohn and Lori Beckstead. But in particular we are indebted to Bev Rosencrans, typist, advisor, "corrector," and source of encouragement. To Ken Dorsher we say "Thank You" for the maps found in this volume. Most of all we thank the University of Mary for shepherding this volume through its publication stages. We appreciate especially the support of Sister Thomas Welder, O.S.B., the University president. Our gratitude goes particularly to Jerry Anderson for coordinating and designing this book. Without his expertise this volume would never have been in print. Many individuals helped with the cost of publication. Their names are gratefully printed in the final pages, along with a complete list of men and women who provided much needed information and photographs.

The collection of materials which formed the basis for this volume will be kept at the Archives of the State Historical Society of North Dakota, Heritage Center, Bismarck.

Some References

The discussion of North Dakota's residents of Syro-Arabic background has been infrequent and very limited. The volume, *Plains Folk: North Dakota's Ethnic History,* W. Sherman and P. Thorson, eds. (Fargo, North Dakota: Institute for Regional History, 1988), contains a brief survey of the subject. Francie Berg's *Ethnic Heritage in North Dakota* (Washington, DC: Attiyeh Foundation, 1983), details some personal accounts and cultural features. Of slight value is Gregory Orfalea's "Mosque on the Prairie" (a publication to be taken guardedly), from *Taking Root, Bearing Fruit: The Arab American Experience,* vol. 2, no. 2 (Washington, DC: American-Arab Anti-Discrimination Committee Reports, 1984).

Regional sources are also few in number. Four special publications must be mentioned: *The Way We Were: Arab-Americans in Central Iowa,* by Lee Tesdal et al. (Grand View College, Iowa, 1993), also "Lebanese Immigration to the United States and the Twin Cities, 1890 to 1924," a 1967 unpublished master's thesis by Carol Jean Landis at the University of Minnesota; also *Cedars by the Mississippi: The Lebanese-Americans in the Twin Cities,* by Viviane Doche (San Francisco, R & E Research Assoc., 1978); and "Middle Easterners," by Deborah L. Miller in *They Chose Minnesota,* June Drenning Holmquist, ed., St. Paul, Minnesota Historical Society, 1981.

There are, of course, classic works that provide general background to the Arab-American migrations and life. Most notable is Louise S. Houghton's "Syrians in the United States," *The Survey* (October 1911-March 1912), so also Philip K. Hitti's *The Syrians in America* (New York: George A. Doran, 1924). In this volume the authors refer to Houghton's and Hitti's publications repeatedly. (Houghton's work is so observant and surprisingly accurate; could she have visited North Dakota?) There are other fine works which help in the understanding of Arabic Midwestern settlers, at least in terms of background; notable are: Abdo El Kholy, *The Arab Moslems in the United States* (New Haven: College and University, 1966); Alixa Naff, *Becoming American: The Early Arab Experience* (Carbondale: Southern Illinois Univesity Press, 1985); Philip M. Kayal and Joseph M. Kayal, *The Syrian-Lebanese in America* (Boston: Twayne,

1975); Yvonne T. Haddad and Adair T. Lummis, *Islamic Values in the United States* (New York: Oxford University Press, 1987); Alixa Naff, *The Arab American* (New York: Chelsea House Publications, 1988); Butrous Dau, *History of the Maronites* (no date, no publisher); Yvonne Haddad and Adair T. Lummis, *Muslim Communities in North America* (State University Press of N.Y., 1994); Eric Hooglund, ed., *Crossing the Waters* (Washington, DC: Smithsonian Institute Press, 1987); Elaine Hagopiad and Ann Paben, eds., *The Arab American, Studies in Assimilation* (Wilimette, Ill: Medina University Press, 1969); Adele Younis, *The Coming of Arabic Speaking People to the United States* (Staten Island Center for Migration Studies, 1995).

Helpful to any research such as ours is the collection concerning Arab-Americans at the University of Minnesota's Immigration History Research Center in St. Paul. The Center in 1994 published, for example, an annotated index to the *Syrian World.*

Small scale Muslim difficulties in cultural maintenance which can be seen in this volume are now of nationwide proportions. See a recent volume: Yvonne Y. Haddan and John L. Exposito (eds.), *Muslims on the Americanization Path?* (Oxford, NY: Oxford University Press, 2000).

A variety of information can be found in occasional journals, but the *Muslim World* and *Aramco World Magazine* are of special value. For a worthwhile overview of materials, see Theodore Pulcini, "Trends in Research by Arab-Americans," *Journal of American Ethnic History,* Summer 1993.

CHAPTER ONE

The Geography of Lebanon

Lebanon, a lovely sounding name, comes from the Semitic language root word laban, which means, "to be white." In Aramaic, the language of Jesus Christ, the word also is translated as "whiteness." Indeed, for some, the name conjures up images of cedar trees in the midst of the snow-capped Lebanon Mountains; yet for others the name evokes the image of Middle Eastern deserts with camels and sand. The reality, however, fits neither stereotype. There are elements of both, but Lebanon defies any simple description.

Lebanon, with 4,015 square miles of territory, is smaller than every American state with the exception of Delaware and Rhode Island. When combined, North Dakota's McKenzie County and nearby McLean County—the home of many Lebanese settlers—far exceeds the size of Lebanon.

Located on the eastern edge of the Mediterranean Sea, the Lebanese landscape extends, at its maximum, 135 miles from north to south. Its average width from east to west is less than 35 miles. Lebanon shares a 200-mile border with Syria in the north and east. There is the 45-mile border of Israel to the south.

The American Arab scholar, Philip Hitti, remarked that the beauty of Lebanon "has never ceased to exercise its charm upon poets and bards from Hebrew to Arab times."[1] Distinct contrasts between land and sea, mountain and valley are everywhere complemented by an array of fascinating colors. When magazine writer William Ellis returned to the land of his heritage he described Lebanon as a "panorama of startling, and often spectacular contrasts, as mountains, creased with lush valleys, pressed down against a jagged shoreline."[2]

Lebanon, within its compact land area, is divided into four geographical regions that are parallel to each other in a distinct fashion: (1) a narrow coastal plain, (2) a coastal mountain range known as Mount

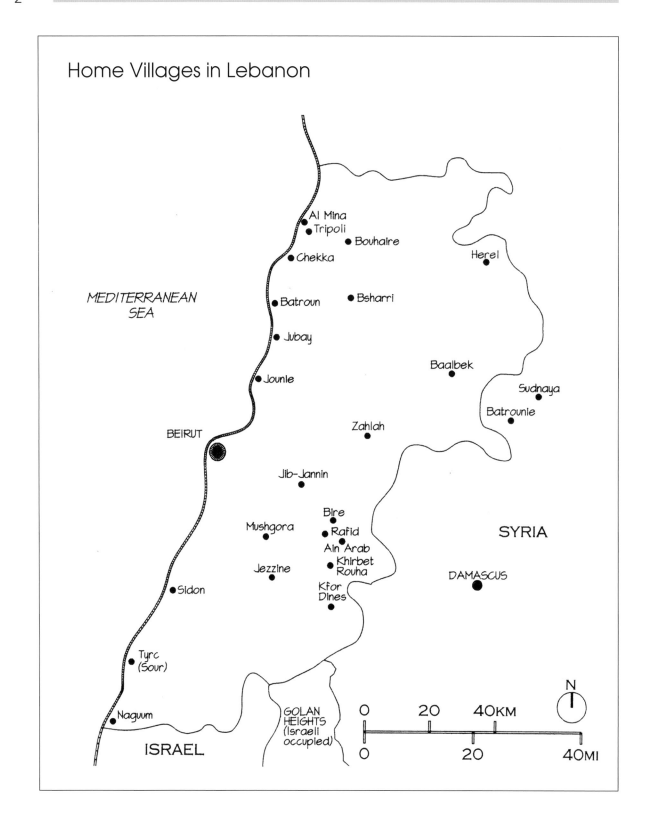

Home Villages in Lebanon

Lebanon, (3) the fertile Bekaa Valley, and (4) a low interior mountain range called the Anti-Lebanon.[3]

Each area has its own characteristics. The first, the coastal plain, is narrow and discontinuous—running the full length of the 135-mile Mediterranean coast. While it is only four miles in width this region contains the major port cities of Beirut, Tripoli, Sidon and Tyre. These large cities, though of great historical importance, provided relatively few settlers to North Dakota. Traditionally, they were the homes for the majority of Lebanon's Sunni Muslims. Today, of course, all sectarian groups reside in these urban areas.

The second region, the coastal mountain range which bears the ancient name, is commonly called Mount Lebanon. This is, in fact, the nucleus of the nation. Within the main range are deep, fertile valleys, which served as a natural refuge for human beings since earliest times. "The Mountain" has always been accepted as "Lebanon" and supports literally hundreds of agricultural villages. It is from this region that many North Dakota and most Minnesota Lebanese immigrants originated. Local, tribal, and religious identifications of the people are deeply rooted in historical tradition and these loyalties reoccur in the American Midwest. It is in this area that we find most of Lebanon's non-Sunni Muslim communities. This region is dotted with settlements of Maronite Catholics, Melkite Catholics, Orthodox Christians, Druze and Shi'a Muslims.

The third area, the Bekaa Valley, is a broad and flat landscape separating the Lebanon and anti-Lebanon ranges. A 1958 *National Geographic* article compared the valley to an "enormous oriental rug unrolled between the mountains." This fertile land produces most of Lebanon's grain, but it is also renowned for its fruits and vegetables. It varies in width from five to eight miles and is watered by two rivers: the Oranti and Litani. The Mount Lebanon regions, with their rugged landscapes, provided safe haven for many political and religious groups. The Bekaa Valley, both prosperous and accessible, attracted invaders and provided minimal refuge for already settled peoples. Over the centuries a succession of forces conquered the region, leaving its security always in a state of jeopardy. Today, the Bekaa is characterized by separatism and on occasion the antagonism of many religious groups such as the Sunni and Shi'a Muslims, the Antiochian Orthodox (often called the Syrian Orthodox), the Maronite Catholics, Melkite Catholics, and the Druze. North Dakota's Muslims came primarily from the towns of Bire, Rafid, Kfar Dines and Khirbet Rouha, all in the Bekaa Valley near the southwestern border of Syria. Most of North Dakota's Orthodox Christians came from the Bekaa town of Ain Arab, just a few miles from the Muslim villages. An assortment of Orthodox and Melkites in North Dakota came from Zahle, further north in the Bekaa Valley.

Finally, there exists the lower interior mountain range called the Anti-Lebanon, which extends along the border of Syria. It is divided by the plateau and gorge of Barada. The southern part of the range features Mt. Hermon, a 9,383-foot majestic peak. The western slope has many villages that sent its native sons and daughters to all corners of the earth. Some few villages, located near present-day Syrian borders, sent people to North Dakota, but they were in small numbers. Those that did go to the American Midwest were mostly Christian, yet a few were of Muslim or Druze background.[4]

The Physical Environment of Lebanon

Attempting, no doubt, to relate to Westerners, writers have referred to Lebanon as being the "Switzerland of the Middle East." They have characterized Beirut as the "Paris of the Mediterranean."[5] If so, a logical question would be why would its inhabitants leave such an idyllic setting and move to remote places such as North Dakota and Minnesota? As will be seen, this exodus was influenced heavily by socioeconomic factors. Yet the physical environment of Lebanon also made the movement possible.

Vegetation zones of Lebanon offer a set of abrupt contrasts. Within sixty miles from the Mediterranean Sea one encounters banana plantations, winter sport resorts and desert oases. The vegetation of the coastal plain features evergreen shrubs and quick-flowering spring plants. Many of the world's main food crops—types of wheat, barley and millet—underwent early domestication there. Also flourishing on the Lebanese landscape are varieties of vegetables, tobacco and ancient fruits including figs, olives, dates and grapes. Other crops have been introduced by conquering forces or by trade.[6]

The crests of Lebanon's mountains suffer low winter temperatures that are inhospitable to the temperate zone shrubs and subtropical palms. What do survive the higher altitudes are hardy figs and cedar trees. Lebanon is, of course, renowned in history for its magnificent cedars. This tree provided the early Phoenicians with the finest of timbers for their seafaring ships. Ancient prophets wrote of its durability and carving suitability. The Maronite Christians have long used the cedar as a religious symbol. The American University of Beirut employs it as type of logo and the Republic of Lebanon adopted it as a centerpiece on its national flag.[7]

It is unfortunate that the glory days of the Lebanese cedar have passed. Today it survives in only small groves. The best-known cluster is above Becharre (Bisharri), birthplace of the mystic poet Kahlil Gibran. (Incidentally, this village area is the ancestral home of America's popular Danny Thomas.) As they still exist, overlooking the beautiful "Wadi Qadisha" or "Holy Valley," these trees continue to evoke a powerful emotional response.

Climate

Western visitors to Lebanon soon become aware of the fact that some Lebanese residents have two residences, one for the winter, the other for summer. Typically, a Mediterranean climate along the coast offers a hot, humid and sometimes nine-month summer along with a moderate rainy winter of three months. Thus, the cool and invigorating mountains attract people during the Middle East summer. But when the snows of winter fall, residents soon seek refuge on the coast.[8]

The Bekaa Valley in some ways is comparable to the Midwest of the United States in terms of a routine agrarian lifestyle. Its past, however, in contrast to that of the relatively peaceful American frontier, has been marked by conflict on countless occasions. As will be seen, for centuries the desert occupants along the Syrian border have looked with covetous eyes on the lands "flowing with milk and honey."[9]

The average annual temperature in Beirut is 68 degrees Fahrenheit, but at times the dust-laden winds of Damascus bring an intense summer heat. The winters are generally mild. This contrasts starkly with the extremes of North Dakota's harsh continental climate. (One wonders how the early Great Plains immigrant adapted to the particular challenges, for example, of a long and sometimes brutal winter.)

As Lebanon's prevailing "westerlies" sweep over the Mediterranean they fill with moisture. Records show Beirut receives about 36 inches of rain annually, which is more than twice as much precipitation as southern California's coastline. When the winds encounter the Lebanon Mountains they lose moisture. Much of the rainfall is lost when it percolates through limestone rock. Some of it is evident in Lebanon's gushing springs.

Land productivity has declined due to improper soil conservation, deforestation and overgrazing. Although originally covered with forests, erosion has taken place and in recent centuries the higher mountain slopes are often bare and desolate.[10]

The discussion of Lebanon's geography sketched in the previous pages is presented for two reasons. The first is to give the reader some sense of the unique physical setting in which North Dakota's Arab settlers spent their younger years. Many observers have remarked that "the physical surroundings of our youth affect our character"; whether slightly or greatly is a matter which the "experts" frequently debate. Second, the contrast of the two worlds, Lebanon and the Dakotas, becomes apparent. But the contrast is not as dramatic as one would expect. Lebanon was neither a Mediterranean beach resort, nor a land of drifting sand dunes and oases. It too had its rugged landscapes, its harsh extremes. And Great Plains phenomena such as grain and livestock, not to mention aridity and precarious agricultural markets, were often part of the Lebanese small town and farming scene. Life in Lebanon could in some ways be as difficult as life on the primitive prairies of the Dakotas.

Lebanon: Its Multi-colored Past

An encyclopedia says, "The Lebanese are a Semitic people, descended from Phoenicians, Hebrews, Arameans and Arabs of ancient times with a mixture of non-Semitic conquering peoples."

Who were the conquering peoples? The earliest seem to have been Hittites, Egyptians, Greeks, and Romans with a continuing influx of tribes from the Arabian Desert. Since the 16th century the Ottoman Turks, France, and England have each ruled the area.

In recent decades, Syrian and Israeli armies have been active in some Lebanese territory. So also the United Nations has had "relief camps" on Lebanese soil. And not to forget the U.S. Marines, who, on two occasions, have occupied parts of Lebanon to help bring stability to the region.

Cedars of Lebanon

Something like 400 cedars are carefully preserved, especially in the Bisharri region of Lebanon. These are all that remain of the rather extensive forests of pre-Christian days. The handsome trees are now found at 6,000-foot altitudes. Their height today is from 60 to 70 feet, but in ancient times they could grow as high as 100 feet. The aromatic and durable wood was excellent for beams in large buildings and, not surprisingly, the Egyptians, Babylonians and Assyrians made use of the cedar centuries before Christ. Some reports say the timbers were in Middle-Eastern use as early as 2000 B.C. (The huge tree trunks were dragged down the mountainsides and floated down the rivers.) King Solomon, in the Old Testament, used cedar panels and beams in his temple. Biblical accounts revere the cedars of Lebanon as symbols of strength and prosperity.

The Isaacs of Crookston

Bob Isaac was born in Crookston, Minnesota, in 1951. His life reflects both loyalty to Lebanon and the intermingling of cultures which occurs with the passing of generations in America. His mother, Sally, was Polish from the Senske-Rebelski clan; his father, John, was the son of Jacob and Rose Isaac, who came from Bouhaire, Lebanon in 1909 to join relatives in Crookston. Jacob and Rose left two small children in Lebanon with their parents, only to have both die during World War I. Bob said the sadness never left his grandparents' eyes.

Bob's grandfather, his Dad, and he himself were long-time Great Northern Railway employees. Of Maronite Catholic heritage, the Isaacs often spoke Arabic at home and cooked Lebanese foods such as kibbi and kousa. Grandfather Jacob Isaac's sister Christine married Michael Noah and raised eleven children. Jacob and Rose's daughters also lived in Crookston with Sadie marrying Peter George and running a grocery store.

Bob Isaac's parents raised ten children and the family followed railroad jobs to Rugby, Sauk Centre, and finally to Fargo. Retired now, Bob he sees his life filled with family allegiance, religious faith, and mobility: all traits which epitomize the Lebanese character.

Vernon and Karma Deane Owan

In the late 1970s, Vern and Karma Owan of Williston traveled to the land of their ancestors. They had little inkling of the good fortune that awaited them. They visited Saydnaya, Syria, a famous place northeast of Damascus, which was known as the site of many miracles. (Jesus and the Virgin Mary had been there 2000 years beforehand.) Saying their prayers, accordingly, they toured the local Greek Orthodox convent. It was at this spot that they received word from North Dakota that a baby had been born. The adoption agency said it was to be their child. The Owans were thankful and overjoyed. (The "miracle" child would receive the name Waheide (or Wendy). She has since blessed Vern and Karma with other "miracle" grandchildren.)

CHAPTER TWO

CHAPTER TWO

History

Modern Lebanon, at least in the minds of many people, plays a highly visible and even integral role in the life of the greater Arab world. But it would be a mistake to extend this present-day perception too far, certainly when one analyzes the nation's complex geographical, historical and cultural roots.

Geographically, Lebanon's 4,015 square miles of territory are few when compared to the 5.25 million square miles of entire Arab world. While what can be called the Arab nations extends several thousand miles from Morocco in the west to the Arabian Sea in the east, Lebanon is only thirty to forty miles wide in most areas. North to south the Arab world encompasses the land from the Mediterranean Sea to Central Africa. By contrast, Lebanon makes up only 135 miles of this longitudinal spread.[1]

Lebanon occupies a tiny portion of the globe, yet rivals many larger nations when it comes to natural beauty and history. Traditionally the Lebanese were considered "middlemen" or "tradesmen." This is no accident. Their land was small in size yet it proved to be the meeting place for Asian, Mediterranean and African worlds.

The Phoenicians

Lebanon can, in fact, be best understood as a crossroads of culture and commerce. Indeed, this strategic position proved to be its lifeblood for many centuries. As early as the twelfth century B.C., recorded history tells us that people traversed the lands of modern Lebanon. Archeologists suggest that some settlements may have been inhabited continuously for more than 7,000 years. Lebanon's first permanent inhabitants referred to themselves as Canaanites, whom the Greeks later called Phoenicians. Along the coastal plain these early settlers established the great city-states of Tyre, Byblos and Sidon. These people represent the earliest ancestors of many of today's Lebanese residents. Archeological discoveries support their fascinating story.[2]

Because the Phoenicians are so central to the Lebanese self-concept (at least for the Maronites), a few words on these early people would be in order. In ancient times, Phoenicians abandoned the inland mountain barriers and turned instead to the sea for their livelihood. Besides creating their fabled twenty-two letter Semitic alphabet, they formed trading relationships with distant lands. Their prowess as navigators was legendary. The Phoenicians eventually established colonies across North Africa, including Carthage, a rival of the Roman republic. Their cargo ships traded goods such as glass, dyes and textiles as far away as the British Isles. Historians have often noted the ways in which Phoenician achievements left their legacy on many early moments of Western history. Not the least was the fact that East and West were brought into closer contact by these seafarers as they established their wide network of trading posts.

In the eighth century B.C. the Assyrians, followed thereafter by the Babylonians and Persians, conquered the Phoenicians. From Macedonia came Alexander the Great who captured Phoenicia in 322 B.C. His successors would rule until 64 B.C., when Pompey would bring it under Roman control. Archeological sites throughout Lebanon attest to these various periods. The Baalbek temple ruins, for example, are among the most impressive vestiges of the Roman period.[3]

But it was not only political and commercial forces that shaped the land. The myriad of Lebanon's religions would provide deep-seated and continuing influences. Christianity can trace some of its earliest and even grandest moments to this land. Indeed, the Maronites represent an indigenous Lebanese church dating to the fourth century A.D. This religious group never separated from communion with the Holy See. Not surprisingly, it endured many centuries of persecution for its loyalty to Rome. And accordingly, "Latinization" has often been a problem. With the arrival of Byzantine invaders came various Eastern versions of Christianity. These groups continue to flourish in Lebanon. This fact alone would serve to place Lebanon into a specific category when discussing what is called the Arab world. Christianity not only flourishes in Lebanon, but its membership in recent centuries has often been equal to and sometimes even surpassing that of Islam in statistical totals.[4]

By the seventh century A.D., the Muslim faith came on the scene with the expansion of the Umayad Empire. The Arabic language and the Islamic religion would be powerful unifying factors throughout Southwest Asia and into North Africa. In later centuries the Abbassides and the Fatimads ruled Lebanon. Conflict with Christian crusaders would force Muslims to temporarily relinquish territory but, by the end of the thirteenth century, Lebanon would be incorporated into the Egyptian Mameluk Empire. At that time the Maronites were concentrated in the northern mountain region, or what was previously described as the Mount Lebanon region.

The modern pattern of Christians and Muslims living throughout Lebanon had certainly been shaped by these early experiences. It is true there were times when Muslim caliphs and Christian princes were rivals for power, but there were also times and regimes during which all groups lived in peaceful coexistence.

In 1516 Lebanon became a subdivision of the Ottoman Turkish Empire. While a certain degree of autonomy was granted from the seventeenth century on, later years would witness a growing resentment toward Turkish domination. French soldiers intervened in 1860 and established Mount Lebanon as an autonomous principality. Although Arab nationalism had not yet emerged, this action was viewed as European interference, particularly by Muslims. World War I saw the Ottoman Empire side with the Central Powers. The resulting peace settlements witnessed the dismemberment of the Ottoman Empire. A League of Nations mandate brought French rule to Lebanon, but a distinct Lebanese identity was soon to be asserted. In 1926, the nation was proclaimed to be the Lebanese Republic. Full independence, however, was not acquired until 1943.* This occurred in the midst of World War II and Lebanon found itself occupied by French troops until 1946. Only then did it see itself as a completely free nation.

The post World War II era witnessed Lebanon's religious mosaic give way to sectarian strife. As is well known, a bitter civil war based upon religious allegiance ensued throughout from 1975 to 1990. It was a confusing period, Christians pitted against Christians, Muslims against Muslims, and some groups such as Orthodox adherents and the Druze were caught in-between. (United States Marines arrived in 1958, hoping to stabilize the situation.) Lebanese foreign relations hardly fared better with an Israeli invasion in 1982 and the subsequent arrival of another group of American marines. The violence of those two decades turned Beirut from the "Paris of the Mediterranean" to a war-torn city filled with ruins. In short, political, economic and cultural chaos had confused the whole issue of Lebanese national identity. Yet Lebanese ethnic perseverance seems to have deep roots. Signs of resurgence keep appearing.[5] This national identity is evidenced not only in Lebanon, but wherever its immigrants have put down roots, including such distant places as Minnesota and North Dakota.

---

* The census nomenclature difficulties which emerged at a later date in America have their origins in these shifting political centers: "Turkey in Asia" in the 1910 Census; "Syria" in the 1920 Census; "Lebanon" after 1926.

Home Villages

The history of Lebanon and the geography of Lebanon were present in the lives of early Great Plains Syrian-Lebanese settlers in a very personal and localized perspective. They had some notion of the centuries- old past and some appreciation of the broad sweep of their home country's terrain. But all this was seen through the focus of their home village. For that reason the authors chose to discuss, early in this volume, the villages that are most often mentioned as places of birth and departure points for Lebanese emigrants who journeyed to the New World.

A village loyalty was not unique to American Lebanese. It was basic to almost every immigrant group. Will Herberg, in *Protestant, Catholic and Jew*, says quite bluntly: "Immigrants were men of their village and region."[6] Herberg insists that only after a period of residence in pluralistic America did the immigrant begin to identify with others of their national group. In America they discovered what it meant to be members of a homeland, whether a kingdom, a nation, or a particular country.

Zahle

The largest city in the central Lebanon Mountains is Zahle. This beautiful city is on the edge of the fertile Bekaa Valley, thus making it the center of a large trade area. It is also the largest town between Beirut and Damascus. If Beirut were known as "the Paris of the Mediterranean," Zahle would be "the Venice," for the city contains many "canals," making the aquatic scenery quite similar to its Italian "sister city."[7] Zahle is of particular significance to North Dakota. Hundreds of present-day residents remember it as the "home of my ancestors."

Zahle, at least in the nineteenth century, was located in an "autonomous" zone of the Ottoman Empire, an area that gave the residents religious and a certain political freedom (even, for a while, exemption from the draft). Sometimes, when asked their nationality in the early U.S. Census, the immigrant would say "Mount Lebanon."

In 1940, Mrs. David Kalil of Williston, remembering her youth, recalled that it was a "nice place to live," not very warm and not very cold. She remarked that it never froze there but "it did get chilly sometimes." If it snowed it would melt quickly. Mrs. Kalil's birthplace was in the mountains just outside of Zahle. Her father raised wheat, cattle and silkworms. The family made raisins, wine and syrups too; figs, peaches, apples and walnuts were also common.

Zahle is largely a Christian town; in fact, the largest Christian town in Lebanon. A prominent religious group in Zahle is called Melkite, an eastern rite in the Catholic Church, sometimes referred to as "Greek

Catholic" because of its historical roots and Byzantine-style liturgy. Also found in Zahle are members of the Orthodox Christian tradition, both Greek and Syrian. In addition, there are Maronites and Latin Rite Catholics and even some Protestants.

The customs and landscapes of Zahle were well recorded in the Works Progress Administration (WPA) interviews conducted during the late 1930s in North Dakota. John Kassis of Williston, for example, remembered his youth in Zahle:

We had hunting and swimming, that's about all the recreation we had. They don't have any parks like in this country, but places we could go along the river and make dams with stones, and then swim in it. They don't have girls and boys play together, one place for girls and one for boys.

Another Williston resident who recalled Zahle's recreational life was Edward Nedoff. Prominent in his memory are small streams with the people listening to music and sometimes dancing and drinking. Syrian dances such as the "debke" were most evident during weddings. Since he was the son of a priest he spent "plenty" of his time in church as an "altar boy."

A relatively large number of Zahle-born immigrants settled in the Rugby area of Pierce County. Perhaps half of the Lebanese settlers in that county were Orthodox. A great proportion of the others were Melkite.

Further east in North Dakota, Walsh County saw other Zahle families such as the Abseys, Deraneys and Fayettes. (Abseys were probably the first Walsh County "Syrian" settlers.) In 1863, Nassif Freije was born in Zahle to Elias and Sadie Freije. He left beautiful Zahle in 1890 for St. Paul, Minnesota. Within a short time he embarked upon a journey that would take him to rural North Dakota. The Orthodox Freije clan first settled in Walsh and later moved to Ramsey County.

In Towner County the Auseys from Zahle were amongst the state's first Arabic homesteaders (later changing the name to Nicholas). The descendants of the above mentioned Auseys, Freijes, and Abseys still cook a specialty of Zahle called *kibbi* (ground lamb, either raw or cooked, mixed with bulghor wheat, onions and pine nuts). *Tabbouli*, another Zahle favorite, is also featured (crushed bulghor wheat mixed with parsley, mint, onions, tomatoes, and olive oil). Exotic foods, at least to the American eye, abounded in Zahle and it is no wonder that this city, built amid picturesque mountain scenes, should be famous for its brightly painted open-air cafes.

Muslim Villages

North Dakota's earliest Muslim residents came primarily from the Lebanese towns of Bire, Rafid, Kfar Dines, Khirbet Rouha, Jib (Joub) Jannine, and Karoun. These small cities are located in the southern part of the Bekaa Valley not far from the Syrian border. With the exception of Karoun the towns are clustered only a few miles apart. They are about 40 miles southeast of Beirut, 20 miles south from Zahle and three miles from Ain Arab. A few miles to the east is Damascus, Syria.

These agricultural villages, with their land nearby, supported small crops such as fruits, figs, grapes and beans. Wheat and barley were staples and typically were planted on what amounted to only a few acres of land since the mountain ranges are nearby. Some wheat was actually planted on the rocky landscapes. Animals such as sheep, goats and cows helped support what Ghali Abraham of Binford, N.D. still remembers as a "difficult way of living."

During the 1890s, conditions in many of the Muslim villages were such that the scene was set for the people to think in terms of America. In a series of late 1930s WPA interviews, a number of North Dakotans recalled the land of their birth. One such person was Mrs. Mary Juma of Ross, who remembered Bire, Lebanon, as being a village located in a valley. "The land surrounding the village was level, extending two miles on each side of a river meeting rougher and more rolling land." Mrs. Juma said her husband's farm was so small that mere survival was difficult. Many people in the vicinity were "migrating to America." With letters arriving about the new riches almost everyone at least contemplated leaving Syria and moving to a better part of the world.

Another resident of Bire was Husien "Sam" Omar who grew up in a local farm family. Years later, in North Dakota, he recalled the Old Country meals which consisted of mutton, beef, goat meat, vegetables and bread. No liquor was served. Since he rented land he had nothing to sell when he left for Mountrail County, North Dakota, in 1902.

Allay Omar of Ross, in the WPA interviews, stated that the homes of Bire were surrounded by orchards that made for a "lovely village of about 1,000 people." His father's farm consisted of 40 acres of wheat, 35 acres of oats, 20 acres of lentils and 5 acres for cattle feed. A team of oxen with a wooden walking plow was used for tillage. "Seeding and harvesting was done by hand."

A few miles away, to the south, was the town of Rafid. Side Abdallah of Ross, North Dakota, when interviewed, said his family lived near Rafid on "level land that was surrounded by hills." All in all, they owned about one hundred acres. The family was kept busy growing wheat, oats, and beans. They also had 200 goats, sheep and chickens. Cheese, butter and fruit were occasionally hauled to the market on a donkey's back.

Another Rafid immigrant was Hassin Alla Juma who in a WPA interview said his farm home was a two-story rock house with a roof made from earth, brush and poles. Filling the countryside were fig, peach, apple and pear trees. Grapes were plentiful as well. The domestic foods consisted of ground wheat, mutton, olives, along with jellies and jams. He remembered, "At mealtime, everyone in the family ate together."

Amid "Mike" Abdallah of Ross was born in Rafid about 1886. He remembered, in a 1940 account, that the village had a population of about 400 people and that most of the houses were constructed on level land near the mountains.

My home was a one story six-room stone building, about 30 x 40 feet. The floor was made like all the other homes in the Old Country, poles about six inches in diameter were laid side by side on the ground, then space between the poles was filled with smaller poles and branches. Then we mixed clay with water till it made a very thick mud. This was packed in between the poles and on top of the poles with a very heavy roller, then lime was spread on the top of the clay while the clay was still wet. Then the heavy roller was used more until the lime was worked into the clay. When this became all dry it would harden like cement. The floors for the second story were made the same way.

These are the recollections of actual villagers who left their native Lebanon and found themselves in a very different world: North Dakota. As if to put things in perspective, Kassem Ramadan, of Muslim background, when reminiscing with an interviewer at Bowbells, ND in October 1939, recalled his home village in Lebanon: "hilly and mountainous," "much like California."

I was born March 10, 1892, on a farm near Damascus, Syria. My home was a large stone house in which there were three rooms upstairs and three rooms downstairs. The rooms were rather large, being about 18 ft. by 20 ft. each. These rooms had fireplaces in which we burned hickory wood or charcoal. I lived three miles from a river. … The climate was very warm—much like California. Sometimes during the winter we would get two or three feet of snow, but it would all disappear in a day or two.

Later in the book other personal accounts will deal with villagers' memories of social and economic circumstances.

Ain Arab

Situated in the midst of this cluster of Muslim towns was the Christian village of Ain Arab, a village whose name occurs in dozens of North Dakota family accounts. Located about 40 miles southeast of

Beirut, the major Ain Arab Christian churches in town were of Orthodox affiliations. Muslims lived in the town but were a minority.

At least from a Dakota perspective, the most prominent family in Ain Arab was the Attiyehs, descendants of a Christian Arab tribe that ruled the southern Syrian desert in the eighth century A.D. Waves of Islam spread through the area and many of these nomadic tribesmen were converted to that religious tradition, yet most were to remain Christian. The Christian Attiyehs sought refuge over the centuries in a number of villages in Syria and Lebanon. Eventually, however, many, if not most, came to regard Ain Arab as their home.[8]

In the 1890s, Ain Arab was a well-established village consisting of about 60 limestone houses. Many of the homes had the red-tiled roofs that seem to have been typical of the region. Today, although a number of clans reside in Ain Arab, numerically the largest seems to be that of the Attiyeh, whose modern North Dakota surnames include the Nassifs, Boutrous, Sabas, Skaffs, Nicolas, and Kellels.

Thomas Nassif of Bismarck grew up in Ain Arab. In August 1939 he remembered the following:

> *I was born in Ain Arab, Lebanon, Syria in 1893 or 1894. Ain Arab at that time had a population of about five-hundred people, mostly consisting of farmers, although there were a few storekeepers, a few tradesmen, flour mill operators, winery and distillery operators and men who made cooking utensils of brass and other metals. The people lived in the village but their farms were situated on the outskirts of the small town. The raising of grapes, olives, figs and fruit is the main industry in this section of the country, however a certain amount of farming is also done.*

Ain Arab is positioned on relatively flat ground in a mountainous area situated in the southern portion of the Bekaa Valley. North and east of the city are high mountains; an extensive forest spreads to the east of town. The most common turn-of-the-century travel methods were either by foot, horse, or donkey.

Aware of the American practice of living on isolated country farmsteads and journeying on rare occasions "to town" for special needs, Louie Nassif of Bismarck in August 1939 describes the Ain Arab of his childhood:

> *I was born on September 1, 1909 in the Ain Arab, Lebanon, Syria. Ain Arab at that time had a population of about five-hundred people, most of which were farmers. However, there were a few storekeepers, a flour mill, and some wineries to make wine out of the grapes raised by the people on the farms which surrounded the farm [sic]. Farming is the chief industry in this vicinity and all of the people live in town instead of on their individual farms.*

George Saba was the son of Ain Arab settlers who came to North Dakota at the turn of the century. Born in the United States in 1903, he returned with his family to Syria in 1906. In 1935 he came back to the country of his birth, settling eventually in Bismarck. As an adult he experienced the contrasts between the two worlds. In July 1939 he said:

Ain Arab has a population of about 500 people and is located in the farming region; the people live in the town and farm the land surrounding the village. Arrac, which is the favorite drink is manufactured in Ain Arab as are other wines and it is made from the grapes which grow so bountiful here. Then there is the flour mill which my father owned and outside of this there is very little manufacturing of any kind going on. However, there are some hand manufacturing of kettles, and other utensils from brass. I have a coffee pot and a coffee brewer which are made of brass and are over 150 years old. It has been owned by my people all that time having been made by a distant relative of mine.

One may speculate that the confusion of Ain Arab's historical influences may have played a role in its residents seeking "greener pastures" in the United States. An Attiyeh Society history reminded its members that "some 2000 years ago, the imperial Romans gathered much of their grain in this region. Hordes of Bedouins of a later date traditionally escaped the summer heat here, entering the region through mountain passes. Waves of invaders and traveling merchants crossed the Ain Arab countryside."[9] Mobility was clearly a theme of the past. To move to a new world or to a new "home village" was a possibility that could be both attractive and attainable. George Saba, of Ain Arab, speaking in 1939, said that the Attiyeh Society, is "an organization of my relatives here in the United States; brothers, cousins, 1st, 2nd, 3rd, uncles and so on. They number now something over a thousand."

Maronite Catholics in Minnesota

During the 1950s Thomas Abercrombie, a foreign editor of *National Geographic,* visited Lebanon. While hunting with President Camille Chamoun he was asked by his distinguished companion, "Just where in the United States are you from?" Abercrombie responded, "Minnesota," whereupon Chamoun said "Land of Ten Thousand Lakes. I've been there. Some of the best duck hunting in the world."[10] As it turns out, Camille Chamoun had not just ducks on his mind when he thought of that American state; a surprising number of Lebanon's American grandchildren call Minnesota their home.[11]

Since the major focus of this book is about North Dakota, the Minnesota section will understandably be less in size. Nevertheless, there is a very real connection between Minnesota and North Dakota, both in trade and in cultural linkage. The reader will note later in this volume that St. Paul and the northwestern town of Crookston, Minnesota were of particular significance in the Lebanese movement to and from North Dakota.

The portion of Lebanon from which many Minnesotan Lebanese migrated is called "Aiz al Rabb" or Cedars of the Lord. Ancient Phoenicians cut timber there as they constructed the famous galleys that allowed them to roam the seas. King Solomon embellished his temple with specially chosen cedar from these woods. As has already been mentioned, the trees today are tragically scarce, yet they remain something of a national treasure.

In the midst of this region, slightly north of the cedars area, the villages of Bouhaire and Toula are located. These towns supplied nearly all of Crookston's Lebanese community and many of St. Paul's as well.

Bouhaire, Lebanon, is a town of roughly 2,500 people located in a beautiful mountain valley. Landscapes in the region abound with waterfalls that tumble down from the nearby hillsides. The most famous river in the area is named "Ain Gubash." George and Sarah Gubash of suburban St. Paul know it well since their families originated there. The Gubashs, through the decades and today, regale their listeners with stories that express their great affection for their village. It was a city of beauty, without lawns but replete with gardens. It was a city widely known for the quality of its apples, which were a thriving part of its regional trade ventures. Water, a priceless resource in the Middle East, flowed in copious quantities in Bouhaire. Not surprisingly, tensions often arose over possession of such a commodity. Gubashs remember that the neighboring village of Aslout, with about 800 people, often bargained and sometimes threatened Bouhaire residents over the matter of water distribution.[12]

The first Lebanese in Minnesota were probably two brothers from Toula, John and Sarkis Peter, who arrived in St. Paul in 1882. While establishing themselves they wrote letters to the "folks back home" about the economic opportunities in St. Paul. Within a few years the two men were joined by a great number of their former neighbors from the "triangle villages" of Toula, Bouhaire and Hadchit. (Some also came from Aslout.) Minnesota and the Dakotas had proved to be fertile ground for peddling and other easily accessible occupations. Some peddlers eventually "took root" in the Twin Cities, some in Crookston, and some in North Dakota. Enough money could be made in a reasonable amount of time for the peddler to become part of a community, buy a home, and eventually educate his or her children. These profoundly religious people were almost exclusively Maronites.[13]

Minnesota, a land of lakes and prairies, would prove to be sometimes similar and sometimes decidedly different from the home regions of Lebanon. Minnesota farming methods they encountered on arriving in America mirrored very often the practices that were part of the newcomers' younger years: the one-bottom plow, the harvest tasks, "wheat, barley, and oats." The similarity stopped, however, when they found the New World had few "grapes" and no "figs and dates."

The memory of farming in Lebanon, as recorded by Louis Nassif of Bismarck in August 1939, probably reflects the sentiments of the Bouhaire and Toula immigrants.

Our method of farming was rather primitive as we used an old fashioned plow which was made of wood and an iron point or plow share fastened to the end of the plow beam. The plow did not turn the land over but dug a shallow ditch somewhat like our modern cultivators. The grain was then broadcast on the field by hand as evenly as possible. ... The threshing was done by clearing a small portion of the field and laying the bundles on the cleared land and making the cattle trample on it. The grain was cut with a hand scythe and gathered into bundles, then loaded on mules or horses and taken to the field where it was to be threshed.

A Tribute to Our "Roots"

A Poem by Floyd A. Nassif, M.D., 1981

Ain Arab,
- Its very name affects one's heart,
And stirs within us
- memories that never part,
Ain Arab,
- a village, cradled in mountains high,
Within whose boundaries
- our beginnings lie.
Its historic site, in Lebanon
- lies where Crusaders chose to be;
Rustic, ancient beauty is there
- for all to see
Ain Arab,
- where our ancestors lived, so long ago,
Still lingers in our memories
- which, forever, cast their glow.

Emigrants, at the turn of the century
- left this village home,
To journey to far away places
- they had never known.
Courage to seek new opportunities
- overcame fears within the heart;
When from their parents and loved ones
- they would, forever, part.
Many of our fathers and mothers
- told of that one last look, behind;
The sight of stone houses
- that would always live in one's mind.
Time cannot erase that Ain Arab
- still casts its touch,
Upon those for whom Heritage
- meant so much.

Ain Arab,
- graceful in its vale on mountainside,
Still bears the same image
- that time could never hide.
Stone houses still stand in places
- its children knew, so well;
The sorrows within their bosoms
- one could never tell.
The mountains still shelter the village
- with its stately view;
The colorful plains still glimmer
- under the skies, so blue.
The picture still lives of mountain shadows
- from darkening skies, as they fell;
Caressing the village in colors
- that words could never tell.

Ain Arab, mother of many
- has spread its heart on earth;
To many famous and successful people
- it has given birth.
Strength, forged in the flames of hope
- has marked their life;
The will of its children to be free
- came from times of strife.
The century is fast closing
- upon those who left, so long ago;
The Torch of Heritage from their hands to ours
- will always glow;
We will always respect these pioneers
- whose heads were held high,
And they will live, forever, in our hearts and thoughts
- and so will never die!

CHAPTER THREE

Religion

The label "German" in North Dakota—and for that matter, much of the United States—is used to describe a variety of independent groups. At least a dozen different kinds of Germans with varying pasts and religious affiliations exist in North Dakota. We should not be surprised, therefore, that the term "Syrian" embraces also a variety of unique peoples. The word Syrian or better still, Lebanese, refers to people not only from a certain geographic origin, but also to adherents of a number of religions, all inherited from the Old Country: Orthodox Christian, Eastern Rite Catholics with ties to Rome (Melkite and Maronite), and Muslim.* [1]

At least a thousand years of religious and political tension stand behind the various divisions. The Christians, for example, can be classed as Semitic in origin. As seen earlier in this volume, some claim that they are the descendants of the Phoenicians of Greek and Roman times. The Arab conquest of the Near East in the 8th century brought Islamic religious traditions in its wake, and although there were periods of suppres-

---

* A note on religious nomenclature: The Maronites were the most numerous of Arab Christians at the turn of the century, both in Lebanon and in early migrations to America. They came often to the New World with the Melkite Christians. Sometimes the Melkites are called Greek Catholics, but that too is confusing. Ukrainian Catholics and other groups have at times been labeled as Greek Catholic. Both the Maronite Catholics and the Melkite Catholics are affiliated with Rome.

Lebanese of Orthodox persuasion have also been called Greek Orthodox. They were at one time part of the international Greek Orthodox Church which before World War I looked to clergy in pre-Communist Russia for guidance. After that war, the Arabic-speaking Orthodox recognized the patriarch in Antioch as a spiritual leader. They are sometimes referred to as Antiochian Orthodox or Syrian Orthodox.

Needless to say, the variance in affiliations of both the Orthodox and Rome-affiliated Catholics led to some confusion among early midwestern Arabic immigrants.

A tiny proportion of Lebanese Christians were of Coptic and Armenian background. These individuals are seldom if ever highlighted in the American Lebanese experience.

Muslims who came to the Dakotas were invariably identified as Mohammadans. This term is unacceptable today. Muslim refers to the person and Islam is the name of the religous tradition. The division Shi'a and Sunn'i, used often in today's news accounts, seems to have little meaning in terms of early-day Muslim experience in midwestern America.

sion, scholars say that the Muslim armies and regimes were remarkably tolerant of Christian and Jewish religious convictions. Only rarely were serious attempts made to force conversions. The Koran, in fact, forbids such compulsion. Both Jews and Christians are "people of the book."[2]

Of particular significance to North Dakota were the religious affiliations of the Christians from Syria. Philip Kayal says that "nearly 90% of all Arabic-speaking immigrants arriving before 1924 were Syrian Christians.[3]

Religious affiliations in the United States, influenced by the memory of the wars of religion after the Reformation and moderated by the American sense of pluralism, led the usual American resident to see religious adherence as a quiet and personal matter. Observers of the Old World Syrian scene say that, in contrast, religion in the homeland elicited an outspoken and immediate sense of meaning and belonging. A resident of Syria, a land of shifting political and residential allegiances, wore religion on his or her sleeve in a very up-front manner.

Indeed, the Syrian was the proverbial "man without a country," and thereupon never had a highly developed sense of a "national homeland."[4] Family and religious loyalties rather than an ethnic homeland were the center of the Syrian sense of identity. (This may explain why there never developed in the United States a type of Arabic "Zionism." No unified expression of Syrian support or outrage has occurred in recent decades in spite of the turmoil in Lebanon and in Israel).[5]

As seen elsewhere, the first permanent settlers in North Dakota of Syrian ancestry seem to have been a handful of homesteaders who in 1897 took land in Shepherd Township on the west side of Walsh County. These men and women were of Melkite background (although some Orthodox were present too). That same year, the Pierce County settlement took place. Here, side by side, on homestead plots, were Melkites and Orthodox from Syria, and nearby (perhaps a little later) were Syrians of Muslim background.

Although figures are hard to come by, it has been estimated that in the decades immediately before World War I—the time period which brought the major wave of Syrians to North Dakota—perhaps half of the population in the Mount Lebanon portion of Syria was Christian; of that number, Maronites were the most numerous, then the Orthodox and finally, the Melkites. These proportions varied somewhat on the Dakota Plains.

The following paragraphs will attempt to describe the differences between the three Christian groups.

The *Maronites* were followers of an ascetic fourth century monk, St. Maron of Cyr, whose life and teaching gave rise to a vibrant Christian group. By the eighth century, after much persecution, they settled in the Qadisha Valley of northern Lebanon. There they prospered. The Church's official langauge was and still remains Syriac (close to Aramaic, the language of Christ). Maronites today, and through the centuries, have been numbered among the Catholic Eastern Rite churches. The affiliation with Rome has led to the introduction of Latin Church practices: vestments, the Creed and sacramentals. The Mass, nonetheless, followed the liturgy of St. James. Baptism and Confirmation (called "Chrismation") were administered in the same ceremony. Priests were often married in the Near East. Such a thing was absent in America.[6]

Already in 1854 a Maronite man was studying in a New York seminary—he became ill and was buried in Brooklyn in 1856.

"Between 1875 and 1889," Philip Hitti said, "two or three Maronite priests had been to New York to raise money." Apparently they did not stay long in America. In August 1891, a Maronite priest arrived and remained in that city to care for the incoming Syrian Catholics.[7] We know that by the turn of the century New York and Massachusetts had active Maronite congregations. By 1906, St. Maron's parish was organized in Minneapolis. Philip Hitti gives the names of 43 Maronite American clergy in 1924. They were located in 12 different states and included one priest each in Minneapolis and St. Paul.[8]

The *Melkites* were at one time part of the Orthodox tradition. In the mid-eighteenth century, influenced by Jesuit missionaries, they broke from their parent organization and were united with Rome. They retained much of the language, ritual, vestments and symbols of the past. Greek is used in their ceremonies. An Iconostasis reflects a Greek past. Their liturgy is that of St. John Chrysostom and St. Basil.[9]

The divisions between the Maronite and the Orthodox from Syria have always been pronounced. The Melkite and Orthodox traditions, sharing much of the same language and ritual, find their differences, both personally and at an ecclesiastical level, much less clearly defined.[10]

Early memories of non-Orthodox North Dakota "old settlers" are blurred on the question as to whether their ancestors were of the Melkite or Maronite tradition. Zahle, the hometown of so many, was known to have a preponderance of Melkites; some called it a Melkite "stronghold." (One estimate of Melkite Catholics in Zahle puts the proportion of Melkites at over 80 percent.) One would think the terms Melkite or Maronite would occur in early accounts, but they don't. Catholic, Muslim, Orthodox affiliation, yes, but little, if anything, concerning further religious subdivisions.

We know that religion was central to their lives. North Dakota memories of the past in Zahle often dwell on the subject. Mary Ferris of Williston, in a 1939 WPA interview, recalled:

The church, it's five-six blocks from my home. We go two times a day— morning and evening—on Sunday. Everybody go. In Lent we don't eat no meat, no eggs, no milk—just fry everything in olive oil. We go to church morning and evening—everybody go, two times every day. For seven weeks we don't eat no breakfast 'tall, just dinner.

Mrs. Libbie Layon when interviewed at Williston in March 1940 says of her childhood in Zahle:

"That's the Catholic Church, and we got nice, big church. We got about fifty churches in Zahle. That's a big place. We go to confession and Communion every Sunday; if we don't the priest scold us good. Here it's once a year sometimes."

"We were members of the Roman Catholic Church and attended church every Sunday." So said Joseph S. Salmon, a native of Zahle, when interviewed by the WPA at Bismarck in August 1939. He continues, "The services are the same as Catholic churches here in America, except they use the Syrian language, not the Latin language.

Libbie Layon and Joseph Salmon both avoided any reference to Maronite or Melkite, but they are clear on the relationship to the Roman Catholic Church.

Today, "Maronite" is a word that is often used to describe the religious roots of many of current North Dakotans. Why the absence of the term Melkite? Could it be that in the "Old Country" these words were never used? Bishop Nicholas Samra, archivist for the Melkite Church in America, has some observations that help clarify the matter. He says the term Melkite was seldom used in the Middle East. Instead the religious group was known as either "Rum Catholic," "Greek Catholic" or just "Catholic." [11] Perhaps the term Maronite has become popular through the news reports of more recent religious conflicts in Lebanon, for indeed, television commentators use the word "Maronite" with great frequency. Yet the first reference to Lebanese (Syrian) religious activity in North Dakota occurred in the *Fargo Forum* of March 18, 1893. (This date is only four years after statehood.) The occasion was a Mass in the local Catholic church by Rev. Basil Sowaya, "a Melchite [sic] priest from Mount Lebanon, who came to look after the fifteen or twenty Melchites who live here." Most of the individuals attending the service were probably men listed in the *City Directory*; they were classed as "peddlers." But what happened to them? What happened to the "Melkites" in later-day North Dakota? As will be seen later in this volume, it's a question that's hard to answer.

We know, however, that Melkite families were interspersed with Maronites in homesteading times. The Melkite priest, Father Seraphim Roumie, came to North Dakota, built a country and (later) a town church at Rugby, and served Syrian Christians all along the Northern Pacific main line, to Williston and perhaps into Montana. Father Roumie, who arrived in Dakota in 1903 (possibly 1902), was preceded in Rugby by Father Aakel. Both priests were sent to the parishes by the Melkite Patriarch of Antioch who was himself from Zahle and was concerned about his fellow religionists. Father Roumie took care of Melkites and Maronites (and often Orthodox) wherever he went. Ed Absey of Grand Forks recalled Father Roumie offering Mass in the farm home of his parents in Walsh County; his father was the Mass server. And yet the descendants of the Absey family today do not remember a Melkite-Maronite distinction.

Bishop Nicholas J. Samra has followed the life history of many Melkites in this country. Several decades ago, while a parish priest in Chicago, Bishop Samra's interest in the Dakotas was aroused when he found a number of Chicago Melkite families who mentioned an early time period during which their forebears resided in North Dakota, so there is no question that Melkites were on the prairies.[12]

Pertinent to the matter of the blurring of Melkite-Maronite distinctions may have been the presence of a Maronite priest and parish in Minneapolis (St. Maron's) in 1906, a very early date. The nearest Melkite congregation was in Omaha. The flow of people into and out of North Dakota was most often through Minneapolis and St. Paul, not northward from Omaha.

Clearly part of the problem is the fact that, with the decline of their numbers, both Melkite and Maronite Catholics eventually found their religious home in North Dakota in the local Latin Rite Catholic congregations which were everywhere present and which served the wide variety of European Catholics who settled on the prairies. This later "common religious ground" softened the differences of the past.

The attraction of the Maronite label might also have been influenced by the fact that a certain amount of Latinization had occurred in the Maronite tradition: Rosary, Stations of the Cross, and Benediction were present. The shift into Latin Rite practices was gentler and Maronite could have been a convenient identification label to adopt.

The Melkite tradition was very much present elsewhere in America at the time North Dakota Syrian farm families were flourishing. Philip Hitti, in 1924, lists 23 Melkite priests at work in 12 different states. (One could be found not only in Omaha but also in Chicago.)[13] The Melkite priests in America must have been somewhat peripatetic for, as mentioned above, Rev. Basil Sowaya offered Mass in Fargo in 1893 for "fifteen or twenty Melkite residents."

The distinction between the various Lebanese Christian groups, without doubt, blurred with the passage of time. John Kassis, when 60 years old (1939), recalled his home town in Syria:

I was born in Zahle, Syria, 18th day of May, 1879. That's the largest town in the Lebanon Mountains. We lived right in town there for sixteen years and I went to school. Our town happened to be all Christian—Roman Catholics, Orthodox and Lutheran. They was all different than here, more or less all Christian.

After 40 years in America, in Williston to be exact, Mr. Kassis, as seen above, is not clear as to religious affiliations. The words "Roman Catholic" could mean anything: Melkite, Maronite, or Latin Rite. The term Lutheran is most likely his generic term for Protestants. Living in western North Dakota, a "Lutheran" part of the state, all Protestants to him probably became Lutheran.

It's interesting that Maronites emerged as the prominent tradition in Minneapolis-St. Paul, the hub cities for much of North Dakota and northern Minnesota Syrian development. Writing in 1967, Carol Jean Landis said in her master's thesis which dealt with Twin City Lebanese: "There has never been a Syrian Protestant or Syrian Orthodox Church in the Twin Cities, but each city has a Maronite Church: St. Maron's in Minneapolis and Holy Family in St. Paul."[14] St. Maron's Church was organized in 1906 with 100 members and Holy Family in St. Paul began in 1915 with 300 members.[15] These congregations are flourishing today. (Carol Landis was not correct in regards to the Orthodox Syrians. In 1913, a St. George Syrian Orthodox congregation was set up in St. Paul. In 1952, a St. Mary's Antiochian Orthodox Church came about.)[16] Yet it remains clear that the Maronite Catholic members have occupied center stage, both in terms of name recognition and congregational adherence.

Orthodox

Orthodox Christians were present, as mentioned earlier, throughout North Dakota. They were sometimes mixed with Maronites and Melkites in the Rugby and Williston areas. They were present in an almost exclusive fashion in Sheridan County, in what has been called the McClusky settlement.

Edward Nedoff of the Williston Syrian community recalled his early life in the 1940 WPA interview:

I was born in Zahle, Syria, on March 30, 1887. We had six boys and one girl in our family. I was the oldest one. We belong to the—what you call our religion—is Oriental Catholic. My dad was priest of the church and I used to be an altar-boy—used to serve Mass. Church was right by the house.

"Oriental Catholic" is the term Edward Nedoff used to describe his church affiliation in Zahle. This word has no meaning in modern

Orthodox priest
baptizing children
in early day
Williston.
Courtesy: Chuck
Joseph

American parlance. It does point out a difficulty that arose from the earliest times in the United States. What is an appropriate title for Orthodox of Syrian background? The term Greek Orthodox appears. Indeed, Thomas Nassif of Bismarck told the WPA interviewer in 1939: "We were members of the Orthodox Church which is a branch of the Orthodox Greek." But competent authorities warn us that this is a confusing label. It is true that at one time the Patriarch in Constantinople claimed jurisdiction over the Syrian Orthodox and in fact all Orthodox of Greek and Russian background, but this was a historical moment that had no contemporary validation.

Lines of authority among the early Orthodox in America varied over the decades. Philip Hitti says the earliest arrivals "leaned toward dependence upon the Russian Church." The first head of what was to be called the Syrian Orthodox Church in America was a priest (later bishop) who studied in Russia and had his headquarters in New York. He came to that city in 1895 and died in 1915. After some confusion, many of the Orthodox from Syria placed themselves under Archbishop Germanos of Selefkias, an Eastern Mediterranean bishop, who presided over what was to be called the Antiochian Orthodox Church. This conformed to the Old Country practice of locating authority in the Patriarch of Antioch. Hitti does say that at the date of his writing (1924), 19 Syrian churches saw Antioch as their center of authority and 11 looked to the "Russian Synod."[17]

As can be seen, the switching of allegiance in the United States points to a complex historical set of events. Alixa Naff describes the background of the Orthodox tradition in a review of Arab-American history. She writes:

Eastern, or Greek Orthodox, is, as its name implies, the Eastern half of the universal Christian Church which officially split in 1054. At the time of the schism, the Western half, centered in Rome, evolved into the Roman Catholic Church, while the Eastern half maintained its Byzantine reference. The divergence between the churches remain broad and deep on a number of doctoral as well as ceremonial and disciplinary matters. Moreover, Latin becomes the official language of the Roman liturgy, while Greek remained that of the Byzantine. After Greece gained independence from the Ottoman Empire in the early nineteenth century and the church hierarchy in Syria became Arab, Arabic gradually dominated Greek in the liturgy in that region. The Eastern church, as might be expected, rejected the Western church's claim to universal papal supremacy.[18]

Just how much communication there existed between the North Dakota Syrians of Orthodox background and the American church authorities is hard to determine. We know that the Orthodox hierarchy tried to keep in touch with their affiliates on the Dakota prairies for a newspaper account describes and, indeed, shows a photograph of a "Greek Orthodox priest and archbishop from St. Paul, Minnesota" holding services in 1914 at the Reno Valley township school south of Rugby.[19] Orthodox priests visited Bull Butte Township near Williston early in the century. Monsignor Abramhous is pictured in a local history as homesteaders gathered for the baptism of a child.[20]

Some reports mention Orthodox priests who came to Sheridan County, a community with close ties to Sioux City, Iowa, through the Ain Arab connection. Father Tom Skaff is remembered as coming from Sioux City and a certain Father Yanney came from Nebraska.[21] A question

Orthodox Archbishop at a gathering of his "faithful" at the Reno Valley School south of Rugby, N.D., in 1914.

Courtesy: Minot Daily News

remains: what Orthodox jurisdiction was responsible for their fellow religionists in the Dakotas? Who sent the priests to the prairies? Some other study will have to clarify this matter; nothing in regional archives seems helpful.

Plains Folk: North Dakota's Ethnic History says this about the Sheridan County Syrian Orthodox:

> *"Owing to the difficulties of the situation [the remoteness and scarcity of clergy] the Orthodox Bishop suggested that they should attend the local Episcopal churches."*

Plains Folk says further,

> *"Some of the staunchest members of the Episcopal church in present-day Bismarck are the children and grandchildren of the original Sheridan County settlers."*[22]

Families such as the Nassifs, the Boutrous, Nicolas and Sabas joined St. George's Episcopal Church in Bismarck. (St. George's altar and stained glass windows are memorials to Sheridan County pioneers.) The same can be said of many Orthodox Syrians in the Williston area. Whether with or without the Bishop's approval, they eventually found their way into the St. Peter's Episcopal Church of Williston and some of their descendants are still on the rolls of that congregation. St. Peter's numbers the Owans, Barkies, Seebs, and Alberts among their members. Jabour Munyer of Williston recalled his Lebanese childhood in a February 1940 interview:

> *They sent me to schools all over the city, but I only stay three, four days. I just run around pass the time—the boys scared me. Church—that's only*

Burial service with Sheik "from Canada", Ross, ND Cemetery

Courtesy:
Rosie Juma Chamley

place I used to go. That was Greek Catholic church; it's Episcopalian here I go—ain't got no Greek church here. It's one in Chicago, but it's too far.

This picture of a Syrian Orthodox association with the American Episcopal church is not unique. Such a thing happened in such diverse places as New Hampshire, Oklahoma and St. Paul, to name only a few friendly affiliations. Sarah John, in her study of Syrians in El Paso, Texas, notes that the local Orthodox were welcomed in the Episcopal Church and an occasional Mass was performed by an "itinerant Greek Orthodox Bishop." In time many of the Orthodox became full-fledged members of the El Paso Episcopal congregation.[23]

Needless to say, not all Lebanese Christians found a home in an American church affiliation, whether Episcopal or Catholic. Some drifted into their own non-identifiable categories. Joseph Abraham of Williston said in August 1940:

I belong to Greek Orthodox Church; we got no church here and I can't go to Minot. I go to Catholic church before, but I don't understand, so I get sleepy and now I don't go.

Muslim

Muslims* in North Dakota were noteworthy in that they came in substantial numbers early in the Lebanese migration stream to America. As seen frequently in this book, they came at a time when Muslim immigrants were relatively rare. A handful of Muslim men were taking land in or near Elling Township, Pierce County, in 1902. That same year at least a dozen filed for land in Ross Township, Mountrail County. (There is some evidence that several Muslim men were in the Ross area even in 1900 and 1901.[24] Hassen Jaha, for example, filed his first naturalization papers in Mountrail County in October 1901.)

It is safe to say that Muslim men came to these central and western Dakota lands not as "late comers." They were true pioneers, among the earliest of "sod busters." And they remembered their past. Allay Omar of Ross recalled in 1939 his childhood in turn-of-the-century Bire, Syria:

---

* A rare Muslim immigrant came from a Druze background. This Islamic sect took form in Egypt around the year 1000 A.D. Their religious perspective differs substantially from that of other Muslims. It is a closed religious system with great stress on the Druze community. It has rules against conversion and intermarriage, and monogamous marriage is part of their life. There are no mosques as such and, in keeping with their Muslim roots, there is a ban on pork and alcohol. They have a belief in transmigration of souls. Numbering only seven percent of Lebanese population, they live often in a mountainous portion of Lebanon. This allows them to preserve a measure of independence in today's world. Yet they are not afraid of the modern world; education at least on a local level, is highly esteemed.

Cedar Rapids, Pioneer Mosque, the religious home for many Islamic faithful on their way to settle in North Dakota.
Courtesy: John Guerrero

We attended the Moslem Church, and services were held every day. Friday's services were the most important, however. We did not sing any hymns at the services.

Amid "Mike" Abdallah, also of Ross, remembered his childhood in a village he named as Rufage (Rafid), Rushia, Syria:

We had church services every Friday. I belonged to the Moslem Church in the Old Country. The same as I do in this country. We didn't have anything like confirmation.

It goes without saying that Muslims, often called Mohammedans in early-day North Dakota, came from a religious tradition that differed substantially from that of the Protestants and Catholics who made up most of the state's inhabitants. They followed the teaching of Muhammad, the "last prophet," who in the seventh century was inspired by God to bring the ultimate spiritual way of life to humankind.

Muhammad, one may recall, grew up in a fragmented Near-Eastern culture which was marked by a wide variety of tribal and animistic religious beliefs. Acquainted with the Jewish traditions and Old Testament writings, and well aware of the Christian sects which were scattered throughout the Middle East, Muhammad's religious prescriptions reflect something of both the Jewish and Christian antecedents. As it developed, Muhammad accepted concepts such as judgment day, the person of Jesus, the virgin birth from Mary.

Significant to the Muslim experience in North Dakota were certain basic religious concepts. Centuries of tradition determined that the Muslim way of life required abstinence from such things as pork and intoxicating beverages. Muslim adherents lived also with some very definite laws concerning inheritance, marriage, and divorce. There were also serious punishments for theft, adultery, usury, and bribery.[25]

All Muslims are required to incorporate into their lives a set of practices, which are sometimes called the "Five Pillars." The first, and indeed the most important, is the Profession of Faith. A Muslim must profess belief in the unity of God and the prophecy of Muhammad, thus the saying, "There is no God but the one God and Muhammad is his messenger." Second, the Muslim must pray at prescribed hours, after he or she has carried out an ablution ritual. The holy day of the week, the prescribed day of prayer, is Friday. The prayers, in Arabic, are recited five times a day: morning, noon, mid-afternoon, sunset and night. These are accompanied by a number of bows to Mecca. The prayers take place, whether indoors or outside, in a clean or uncontaminated environment. Accordingly, prayer mats are often used. Of special value in the Dakota pioneer environment is the belief that, although the mosque is the central sanctuary of prayer and meditation, attendance at a mosque is not obligatory. Also of significance in North Dakota is the fact that prayer is considered an individual matter, even in mosques. The Muslim faith has no formal clergy. An imam, who often leads the prayers and delivers the sermons, is not an

The Muslim cemetery today, near Ross.

Courtesy: William Sherman

ordained priest; he performs marriages, burials, and teaches the Koran. Women, when praying in a mosque, are segregated from men.

A third pillar of the Muslim faith is charity. Almsgiving and the feeding and clothing of the poor are necessary parts of religious life. An act of charity—assistance in building a mosque or school or hospital— can compensate for failure to perform other religious obligations.

The fourth pillar is total fasting—both food and water—from sunrise to sunset during the holy month of Ramadan. This, as the reader can imagine, could be a considerable burden on the Dakota prairies, with their long spring days and limited hours of nightfall.

The fifth pillar is the obligation to make a pilgrimage to Mecca at least once during a lifetime. Again, this poses problems for North Dakota residents. Mecca is halfway around the world.[26]

The reader will notice that the Muslim tradition is a remarkably mobile way of religious life; the adherent carries his or her beliefs within themselves. Priesthood and church buildings are not essentials. On the primitive homestead frontier this could give them special advantages.

And indeed Muslims came to the Dakotas in large numbers. In the appendix of this volume, census and naturalization lists of "Syrian" men and women are recorded. Over 1,000 names can be found. That figure is, without doubt, too small. The "1,000" is based on actual records, those individuals who can be found in census, naturalization, or land office records. But what of the mobile peddlers, coming and going in the years in which no census was taken, what of those who chose not to take land or become a citizen? The total could easily reach 2,000 "Syrian-born" in North Dakota. Elsewhere in this book it is stated that probably 30 percent of the state's Syrians were Muslim. If we accept the 30 percent figure, we could credibly say that perhaps 500 Muslims were at one time or another in North Dakota. That makes the early North Dakota experience a truly remarkable thing.

Many Muslims were peddlers, some were businessmen, and some were working folk, but as we shall see, Muslim homestead clusters sprang up in Pierce and Rolette county regions in the middle of the state, in McIntosh County in the south central part of the state, and in Mountrail County in North Dakota's western regions.

The authors found no instances where Muslim immigrants hid their faith in North Dakota. Such a thing may have happened in the second generation. In fact, one would expect it to happen when the "children" began to experience a life in which they had one foot in a decidedly different Old Country family world and one in the non-Muslim American world of school, jobs, and neighborhood relationships. Almost every Old Country religion—Catholic and Jew especially—lost adherents in the second-generation period.

But the Muslim immigrant was forthright in his or her religious adherence. Mary Juma of Ross in 1939 (without any apology) told her interviewer: "My religion in the Old Country was Moslem. We attended services every Friday, the same as we do here."

Kassem Ramadan, an isolated Muslim in the decidedly "gentile" world of Lignite, North Dakota, told his interviewer in October 1939:

We attended the Mohammadan Church and we had church every day. The services lasted about thirty or forty minutes. During these services the congregation would kneel, with their heads bowed to the floor and pray, while the preacher chanted hymns. Our Sabbath came on Friday instead of Sunday.

Mr. Ramadan's thirty years in America did bring about some change, at least in religious terminology; the "Mohammedan" (an American phrase), the "church" and "preacher" (both American terms) appear in his account.

Others, too, adopted the American vocabulary. Bo Alley Farhart of Ross in November 1939 used the terms "church" and "hymns."

We attended the Moslem Church in the Old Country, and services were held every Friday. Men and women prayed separately, and no hymns were ever sung.

Minnesota

Reference to Minnesota will occur frequently in this discussion of Arabic people in North Dakota. It was the pathway to the "West." Some note on the Syrian religious situation in that state would be in order.

As mentioned in previous pages, the Maronite Christians established their early congregations in Minneapolis in 1906 (St. Maron's) and in St. Paul in 1915 (Holy Family). By 1913, the St. George Syrian Orthodox Church was organized. The Arabic-speaking faithful used Syriac and Greek in their liturgy.[27]

Closer to North Dakota was the Minnesota town of Crookston, which became a "hub" community of Syrian-Lebanese people primarily because it was a natural "crossroads" between northwest Minnesota and North Dakota. Two major railroad lines went through the town: the Great Northern and the Northern Pacific. Many Syrian immigrants journeyed through Duluth or St. Paul, and thereby arrived by rail at Crookston. Many, perhaps most, intended to move into the Dakotas, to Montana, and even beyond. Melkites, Orthodox and Maronites were present, but a significant number of Muslims also passed through the city on their way to homesteading areas. A few Muslims, in fact, chose to stay and find work. Both Christians and Muslims worked on railroad jobs, some peddled and some even established wholesale and small retail firms.

As early as the mid-1890s, Tannous Noah from Bouhaire, a Maronite gentleman, had set up a store in Crookston. Charley Joseph from Bouhaire arrived in 1898. He is remembered as a long-time railroad employee. Charley's sister, Lateefe Joseph, came to Crookston in 1913 at the tender age of fourteen. Like most Lebanese Maronites, Lateefe was profoundly religious, attending Mass daily at the Latin Rite Cathedral of the Immaculate Conception. (The rituals and language were different, but there were other problems too. At first, many Latin Rite Catholics refused to believe the Maronites were "legitimate" Catholics.)[28]

The great majority of Crookston's Lebanese were Maronite. And it was from Crookston that many Lebanese moved throughout the northern portion of North Dakota. These Maronite pioneers could tend to overshadow the Dakota Melkite and Orthodox presence. Crookston's early families include the Noahs, Josephs, Salems, Amons, Isaacs, Georges, Mikes, Anthonys, Solomons, and Romances. A relationship of at least friendship existed between the Crookston people and those who lived in North Dakota's Walsh and Pierce counties.

Rev. Seraphim Roumie

Peter IV Geraigiry, the Patriarch of the Melkite Catholics of Antioch, Alexandria, Jerusalem, and all of the East, at the turn of the century was concerned about his fellow religionists who were migrating to the American Great Plains. Peter IV's attention must have focused on North Dakota because he himself was a native of Zahle, Lebanon, and by some estimates a possible 50 families from Furzol and Zahle had moved to the Rugby area of North Dakota.

In 1902 the Patriarch sent Fr. Elias Aaguel to Rugby. This man set up a Syrian Catholic congregation named St. George. (One account said he started construction of a church.) But after two months Fr. Aaguel returned to Syria (most likely because of the death of Peter IV).

In May, 1903, a second Melkite priest arrived in New York on his way to Rugby: the Rev. Economos Seraphim Roumie of the Basilian Alleppian Order. By mid-June Fr. Roumie stopped in Fargo to present his introductory credentials to Latin Rite Bishop John Shanley.

In the Rugby area the priest found himself with at least 75 Lebanese men and women who had filed on the free homestead land claims. With an amazing burst of energy, Fr. Roumie himself filed on land in Williams County and brought about the completion of St. George's Church in Meyer Township, some ten miles southeast of Rugby. The Lebanese informational "grapevine" alerted the priest to the existence of Lebanese settlers throughout northern North Dakota. Early reports have him holding services as far west as Williston, but also in eastern North Dakota's Walsh County.

By 1906 Fr. Roumie had moved to Chicago to take charge of the St. John the Baptist congregation. A 1910 Bulletin of the Diocese of Fargo says the priest sold his North Dakota homestead for $400.00 and used it to assist his Chicago parishioners as they purchased a $1,500.00 building which became, in effect, the first "Syrian Church" in that city.

Fr. Roumie's concern for his North Dakota parishioners

Fr. Seraphim Roemie, pioneer Melkite priest and homesteader in Williston area.

Courtesy:
Joe Nicholas Family

continued. Even though a Lebanese Fr. Timothy Joch often came to the state through the rest of the first decade of the century, Fr. Roumie would periodically leave Chicago and journey across North Dakota. (A Williston newspaper of 1907 said he was spending two weeks in that city.)

Fr. Seraphim Roumie died in Chicago in 1940. The Latin Rite Archbishop of that city officiated at the funeral service. Fr. Roumie, by that time, was the Rt. Rev. Archimandrite Seraphim Roumie, a high ecclesiastical rank, which is comparable to a Western Rite Monsignor. He was revered by many Chicagoans as a saint, a man who reputedly performed miracles of healing.

Noah Brothers
(of the Crookston,
MN community)
Fr. Timothy Noah,
John Noah,
Fr. Daniel Noah
Courtesy:
John Guerrero

John Noah

When Maronite Catholics left the Lebanese mountain village of Bouhaire for the northwestern Minnesota town of Crookston, their Arabic name translation seemed to come right out of the Bible. Amongst these immigrants were families such as the Noahs, Isaacs, Josephs, Thomases, Peters, Salems, Solomons. One of the early marriages was between Michael Noah and Christine Isaac. Out of that union came eleven children including two priests, two hairdressers, one judge, one accountant, and an

Olympic hockey star. Faith, family, and education were foremost in the Noah value system. Perhaps the most famous of the clan was John Noah who graduated from Cathedral High School in 1946. He went on to join UND'S first hockey team and eventually captained the team to a NCAA championship over Michigan. John was named UND's "first All American hockey player" and to this day is introduced by former college president Tom Clifford as the "first Arab All American hockey star in the world."

After college he led the Crookston Pirates city team to the 1951 U.S. National Championship. In 1952, John played a vital role on the silver medal U.S. Olympic hockey team in Oslo, Norway. He then spent two years in the army and later married Mary Kelly of East Grand Forks. They raised a family of seven boys and one girl in Fargo while John became the chief U.S. probation officer for North Dakota. Two of his "clients" were the very newsworthy Gordon Kahl and Leonard Peltier. For most of those years John worked for federal judge Ronald Davies who he said ran a "tight but fair court." John's common sense in rehabilitating criminals was summed up with "some want help, some don't, and the rest you pray for."

In 1989, John went on to become manager of the Fargo Civic Center, which lasted until "retirement" at age 68. His busy life has included a run at a statewide political office and being an active member at St. Anthony's Catholic Church in Fargo.

CHAPTER FOUR

The Village Life: Marriage and Family

Seventy-five percent of the Lebanese population were village people, so says a report in the 1940s. They, like most of Europe's people whose roots were agricultural, lived not on isolated farmsteads but in central settlements with farmlands spread throughout the adjacent countryside.

The Lebanese village consisted of a cluster of houses which one visitor said resembles "southwestern pueblos in degrees of compactness." The visitor said further, "One finds one's way from home to home by a maze of twisting paths, which become alley-ways in the larger towns." An open area occurred here and there and in these spaces could be found a church or a mosque with some adjacent small shops.[1]

After living through the difficult homesteading decades on the North Dakota prairies, in 1939 Allay Omar, a Muslim from the Ross community, recalled with some nostalgia Bire, his Old Country village.

> We lived in a lovely village in Syria. It had a population of about one-thousand people, and everyone's home was built of stone. Our home consisted of four rooms, and the entire building measured 30 x 40 feet. All the homes were surrounded by trees and many had orchards, and the whole effect was pleasing to the eye.

Mrs. David Kalil, who came to America as a young lady, remembers her home village, a Christian one, in Lebanon where the snow "melts quick." In August 1940, she told the WPA interviewer:

> I'm born in little town, big as Williston, close to Zahlia [sic], in Syria.... We live close to mountains and my father have farms and cattle. We raise silk-worms too; we wait for our crop every year; some year we have failure, some year good. We raise grapes, and make raisins and wine and other drinks, and syrup too. We have figs, and peaches, and apples and we raise lots of walnuts too. My father have six or seven cattle,

two or three milking cows, and they plow by cattle, you know. It's a nice place to live in Syria—not very warm, and not so cold. It never freeze there—just get chilly sometime and when it snows, it melts quick. We can go without stocking sometimes.

The villages were usually in the valleys, but sometimes on the hillside and occasionally were positioned on surprisingly high mountain slopes. The houses, as is frequent in the Middle East, were flat-roofed, often two-story in design, with exterior staircases. Stone and earthen materials were the common features of floors, walls, and sometimes roofs.

Conscious, no doubt, of the flat terrain in which he had been living for about 40 years, Side Abdallah, a Muslim from the Ross area, recalled in 1939:

We lived in a village [Rafid], and the land surrounding us was very level, but a few miles outward, the land became of a hilly nature. Our home was built of stone, two stories high, and measured 30 by 48 feet.

Mary Juma, of Ross, North Dakota, in a 1940 interview, remembered her home in the village of Bire:

My home in Syria was a large, one-story stone house. The floors were made of logs (about the size of our telephone poles), and the space between the poles was filled with smaller poles. Branches were used to fill small unfilled parts. A mixture of wet clay and lime was spread over the poles and branches, packed in hard, and smoothened by running a heavy roller over the floor. This was allowed to dry, and the result was a hard floor looking like cement. The roof was made in the same way.

In 1939, Bo Alley Farhart of Ross remembered his home village. In stark contrast to his tiny (12 by 14 feet?) Dakota homestead shanty, Farhart says his two-story home measured 34 by 50 feet, with "large porches."

I was born on June 23, 1883, in Rafieg [sic], Syria. We lived in a city, and the land surrounding the village was level and a few hills could be seen in the distance. Farms surrounded the town, but all the farmers lived in the village. Our house was built of white rock, two stories high with three large porches. The house measured 34 by 50 feet.

Agriculture was the basis of all Lebanese village life. WPA interviews give us some glimpse of the type of farming that dominated turn-of-the-century Syrian life. Thomas Nassif, a native of Ain Arab, recalled in an August 1939 interview:

The farming was rather primitive as we did not have any of the modern equipment. Our land was first broadcast with seed and then plowed with a wooden plow which was drawn by oxen or cows. This plow was made out of a piece of timber and was four or five feet long. On the end of this beam there was placed a sharp piece of metal or the plowshare.

Mr. Nassif continues his reminiscence by describing the threshing and winowing of the grain:

In the fall when the crop was ripe it was harvested with hand scythes; the harvester would grasp a bunch of grain in his left hand near the heads and cut it off with a hand sickle in his right hand, and then throw it on the ground. After it was all cut it would be gathered up in a sort of a cradle made of short pieces of wood tied together with ropes. These were then loaded on donkeys or mules and taken to the threshing ground. A hard surface was located on the field which served as a threshing center. After a thin layer of the grain had been spread on this spot in a circle, a horse or an oxen was hitched to an implement somewhat resembling a stone boat. This boat was made of lumber in which holes had been bored and small stones about three inches in diameter inserted in the holes so that they projected on the other side. This implement was dragged over the grain until it was threshed. This was kept up until the whole pile had been threshed. The threshed grain being pushed to the outside of the circle as they went along until it was all on the outside of the circle. Then the same procedure would be done all over again, the re-threshed grain would be piled in the center of the circle, so that when the second threshing was completed the threshed grain, straw and chaff would be in a pile. After this process the grain, chaff and straw would be thrown into the air with a fork letting the wind separate the grain from the chaff and straw, the grain would fall straight down and the wind would carry away the chaff and straw to one side.

When the Lebanese homesteader came to the Great Plains, America's "wheat country," he or she was not entering an entirely unknown world. Wheat had been a staple product in the Old Country. But there were other farm products that were decidedly different. In August of 1939 in Bismarck, Mrs. Mary Saliba, an Ain Arab native, recalled:

"We also had goats which were milked and the milk was churned into butter and also made into cheese." Joseph Abraham, born in 1860, "two hundred miles north of Jerusalem," reported in Williston, August 1940: "We have trees, we raise silk [sic], worms get in these. It's like Russian trees we have here. We raise a little wheat—winter wheat—by hoe; we can't plow there."

Thomas Nassif adds to the description of Syria's basic agricultural crops. Reported in August 1939 at Bismarck, he said:

We raised the same grain that is raised in this country with the exception of "Hammos" [hummus] which is a grain that they do not raise in America. This plant is something like beans but there is only one kernel in each pod. The taste resembles beans or peas. These kernels are roasted and salted and they taste very much like nuts. We also raised some poultry, some goats as well as sheep. Also fruits of all kinds, figs, olives, grapes, dates and practically every kind of fruit grown in California or in the Southern States. The climate here in Syria is somewhat like the climate of California.

Characteristic of Old Country village life at the time of the first immigration wave was a group loyalty, a loyalty which was integrally woven into the community fabric. Since farming was a basic to survival, land was of supreme importance. And it was an extended patriarchal family that lived on the same land through many generations. In the center of town was the church and very often the majority of neighbors belonged to the same faith. As in many cultures, more emphasis was placed on the extended family than the actual biological family.[2]

Philip Hitti, in an oft-quoted phrase, puts the matter succinctly: "The Syrian is a man without a country par excellence. His patriotism takes the form of love of family and sect."[3] With a background of changing political scenes, of invasions and occupying forces, of the varying national jurisdictions, the extended family loyalties not surprisingly became central to the Lebanese sense of identity. Lebanese men and women lived in continual association with their kinfolk. This meant a deep awareness of aunts, uncles, cousins, and grandparents. Alixa Naff, in the *Harvard Encyclopedia of America's Ethnic Groups,* spells out the implications of this set of allegiances: "The enhancement of family honor and status is an inviolate trust for its members; in return for protection, the family demands a conformity and a sublimation of individual will and interests. The honor or dishonor of an individual reflects on the entire family."[4]

Part of the family perspective involved religious affiliation. Given the mixed condition of the country—Orthodox (Greek or Syrian), Maronite, Melkite, Islamic (Sunni or Druze)—the specific religious tradition with its ritual and beliefs became of paramount importance in defining family life. Indeed Philip Hitti introduces a discussion of homeland life in his book, *Syrians in America,* with the phrase, "Religion, a sort of nationality."[5]

Lebanon was a land of diverse loyalties and yet the groups seem to have lived together with relative peace and tolerance. A number of scholars have remarked about the ease in which people forming a religious mosaic could, at the same time, show great cohesion.[6]

Allegiance to the village was the next rank of loyalty after religion and family. This is not surprising in an age before the modern media and rapid means of transportation, an age in which generation after generation unfolded under the same economic and social conditions. The village therefore had its common history. It was actually a collection of family histories. And further, it was the site of both family and church events.

Original North Dakota settlers, when thinking of the "Old Country" expressed some bitterness as they considered some of the harsh conditions of the day: Turkish rule, for example, and the relative poverty of Syrian life. Yet these seem to fade into the background as they thought of the special happy moments. Dancing and feasting, in particular, brought joy to the meagerness of their village surroundings. In 1939, Abe Mikel, a Christian from the Williston area, said:

> They had lots of dances, parties and good times. Went from house to house dancing, one house one night, another next night. There was no dancehalls like they have here, or at least I did not see them. We dance mostly the waltz and square-dance. People seemed to have more time there to have a good time. I don't know much about the weddings, but when my brother was married I know they celebrated a week or ten days. It cost him about five hundred dollars. They had a big feed and invited lots of people; eating and drinking, mostly drinking, anything you wanted to eat and all different kinds of liquor.

George Saba, born in North Dakota, raised in Ain Arab, and a returnee to North Dakota in 1935, described Old Country festivities in a July 1939 interview at Bismarck:

> The instruments played were the harps, zithers and an instrument [nai] similar to the piccolo. The dancing is quite different than the dancing in this country, in that there is only one dance where a man and a woman dance together. This dance is something like the American two-step. The man holds the lady's right hand in his left hand and they dance sided [sic] by side, the man waving something in his other hand, usually and [sic] handerchief [sic], flag or a tamborine in time with the music.

> There were several dances when the man danced alone and the steps are hard to describe. But some of them resemble the Highland Fling and some are similar to some of the Russian Cossack dances. Often the ladies dance alone too and their dances are of the Oriental class. They wave their hands and arms gracefully and move their bodies to the rythm [sic] of the music with very little movement of their feet.

Muslim memories, too, recalled the dances, but with what must have taken slightly different traditional forms. Mike Abdallah, of Ross, North

Dakota, when interviewed in December 1939, recalled:

When dances for everyone were held, the people did not dance in couples but danced single. Then there was a dance where a group would clasp hands and dance much similar to the square dance in this country.

Mike Abdallah's description of one Old Country dance caught the attention of his non-Syrian WPA interviewer when Mike said: "For recreation we had parties, dances, feasts. The parties were mostly like celebrations in this country, and would consist of competitive games and feats of athletics and strength [including] the sword dance. . . ." The American interviewer, who through his report had put on paper the exact words of Mr. Abdallah, injected at this point his own observation:

The sword dance, as described to the field worker, was much the same as fencing in this country, except that it was done to music and they danced among the crowd. The dance continued until such time as blood was drawn by one competitor. A scratch of a finger would be enough. This dance was done by only certain men trained for the dance, it wasn't everyone that could do it.

The central agriculture town pattern of life was almost universal in Europe and the Middle East. The mother and children spent their days in the cluster of village homes while the men and boys (and sometimes girls) labored on the family land out on the countryside. The family was reunited at the end of the day, and evening social life took place in a community atmosphere.

Every student of midwestern settlement history has commented on the sometimes wrenching experiences that burdened new-comers as they first faced the realities of the Great Plains. Homestead laws insisted that the individuals reside on their respective land claims. In the Dakotas that often meant living a mile from one's neighbor and many miles from town. Some commentators have spoken at length concerning the resultant sense of isolation and loneliness, compounded at times by the flat terrain and seemingly endless expanse of sky.

Though many of the first land-takers were unmarried and remarkably mobile, Lebanese, like people of almost every background, were affected by the empty land sentiments to some degree. A review of Federal Land Office records show dozens of Lebanese who filed on their claim, and either relinquished it or just plain "gave up." Names are on Land Office initial filing records, which never appear again in census reports, in news reports, or the memories of "old timers." Obviously, the acquisition of 160 acres of free land was not worth the stress of the isolation, the big sky, or the winters.

Wedding Customs

The dances and celebrations mentioned in the previous pages took place very often in Syrian village life but nothing called forth such elaborate festivities as the occasion of a wedding. Such traditions were not unique to the Lebanese. North Dakota "old-timers" still recall the "two-day, three-day" weddings among early-day Poles, Ukrainians, and German-Russians. Perhaps it was part of an across-the-board Eastern European tradition. Weddings and rather exuberant fun-filled moments went together.

Given the diversity of religious traditions, it is difficult to describe specific marriage procedures, but memories of Mid-western Syrian settlers spell out in some detail a few of the customs of the past. Mary Juma recalled weddings in her hometown in a 1940 interview:

A wedding in the Old Country was just the same as a Moslem wedding anywhere. There is no courting before the wedding. When a boy decides to marry a certain girl, he goes to her parents and tells them about it.

Sam Omar, of Muslim background, gives his recollections of Old Country marriages. He said in 1939:

In asking for a bride, a Syrian boy (if twenty-one years of age), approaches the mother of the girl he wishes to marry and makes the proposal of marriage. If, however, the boy is not of age, his mother acts in his stead. If the two parties can agree, a stated amount of money is set aside, so in case of a separation and it is caused through the fault of the man, the bride receives the money. Before the ceremony, the bride names two people she wishes to witness her marriage, retires to another room so as not to witness the ceremony, her father clasps the hand of the groom over which a handkerchief is draped and the ceremony is read. After this, there is much feasting and celebrating for many days.

Also remembering Muslim weddings in the Old Country, Amid "Mike" Abdallah of Ross, in a 1939 interview, said the following:

After all arrangements for the wedding were completed, such as the consent of the girls parents, amount of money set aside to provide for the bride in case the marriage proves a failure because of some fault of the groom, or desertion by the groom; this amount is set according to the financial condition of the groom. Then a feast is prepared for the crowd that is invited, the table remains set with all the food during the whole time of the celebration and the people can and do eat whenever they want to. A man, or boy may make arrangements for the wedding whenever he sees a girl that he wants as his wife, the agreement is made between the man and the parents of the girl, or if the man is not of age, the boy will tell his parents that he desires a certain girl and then his parents will make the arrangements with the parents of the girl. This agreement is some times made when the girl is only a few years old. When the ceremony takes place the bride goes to a room by herself and remains there alone until after the ceremony, she has named witnesses to act in her behalf. The father of the bride then clasps the hand of the groom and a cloth is drapped [sic] over the clasped hands, the ceremony is then read from the Koran (our Bible). Then there is dancing and feasting for sometimes many days and nights.

In North Dakota, it must be mentioned, the Muslim couple went to a local civil officials—a judge or magistrate—sometime during the wedding event. Yet the revered traditions were carried on as much as possible. The formality of asking the bride's parents for the hand of the bride was observed. The ceremonies took place at the bride's home and a community religious leader would provide the special readings from the Koran. An array of festive celebrations would follow.

Yet a civil license for marriage was not unknown among Muslims (and probably others) in the Old Country. Kassem Ramadan, a Muslim, described the wedding details from his perspective when interviewed at Lignite, ND, in October 1939. He mentions the decorative veil on the face of the bride. Mr. Ramadan said he was born on a farm "near Damascus."

When the boys were old enough to get married, the parents would pick out a wife and make arrangements with her parents for the marriage. They must have a license which was issued by a judge. Then, for three Fridays, the engagement would be announced in the church. Most weddings were held on Friday, as that was our holy day. When I was a boy, the women in my country always covered their faces with veils at all times. Veils of brides were decorated with green flowers.

From an Orthodox Christian perspective, the wedding centered in the church, but the festivities spilled over into what could be a week of celebrations. Attas Boutrous, in 1939, recalled the event in his home village, Ain Arab:

The weddings in my country are always held in the church by the priest and on Sunday. There are no civil marriages in Syria. On Saturday preceding the wedding the bride and lady friends are invited to her home, and the groom and his friends are invited to his home. They stay here, feasting, drinking and visiting until time for the ceremony when they are escorted to the church and the ceremony performed. After the ceremony those who can afford it put on a large celebration which is usually held at the home of the groom.

A week or a two-week celebration is fixed in the memory of Samuel Nicola, Orthodox and a native of Ain Arab. The couple "was not compelled to marry" but they had a "lot of respect for their parents." In July 1939, Mr. Nicola reported:

> *The weddings were held by the priest in church and after the ceremony there would always be a long celebration lasting sometimes a week and sometimes two weeks. The young people tried to please their parents when getting married, however they were not compelled to marry whom they did not wish. The children had a lot of respect for their parents and they always tried to please them in everything. Usually the celebration would be held at the bride's home or at the groom's home and would last quite a while depending on how well fixed the couple's parents were.*

Mary Farris, of Catholic background, recalled a Zahle wedding in a 1940 interview in Williston:

> *My folks is well off—just small family—I didn't do nothin' before I married. Old Country work awfully cheap—you work all day for ten cents. Everybody got wheat, take it to mill and make flour. My father he make good livin'. We got no show, no car, just big time when weddin'. You know rich people—weddin' a week. Poor like us (now) just one night. Lots fun. One evenin' when I got married. Girl stay home all time in Old Country—not like here. I don't like dat. I glad I got no girl now. Old Country no fun only when weddin' or somethin'. Time I married I'm 18 year old.*

George Saba, whose infancy was in North Dakota and young adulthood was in Ain Arab, indicated in a July 1939 interview at Bismarck that times were changing in "Syria." The dowry for the bride was becoming a less frequent part of marriage arrangements.

> *The marriage ceremony of the Christian Syrian is conducted in the church and in the early days in Syria the contracting parties were brought together by the parents and usually the groom's parents would pay some money to the bride's parents, in fact really purchasing her for their son. However, this practice has been discontinued among the Christian Syrians but is still the custom among the Druse [sic] Syrians who are a tribe living in the mountainous regions of Syria, and who are Mohammedans.*

In 1949, Sam Eli went to Lebanon with his father Hassen (originally Hassen Ali el Kadry) to visit their kinfolk, but the pair made the trip for an additional reason: to obtain a wife for the widowed Hassen. They left Glenfield, North Dakota, took the long journey and arrived at the village of Hassen Eli's birth, Kfar Dines, Lebanon. While there they witnessed a three-day Muslim wedding in which over 2,000 Muslim, Christian, and Druze took part. The groom was not allowed to see the bride for 24 hours prior to the event. The prospective husband arrived riding backwards on a horse and did not see the bride until the vows began. Some villagers asserted that the bride's mother kept vigil outside the house on the night before the wedding to make sure her daughter remained a virgin.[7]

Between the lines of Old Country memories, the presence of what scholars call arranged marriages can be detected. Given the fact that the family was of paramount importance, such a set of customs would seem entirely appropriate; in marriage, one took not just a new bride or groom, but also adopted an extended family. Obviously the family would have a role to play in mate selection.

Needless to say, arranged marriages elicit a disagreeable reaction in modern America. It's obvious that "old settlers" do not like to emphasize their early associations with it. Yet it is still the way in which many of the world's marriages take place. Such marriages can vary from family to family and probably in Lebanon from religion to religion. In some cases it may have been a gentle nudge, pointing to a suitable prospective spouse. At times it may have involved a "matchmaker," an in-between person, who brought about a satisfactory union. The individual usually retained a "veto" power. But there were instances, it seems, in which the couple had no choice in the matter.

In the United States, choice of a mate is often the exclusive prerogative of the individual. This would become a problem for many immigrant groups. Lebanese were no exception. Family memories do not dwell on the difficulties that may have risen. There is plenty of evidence that among Lebanese some second-generation young people in North Dakota did actually have mates who in one way or another were "chosen for them." We might add that other North Dakota ethnic groups also had a form of arranged marriage in the early settlement years. Yet "parental choice" might be too strong a phrase to use in America. "Parental preference" is probably more correct. And for many second-generation young people such a preference was sufficient to indicate the acceptability of a potential mate. In time, however, the spirit of freedom and individuality that blew with the winds of the New World certainly affected America's children of every national origin. Dictatorial measures would increasingly be frowned upon.

In fact, an alleged attempt to coerce a Dakota Syrian girl into marriage and the subsequent brutality of the husband appeared in several North Dakota newspapers in February 1910. It came to the attention of local officials:

The husband of the girl claimed to have purchased her for $1625. They have been married about a year. The girl's parents finally induced her to leave him on the grounds of cruelty, and took her home with them. The husband claimed to have the right to his wife, as according to the custom of their race her price had been duly paid and she belonged to the person who bought her.[8]

The Gackle, ND, newspaper, when reporting the above-mentioned incident, said the parties settled their dispute amicably. They also left the state, probably after a strong admonition from the State's attorney as to the way "we do things in America."

This discussion of arranged marriages would be deficient if it led the reader to believe that women in Syria were mere pawns in the hands of male family members. Old Country gender ways were fashioned through the centuries by a sense of struggle—a matter of survival—in difficult sets of political and often geographical difficulties. Never in any WPA interviews and never in any of the authors' conversations with "old-timers," was there a suggestion that women were somehow less than men in terms of human dignity.

Women in the original Lebanese villages and cities had their distinctive role to play, and not surprisingly, the women's portion of life centered in family matters. But women were also an economic asset to family and clan. As in most Middle Eastern, and probably most European households, the women managed the home, made clothing, cooked and baked, and handled the affairs of the children. In rural regions, she sometimes helped in the fields alongside her husband.

Marriage did subordinate the woman to her husband; yet motherhood gave her a special role that was regarded, by one writer, as "something almost sacred."[9]

Whether Christian or Muslim, the family in Syria was patriarchal in orientation, but generational bonds were also of paramount importance. The elders thereupon had a controlling voice in family matters. In the Muslim family, for example, the mother had the task of "screening" potential mates for possible marriage. The father made the final arrangements. The same was most likely true in Christian families as well.[10]

Jabir Shibli

A truly diverse and fast-moving man, Jabir Shibli was born in Btighreen in Lebanon in 1886. At the age of 22 he came to the United States and by his late 20s had already attended a Presbyterian theological seminary and was pastor in a Presbyterian church in McIntosh, South Dakota. Receiving a master's degree from the University of North Dakota in 1918, he became professor in the Fargo College where he stayed for three years. With further study at the University of Wisconsin, he subsequently earned his doctorate at Columbia University in New York.

For 27 years he was professor of Mathematics at Penn-sylvania State University and among his many publications was a basic textbook on trigonometry, which was used in nearly 500 colleges. A university chair in the Mathematics Department is dedicated to his name.

His career as a university professor did not diminish his concern for the Presbyterian ministry; he was continually involved in religious affairs, sometimes temporarily occupying the pulpit in churches and teaching Bible classes. (In a two-year period he gave illustrated lectures on the Holy Land at 50 central Pennsylvania churches.)

Jabir Shibli married Adma Hamman, born in Shwier, Lebanon, and their three children excelled in academic life. One son, the late Raymond Nadeen Shibli, was a distinguished attorney in the Washington, DC area. Another son, David, was a professor of history at Santa Monica College in California.

Jabir Shibli's love for Lebanon never diminished. He returned to Lebanon to teach at his alma mater, the American University at Beirut, in 1950. He died in Btighreen at the age of sixty-eight.

Jabir Shibli: early Dakota clergyman, professor at Fargo College and distinguished faculty member and author at Pennsylvania State University.

Courtesy: David Shibley

CHAPTER FIVE

Schools

Schools in Lebanese villages were of two types, native and mission. The native schools were often run by local priests, whether Orthodox, Melkite or Maronite. The school building was usually a one or two-room structure, neat and equipped as well as local resources could provide. Needless to say, a religious component was often part of the curricula. The quality of the schools varied from town to town and understandably depended on the abilities of the teachers. The mission schools were set up by foreign groups: American, British, German, Russian, and especially French. Remembering his childhood some 40 years before, Abe Mikel of Orthodox background and a long-time resident of Williston, North Dakota, said in 1940, "Sure we had good schools there, all kinds, English, French, Russian and Syrian. I went to school and studied hard till I was thirteen or fourteen years old."

More details concerning the schools of Zahle in particular were given by Joseph Azar who, in Bismarck in August 1939, remembered:

> I attended a public school until I was 8 years old and when my father died, I quit. The school building was a large brick building, similar to those school buildings in the United States. There were also several colleges where one could obtain a good education, but I did not attend any of them. Most of these were conducted by the Latin Catholic Church and the pupils lived right in the colleges, like they were in a home. Some of the children from the country towns came to the schools and stayed the whole year. Several of the colleges were conducted by the Greek Orthodox Church.

Zahle, the hometown of Joseph Salman, must have been a regional educational center. Mr. Salman, in an interview in Bismarck in August 1939, recalls his childhood training, which seemed comparable to the private school system in America.

I attended a parochial school for 7 years and completed the fifth grade. The Catholic Church under the direction of the priests conducted the school. The subjects were about the same as they are here with the exception of the religious training we received. We were taught only the Syrian language at that time. The boys and girls were separated and were placed in different rooms. The school building was attached to the church and was a very large building made of brick.

Louie Nassif, a native of Ain Arab, considered his educational experience as equal or better than those of contemporary American standards. In Bismarck, in August 1939, Mr. Nassif said:

I attended a public school for six or seven years and I don't know what the grades were known as there. We were under very strict discipline while attending school and we had to study hard and know our lessons well, while we were going to school. I believe that most of us learned a good deal more rapidly than the children do in this country.

School support and standards in Ain Arab did not seem to be a matter involving the direct concern of either state or community officials, but were more a family preference. Thomas Nassif of Bismarck in August 1939 reported in an interview:

Howell Township School, north of Bisbee, ND
Pupils seated on ground include Joe Nicholas and Jim Nicholas
Courtesy: Gene Nicholas

I attended school for two and one half years. The parents hired the teacher and paid him and also arranged for the school house. If the parents did not have money so they could pay their share of the teacher's salary they were just out of luck for education for their children. The government did not help the children get an education at that time and it was not compulsory for the children to attend school. The teacher was paid the same way as the priest, each parent donating as he could. We were taught reading, writing, arithmetic, and the Syrian language.

Levels of education, it is clear, varied with the differences of family preference, family income, and with local circumstances. Kassem Ramadan of Bowbells, ND, a Muslim who was born "near Damascus," explained in October 1939:

But they do not have free education in that country. Instead of paying taxes to run the schools, as we do here, the parents paid the money to those who had charge of the schools. The amount each parent paid depended on how many children he sent. My father had to pay about ten dollars a year for my schooling.

Kassem Ramadan said he attended school for only one year. Bo Alley Farhart of Ross said in November 1939 that his family had private instruction:

A private tutor was hired by my father to teach us children to read and write and learn the Koran.

Joseph Abraham, of Christian background, told the WPA interviewer in 1940, "My mother's a teacher, and she learn us right in house; we got school two, three months every year." Another North Dakota settler, H. A. (Hassin Alley) Juma, said in 1939, "I had a private tutor to teach me for two years. We were taught to read and write the Koran." Reminiscing in the same year, Sam Omar, a Muslim of Ross and a native of Bire, said: "I attended a parochial school for two years in the years of 1888 and 1889. Our school building was small and we were taught arithmetic, geography, and religion. Our teacher was a native."

Formal education, whether for few or many years, put the emphasis on what Americans would call "The Three R's"—reading, writing and arithmetic. But the trade skills were taught in Syria, and throughout the rest of the world, through various apprenticeship programs. George Saba, a native of Ain Arab and a resident of Bismarck, said in July 1939:

When one wants to learn a trade in Syria it is necessary for the person to work for one who has been a tradesman for a long time and knows the work. He works for a year or so until he has learned the trade. The appren-

tice never gets any money for the work while learning the trade, but receives his board, room, and clothing and maybe a little spending money.

As is apparent in the preceding paragraphs, much of the more sophisticated (and more urban) education in Syria seems to have taken place under the auspices of religious groups. Indeed, a Presbyterian missionary school was established in Beirut as early as 1830. As time went on, other denominational colleges arose. Alixa Naff, in her book, *Becoming American,* said that "by World War I, the Levant Coast, according to one observer, had over three hundred foreign schools educating more than fifteen thousand students." Naff says further that Zahle in the 1890s, for example, had a British Anglican school, an American Protestant school, two Jesuit boys schools, a Catholic girls school, and a Russian Orthodox school. In addition, Zahle had a Jesuit college.[1] Beirut is still renown for its famous American University (originally known as the Syrian Protestant College). Through the years this school has produced scholars recognized worldwide for their abilities.[2]

Philip Hitti says that American and English missionaries never encouraged young people to move to the United States; rather, they discouraged such an endeavor. Nonetheless Hitti says that by teaching English and introducing the students to the geography and history of America and England, they indirectly made movement to such countries a more tempting possibility.[3]

In a study of the backgrounds of Syrian immigrants to America, Samir Khalaf seems to discount the effect of education in stimulating the early waves of migration. Quoting approvingly from Hitti, he says the early movement to America involved "Youths in their mid-twenties drawn from the lower strata of society. … The bulk was poor peasants without formal schooling."[4] Khalaf's comments do not completely fit the North Dakota scene; the majority of Syrian settlers were anything but "peasants without formal schooling." Most of the WPA interviewees—male, at least—had some school background.

Nonetheless, Attas Boutrous of Bismarck, when interviewed in 1939, described education in Ain Arab in a very pessimistic way:

I attended a public school for two weeks and did not complete any grade. There was a small one-room school house in Ain Arab; and a teacher was employed by the people who had children going to school. The teachers usually did not know much about teaching, but simply tried to teach the best they knew how. In the town of Ain Arab at that time, I don't believe there were more than five or six people who could read or write. The teachers were certainly not eligible to teach, but they tried to teach some first grade subjects which they did not understand very well. There were no regulations governing the qualifications of the teachers then.

This does bring up the matter of literacy. How many Syrians could actually read or write when they arrived at America's shores? Records must be taken with a certain degree of caution, for language barriers, individual preconceptions, and other such circumstances cloud the judgment of the interviewers. Louise Houghton, using Immigration Department figures, says, "56 percent of the Syrians were illiterate upon arrival in the United States." Houghton says further that their literacy rate was lower than any other immigrant group except Lithuanians. But in perspective she says that upon arrival, "Syrian immigrants openly covet education for their children."[6] She makes the statement that "The truant officer had no dealings with these children."

A 1903 study of New York City found among the "Syrian" residents that 60.9 percent could read and write Arabic; 59.9 percent spoke English and 32% could both read and speak their new country's language. When tabulating female adults the study found that 41 percent spoke English, 27.8 percent read and wrote in Arabic, and 23 percent could both speak and write English.[7]

What of North Dakota? Especially what of the women who came to North Dakota? WPA reports vary on the subject, but it's clear that education for boys rather than for girls in the Old Country was a preference; in fact, it was almost a necessity. In January 1940, Mary Farris, a Williston resident of Christian origin, remembered, "Not much school dat time and dat time people didn't care for girl to go to school, and boy—some people—when get old enough, go to work. Not care much for school dat time."

Mary Juma, a Muslim from Bire and housewife in Ross in 1939 said, "I received no education, as our people thought it was a waste of time and money to teach a girl to read and write. There were no schools in our village, and those that were taught to read and write were taught by a tutor."

"I'm the last one to leave," Mrs. David Kalil, a Christian of Williston said in 1940. "I go to school a little, but in Syria they don't send the girls to school." Mrs. Libbie Layon of Williston, formerly of Zahle, remembered her childhood in a March 1940 interview. She said:

I don't go to school 'tall in Old Country, girls don't go to school. They stay home, learn to do house work, sewing, fancy work, take care children.

In contrast, Mrs. Mary Saliba, native of Ain Arab, said the following in Bismarck in August 1939:

I attended a public school for four or five years, and really did not get much of an education. Our school house was a one-room stone building which was used for a school. The teachers were paid by the parents who had children in school, much the same as the collection received in the church, but they paid, or donated according to the amount of children in the school. If they couldn't pay their share the children received no schooling. I think this has been changed since I left the Old Country, and now the schools are owned by the city or government who give the children free education, or education which is paid for in terms of taxation. I know they have wonderful schools there.

It is clear from the memories of North Dakota's first Syrian settlers that in the Old Country schools were available for both men and women, and that family circumstances dictated the extent and quality of school attendance. It is also clear that men had the advantages. Women were to be taught the skills of a mother and wife. The North Dakota reports also seem to imply that Christians in Syria put more emphasis on basic education, but this was oriented particularly for boys.

Seen from the vantage point of several American generations, this apparent lack of women's education in Syria could be of great disadvantage in North Dakota. (This matter will be discussed later in this volume.) The transmission of cultural and especially religious values from the old to the young was often a mother's task. Without written texts as reference guides, the traditions would have to be passed to the children from memory. Other ethnic groups had an array of catechisms or prayer books. For Muslims, especially, living in rather isolated circumstances, the lack of literacy could present special problems. Generational cultural continuity could be in jeopardy.

James Kallod Jr.

When Jim Kallod's father left Batrounie, Syria, in the early 1900s, he was about to be drafted into the Turkish army. At only 14 years of age, Ibrahim Sheban worked his way across the Atlantic on a cargo ship destined for Brazil. He stayed a short while in South America, only to hear about other Syrians working in Sioux City, Iowa, stockyards. So young Sheban made his way to yet another continent.

While there he bought a peddler's cart that was previously owned by James Kallod. Taking not only the cart, he also took the cart's lettered name for his own. And so the newly named immigrant peddled his way to Tokio, North Dakota. There he established a store on the Ft. Totten Sioux Reservation, which today is called Spirit Lake. He would sell groceries and dry goods there for over 40 years. His wife was of French-Indian (Metis) ancestry.

Ibrahim Sheban (James Kallod) and his "French" wife, Mary, in 1920; long-time merchants on the Sioux Reservation (at Tokio, ND).

Courtesy: Jim Kallod, Jr.

In 1920 a son was born and named James Kallod, Jr. He would proudly become known as "Tokio Jim." He went on to become a World War II hero on the front lines of General Patton's fabled army. One of his army pals was the famous boxer, Joe Louis, with whom he kept in contact. Upon returning from the war, Jim founded Kallod's Carpets of Fargo, which today is operated by his sons. He delivered Christmas presents to several area Indian reservations for many decades.

His advice to young people is to be proud of your heritage, work hard, and save your money. Despite many health problems, Jim said, God had been very good to him.

CHAPTER SIX

Unrest and Departure

S ome have said the legacy of a Phoenician past has left its imprint on Lebanese culture in something that might be labeled "an emigration way of life." Indeed, if one is inclined to believe that certain predispositions can be hidden in a people's nature, the nomadic history of the Lebanese people would seem to point to the Phoenician past. Most scholars, however, would argue that the socioeconomic, political, and historical forces ultimately determined the various elements of the Lebanese character. These circumstances, they say, either "pushed" or "pulled" the Lebanese away from their native land and these factors account for their dispersal to distant global corners. Whatever the case, the Lebanese record in the Americas is replete with fascinating migratory accounts.

There are fragmentary reports of very early Middle Eastern people arriving on American shores. Luis deTorres was an Arabic-speaking gentleman who accompanied Christopher Columbus in his 1492 voyage to the Caribbean Islands. DeTorres was to be an interpreter when Columbus met the "Grand Khan of the Orient."[1] Frequent reports mention "Arab seamen" who jumped ship in the America's of the 1800s. (Descendants still live on Ocracoke Island, North Carolina.) At a later date, 1866, and of some historical fame, was Hadjj Ali of Arabic background who came to the American West with a shipment of animals as the Americans experimented with camels in what was considered, at that time, the "Great American Desert."[2] Mr. Ali became known as "Hi Jolly," and he is still mentioned in western history books.

Others can be added. Arabic-speaking people are said to have been at the British fur trade posts on the Hudson's Bay in the earliest part of the 19th century. Mary Sawaya, a Lebanese lady, appears in the Detroit, Michigan, records in 1856.

Most historical sources start the discussion of Lebanese emigration to the United States with the story of Antun Bish'alani. This individual is considered the "first officially recorded Arab immigrant" to this country. A resident of Salevia, Mr. Bish'alani arrived at Boston in 1854 and tragically died two years later in New York.[3]

In 1864 a Syrian, Sahli Sabrinji, spent time in New York to help with an Arabic translation of the Bible.[4] The first Lebanese immigrant family of special note however seems to have been that of Joseph Arbeely, who came to this country with his wife, six sons, and a niece. He came in 1878 as a professor who would teach Arabic to American missionaries. Two of his sons are remembered as the founders of the first American Arabic newspaper, *Kowkab Amerika* ("The Star of America").[5]

A memento of the "Old Country" from the Joe Nicholas Family collection

Courtesy: Joe Nicholas

The activity of some church officials may have focused the attentions of some early Lebanese immigrants toward America. In 1849 (?), Father Flavianus Kfoury visited in New York to raise money for a Syrian monastery. Welcomed by bishops in New York and Canada, Father Flavianus offered Mass on many occasions in his own rite. These may well have been the first Melkite services in America.[6]

The Philadelphia Exposition in 1876 had a number of Syrian citizens helping with displays. Certain emissaries of the Ottoman government arrived at times for ceremonial visits. These travelers seldom, if ever, stayed, yet information moved through them to their fellow countrymen back home in Syria.

The first Lebanese arrivals in North Dakota were probably peddlers passing through during the 1880s and 1890s. The naturalization records show a certain Joe Paristuin, from "Turkey," filing his second papers for citizenship in May 1898 in Cass County. In the same year, Charles Turk filed his second papers in that county. No Syrian agricultural settlement was nearby. These must have been peddlers who already had five years of American residency.

News concerning the "free lands" in western America was not unknown to the Syrian public. By 1869, Adele Younis says that "rumors had reached

Syria that in America the [president] under the Homestead Act was dispensing valuable lands." "Brave young souls," she says, "began to seek acreages." "Michigan, Ohio and Indiana lands proved attractive."[7]

"Letters from America" is a familiar theme in early settler accounts. "Others can do it, why can't I?" This was especially attractive if the letters came from friends and kinfolk. Louie Nassif of Bismarck said in an August 1939 interview:

The reason I came to this country was because I had some brothers in America who had come to this country some time before and they had written to me telling of the wonderful opportunities that existed here. They wanted me to come over so I did, and I am not sorry either.

Mary Juma, one of the very first settlers in the Ross Muslim community, in 1939 told a WPA interviewer:

The people in our vicinity were migrating to America and kept writing back about the riches in America. Everyone wanted to move and we were a family of the many that contemplated leaving. We sold all our possessions and borrowed two hundred dollars from a man, giving our land as a collateral.

The modern reader may wish some notion of the costs involved in making the one-way trip to the United States. Viviane Doche quotes a John Thomas who came to New York about the same time as the majority of North Dakota immigrants were arriving in the New World. Mr. Thomas traveled on a French ship to Marseilles, then by train to Cherbourg and thence to New York. He said, "It cost me approximately $75 or $80. There were about 300 immigrants on this ship and we stayed in large compartments below deck and slept in bunks tiered three high."

During the nine years between 1899 to 1907, of the 41,404 Syrians who came to the United States, 2,055 individuals listed their destination as one of the four north-central American states. These figures come from the Department of Commerce tally sheets. The East Coast might have been the initial entry point but it's clear that many Syrian immigrants were already thinking of some specific midwestern place of residence.

The lure of "streets of gold" emerges frequently in early immigrant accounts. Viviane Doche, in a discussion of Twin City Syrians, found the theme in the story of a Mr. Lyons (Aziz Layvoun) whose parents homesteaded in North Dakota. The family left Lebanon because "in America all you had to do is pick gold in the streets."[8]

Bo Alley Farhart, of Ross and of Muslim background, told the WPA interviewer in 1939:

Stories of the wonderful opportunities in America caused me to migrate to this country. I had thoughts of becoming rich and returning to Syria to live in luxury for the rest of my life, and I expected to find opportunities, good wages, and much of everything wherever one turned.

By the early 1890s, every village in Lebanon could claim at least some sons and perhaps daughters who were living in the United States. The exodus would almost double by 1900. It would be a gradual exodus for most of Lebanon, yet the outmigration continued into the ensuing decades and some villages would eventually lose a very large percentage of their inhabitants. Zahle, for instance, saw more than one-ninth of its population depart in eleven months.[9] Alixa Naff quotes a man who left Lebanon in 1891: "All of my village of Ain Arab rushed to America. It was like a gold rush." Many of the emigrants were among the most industrious; their departure, as one would imagine, created some readjustment and even hardships in the affected villages.[10]

All the while another influence began to encourage outmigration: successful emigrants began sending back to the Old Country some of their American earnings. This, of course, was in the background of almost every national group that came to the United States. The first arrivals had often been helped by their family and friends to make the journey to the New World. In return, a steady flow of American dollars was sent to relatives at home. Carol Landis quotes a source which said that in 1924, 19 million dollars went back to Lebanon in what Landis calls "remittance from abroad."[11]

"They sent for me" is a phrase that reoccurred in early accounts. Edward Nedoff, a native of Zahle, said in a 1939 report from Williston:

I'll tell you how it happened when I came over here. Kassis brothers was on a farm at Rugby (N. Dak.). They sent for me and my brother to help our family out. My dad didn't make much money. I and my brother Mike, they sent us the fare and we came over.

The memories of Mary Saliba of Ain Arab were recorded also in Bismarck in August 1939:

My father had gone to America quite some time before. I came, because I was quite young. He had homesteaded on some land near Denhoff, North Dakota, and of course he sent for us when he had the house built and was sure of a living for us.

The village of Ain Arab, the home of the Attiyeh family, is of special interest. As noted earlier, this town lost large numbers of its more adventuresome men and women. They seem to have avoided the large eastern seaboard cities, at least in terms of permanent residence. Rather they sought out midwestern U.S. cities such as Cedar Rapids and Sioux City. Many eventually found their way to the North Dakota counties of Sheridan and Burleigh. Estimates say that 1,500 American men and women today claim heritage from a common ancestor named Attiyeh Hanna Mahfouz Attiyeh.

Emigration from Lebanon (Syria) to the United States, 1887-1920*

Year	Number	Year	Number	Year	Number
1887	208	1899	3,708	1910	6,317
1888	273	1900	2,920	1911	5,444
1889	593	1901	4,064	1912	5,525
1890	1,126	1902	4,982	1913	9,210
1891	2,483	1903	5,551	1914	9,023
1892		1904	3,653	1915	1,767
1893		1905	4,882	1916	676
1894		1906	5,624	1917	976
1895	2,767	1907	5,880	1918	210
1896	4,139	1908	5,520	1919	231
1897	4,732	1909	3,668	1920	3,045

*Source: National Bureau of Economic Research, Statistics, vol. 1 of *International Migrations,* ed. W. F. Willcox (New York: National Bureau of Economic Research, 1929), pp. 384-88, 432-43 (as found in Eric Hougland, *Crossing the Waters,* pp. 20-21).

One striking feature of Lebanese immigration is that, at least in the earlier stages, it was largely a Christian phenomenon. The Mount Lebanon portion of Syria experienced severe civil and religious hostilities during the years 1841, 1845, and 1860. Christians saw themselves as a persecuted minority within the larger Muslim-oriented Ottoman Empire.[12] A massacre of Maronites and Orthodox in certain villages—a matter of thousands of deaths—took place in 1860. These events left a decided unrest in the Middle Eastern Christian world. Economic factors were also aggravating the scene. And at the same time steamship agents were recruiting labor for American industry. The efforts of Lebanese brokers and, in time, the return mail filled with letters (and with money orders) combined to begin the series of sizable emigrations from Mount Lebanon.[13]

Why the delay of Muslim outmigration? Some historians speculate that Islamic Lebanese were fearful of losing their religious traditions if they were to move to a western Christian society like America.[14] This would be a concern for it meant a loss not only of religion but of the entwined culture as well.

Another explanation holds that Muslim peasants when compared to Christians had lower socioeconomic status and thus had greater difficulty in obtaining the funds for an overseas voyage.[15] And it may be true that the Christian Lebanese had an advantage over their Muslim compatriots, for if the Christians were more in tune with Western schools and the European-American business world, they would have easier access to migration routes. And since Christians came earlier the flow of "letters" and the flow of "remittances" would give them a head start.

This we know, the early Lebanese emigrants tended to be young, unattached males, some of whom had low skill levels and minimal educational backgrounds.[16] Accordingly, many would mortgage property, borrow money from relatives, or pledge indentured labor in return for the costs of their overseas voyage. Their hope was to generate as much wealth as possible, in the shortest time, and then return home to live with a certain degree of ease. Family resources therefore often financed emigration. If the emigrant returned home with wealth and prestige it was considered to be a good investment. If the emigrant stayed in America there was the well-founded hope that money would be sent back to the "folks at home" in Syria.[17]

The migration of such a vital portion of the population brought about changes in the Old Country way of life. Many parts of the Syrian culture would be affected by the decline in the work force. Some towns, it is said, became almost homes for the aged rather than homes for the youth.[18] Wage conditions would have to adjust. The "word from America" would change the things. Education would become more meaningful, certainly the status of women would be affected, for in America Lebanese men quickly saw how the economic value of women could bolster a family income: women not only crafted things but they often left home and peddled in their own "territories."

By 1910, thirty-two percent of the total number of "Syrian" U.S. immigrants was female. The average female proportion of all arriving ethnic groups in that year was 30 percent.[19] Philip Hitti points out that the female proportion would have been much higher by that time period were it not for the fact that the earliest Muslim and Druze migrations brought only several dozen women to America. In contrast, thousands of their male coreligionists were arriving.

The Holy Family Maronite Church in St. Paul listed reasons for emigration from Lebanon in its *Golden Jubilee* booklet. There may be some exaggeration but the publication mentioned that first in importance was religious persecution suffered at that time under the "Turks," the Ottoman Turks. Remembered particularly was the fact that no church bells were to be rung, no cross could precede a funeral, and a license was needed to bury the dead. Moreover, it was claimed that the Maronite Patriarch had to accept orders from the Sultan of Constantinople. Other restrictions were said to have been placed on Christian shoulders such as a prohibition of green colors, walking on the left side of the street in the presence of Muslims, and the denial of Lebanese identity in favor of the offensive phrase "Ottoman subject."[20]

Religious massacres have played a very definite role in Lebanon's history. (They have occurred in recent years as well.) In spite of long periods of relative peace there were times, such as the 1860 massacre, when religious motives stirred up unrest even more than economic factors.[21] Philip Hitti, the renowned student of Syrian immigration history, stressed the persecution factor. Other scholars, such as Hasib Seliba, argue that oppression was a secondary motive. He is convinced that it took until the 1890s for substantial numbers of Christians to leave Lebanon and by this time religious problems were minimal. From a North Dakota perspective, Seliba seems to be correct. No Christian complained in the 1939-1940 interviews of religious persecution. In every case, whether in Crookston, Minnesota or North Dakota, it was political and economic oppression by the Ottoman Turks, not so much religious difficulties, that were paramount and reoccurring themes in settlers' accounts.

The recollections of North Dakota's "old time" immigrants from Lebanon, as recorded in the 1939-1940 WPA reports, are filled with memories of relative overpopulation and land shortages. Mary Juma at Ross, North Dakota, wrote: "My husband's farm was very small. I don't know the number of acres, but it wasn't enough for us to but barely exist on."

Bo Alley Farhart, also a Muslim from Ross, reminisced in November 1939:

> *My father was a farmer, and I herded goats and sheep for my parents. Wages for a goat herder amounted to $8.00 a year with board and room. Father owned one-hundred and twenty acres of land, and sometimes rented more land. When he rented, it was on shares. The owner got one-third and Father got two-thirds. Taxes for one-hundred and twenty acres were three or four dollars.*

A political factor that emerges frequently in immigrant recollections was a desire to escape military conscription. The Ottoman Turk Constitution of 1908 made not only Muslims but also Christians subject to the military draft. Christians had been exempt through many centuries of Muslim rule. Conscription, understandably, was a universally disliked measure. Not only was it an economic drain on a village but also it meant prolonged isolation from close kinship groups.[22]

Both Christians and Muslims hated the draft and reports say that many went to great extremes to avoid service in the military. Examples included such things as hiding in caves, sailing out to sea, or going to foreign consulates or embassies. Some Druze resorted to bodily mutilations. There were severe consequences for those who concealed or aided any one who would seek to avoid the military conscription.[23]

Allay Omar, of Muslim background, remembered Old Country problems when speaking to an interviewer at Ross in 1939:

> I left my country of birth because I thoroughly disliked and disapproved the government of Turkey and the control they had over us. They forced the young men to join their army, and they taxed us until we bled, and we never could understand what they used our money for as no improvements were ever seen anywhere.

Some early North Dakota Lebanese, both Muslim and Christian, did not know their true age because the Turkish Army forced teenagers into military service. (The age was 14 years!) Sam Omar of Ross said he had no idea of his age because his parents in Lebanon concealed all information concerning births from Turkish military authorities.

Reiterating the same thing was Side Abdallah, a Muslim of Ross, who recalled sadly in a 1939 interview:

> I was born in Rafieg [sic], Syria, but cannot say how old I am because when we were under the Turkish rule, no age records were kept. Parents tried to conceal the ages of their children so as to keep their sons out of the army.

Restless under Turkish political and economic rule, Mike Abdallah of Ross, a Muslim who came to America in 1907, said in an interview 32 years later:

> In the Old Country I only had forty acres to farm and only one cow so it was very hard to make a living. A man couldn't make a living by working out. Quite a few people from our town had already come to America and their letters told of lots of work for which they got big pay, free land to farm and live on, and much freedom. We didn't have any freedom in the Old Country as we were under the Turkish rule and we even had to be very careful what we said and the taxes we paid were taken by Turkey and we never got anything back for the taxes we paid. Our roads were

terrible. Then the Turkish government made our men and boys serve in their army for sometimes many years.

Over and over again the theme of governmental economic oppression occurs in the memories of Syrian immigrants. Mary Juma, at Ross, ND, made the following observations in 1939:

There is too great a comparison to say much about America and my native land. This country has everything, and we have freedom. When we pay taxes, we get schools, roads, and an efficiency in the government. In the Old Country, we paid taxes and Turkey took all the money, and Syria receiving nothing in return. We were repaid by having Turkey force our boys to join her army. The climate in the Old Country was wonderful, but we have such a climate down south.

The Mount Lebanon area, with its mountains and valleys, had, for years, a serious dependence on silk. After four decades of civil unrest, national and international factors changed the silk industry drastically. Silk production declined, placing an added burden on the valley and mountain people. Problems began to accumulate: high domestic taxes, the absence of protective tariffs, and the change in European clothing styles. When the Suez Canal opened in 1869 it struck a near fatal blow to silk merchants of Mt. Lebanon. Not only were the trade routes shortened but also the Far Eastern silk was of good quality and sold for a lower price.

Perhaps Lebanon's most damaging hardships came after the North Dakota immigrants had left Syria; the problems came with World War I and its devastating aftermath. The volume, *Crossing the Waters*, says:

Foreign remittances, tourism, and revenue from summer resorts, by then major sources of national income, came to a sudden halt. A tight blockade was imposed on food, medical supplies and clothing. Staple items and basic commodities were scarce; prices rose, and shortages became more widespread. By the fall of 1916, famine, successive swarms of locusts, and epidemics hit an already enfeebled and demoralized population. Entire villages were deserted. Others were left in partial ruin.[24]

Not surprisingly, when the war ended and people could again resume safe travel, a large number of immigrants fled Lebanon in desperation. Unfortunately, by this time many would encounter new immigration laws and restrictive quotas in the United States, so instead they went to South America and Africa. North Dakota received few, if any, of these post-World War I "refugees."

The Departure

As various Muslim groups of the Bire and Rafid vicinities said goodbye to their Lebanese homes, the occasions were, to say the least, filled with great emotions. Mary Juma of Ross remembered it very well. A group of townspeople gathered and a large farewell party was given in their honor. Although it was a sad occasion for friends and relatives, there was still a feast with foods and dancing. The activities included games in which the men competed in feats of strength and endurance.

Allay Omar, a Ross resident, remembered a 1907 farewell party given to honor him and seven other individuals as they left Bire. "It was sad, indeed, for our relatives didn't want us to go such a distance." But there were lots of handshakes and many gifts were presented. They were laden with food and their suitcases were full of clothes. His group left Beirut in August 1907. Omar remembered that the ship's quarters were good but that he was too seasick to eat the foods. The eight men came directly to New York. He thereafter took a train to Grand Rapids, Michigan, where he visited friends and relatives. He then went by rail to Stanley, North Dakota, and there his brother, Sam, was waiting for him.

Side Abdallah's WPA story is a rather sad one. After marriage in Rafid, Lebanon, in 1902, he came to America, the land of gold in the streets. He intended to send for his wife when he had accumulated sufficient funds in the New World. Later, after homesteading in Ross, ND, he sent money but she didn't come. The Dakota farm work, he said, was not as easy as he had been led to believe. Side stuck it out and continued to live in North Dakota until old age.

A more fortunate immigrant was Rafid resident Hassin Alley Juma who was born July 2, 1888. Interviewed in 1939, he remembered no farewell party but did recall the trip across the waters. Amid Abdallah, Bo Alley Farhart, Alley Omar Sage, and others came with him on the 1907 journey. The first stop was Naples, Italy; then Paris, France; then London; and finally Halifax, Canada. He remembered storms and seasickness on the voyage. En route to St. Paul, Minnesota, he fell asleep and some of his money was stolen. He arrived finally at Ross, North Dakota, and became part of the local Muslim community. Hassin Alley Juma was disappointed at the barren land and went through difficult times on his prairie farm, but his life had a happy ending. His descendants grew up in this country to become successful citizens.

The departure from the Old Country was never pleasant. WPA interviews in 1939-40 showed instances of intense heartache. Several families left children in Lebanon. Mrs. Mary Juma left two daughters there, one died, the other continued to live in Bire. Husbands left wives, brothers left siblings, and children left parents. Sometimes they would never see each other again. Such was often the price of emigration.

Perhaps because of the Turkish draft, or perhaps because of recriminations toward the family, Bo Alley Farhart left Rafid in secret. In November 1939 he reported in a Ross interview:

My mother financed the trip to America, and I brought only my clothes with me. Not anyone was allowed to leave the country at the time I wished to depart, so I did it stealthily. No farewell party was given in my honor, but there were many tears shed by everyone. I was the only one leaving that community at that time, although a brother of mine did migrate to Ross, North Dakota sometime before.

Thomas Nassif of Ain Arab, Lebanon had heard tales about America's opportunities through letters from his father who had gone earlier to the New World. Describing his "round about" way to meet his father he reported, in 1939, that he left the port of Beirut in July of 1909 and traveled to Alexandria, Egypt. The steamboat then went to Naples, Italy. From there he traveled through Germany to LeHavre, France, by railroad. Then a ship took him to Liverpool, England, and finally to Halifax, Nova Scotia, Canada. Nassif recalled the hassles of passports and stressful baggage searches. Mr. Nassif believed his father resided in Cedar Rapids, Iowa, so the railroad took him to that city. As it turned out, his father was farming in Kief, North Dakota. Finally, in a matter of days, Nassif and his father were reunited at that tiny prairie town. Back in Ain Arab he believed American farmers were shoveling money into their pockets without too much work. Disappointment set in quickly as Nassif took up farming on the North Dakota plains. But, he says, "I really do like it now."[25]

Shaker Nassif of Orthodox Christian background, left his wife and four children in Ain Arab, Lebanon with the promise that he would send money to the family to make life easier. After many adventures he finally ended up on a homestead near McClusky, North Dakota. (Shaker reported that Arab immigrants had a relatively smooth trip to their New World destination if a note was pinned to their clothing indicating that already established relatives awaited their arrival at a particular American destination.)

Shaker Nassif worked hard in North Dakota. Faithful to his promise, he did send money back to the family and after four years in North Dakota returned to Ain Arab to build a stone dwelling for his wife and children. He returned to America with a son and daughter and lived to be 94. He was never again able to see the rest of his loved ones in Ain Arab.

A grandson of Shaker Nassif, George Skaff of Bismarck, tells this story of his grandfather's journey—on foot—through eastern America to North Dakota:

The only way he could make it was to take merchandise which he bought for pennies – like thread, scissors, and small notions that people would buy readily. He put them in a big bundle on his back and walked all the way from New York, stopping at villages and farms along the way. It took him nearly two years before he reached St. Paul. There he got more merchandise and trekked westward into the Dakotas because he had heard that there was free land. He kept selling merchandise which he carried on his back and made a few dollars.[26]

A WPA field worker interviewed Mrs. Mary Farris of Williston in 1940 at the end of the Great Depression. In broken English she told of leaving her two children with her parents in Lebanon and her intense yearning for them. Her intention was to make money for a couple of years in America and go back home. She spoke of the long hours spent in producing needlework for her husband's peddling rounds, which often took him away from home for several weeks at a time. From 6 a.m. to midnight she would crochet her small textile items. This work was often accompanied by periods of crying. In an understatement, which summed up the experience of many Lebanese, she said, "those were hard times."

Titanic's Fate Haunts Minot Man

Mike Fedorchak of Minot has a special connection to the story of the Titanic. Fedorchak's grandmother, Thelma Thomas, was one of only 700 or so people who survived the doomed ship's first and final voyage. On April 15, 1912, the Titanic slammed into an iceberg and sank off the coast of Nova Scotia. The disaster claimed more than 1,500 lives, and the mystery of why the ship sank so quickly endures to this day.

Fedorchak's grandfather had immigrated to the United States and arranged to marry Miss Thomas in Lebanon where she was from, and eventually bring her to the states.

The two married in Lebanon and conceived a child. While Thelma Thomas was pregnant, the groom needed to return to the United States to work. He later sent his brother to Lebanon to return with Thelma and their newborn son, Essid.

Thelma, the newborn, and 12 other relatives went from Lebanon to France and boarded the Titanic, sailing for the United States. The 12 relatives didn't make it to the United States, dying in the frigid arctic waters when the mighty Titanic broke in half.

"When the ship was going down, my grandmother threw the baby to a woman in one of the lifeboats," Fedorchak said. "She thought she was going to die. But she managed to get onto another lifeboat. She and her baby were reunited in New York, with other survivors.

Fedorchak said he is still haunted by the thought of the sinking vessel. Until her death in 1972, Thelma Thomas participated in numerous ceremonies marking the anniversary of the demise of the giant ship.

(Courtesy of Mike Fedorchak and the Minot Daily News)

Profile: Joe Ausey-Nicholas

One of the children born of Arabic heritage in North Dakota was Joe Nicholas. His immigrant parents were from the Zahle area in the northeast part of Lebanon's Bekaa Valley. Joe's father,

Mother of Nicholas Ausey in Zahle with son Joseph

Courtesy: Joe Nicholas

Nicholas Ausey, had arrived with his brother Sam in Towner County in the 1890s. They homesteaded literally "where the wagon wheel broke." Years later, the son, Joe, would wonder what strange urge led his parents to leave a comfortable Mediterranean climate for that of harsh North Dakota winters. Joe figured it must have been political and economic factors that motivated their move.

Joe's mother's maiden name was Mary Absey. She left Lebanon and moved to St. Paul, thereby joining her brothers and father. The family moved to Walsh County, where they set up a business. Mary Absey and Nicholas Ausey married in Grafton, ND. When Joe was born in 1898, North Dakota was predominantly northern European in ethnic background. Names changed in the new environment. Many children took their father's first name by custom in Lebanon. Many, when they came to America, Anglicized their names. Nicholas Ausey's son, accordingly, became Joe Nicholas.

Not only names changed in the New World; other labels were adjusted. In Zahle, the family had probably been of Melkite Catholic Rite. (Fr. Seraphin Roumie, a Melkite priest would visit their North Dakota farm.) Nicholas Ausey helped build Fr. Roumie's St. George Church in rural Rugby. The Melkite priest was eventually sent to Chicago to meet the needs of other arriving Lebanese. Soon the Ausey-Nicholas family became Latin Rite Catholics. The family still finds its home in that tradition.

Looking back at his life, Joe finds it difficult to believe his parents with four boys and four girls could have made it through the ups and downs of Dakota farm life. Their house now "would not be used as a chicken coop."

Joe and his wife had three children: Gene, a prominent Cando businessman and a long-time legislator in the North Dakota House of Representatives; Loretta, in the Minnesota school system; and Dan, with the North Dakota National Guard.

Zahle and the broken wagon wheel are key parts of the Nicholas family heritage.

Hi Jolly and the Camels

Hadji Ali (known to southwestern Americans as Hi Jolly) came to America from his native Syria during the mid 1850s with a score or more of North African camels. They had been ordered by the U.S. Army for a desert experiment, and Hi Jolly was hired as the chief camel driver.

The Army hoped that the camels would make excellent beasts of burden in the desert. However, the camels were not compatible with the Army's mules and the entire plan was junked in 1864.

On February 26, 1864, thirty-four camels were auctioned off at Benecia, California. The remaining sixty-six camels were auctioned off at Camp Verde on March 18, 1866. Some camels found homes in zoos, while others were bought by circuses and side shows, eventually being turned loose in the desert.

Hi Jolly kept a few camels and tried to operate a freighting business between Colorado River port cities and the mining camps to the east. Although the camels could carry up to 600 pounds of goods and travel more than 60 miles a day without water, his plan, like that of the Army, did not work out. In 1868, Hi Jolly went to work prospecting and scouting for the government.

Hi Jolly died in 1902. His grave in Quarzsite, Arizona is marked by a large pyramid made of the stones from the area, and is topped by a copper camel. *(The above information is from the Quarzsite Chamber of Commerce)*

CHAPTER SEVEN

Passage to the New World

Once the movement to the United States began a series of "services" developed on both sides of the Atlantic. Steamship companies, which had profited from the transport of European peoples to the American shores for two decades, turned an eager eye toward Syria. Through their facilities emigrants moved towards ports in Latin America, the Caribbean, and to the major eastern American cities.

For a few the trip was somewhat commonplace, even an almost enjoyable experience. Edward Nedoff, originally of Zahle, recalling his personal "epic" journey some three decades after the event, said:

> They sent us the fare and we came over. We came to Rugby. We sailed from Beyrouth, Syria. It took us 16 days to cross the ocean. We brought along clothes, biscuits and stuff like that. We had nice weather. I was seasick one or two days. Nothing special happened on the day except they used to gather up and have good times—sing and dance on the boat.
>
> We landed in New York in April, I don't remember the exact date, in 1902. We thought it's a nice country, big buildings and stuff, lots of lights. We didn't have no electric lights where I come from. First we didn't see much of the country after we went to Rugby. We were on a farm at that time.

Mike Abdallah, of Islamic background, remembers his trip to America. He left Rafid and then Beirut in 1907. His memories, in 1939, dwelt on everything except the actual cattle boat passage across the Atlantic. Was it so bad he blotted it out of his mind? Was it so routine it left no impression?

> When I left for America, I gave my land and things to my mother and sister, my father was dead. I borrowed seventy-five dollars besides the money I had saved, to make the trip. I brought only some clothes and enough food to last until I got to France. There were fifteen of us that left from our town at that time, H. A. Juma and Alley Farhart were in the

group, I don't remember the names of the rest. We left from Bayruit the spring of 1907 and sailed to Naples, Italy on a cattle boat, from there we traveled through France by train and took a boat to Liverpool, England. I can't remember sailing from England to Montreal, Canada, it seems to me that I was only on a boat two times on the whole trip. (Interviewer Note: "Mrs. Lila Abdallah, Mike's wife, tried to convince the informant that he must of crossed the ocean on a boat, but he could not recall it.")

Seasickness was almost a universal affliction and it intensified the sadness of leaving home. Mary Farris of Williston, in a 1940 WPA interview, recalled:

On trip I'm sick all time. If I see ocean before, I never come. I cry all the time. I'm sick. Everybody scared. Boat not like now—safe. My husband not sick. He's good on water. He buy me somethin' good, I eat it and I like it.

A series of honest and sympathetic individuals could be found along the transit lines, but unscrupulous "con men" and outright thieves also stood by looking for potential victims. Hassin Alley Juma, mentioned on previous pages, said,

I stayed in Halifax, Canada, for three months and then came to St. Paul, Minnesota. Enroute to St. Paul, I fell asleep on the train and some of my money was stolen.

Theft was part of Deeby Sine's journey to America. The WPA interviewer at Williston recorded her memories in November 1939:

That was about 1900, and went by train to France and sailed from there. I had sold my household goods and even some of my clothes to pay my passage and keep me until I found work in this country. Besides, I wanted clothes of American style, so needed only a few of the ones I had, and also brought a case of laces and fancy work, but this was stolen on the voyage. We were two weeks on the way, and when I saw the statue of liberty welcoming me I was very happy.

The steamship companies, in the main, tried to provide proper transportation. Horror stories abound, however, concerning some of the less-than-honest steamer firms. Overcharging, dreadful voyage conditions, and long delays are remembered by many of the first American arrivals. On one occasion, a newcomer was deposited at the wharf in a Latin American country, the migrant assuming that he or she had arrived in the United States. The opposite was true of three male members of the Nassif family who came, perhaps by accident, to America and North Dakota. A grandson, DeLayne Nassif of Fargo (in 1995), tells some of the family lore:

These young men left their home in Ain Arab and traveled by horseback through the mountains to Beirut. They went by steamship, stopping at Alexandria, Egypt and at Marseilles, France. Upon arriving in that Mediterranean French city, they decided to obtain some of the latest French clothing. Later that evening they were arrested by French police. As it turned out, they were wearing indecent garb, what Americans call long john underwear! The next morning they got out of jail in time to catch a ship which they believed headed for Venezuela. That, too, was a mistake, because upon disembarking from the boat they were surprised to see they were in New York City, America.

In Syria, steamship brokers solicited customers en route to the New World. Well-dressed recruiters returned to the Syrian cities and villages, seeking prospective peddlers for various suppliers in American cities. A trade in illegal passports and even naturalization records developed. (Some American politicians distributed passports in return for vote.) Bribery, of course, was a common part of the process at every stage of the journey. European ports, often a way station on the journey to America, subjected the traveler to a bewildering array of language difficulties, poor foods, and decrepit hotels.[1] But this was not just a Syrian problem. Stories concerning such difficulties can be found in the life experiences of every national group as they journeyed to their New World homeland.

Through an interpreter, Annie Aboud of Williston described for the WPA interviewer the muddle of events that brought her to the Midwest (and eventually to Williston). In January of 1939 she said:

Mother sent ticket for us. Took eighteen days to go from Bania (?). Syria to Marseilles; boat broke, lots of trouble. Left house for cousins in Old Country. Come to Chicago, 1898. Lots relations there that time. Stay there three months. Go to Springfield, Illinois. Husband work in iron factory seven years. I sell laces one year.

Confusion at its maximum is illustrated in the story of Mrs. David Kalil, who recalled her turn-of-the-century journey to North Dakota. This heroic lady left home in Zahle:

So I work four years and save money to come to this country. My father say I can go with [some people] to this country. I leave in September— that's when everybody come, when the water is still. And I come for half ticket, even on train in this country I pay only half-fare. We come to Italy and stay fifteen days there, because somebody got measles and you can't go on boat when somebody sick like that. We stay in Naples, and I learn to talk lots Italian words when I'm there. We have nice trip on ocean; I never get sick, but we have storm one time. Everybody have on life preservers two days, then it get nice and still again. Before we come to New York we stop on Ellis Island and there they put us in big corral like cattle—Syrians in one, Italians, Russians, Irish and every body, all in different corral. I get lost from people I come with and they put me in Italian corral because I talk Italian. They examine everybody there and see how much money you got, where you go and everything like that.

A man come to me and say "how much money you got?" I show him; I got twenty-five dollars in gold—five-dollar gold pieces. He say "you bonus" (that's good). Then a man come take me down about twenty steps and put me in room; he leave me there and I don't get nothing to eat and I'm there about eight hours. Then in the night a man take me and put me on ship and I'm afraid they send me back to Old Country, and I cry. In morning he take me out and put me in depot and say "stay there." And that's New York, but I don't know it. If my aunt know I'm there she come to meet me, and she find me if I'm with Syrians, but I get lost from people I come with. I don't have nothing to eat and I sit in depot and cry. After while I start out and pretty soon police come and grab me and say "who are you? where you going?" And I can't talk to him; he take me back to depot and he say "stay there," so loud. Then I stay there about two hours and they put me on train. After I ride all night, I come to where my brother live in Massachusetts. The man I come with to this country give me wrong address for my brother. They take me in taxi and the man drive around till noon and he can't find my brother. He take me back to depot and just let me off outside.

Italian woman come and ask me where I want to go when she saw me crying. I can talk Italian to her, and I tell her I want my brother and my uncle. She know my uncle when I tell her his name, and she take me there, and then I go to my brother too. I don't see much of this country; I see more in Egypt than here. After while I start work in corset factory and work about month and half. The first week I don't make anything 'cause I don't know that work; next week and after that I get four, five dollars. Then after I know the work, I came here [to Williston].

Every new arrival in the United States had the suspense, even terror, of going through the immigration processing inspections. Ellis Island is the name that comes up most frequently. It contained the "big corral—like cattle" atmosphere of which Mrs. Kalil speaks. Yet something of the same was experienced by those who came through Castle Gardens (the Ellis Island predecessor), Halifax, or Galveston.

As can be seen in WPA and Census accounts, some Dakota immigrants took the Canadian route. Were the immigration requirements less stringent in that country? Mary Juma, in 1939, said in a Ross interview:

We went to Bayruit, which was about thirty miles from our home, and caught a boat to France. It took us about three weeks to travel through France. I do not remember the name of the boat we took from there to America. It took us three weeks to come from France to Montreal, Canada.

Vernon Owan's father arrived in Williston in settlement times but came into the United States by way of Juarez, Mexico. The father's explanation, as he reflected on it in later times, was that it "involved less red tape." The father admitted that many of his "Syrian" countrymen came across the border simulating a Mexican ancestry, even "wearing a sombrero on the bridge between the countries."[2]

For the Syrian immigrant, these frightful entry-time moments were compounded by language difficulty. The Scandinavians or Germans at the depot or on the street could find early arrivals that spoke a dialect that contained some recognizable words. So also Italians and southern Europeans. But the late-arriving Arabic people had few, if any, countrymen who "arrived earlier" and certainly their language was seldom akin to that of the Americans they would encounter as they struggled to find their destination in Midwestern America.

Although government policies varied with the times, it seems that on occasions a certain amount of money, or at least some contacts in America, were essential for admittance into the United States; the government did not want to add another individual to the welfare rolls. The reminiscence of Joe Albert at Williston in February 1940 gives an example of someone who was "sent back" to Europe.

I had friends over here in the United States and they had been writing to me what a wonderful country this was, and I couldn't see how a man would ever make it over there, the Turks taking everything, and there were no opportunities there to give a man a chance for any kind of living. So I decided I would come to America. My father gave me the money for the trip. I got on a boat for France—I can't remember the name of boat but I know it wasn't clean. I then sailed from France to New York—the same thing, everything was dirty. We had pretty good weather coming across to New York; we were about twenty days coming over. When we get to New York or wherever they examined me, I did not have enough money and they would not let me come in. They kept me there three weeks and then shipped me back to France. When I got back to France, my friends over here had sent me money, so I get on boat second time and come across. This time I get through alright. I came alone—none of my family ever came over here but me. I did not bring anything but my clothes and not many of them. I can't tell you exact date, but it was in spring of 1901. It was a good boat I came on second time—everything clean and everybody having a good time. There were five or six Syrians came on the same boat but we did not have a good time. I knew I was worrying all the time for fear I couldn't get in again. When I arrived in New York everything looked big and people rushing around. I had my ticket bought the second time to Sioux City.

Abe Mikel, of Orthodox background, recalled his rather "exciting" journey to St. Paul some forty years earlier. He spoke to a WPA interviewer in 1939. (Mr. Mikel took land near Williston shortly after his arrival in Minnesota.)

The reason I came over here, my mother and brother had been over here quite a while and left me with my other brother. They were at St. Paul, Minnesota. There was fourteen of us in the family and I was the youngest. My sister staid [sic] with my married sister. Her and I were the only single ones; the rest married. My mother sent me the money to come to the United States. I got on Paris boat and went to France—took me seven days from home to France. I got on boat in France—U.S. American Line—and it only took me seven days from France to New York—fourteen days altogether to get from home to New York. We didn't have any storms and I was too much scared to have a good time on boat, although everybody else seemed to have a good time. Before we got into New York City, they took me in some guard thing or other to be examined. They didn't find anything wrong with me and the doctor took me by the hand and told me to sit down. I was so scared I kept running around showing my ticket and saying "St. Paul." I finally got to depot in New York. I was talking Syrian all the time; he was talking English. I had to wait in depot two hours; I got tired waiting and thought I would take a walk and get a drink of water. I showed the man at ticket window and told him St. Paul. I thought I had to show him ticket before I could leave depot. He came around and grabbed me and set me down. I got up and went for water and when I came in train was waiting, so somebody led me to train and got me a seat and say "Chicago." When I got to Chicago depot conductor took me in and I had to wait two hours there. I kept saying St. Paul to everybody and everybody was looking at me, thought I was crazy, I guess, and I pretty near was. Somebody finally got me on the train for St. Paul. The train was supposed to get into St. Paul at ten o'clock at night, but didn't get there till one in the morning. My brother was supposed to meet me at depot, but he wasn't there. There was only a few in depot. There was a big cop there and I bet he weighed three hundred pounds. He knew I was Syrian so he took hold of me and led me out of depot. He walked ahead of me three blocks from depot to Robert Street. When we came to bridge I was so scared I thought he was going to throw me in the water. We finally came to an Italian saloon. The saloon-

men talked Italian and I talked Syrian. The officer then took me to drug store and they told him Syrian people live two blocks from there. We came to a big two-story building and here came a fellow to the door that I knew. He yelled, "is that you, Abe Mikel?" And then my brother and mother came running down the stairs. Maybe I wasn't glad to see them so I could talk to somebody! All I could say in English was "St. Paul," and I'd been saying that ever since I left Syria. I came all the way alone. I didn't bring anything with me but my clothes. It was in 1899.

The "journey to America" stories are often heartrending. Aziz Layon (now Lyons) is quoted by Viviane Doche as he describes the trip made with his brother to the New World to rejoin their parents in North Dakota by way of Duluth, Minnesota:

They left us with our grandparents and two years later they sent for us. My brother and I traveled the 7 seas alone. We were put on the ship and wore a tag where was written: Destination, Duluth, Minnesota. We landed in Marseilles and Le Havre. Once while in transit, we strayed away from the ship. Here we were in a strange country, not knowing French nor a soul, not knowing how to get back to the ship. We were hungry, thirsty, dirty. It got dark, we were fatigued and started crying like crazy. A young man happened to stop by, he talked to us in French, we answered in Arabic. When he saw the tag, he led us to the boat. On the boat I used to beg food from the sailors but soon became friends with the cook's son. When we arrived in Duluth, we sat at the train station not knowing where to go. Finally a woman came towards us, it was my mother, I had forgotten her face and was surprised when she recognized me.[3]

Ports of entry, as seen through the above pages, ranged from New York, to Montreal in Canada, to Galveston on the Caribbean Coast. Sara Elizabeth John, in her story of Lebanese in the El Paso, Texas region, details the overland Mexico route which some preferred. She says, without qualification, that Mexican immigration requirements were less strict than those of the United States. Ms. John also mentions the advantage of a dark complexion. The Lebanese would blend more readily into the flow of Hispanic people coming across the American border. And she, too, spoke of Syrians who crossed the border wearing sombreros.[4]

Viviane Doche records Martha Aussey's recollections. This lady came as a child to North Dakota and then moved to the Minneapolis-St. Paul area.

My parents left the Old Country and sent for us, one daughter after the other. My father went to Mexico first because it was easier to enter the United States. But he died in Blad El Spaniol *(Mexico). I met my*

husband there. He came around the turn of the century, he was
from Ferzoul, a village close to Zahle where I came from. An Abn Arab
(son of the Arabs) from Mankato helped my mother come over to North
Dakota.[5]

A careful look at the U.S. Census reports in 1900, 1910, and 1920 found no North Dakotan indicating Mexico as a birthplace of a child; Canada, yes, but no Latin American country. North Dakota's immigrants traveled through Mexico but didn't settle there. They were in a hurry to get to the land with "streets of gold." As previously noted, Charlie Owan of Williston, hastened across the bridge into El Paso at Juarez. Louie Nassif did the same. In a Bismarck interview Nassif recalled the journey to America through Tampico, Mexico. In August 1939 he said: "I left the Old Country in 1928 and departed from Bayruit, Syria, and traveled to Marseilles, France and from there I took a boat and landed at Tampico, Mexico, and came from there to St. Paul, Minnesota by train."

Some hopeful individuals were turned back, even at the doorstep of North Dakota. The North Dakota newspaper, *The Search-Light*, reported on October 13, 1906: "A party of Assyrians en route to Bisbee were stopped at Killarney [Manitoba] and were required to return to Winnipeg for examination."[6] We know nothing more about the group except to say that other Lebanese had already settled near Bisbee.

In perspective it is clear that the great majority of North Dakota Syrian immigrant accounts mention New York City as their American port of entry. No doubt their experiences in that particular city were forever engraved in the newcomers' minds. This was certainly true of Mrs. David Kalil, whose recollection is noted on a previous page: "We stop on Ellis Island and there they put us in a big corral like cattle— Syrians in one, Italians, Russians, Irish and everybody, all in different corral. I get lost from people I came with …"

Edward Wakin is an American of Lebanese background. In his volume *The Immigrant Experience,* he describes the new arrivals' first moments at Ellis Island:

Once transferred from the ship on which they arrived to a boat or barge,
the immigrants were taken to Ellis Island, which became known as the
Island of Tears to those turned back. They were taken to the Main Hall, a
huge red-brick building with limestone trim and domed towers. Inside,
five thousand at a time were crowded into what was the largest room most
of the immigrants had ever been in. They filed into a maze of passage-
ways made by metal railings, walking twenty feet apart as U.S. Public
Health doctors watched for signs of medical problems.

Chalk marks were used to label those who appeared to need more careful examination. "L" for lameness, "X" for suspected mental defects, "F" for a bad rash on the face. A second doctor looked for specific diseases that were reasons for exclusion, such as tuberculosis and leprosy. A third examined their eyes for symptoms of the blinding disease, trachoma. Where this was suspected, "E" for eyes was chalked onto the immigrant's clothing.

Those with chalk marks were shunted aside for further medical examination, some to be deported. Only about two out of ten actually were detained for more than a few hours at Ellis Island and not more than two out of a hundred actually were sent back. But the arriving strangers knew nothing of the odds in their favor. Each worried about his or her own destiny.

The final test began when the waiting immigrant was summoned from a wooden bench in the giant Registry Hall to appear before an overworked and harried inspector. Looking first at the name tag on the immigrant he then examined the ship's manifest which contained the immigrant's name and twenty-nine pieces of information. With the help of an interpreter, the inspector hurriedly checked the key pieces of information and in less than two minutes made the decision mandated by U.S. law: whether this stranger was "clearly and beyond a doubt entitled to land."

It was almost invariably a quick yes, but that did not lessen the tension. So much was at stake. Bridges had been burned, money scraped together, uprooting completed. For each immigrant it had to be a peak moment.[7]

The next step in this bewildering process was to encounter the city of New York, the number one city in this fabled land of wealth and promise. Reactions, as one would expect, were mixed. Mrs. David Kalil, mentioned above, said that after the entry examination a member of the Ellis Island staff put her on a ship and "I'm afraid they send me back to Old Country, and I cry." She was deposited in New York but alone and confused. "I don't have nothing to eat and I sit in depot and cry." Finally the police came to her assistance and she eventually found her way to her New World friends.

For Sam Omar of Ross, impressions were different. "I was not in the least disappointed about New York because everything looked so new." Joe Albert (not the bear wrestler) said, "When I arrived at New York, everything looked so big and people were rushing about. I wasn't used to that, but everything looked good to me."

The hectic pace of New York—a characteristic of the city even today—made a deep impression on another newly arrived turn-of-the-century immigrant. Mike Abdallah, a Muslim who was to become a permanent resident of Ross, said in 1939:

When I first came to America, I thought America was pretty funny. The way people done things seemed funny. The people were always in a hurry and when they got done there didn't seem to be any reason for the hurry. When they went someplace they were in a hurry; everything in the Old Country was much slower and people weren't in a hurry. I didn't like it for the first two years I was in America and many times I felt like I wanted to go back to the Old Country.

Edward Nedoff, mentioned on previous pages, was impressed, not by the pace of life, but something more basic—electric lights. This future North Dakota farmer, who arrived in 1902, said: "We thought it's a nice country, big buildings and stuff, lots of lights. We didn't have no electric lights where I came from."

Nations with Significant Lebanese Populations

Latin America
1. Brazil
2. Argentina
3. Mexico
4. Columbia
5. Venezuela
6. Chile
7. Ecuador
8. Cuba
9. Paraguay

Europe
1. France
2. Italy
3. Great Britain

Other Areas
1. Australia
2. New Zealand

Africa
1. Egypt
2. Ivory Coast
3. Senegal
4. Liberia
5. Nigeria
6. Gabon
7. Ghana
8. Congo
9. Sudan

Asia
1. Cyprus
2. Saudi Arabia
3. Kuwait

World Cities Outside of Lebanon-Syria with Substantial Lebanese-Syrian Populations

Latin America
1. San Paulo
2. Rio de Janeiro
3. Buenos Aires
4. Mexico City
5. Caracas
6. Bogota
7. Quito
8. Havana
9. Juarez
10. (Other cities)

North America
1. Detroit-Dearborn
2. New York
3. Montreal
4. Calgary
5. Edmonton
6. Toronto
7. Los Angeles
8. Houston
9. San Antonio
10. Pittsburgh
11. Toledo
12. Paterson, NJ
13. Chicago
14. (Other cities)

Africa
1. Cairo
2. Dakar
3. Monrovia
4. Abidjan
5. Accra
6. Lagos
7. Libreville
8. Brazzaville
9. Khartoum
10. (Other cities)

Europe
1. Paris
2. Rome
3. London
4. (Other cities)

Asia
1. Nicosi
2. Riyadh
3. Kuwait City
4. (Other cities)

Other Areas
1. Sydney
2. Wellington

CHAPTER EIGHT

Lebanese Dispersal: America, North Dakota

L
ebanese are mobile people. Every modern descendant who has looked closely at his or her past and present has made this observation. It is still debated whether this is a matter of political or economic pressures or, as has been suggested, some innate urges. Certainly one cannot overlook the matter of geography. Lebanon is at the crossroads of three continents and is tucked into the eastern edge of the Mediterranean Sea. Like it or not, its residents have been forced by their strategic location to think in terms of a wide world of diversity.[1]

Whatever the case, the last century has seen Lebanese migra-tion to every part of the world. More Lebanese are in residence outside of Lebanon today than the totals of those in their homeland. Lebanon is a relatively new nation and has had its share of wars, divisions, and turmoil. Not surprisingly it has been difficult to gain agreement on what would at first sight seem to be a simple matter: the status of the emigrant.

Lebanese law protects the property of emigrants, even for villagers who admit they will never return. (Old Country residents, hoping to purchase their Lebanese land parcels even today are contacting the Noah family of Crookston, the Aggies of Fargo, and the Omars of Stanley.) The original American settlers refused to relinquish their claims and the younger generation, happily established in the United States, is often uninterested in land issues. Both factors prevent local disposition of the property and this leads to continued confusion.[2]

So both at home and abroad the tendency to "move" has led to diffi-culties. This volume concerns itself with America's Midwest and in particular North Dakota. So we begin this chapter with questions: When did they come? And how many came?

Various authors divide the migration from Syria to the United States in different ways. Philip and Joseph Kayal write of an early movement corresponding to periods of political unrest in the Mount Lebanon part of Syria. The first wave, in their assessment, left the homeland from the 1860s through 1890, migrating, for the most part, to Egypt, with some few going to the New World. A second larger immigration, according to the Kayals, took place between 1890 and the First World War (1914). During these years, the population of Mount Lebanon lost 100,000 residents. Again, these emigrants distributed themselves throughout the world, many to the United States. The majority of these departures were from the Syrian Christian group.[3]

Looking especially at the United States, some have divided the various "waves" into four time periods: the first, from 1875 to World War I (1917); second, 1918 to World War II (1941); third, 1947 to the mid-1960s; and finally, 1967 to the present day.[4]

The last two immigration waves have been sizable in number and include refugees from the Middle Eastern unrest of recent decades. Often, these were people of professional background. The Muslim component has proved to be more numerous during these later years. These most recent waves affect North Dakota only in a minor way; the major universities, for example, have graduate students who remain only during their course of study. An educated guess would suggest that several hundred Arabic students have come to the state and left since 1960. Of more lasting influence, but relatively small in number, are professionals who at times remain permanently: college professors, physicians, and skilled technicians.

How many Arabic-speaking people actually came to the United States? We start, of course, with the U.S. Census figures. Yet, as scholars mention repeatedly in these matters, there is the initial difficulty of determining such things as national labels. The 1920 Census called them Syrian. Before that, they were Turks. Other classifications occurred; on occasion they were Mount Lebanon people, Armenians, Ottomans, Arabs, and even Greeks. With such problems in mind, and with few other places to turn, we consider the census totals. Categorizing as to place of birth, we find for the United States as a whole the following: In 1900 (Turkey) 9, 910; in 1910 (Turkey in Asia) 59,729; in 1920 (Turkey in Asia) 8,610; and from Syria, 51,900; in 1930 (Lebanon) 57,227. The corresponding North Dakota figures are: 1900 (Turkey) 104; 1910 (Turkey in Asia) 392; 1920 (Syria) 289, (Turkey in Asia) 18; 1930 (Lebanon) 239. (For a discussion of difficulties in U.S. Census tabulation figures, see Chapter 15, *Naturalization.*)

The above population totals are, of course, subject to many interpretations. The North Dakota "Turkey in Asia" certainly includes people who are, in fact, Armenians for they were present in the state as railroad workers. It may also include Dobrudja Germans from northern Turkey around the Black Sea. (These German transplants had farming colonies in early North Dakota.)

The well-known problem of language barriers and the peripatetic nature of the peddling profession aggravate the labeling and enumeration problems. Another difficulty was the fact that the census takers depended upon self-enumeration as a method of determining places of origin. How accurate would the newly arrived respondent be when he or she, often ignorant of geography, tried to categorize the village of their birth, the transit locations, the dates or methods of travel?

Louise Houghton is the author of the classic and relatively early study of Arabic people in America. After studying United States Department of Commerce work-study sheets, she calculated that something like 41,000 Syrians were said to have entered the country between 1897 and 1907. Yet other estimates, she says, came to 100,000 immigrants during that time period. Still others have suggested 70,000 for the same time period. One source said that in 1908 between 100,000 and 150,000 Arabic immigrants were in this country. Such an array of diverse figures coming from rather authoritative sources means that the whole subject must be approached with a degree of caution. One must assume, then, that the North Dakota figures would be subject to some similar confusion.[5]

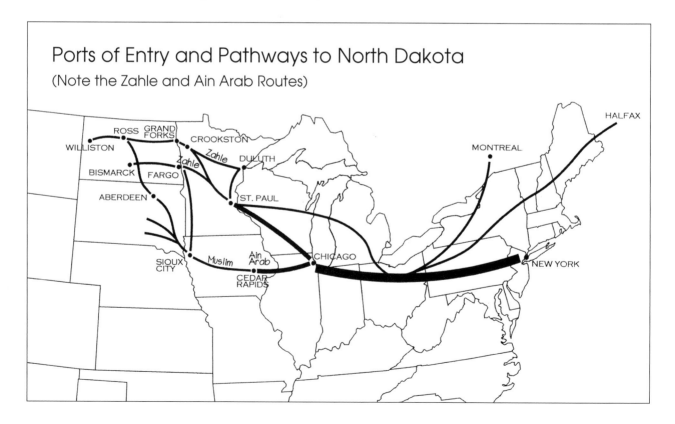

Ports of Entry and Pathways to North Dakota
(Note the Zahle and Ain Arab Routes)

To North Dakota

Whether by way of New York, Canada, Galveston, or Mexico, the Lebanese immigrants spread not only to America's eastern states; they also came, as this book indicates, to a rather unexpected place, the prairies of North Dakota.

Sam Omar's story is typical. Coming to America in 1903, in October 1939 at Ross, Mr. Omar recalled his 1903 arrival moments:

When we landed at New York, I was not in the least disappointed about America because everything looked so new. We took a train to Grand Rapids, Michigan, and visited with Syrian friends for about ten days, and then came to North Dakota. I worked part of that summer near Fessenden and then moved on to Mountrail County. I was attracted to this section of the country because I knew some of the Syrians homesteading there and was interested in farming for myself.

As seen on earlier pages in this volume, many came to North Dakota because a friend or family member was already present. Mrs. Libbie Layon, in March 1940, remembered her first years in an interview at Williston. Her journey took her first to New York, then Chicago, then to Wisconsin (for a nine-year residency). She continues:

When I'm twenty, I get married in Rhinelander, Wisconsin. I live one year in town; then I go out on farm for eight year. We don't do very good, but we make livin' anyway. Then we hear about land here, and we come out to McKenzie county and take homestead. We live about nine miles from Alexander. We get cows, horses, pigs, chickens and we start farm. We got about twenty head altogether. We sell coal and we got spring [for water] there.

Cedar Rapids, Iowa, was a stopping-over place for many future North Dakota residents. George Saba, of North Dakota birth and a Lebanon youth, recalled in July 1939:

I lived in Charlestown [West Virginia] for about two months in the Oriental Rug business and did very well. I then went back to Cedar Rapids and came from there to Bismarck, North Dakota chiefly to see the home of my birth near Denhoff, North Dakota. I came to Denhoff and then went to McCluskey to see an aunt living there. Here I met my wife. Her people are my third cousins. We visited and became quite fond of each other and when I asked her to marry me, she accepted and said, "yes."

Thomas Nassif, from Ain Arab, went first to Cedar Rapids, then to North Dakota. In August 1939 he spoke to an interviewer at Bismarck:

When I arrived at Halifax, Canada, I traveled by rail to Cedar Rapids, Iowa, where I thought my father was located. When I arrived there I found that my father did not live there but I was fortunate in having an uncle in Cedar Rapids. I went to the home of my uncle where I stayed for two or three days and then proceeded to my father's farm in Keif, North Dakota.

Sioux City, Iowa, was another center to which Syrian immigrants came as they adjusted to their new American homeland: Attas Boutrous of Ain Arab, reported in Bismarck in July 1939:

After the usual inspection of my luggage, precautions by the customs officials and questions, I was allowed to continue my trip. I boarded a train and came to Sioux City, Iowa, where I had some friends. My first job here was working in a packing plant for Armour's Packing Company. I do not remember what the wages were, but they were not very large.

St. Paul, Minnesota, was an initial center for some immigrants. A native of a little town "two miles from Zahle," Mary Farris, said in an interview at Williston in November 1939:

We stay in St. Paul three years 'bout. Mr. Farris he go to Wahpeton [N.D.] when he travel. Two, three Syrian families dere. Dey tell him "come here, come here." Mr. Farris have horse an' buggy when he travel. We go to Wahpeton. After four years we start restaurant; we charge fifteen cents meal. First we start we got ten dollars. Man he got building he's good. Everybody say "start restaurant." We buy little bit all time. We stay, I guess, three year eight months. We make money 'cause I work hard. I cook, wash and everythin'. One man he travel, he stop my place, and he tell me 'bout land here. He tell me more people come here. We know some come, we don't know some. I tell Mr. Farris, "go, I stay here." We got good business, we got eighteen boarders. Mr. Farris go; he show him land three miles west Williston. Mr. Farris he like it. Dis man he want sell his right $300.00. Mr. Farris get it $250.00—160 [acres] that claim. He went back, we sell everythin'. We think we keep restaurant in Williston. When we get here and see log houses, we think we make more money we farm. We come here May 19, dat 37 year next May.

Duluth, Minnesota, was another "stop over" center (the name will occur at times in interviews throughout this book). Duluth, in the 1900 census, already had four merchants and eleven "peddlers." Zines, Atols and Bouslimans, all Williston family names, are also in the 1900 Duluth census. Louise Houghton mentioned that in 1911 six or seven Duluth merchants were selling "peddlers' supplies."

Lebanese people seemed to appear everywhere on the prairies, even the small out-of-the-way village of Ashley in the southern portion of North Dakota held its attraction for newcomers. Mike (Amid) Abdallah, who eventually settled at Ross, said in 1939:

I stayed in Montreal for one month and then came to Fargo, N.D. by train. I tried to peddle for about three months but couldn't make a living at that, so I took the train to Ashley, N.D. There were other Syrians already there and I went to work on a farm; worked on farms there for three years, making from twenty-five to thirty dollars a month. In 1911 I came to Ross, I worked out for four years and during threshing I got $1.25 a day, then working by the month I got $30. In 1915 I filed on a homestead sec. 12-157-92. I lived on my homestead for two years and then lived with Frank Osman for a year. I got my naturalization papers Oct. 2, 1916. In 1918 I moved to New Rockford, N.D. I stayed in New Rockford for five months and worked with a section crew. In 1919 I moved to Detroit, Michigan, and worked in the factories for two and a half years. In 1921 I moved back to Ross, N.D. as I got married in 1920 and had to settle down and make a home. I have lived around Ross ever since. I rented three farms and in 1927 I bought the farm we are now living on.

The "moving about" of the newly arrived Syrians is evident in Mike Abdallah's report above. Mr. Abdallah was a Muslim in a Christian world, yet this did not deter him.

Even more remarkable was the itinerary of Hassin Alley Juma, also a Muslim; he lived in at least six different locations and did a stint in the American Army before settling in Ross. His October 1939 recollection is as follows:

In 1917, I moved to Fargo, North Dakota, thinking there was more opportunity there. [Mr. Juma had lived on a homestead claim previously near Medina, N.D.] In 1918, I enlisted in the United States Army, and was discharged in 1919. I came to Detroit, Michigan, but moved to Saginaw, Michigan, where I rented a farm. This was in 1920, and that same year I moved back to Detroit. In 1921, I moved to West Virginia, but returned to Detroit that same year. I again moved to West Virginia in 1921, and lived there until 1927 when I moved back to Detroit. I came to Ross, North Dakota in 1928, and have lived here since, on this farm which is seven miles north of Ross. I do not farm at present.

While moving from one place to another, I worked at different trades. I peddled at some places and worked in an automobile factory for some time. What I wanted to do was to get rich in a hurry and return to Syria.

North Dakota Dispersal

Where did the Lebanese settle, and when? How many came? For answers we must turn first to the U.S. Census and, as has been mentioned previously, this is not always an easy task. National boundaries and self-enumeration confused the census taker as he or she asked questions concerning place of birth, date of arrival, origin of parents, and citizenship application. If the newcomer found that the word Arab or Turkey elicited a negative reaction, it was possible to provide a deceptive answer: "Palestinian," "Austrian," "Armenian," and the like. The use of similar subterfuges took place among other North Dakota residents. In 1920 and in 1940, when the United States was hostile to Germany, many Germans from Russia became "Rumanian" or "Russian." When in 1930 and 1950 the Bolshevik menace was an American preoccupation, the number of "Germans" in American and Canadian census tallies increased considerably.

Where were the Arabic people in North Dakota? When did they arrive? *Prairie Mosaic,* a 1983 ethnic atlas of North Dakota, gives us some answers. Clearly identifiable Lebanese farmstead settlements could, in that year, still be found in Mountrail County (the Ross-Stanley area) and in Williams County (west of the city of Williston). The atlas says further that rural Arabic settlements existed at one time in Foster County, in Pierce County (especially in Meyer and Reno townships), and in Rolette County (the Dunseith-Belcourt area). Settlements had also existed in Stutsman County (Lowery township) and in Ward County (Baden township). *Plains Folk,* the history of North Dakota ethnic groups, lists additional early (and now nonexistent) settlements in Sheridan County and in Walsh County (Shepherd township).[6]

The term "settlement" in the above paragraph refers to homestead communities that varied considerably in size. Some had as many as 100 newcomers living on the land; others numbered a few dozen. The specific settlement circumstances will be discussed in a later chapter. But first let us take a look at the Federal Census information.

Here we are faced not only with the usual nomenclature difficulties, but an additional one, the 1900 U.S. Census occurred in the midst of the Syrian settlement stream that focused on middle and eastern North Dakota; it was too early to record much of the movement to the western part of the state. In 1900 only eight counties recorded "immigrants from Turkey." We know from other sources that eastern North Dakota's Walsh County had perhaps 30 to 40 Syrian-born residents by that time. But even in that county only a few appeared on the census takers' rosters. (Two very early names appear in the Federal Land Office list of those who "proved up" in northern Dakota Territory: Richard Gabriel in 1884 and

Stephen Mahood in 1886; the first in Richland and the second in Walsh County. If these men were Syrian, they represent the earliest isolated newcomers to what is now North Dakota.)

Looking at the 1910 Census gives a more full picture of the Syrian distribution in the state (see the Appendix of this book). A perusal of the county-by-county data totals shows a widespread disbursement of Syrian immigrants. Only 11 of the 53 counties did not have a Turkey-born resident. Cass County (Fargo) had 28; Grand Forks County had 21; Ramsey County (Devils Lake) listed 34; and Stutsman County (Jamestown) contained 24. These more urban county figures were probably recording Syrians engaged partly or exclusively in the peddler's trade.

By 1920, as can be seen in tables in the Appendix of this volume, Arab farmsteads were less dispersed. Some men or women of Syrian background had no doubt acquired their land titles and either sold the parcels or were renting them to former neighbors. In that year, 23 counties had no Syrian-born residents. This contrasts with 1910 when 11 counties had no such residents.

The 1920 Census reveals even more information. The combination of the Syrian-born and the American or Canadian-born children of Syrian parents gives the reader a sense of what was, in fact, the overall Syrian population in the state. The new figures reveal certain surprises: 66 people of Arabic ancestry resided in Fargo in 1920 and 37 lived in Bismarck. This indicates a movement from the homestead settlements to the larger cities. It may also mean that Syrian peddlers by that time were operating from North Dakota's more urban centers. It may show a second-generation tendency to establish permanent businesses in the state's larger towns.

Prairie Mosaic, the ethnic atlas of rural North Dakota mentioned above, takes a different approach to the problem. Using Federal Land Office records which enumerate the original land claimants and coordinating this with extensive interviews, a clearer picture emerges: Walsh County, in the northeastern part of the state, saw perhaps a dozen Arabic settlers taking land in 1897, or perhaps as early as 1896.[7] These were almost all of Maronite and Melkite traditions. Pierce County, with Rugby as the central city, one hundred miles further west, on the Northern Pacific Railroad line, saw Melkites, Maronites, and some Orthodox arriving in 1897. These were the first contingent of what would eventually be a sizable Syrian rural enclave. To be more specific, the atlas says, "At least fifty Syrian men and women filed on Pierce County land." The settlement took place especially between 1897 and 1902. Research done since the atlas was published indicates Syrians had "spilled over" into an adjacent county. Others in Pierce County were also discovered. Adding the nearby McHenry County settlers and scattered individuals, a good estimate says that 150 Lebanese took up land claims in what could be called the Rugby area.[8]

Though Rolette County-Turtle Mountain settlers took land in a rather dispersed fashion, a few, it seems, had arrived already in 1897. Some were Christian; some were of the Islamic faith. They numbered no more than two dozen farmsteads. Farms could also be found in the Perth and Bisbee areas of Towner County.

Some 100 miles to the south, Orthodox Christians, twenty-three men, often with families, settled in Sheridan County starting in 1902.[9]

In Mountrail and William counties, near Ross and Williston, the *Prairie Mosaic* atlas says an estimated 100 Syrian settlers filed for land. (The atlas figure was too low for a later analysis indicates something like 150 took land.) The first arrivals in these counties came in either 1900 or 1901. These came when the land rush was at its highest intensity. The Ross area immigrants were Muslim in background (seventy at least). A little farther west, near Williston, almost on the Montana border, the second settlement of Syrians grew up, and these were of Christian faiths. An eventual 85, possibly more, came, starting in 1903.[10] (Some descendants, as this volume is published, still remain as farmers, both in the Ross and Williston areas.) The location and the numbers of settlers of Syrian background recorded in this chapter and in Chapter 13 (Syrian Enclaves) are probably as definitive as we can obtain, at least for the present.

There are, however, bits and pieces of information contained in early-in-the-century accounts published elsewhere in the United States, which are difficult to verify. Nonetheless, they may have a certain validity, for the reports may reflect information flowing east through a "Syrian grapevine." Louise Seymour Houghton, quoted so often in this volume, says, "Syrian peddlers were roaming over North Dakota in 1888."[11] She says further that, in spite of the good farmland of the Dakotas and the north central states, "few brave the extreme cold."[12] Louise Houghton does, however, state that, "Still colder climates has not kept them out of Canada." The same author, in her basic study published in 1911, wrote that Syrian farm colonies existed in "Iowa, Kansas, Oklahoma, North and South Dakota, Montana, Wyoming, and Washington." She singles out North Dakota, saying that the greatest number were in that state. "In the neighborhood of Williston there were about one hundred Syrian farmers and homesteaders."[13]

What were Ms. Houghton's sources? No published accounts existed in her day. If she is considering the Williams County-Ross area she is correct in saying that one hundred Syrians were on farms near Williston; recent research says as much. Was she just as accurate in stating, "Syrian peddlers were roaming over North Dakota in 1888." We don't know; it's a surprisingly early date. But maybe the Syrian "grapevine" was at work; perhaps her observations were valid.

Louise Houghton has more information. She says, again in 1911, "one Syrian merchant in St. Paul has come into possession of more than 800 acres in scattered quarter sections not far from Rugby, ND, a part of which he rents to a Syrian, and the other parts to Russians and a Norwegian." She says further, "In 1907, correspondence showed [the Rugby colony] to be one of the most flourishing farm colonies of Syrians in the state." Yet she also says "a letter from an American clergyman of the neighborhood says that the Syrians have all sold their farms and moved further West."[14] In terms of recent scholarly research, Ms. Houghton was, for the most part, correct. The Rugby colony did flourish—it built a Syrian church in the countryside—and indeed, the Syrians were surrounded especially by German-Russians and occasional Norwegians. The clergyman is most likely Father Seraphim Roumie, the Melkite priest who himself was a homesteader and a personality who will be discussed elsewhere in this volume.

To continue with Ms. Houghton's observations: "It is worthy of note that a certain Dakota farm colony, breaking up for reasons which do not appear, but probably to secure educational advantages for their children in an adjacent town, moved their church building with them." Again she is speaking of Rugby; the church was, indeed, moved to the city. But was it for "educational advantages"? Perhaps. But we know that other factors—disillusionment with farming, the attraction of major cities—were also at work.[15]

Pathways to North Dakota

The interview accounts done by the WPA in the years 1939-40 and printed in excerpt fashion earlier in this volume show the sometimes-haphazard routes which settlers took before arriving in North Dakota.

Another, perhaps more systematic approach can be used to trace Dakota-bound Syrian pathways. In the following paragraphs we present an analysis of the birth locations of the children, particularly the first child, as found in North Dakota portions of the U.S. Census for the years 1900, 1910, and 1920. (Census lists for these three years are in the Appendix. The lists are not definitive, some families are missing, but it's a good representative compilation.)

In 1900 there were 24 families with children. Of that number, eight listed their first child as born in "Syria" (Turkey, etc.). Ten of the first births occurred in North Dakota, six were in Minnesota and one each in Tennessee and Indiana.

The adage that the American frontier was populated overwhelmingly by single men does not hold true as far as North Dakota's Lebanese census population is concerned. In 1900 there were 29 Syrian-born men in the state who were without a spouse. This contrasts with the 24 men who had wives and children. But the figures may be deceptive. Other single men, no doubt, were "on the road" in peddling ventures, beyond the reach of census takers.

In 1910, 73 families were known to have been present in the state. Of that number, 11 listed the birth of their first child in Syria. Ten were of Minnesota birth (again, the Minnesota "stop over") and 46 were born in North Dakota. One each had been born in Iowa, Nebraska, Canada, Pennsylvania and Illinois. (One child was born "at sea.") The 1910 Census manuscript show in some cases the tangle of previous states which some Lebanese called "home" before they reached their North Dakota settlements. As an example we find Soloman Oman and his wife Lorida, both born in Syria, and now residents of Towner County. One of their children was of Pennsylvania birth, another of Massachusetts, and the third child was born in North Dakota. Salem and Sullava Bahme, of Mountrail County, were of Syrian birth. The first two children were born in Nebraska, the third in North Dakota.

As one would expect, by the 1920 Census, of the 94 recorded families present, most of the first births took place in North Dakota (65). Yet eight were of Syrian birth, so the migration to North Dakota was continuing into the second decade of the century. Minnesota was mentioned eight times as the birthplace of the first child. Canada had five; two were from Nebraska and South Dakota. Yet one each was recorded as being Indiana, Iowa, Wisconsin and Utah. (The Lebanese were a mobile people!)

Bearing in mind that the U.S. Census occurred only every ten years, the reader must be cautioned for the above totals do not represent the full number of Lebanese married couples who came to North Dakota. Some, perhaps many, were never recorded, some came and left *between* the Census tally dates.

But this much can be determined from the above data. Though the literature from studies elsewhere in the United States seems to say that single Syrian individuals were by far the majority of those who came to America, census reports in North Dakota tell us that in the very earliest portion of this century a goodly number of married couples also took the long journey to the New World.

Several other questions arise when considering totals of Syrian settlers in North Dakota. One concerns women. What proportion of North Dakota's immigrants were women?

First, a look at the country as a whole. National figures show that until 1895 relatively few Syrian females came to the United States. Philip and Joseph Kayal estimated the ratio to be four men to one female when considering the earliest Syrian arrival period, a time sequence which included the first twentieth century decade. The U.S. Census of 1920 indicates an evening out of the proportions. There were 51,900 foreign-born

Syrians in the United States. Of that number, 31,240 were male and 20,660 were female.[16]

The North Dakota census, as seen in the Appendix, shows something of the same Syrian-born proportions; in 1900, 217 adult men as compared to 113 adult women. But the gender gap was slowly closing, for the 1920 Census shows 199 men and 117 women who were of Syrian birth. In the census of 1930, the "Palestine-Syrian" tabulations of foreign-born indicates 425 males and 307 females present in North Dakota. This northern prairie state was, of course, a land of newly developing farm life. For the Syrians, it was also a land where peddling was an especially valuable economic enterprise. An increased number of women in the state must have been the wives of farmers or peddlers.

A close look at the Federal Land Office tract books shows that, among those seeking to acquire homestead acreages, a great disparity existed between males and females. In Pierce County, for example, where 68 Syrian men filed for land, only six Syrian women did the same. In Williams County, the Syrian-born variation is less extensive, 66 men and 14 women.[17]

The table that follows contains the North Dakota county total for those of Syrian origin as found in the U.S. Census for 1910 and 1920. (Note: "Syrian" in over 95 percent of the cases means immigrants who came from what is now Lebanon. In 1910, unless noted, Turkey means Lebanon.)

US Census, North Dakota, Foreign Born
(Counties with 5 or more)

County	1910 Turkey	1920 Syria	County	1910 Turkey	1920 Syria
Adams	3	8	Pierce	99	29
Benson	21	3	Ramsey (Devils Lake)	342	
Billings	25	2	Renville	8	0
Burleigh (Bismarck)	6	20	Rolette	8	1
Cass (Fargo)	28	29	Stutsman (Jamestown)	24*	8
Dickey	11	0	Sheridan	42**	3
Emmons	9	7	Towner	12	4
Grand Forks	21	1	Traill	11	0
Kidder	11	7	Walsh	18	12
McHenry	20	2	Williams	121	87
Mountrail	29	22	McLean	14	0
Morton	9	0			

* This figure includes Armenians
**This figure includes some Dubrudja Germans

An occasional Eastern European railroad work crew may be enumerated (for example, Billings and Ramsey County, 1910).

As will be noted often in this book, the U.S. Census tabulations of "Syrians" are frightfully deficient. (See Chapter 15 for an attempt to obtain a more accurate North Dakota count.) Nonetheless, the above table does give at least a partial picture of Lebanese distribution and residency lengths in North Dakota.

The 1920 figures, while reflecting the deaths of some "foreign-born," show the movement away from farmstead residences. Thus, agricultural McHenry County drops from 20 (in 1910) to 2 (in 1920). Pierce County, a relatively rural region, had 99 in 1910; in 1920 it had 29. So also Williams County Syrian-born decline from 121 to 87. Burleigh County, with Bismarck City in its midst, increased from 6 to 20.

Muslim Presence

A second question arises. This concerns the proportion of Muslims compared to Christians who entered North Dakota. First, a look at national proportions. The religious affiliation of Syrians in the United States according to Philip Hitti in 1924 was as follows: "Maronites—45 percent; Orthodox—43 percent; Melkite—5 percent, and Muslims—4 percent."[18]

The low percentage of Muslims was, perhaps, not a surprise for reports stressed the "late arrival" of the Muslims in the migration stream to America. Another author, Linda S. Walbridge, says for example: "Of the approximately thirty-nine thousand Syrian/ Lebanese who entered the United States between 1909 and 1914, only about 10 percent were Muslim."[19] The *Harvard Encyclopedia of American Ethnic Groups* says this: "Fragmentary data suggests that only a few hundred young Muslim men joined the Christian emigrants between 1900 and 1914, most of them after 1908."[20]

Does the North Dakota experience fit this pattern at least with regards to Muslims? Using first name recognition and drawing from extensive interviews of long-time residents, the authors of this volume analyzed the North Dakota's Naturalization Records—especially the initial Declaration of Intention papers. (Christian preference for first names differed in most cases from Muslim choices.) Where possible the "second papers," the Petition for Naturalization, were also consulted. The particular focus of the investigation was the three counties that contained the highest totals of "Syrian" applicants: Williams, Pierce and McIntosh.

Forty-eight first and second papers were given by North Dakota courts between 1894 and 1898. These individuals were all Christian. There were no Muslims. Yet, in these three counties from 1899 until 1917 (the date when the application numbers began to taper off), Muslims appear on the scene in comparatively large numbers: 504 Christians and 294 Muslims sought citizenship through either their first or second papers.

At least in terms of these three rather significant counties, the figures hold true to some of the expectations. We find that the earliest Muslims appear on the citizenship application lists four years later than Christians. Yet when, after 1899, Muslim totals appear on the scene, Muslims are anything but a "tiny minority." They represented 35 to 40 percent of the applicants.

The various totals and the Muslim proportions as expressed above refer to North Dakota's three most populous "Syrian" counties. Does this hold true for the rest of the state? The authors feel it does. An assessment of the Syrian history in the state as found throughout this volume will say as much.

One thing that is clear from the preceding discussion is that North Dakota's proportion of Muslim Syrians, when compared to Christian Syrians in the first two decades of the twentieth century, contrasts decidedly with similar comparisons published concerning eastern American states. Couple this with the fact that the Muslim community at Ross, of good size and completely rural, seems to be the only such thing in America. Add to this the fairly well accepted fact that the first Muslim prayer service in the United States took place in Mountrail County in 1900, certainly by 1901. So also—as will be discussed later in this volume—the nation's first building erected specifically as a mosque was erected at Ross. These historical items lend credence to the statement that Muslims, contrary to expectations, settled in North Dakota at an exceedingly early date and in numbers that go far beyond those found in other parts of America.

A Study in Mobility: Ali Hasen Debaji

In 1884, a son, Ali, was born to Hasen Debaji and Ishie Omar Fadd. The parents' marriage took place in Karoun, Lebanon. As a teenager Ali, about to be drafted into the Turkish Army, promptly left for New York, where he became "Alexander Hansen." Lebanese contacts told him to go to Ashley, ND. He did so. He homesteaded and soon found himself penniless. He returned to Lebanon, saved some money, and came back to America, this time to St. Paul, MN. His name now was Alec Hasen. As he would later say, he and his cousin "went broke in St. Paul" in the linen business. Ali (Alec) then decided to go to Perth, ND, where he became a peddler. Returning to Lebanon once again, he took as a bride a 20-year-old Karoun girl named Sherifee Lyla. The last trip to America led him to establish at Rolla, not far from Perth, the "Golden Rule" clothing store. From the early 1940s to the summer of 2001, the store would stay in the Hasen family. A son, Ramiz, or "Ron," with his wife Freida, became respected community leaders. Their son took the name of his grandfather, Ali Hasen Debaji, and entered college in Beirut, Lebanon. After several years working in the Middle East, he would eventually settle in Seattle, Washington.

CHAPTER NINE

Peddling

No discussion of Syrians (actually Lebanese) in the Dakotas, or for that matter, in rural Minnesota, would be complete without a serious consideration of "the peddler." Like it or not, the term "Syrian" is inevitably linked in early days to an occupation which might today be called the "itinerant merchant."

But peddling was not a recent or unknown thing in the United States. Some background discussion of that "age-old trade" should be in order. We start with the observation that early American life was, for the most part, rural. This was true from colonial days well into the mid-19th century. America consisted of small-sized family plots dispersed throughout the recently settled landscape. There were, of course, villages and country stores at various crossroads, but muddy or snowy trails insured that isolation was a common feature in the life of most of our nation's citizens.

If people did not have access to the merchant, it was natural for merchants to go to the people. It's here that the peddler comes into the American scene. From earliest colonial times, observers have noted the presence of the solitary individual who walked or rode or pulled a wagon from farmstead to farmstead. "Hawkers and walkers" they were called. "Strolling peddlers" was another common term.[1]

Even the country folk of colonial times, self-sufficient as they were, needed certain manufactured commodities: gunpowder, flints, paper, needles and buttons, nails and shot, pots and pans. The lady of the house sought spices, lace, cloth, and domestic niceties.

Industrial growth in the mid-nineteenth century brought cities and shopping areas in its wake. But frontier America, the lands to the West, even with mail order catalogs and gravel roads, still existed in isolation. Certainly the dispersed nature of the Great Plains farmsteads, a midwestern feature until World War II, provided the itinerant merchant with an opportunity that was both profitable and respected.

We know from family memoirs that Jewish homesteaders in the Dakotas very often supplemented their farm income with door-to-door peddling. Many small town Jewish merchants flourished after having learned the American retail system—and often the English language—while visiting prairie farms with a wagonload of small-sized goods. Some Jewish men and women subsequently established major mercantile firms in America's moderate and even large sized cities, using the insights they gained from farm-to-farm merchandising.[2]

Where did the Great Plains Jewish peddlers acquire their proclivity for the merchant way of life? Why did Jewish people find business of any sort a friendly environment? Not every North Dakota immigrant group chose such a mobile and speculative way of earning a living. Germans and Scandinavians, for example, seldom in the first generation left the shelter of their rural farm ethnic enclaves. When such groups did move into the business world they rarely if ever chose mobile selling ventures. Rather, they sought a storefront enterprise, centered in a rather stable village environment.

Jewish peddler accounts and Jewish merchant life have been the object of a considerable amount of historical study. Perhaps the tendency came from the prior trade experience demanded by the wide expanses of Russia or the Near East. Perhaps it was due to oppressive anti-Semetic forces in a previous time period.

It was into this American and Midwestern world that the immigrant from Syria would find him or herself and, like their Jewish counterparts, the Syrian man and woman frequently became a mobile merchant. In fact, almost the minute the newly arrived Lebanese received clearance and stepped off the ferryboat from Ellis Island the prospect of peddling was called to his or her attention. Alixa Naff quotes a *New York Tribune's* 1892 description of the city's Syrian world. This scene, whether in New York or elsewhere, met the eyes of the newcomer and peddling was clearly part of the new and exciting environment. The *Tribune* said:

The houses, especially on the Washington Street side of the block are old, weatherbeaten, dingy and sometimes dirty, the cellars are devoted to trade and packed full of everything which a pedler [sic] can carry in his pack or find a market for in his wanderings, and the first or ground floor is generally used as a display room and office where goods are sorted out and bargains made—and these sojourners from the far East are sharp traders. ...

Go inside one of these stores where pins by the hundred gross rest against shoe-blacking by the case, and scapularies and rosaries, beads and prayer-books are almost hidden from view by boxes of cheap cologne and orna-mental shellwork ...your eyes are dazzled by a great square of yellow

*satin covered with delicate tracery of silver wire. . . . Out from a drawer
. . . is tossed a great fleecy cloud . . . of soft white silk with blue stripes. . . .
Silks and satin lacework, embroideries, follow each other in rapid succession until the eyes are revelling in a bewildering maze of gorgeous,
fantastic and beautiful colors. . . .*

*Pick up a filmy gossamer web of silken lace with a line from the Koran
running around its border and in your ear is whispered the magic word,
"Baghdad." Shade of Haroun-al Raschid! . . . he has some rugs there which
are a delight to the eye. . . .And the quaint specimens of Oriental carving,
the marquetry work, the little tables in which the wood is lost in the wealth
of inlaid pearl with which it is adorned, the long, curved sword of
Damascus steel, whose edge is as keen as a razor. . . . And in the midst of
all this riot of the beautiful and odd stands the dealer, the natural gravity
of his features relaxed into a smile of satisfaction at the wonder and delight
expressed by his American visitor. . . .*

*These wholesale dealers, who will do a retail trade if opportunity offers, are
of great help to their poorer countrymen, often advancing to them not only
goods but money with which to trade, and though there are large sums
outstanding at times, and often goods of much value on hand, the Syrian
Colony has yet to furnish a case of bankruptcy, and the credit of the
tradesmen is first-class.*[3]

The New York experience, repeated in other seaport cities, almost
propelled the immigrant from Lebanon into the "mobile selling" trade.
The monetary advantage must have been apparent from the beginning. A
day's work at peddling could produce five dollars in New York City; in
contrast, an Irish immigrant worker would receive only one dollar for
the same time expenditure.[4]

Three peddlers
wagons: The Tanous
Family working out
of Hettinger, ND

Courtesy: Joe Nicholas

Peddling apparently could be undertaken almost immediately upon arrival. Even without knowledge of English, an awareness of the American monetary system, of price, was all that was needed. Even monetary investment was unnecessary, due to the accessibility of suppliers who were already familiar with the American scene.

As discussed elsewhere in this volume, many—perhaps most—early Arab immigrants did not intend to stay in the United States. (In fact, most did stay.) With return to the Old Country in mind, the Syrian immigrant was inclined to avoid investment in American real estate or any other permanent commodity. The mobile life, with its limited expenditures, would fit well into the hopes of people with such a "temporary" perspective.

Writing in the *American Sociological Review* concerning those who came to southern states in the 1890s, Afif Tannous says practically every man and woman of the original group began their American lives as peddlers.[5] Stories of the first decades of Syrians in Georgia, Iowa, Illinois, Oklahoma, in fact everywhere in the west, include an initial few pages concerning what has been called the "peddler stage." (In the movie, *Oklahoma*, Eddie Albert played a traveling Syrian Oklahoma peddler.) Louise Houghton, the chronicler of early Arab Americans, says Syrian peddlers were out in northern Dakota Territory in 1888. This is possible; the Dakota land acquisition "boom" was underway. Perhaps they visited the new town sites along the Northern Pacific Railway; maybe even along the half-completed Great Northern main line. The 1893 *Fargo City Directory* names seven Syrian peddlers who resided in that city. Five lived together at 110 Front Street.

The Syrian (or Lebanese) story almost inevitably begins with the solitary individual setting out on foot from a city or a farm with a pack on his or her back. Sometimes the initial stage of the journey would be by train but ultimately it was by foot to a number of distant locations. With the passage of time a horse and wagon would appear. But the basics of the enterprise continued: the movement from home to home, from farm to farm, the canvassing of potential customers. The decades brought progress; an eventual truck could come into use, with shelves and cabinets covered from the ravages of weather. Yet the peddler's routine through the decades remained much the same.

Like their Jewish counterparts, the Syrian man or woman might in time set up a mercantile firm in a town or village. Unlike their Jewish friends, however, they were less inclined to abandon the farm and go exclusively into village business pursuits. Again, in contrast to Jews, historical accounts show that first generation Syrians embraced a wider variety of business pursuits when they located in the city. After several decades in America, Syrians could be found running such things as gas stations, boarding houses, cafes, and auto dealerships. Again, in contrast to their Jewish neighbors, Syrian children were less likely to choose university life as a ladder for advancement in the American scene. Rather, the life of a proprietor in a small and eventually large firm was stressed through the various generations.

In this regard, it is curious that North Dakota's Jewish merchants were seldom in direct competition with small-town Lebanese merchants. Not that the two groups were antagonistic; on the contrary, they were often friends. But with rare exceptions, if an Arabic shopkeeper was active in an early-day village, a Jewish merchant would be absent. And this does bring up an additional question. Lebanese peddlers were criss-crossing the countryside with their display of wares, but so also, in the earliest days, were Jewish peddlers. What was their relationship in these circumstances? Was there an implicit agreement that they would respect each other's trade territories?

A modern-day version of such an "arrangement" occurred in Grand Forks. Hal Gershman and Bob Absey, two long-time friends of Jewish and Lebanese backgrounds, owned the Roadking Inn and the Ramada Inn respectively. A large expanse of grassy lawns separated the two motels. In a humorous fashion, Gershman and Absey referred to the area as the Golan Heights and had a "gentleman's agreement" never to build on the property.

But back to the original question. Where did the Syrian newcomer acquire the almost instant affinity for the peddler's trade? Some who write on this subject say that peddling played only a minor role in the life of 19th century Syria. Yet carrying a pack from field to village was not infrequent in Syria; fuel and commodities were often brought from place to place. Joseph Abraham of Williston in August 1940 still remembers a portion of his early life in his hometown, some "two hundred miles north of Jerusalem":

> We have lots of fruit on our place, and I go out selling to other towns, sometimes fifty, sometimes seventy-five or a hundred miles. I have mule to carry fruit and I walk. I have bad trips in mud and snow; sometimes mule get stuck and it's pretty hard to get him out. Some people use camels on level land, but we can't do that.

Nonetheless, it seems that the bazaar-type outdoor markets, not peddling, were the usual method of disposing of Lebanon's agricultural goods. This is not surprising, for such things were true not only of the Middle East but throughout all of European village life. And too, as others have noted, traditional Syrian life was at the "crossroads" of three continents. This gave rise to an expertise in certain business practices which were fundamental to the peddler's trade: bargaining, haggling, a system without fixed prices, a quick wit and ready tongue.

Some have said that peddling came naturally to the Syrian man and woman for there was a sense of "individualism" and an underlying "impermanence" in the Syrian character, the result of Lebanon's repeated experience with invasions and political chaos. Many observers point to the remarkable dispersal of Syrians in their worldwide migration traditions. Syrians seem to have been comfortable moving from place to place.

Taking up the peddling profession, whether at an eastern seaport or in some cases in the American West, was not as random and haphazard an undertaking as one would suspect. Most likely as the new arrival left the boat, he or she had in their pocket the name and location of Syrian friends and even relatives who had already made an adjustment to the American scene. Jabour Munyer, of Williston, told the interviewer in February 1940:

> Then we go to Havre, and then to New York about middle October. Well, New York is alright—nice city—but when you can't talk the language, it's too hard. My cousin he started me out selling buttons, hairpins—notions. He go with me, show me how to knock on door, and what to say.

As can be seen in Mr. Munyer's account, the "supplier" was often already a known figure in the newcomer's mind. This supplier may well have recognized the newcomer as a fellow countryman from an already familiar village or family. The reliability of the newly arrived prospective peddler was therefore authenticated by an informal "grapevine" type of method. The supplier would then advance credit, outfit the apprentice, and send him or her on their way.

Jabour Munyer recalled his first years in North Dakota when interviewed at Williston:

> Then I went to Minot sell some goods, and I lost $375.00 goods. You see, I check some and when I get to Berthold and take my check to get goods, they can't find it. And I have to send New York for some more: I get $500.00 goods there—my credit's good.

As Syrians moved from the cities of the east to America's hinterlands, experienced and successful peddlers assumed the role of supplier in their new environments and in return dispersed newcomers to outlying villages and farmsteads. The process repeated itself as settlement expanded further to the west. Peddler networks developed. St. Paul became a supply center, Chicago had been an earlier hub city. In time, Duluth, Cedar Rapids, Sioux City, and eventually, to a minor extent, Crookston, Minnesota, became distribution points. The 1910 business directory of St. Paul already showed a handful of Lebanese individuals who distributed goods to what might

Sam George's peddlers wagon with playful tustle in the farm yard. Sam Juma, Charlie Juma, and Jack Muffinmeir.

Courtesy: Charlie Juma Family

be called "agents" in the northwest environs. The Duluth business directory also had such firms in its listings.

As one would suspect, the supplier network was often dictated, even controlled, by Old Country family and village ties. An Ain Arab (Orthodox) network moved from Fort Wayne, Indiana, to Cedar Rapids to Sioux City, Iowa, and thence to the Dakota prairies, as far north as Sheridan County, North Dakota[6] A Zahle (Melkite-Maronite) network can be traced from Milwaukee through Wisconsin to Sault Saint Marie to Duluth and St. Paul, thence to Rugby and to Williston on the prairies. But the networks were flexible in their outlines. There was a lot of crossing over and freelancing. One early Ain Arab peddler would leave Sioux City, go to St. Paul, then to Crookston, and then follow the more common "Zahle route" along the Great Northern Railroad to western North Dakota.

Joe Seeb, of Orthodox (Ain Arab) background, recalled his journeys in an April 1940 interview at Williston:

We landed in New York and I think it's nice country. Then I go on train to my brother-in-law; he got store, kind of wholesale business. I work for him about fifteen years, some in store and some out on road. I travel in Illinois, Iowa, Nebraska, North Dakota and South Dakota. I didn't have no trouble, and I had lots of friends all over. I was selling dry goods and clothing and had headquarters in Sioux City for long time. I took my citizen paper there in 1900.

The supplier was a key individual. He knew the potential territories. He also knew the peddlers who already were "serving" various routes. Through experience, he could suggest merchandise that would prove to be of value to the prospective consumers. The supplier also, at times, held the peddler's savings, arranged for housing, dispatched by freight the goods which would replenish the peddler along his or her route, and sometimes mediated with authorities when legal matters arose.

The supplier, therefore, had a substantial amount of power. An irresponsible or dishonest peddler would be "blacklisted" in the Syrian mercantile world; very real conduits of information existed, news passed along the line with great rapidity. But there seems to be no evidence that the Syrian supplier, who functioned often like the Greek and Italian padrone, would abuse his position. Family honor and religious ties enforced a certain sense of loyalty and fair play.

In terms of North Dakota, the peddler obtained his or her merchandise as mentioned above, most often from St. Paul and Sioux City. (Duluth was a minor player in the enterprises.) This is not to overlook Crookston, in the northwest corner of Minnesota, which was significant, especially to the northern North Dakota counties. Old-time memories provide the name of at least one Crookston "supplier" firm: the Abbas and Heider Company. Though most of their patrons were Christian, Abbas and Heider were Muslim. (Comeral Heider eventually left Crookston and took land in Canada. His descendants still reside in Manitoba.) A peddler could leave Crookston and soon be at Grand Forks, his North Dakota departure point. From there he or she would follow the Great Northern rail line to various stops along its route, all the while visiting small towns and farmsteads. Indeed, Crookston supplied peddlers who often visited Montana.

The Syrian North Dakota experience corresponds very much to the peddler trade as described by observers of the Syrian life in eastern American circumstances. Before the Lebanese moved into the prairies, most peddlers already had hints as to how to proceed. Alixa Naff, writing about "backpackers," described what must have been a common occurrence. She said: "Few beginners ventured out unapprenticed or untutored, at least in the preliminaries." One woman said to Ms. Naff, "Those who had been here a month or two would teach them a few words they [the veterans] had already learned—to knock on a door and say 'Buy sumthin, Maam,' or how to say they were hungry or needed a place to sleep."[7]

But some apparently didn't even have that much introduction to the trade. In a WPA 1939 account, Mike Abdallah of Ross remembered his first experience in turn-of-the-century North Dakota:

I couldn't talk or understand the American language when I came here and when I was peddling I had to talk to people by motions and when I wanted to tell anyone the price of a thing, I would take money from my pocket and show them the amount of the price. When I wanted to ask for a place to sleep, I had to lay down on the floor and play that I was asleep and then they knew what I wanted. Nearly everyone felt sorry for me because I couldn't talk their language.

A writer in the program for the Attiyeh National Arabic-American Convention, held in Fargo in 1976, gives more details. In this case the whole family was involved:

They became merchants over night, little kids and all! What kind of a merchant? An itinerant peddler that walked from farm to farm selling notions out of a back pack, winter and summer. Trudging through snow and mud they stayed out all week and would eat and sleep with the farmers. Their average inventory was about $20.00. They would sell out by the week-end and make a net 10 bucks profit, go back to town, give kindly countryman merchant the 20 bucks, save $10.00. Monday morning load up and do the same thing over again. Yes, I said kids too, like 9 and 10 year olds and mothers and fathers and grandmothers and grandfathers and they couldn't speak English! True trail blazer pioneers, paving the way for generations to come. A couple years of this and no more walk, horse and wagon now. Then small North Dakota homesteads. Then, much later, business and professions.[8]

"They couldn't speak English," and the language they spoke did not fit into the German, the Slavic, or the Scandinavian patterns that were to be found spread across the prairies.

Wonder of Williams, a history of Williams County, North Dakota, in assessing the difficulties that the early Syrian settlers confronted, says this:

They learned by watching their neighbors. The Lebanese or Arabic language is much more difficult to translate into English than, for instance, German or Norwegian. The Syrian immigrants were accustomed to using their minds, and this they did. Dave and Jim Kalil learned English by copying labels and prices from groceries onto charge slips when they first came and worked in a store. The Hapips tell how their father watched his neighbors farm and then he did the same. When William Abraham Owan was watching others write their names, he noticed they only had two names so he only wrote two—William Abraham. Some years later he had to change the records to show his correct name.[9]

Learning a non-Arabic language from the farm patrons they met on the road could give rise to sometimes surprising results. Albert Alley, of Muslim background and a native of Bire, regularly carried St. Paul goods on his back through a North Dakota region that was almost totally Norwegian. He learned Norwegian first, then had to master English.

Shabel Freije, selling throughout western Walsh County, an area filled with Czech farmers, spoke Arabic, Bohemian, and English.[10]

Peddlers were amazing people. Their peripatetic ventures to the still primitive farms and villages make the modern observer stand in awe: dirt trails, no conveniences, harsh winter conditions, an alien cultural environment! Old-timers recalled walking 200 miles as they made their customary rounds. Ross resident, Hassin Alley Juma of Muslim background, described the early days on the Northern Prairie in an October 1939 interview:

> *In the first years of peddling, I suffered much from cold because I could not understand more than yes and no. I would ask people if I could stay overnight, and if they would answer in any other way than yes, I wouldn't know what they did say and I'd go on. I spent many winter nights on the prairie.*

Such an enterprise was possible partially because the peddler was, in most cases, a welcome visitor to the farm family. Not only did he or she bring needed commodities from the outside, the peddler was also a walking purveyor of news, of gossip, of national affairs. Women sought the trade goods, children delighted in small gifts, sweets, or toys. The menfolk learned of crops, rains, new neighbors, and the like.

There were not a lot of conveniences on the early farms. The peddler would often sleep in the barn's hayloft, but so did the itinerant hired men at harvest season—remember, this was the time when farm homes were very often two-room shanties. The peddler, of course, had a small gift for the "lady of the house" and would regularly help with the chores. It was standard practice for the outside visitor to eat at the family table.

But things were not always rosy. This becomes obvious if we read turn-of-the-century small town newspapers. The *Dickinson Press* published the following under the title "Abandoned His Children":

> *Five months ago a peddler left three children to be boarded at the residence of John Mura in the northeastern part of Sargent County. The man has never since been heard of. The children are "Arabs," and are aged 10 years, 8 years, and 4 years respectively, one being a girl.*[11]

We have to assume the local village merchants, even though they were miles from a great number of their potential farm patrons, were not always sympathetic to the wandering outsiders who "invaded" their sales territories. Three early-day items from the Fargo *Search-Light* point to at least an occasional aversion to the peddling intruder (in this case we don't know whether the offender was Syrian, Jewish, or Old American). On October 17, 1908, we read: "A peddler at Valley City was fined $5 for failure to secure a license." In the western part of the state another incident occurred a week later: "An itinerant peddler was caught and fined at New Salem. He had failed to provide himself with a license to hunt customers."

Early in the next year (January 1909), the *Search-Light* expressed local business resentment when it reported:

> *A Turkish peddler sold highly colored rugs in Ellendale at $10 per, and one of the merchants insisted he could duplicate the stuff at $4 per dozen.*[12]

All the while a supply network was at work, and St. Paul-Minneapolis are mentioned most frequently in early Dakota accounts. We catch a hint of the Twin Cities scene in this excerpt from the master's thesis of Carol Jean Landis entitled "Lebanese Immigration to the United States and the Twin Cities, 1890 to 1924."

> *In 1895, the St. Paul Syrians had five stores (three dry goods and two confectionery) besides two men whose occupation was listed as "peddlers' supplies." Forty-nine are listed as peddlers, only two as laborers, and one as a shoemaker. In Minneapolis, there was one store, seventeen peddlers, and two farmers. In 1905, St. Paul had four Syrian merchants (only two remaining from 1895), 34 peddlers, 20 laborers, one organ grinder, one clerk, two farmers, one dressmaker, one seamstress, one cook, one bar keeper, and one truckman. Minneapolis had five merchants (one from 1895), 31 peddlers, and 24 laborers.*[13]

The number of peddlers—49 in St. Paul (1895) and 34 (1905); Minneapolis 17 (1895) and 31 (1905)—clearly shows the clustering of this mobile sales force in those two hub cities. And we must assume that this was only a portion of those involved in the trade. The census, taken in the spring of the year, caught individuals tabulated above in the Twin Cities; how many more were out "on the road"?

St. Paul, Minneapolis, Sioux City, Duluth, and Crookston—these were all "jumping off" places in the itinerary of the northern Minnesota and Dakota wandering merchant. But the prairies were not always "unknown territory." There existed, as mentioned earlier, a series of pathways, and along these pathways were well-known stopping places.

The United States Census of Griggs County in 1920 lists Abe Abraham as a merchant at Binford; four other gentlemen were staying at his home, all were classed as "peddler/salesman." Mr. Abraham came to America in 1900. One peddler came in 1894, one in 1905, one in 1910, and the most recent arrived in 1914.

In rural Williston, the Abdula and Sadie Bohamra home was a frequent "half way house." Chuck Joseph, the son, said these peddlers "worked the Montana territory"; Havre and Glasgow especially were their destinations. Chuck Joseph and Vernon Owan both remember that a toast with the beverage *"arak"* was a common part of the peddler's visit; one of the toasts was the Arabic phrase, "Your health is your wealth."[14]

Ali Kamoni is mentioned in the *Wahpeton Times* of April 10, 1903. This gentleman purchased a building for a stock of goods for the "Arabian trade." In this case Kamoni must have served as both a halfway house and a regional supplier. (The Kamoni family is unique in North Dakota. They came to America not with a group, but as an isolated pair of brothers. They were unique also in that they came from Jib (Joub) Jannine. Their North Dakota descendants are today in the well-drilling and ranching businesses.)

In the background of this very admirable prairie hospitality is the fact that one of the "pillars" of Islam insists on kindness to the stranger. For Christians, too, the guest was of special importance. George Saba of Orthodox and Ain Arab background, said in Williston (July 1939):

> The people in the Old Country are very sociable and when one has guests nothing is too good for them; they see to it that the guests have all they want to eat and drink and are entertained in every possible way.

It seems that with rare exceptions every early-day Lebanese home was a haven of hospitality. The lines between religious groups never dictated a violation of this sense of neighborly behavior. Muslims could be found staying with Christians; Orthodox and Catholics were often intermingled. These "visits" were sometimes for a few days, but often they stretched into weeks and months.

The earlier arrival of Lebanese Christian settlers gave them a certain advantage: a degree of affluence, knowledge of the geography, the political system and the language. These families could easily become temporary friendly centers that would assist new arrivals. Indeed the memories of modern-day Christian descendants are particularly filled with childhood experiences like that of Art Deraney who recalled his rural Walsh County home: "people were sleeping on floors throughout the house."[15]

A number of early farm homes can still be remembered as key "hub" centers. The Peter Absey farmhouse in Walsh County is often mentioned. Coming from Zahle and taking land as early as 1896, the Melkite Abseys were in an advantageous position to help regional newcomers. Hassin and Mary Juma of Muslim background (Bire, Lebanon) stayed first with the Abseys on the way to Ross, North Dakota. The Barkie family, Orthodox from Ain Arab, stopped for a time at the Absey farm as they traveled to the far west near Williston. Ed Absey, in an interview October 23, 1983, said his mother would feed the travelers "whether Christian or Muslim, even if she had to kill her last chicken."[16]

A well-known "halfway house" was the Nicholas Ausey farm in Towner County north of Cando. Taking land in 1898, the Auseys, of Melkite background, had a continuous stream of Lebanese at their place: landseekers and often itinerant peddlers. (The last name "Ausey" gave way to "Nicholas" in subsequent generations.) Joe Nicholas, the son of Nicholas Ausey, remembers "over one hundred" peddlers who came in and out of our "home place" through the 1910s, 20s and 30s. Whether Christian or Muslim, "they slept in the barn and helped with chores." Ali Hasen Debaji (who took the name Alec Hasen) lived and worked intermittently out of the Ausey home. Of Muslim background, in 1943 Alec set up the Golden Rule store in Rolla, North Dakota (an establishment which flourishes today).[17]

The Kalil Store, established by David Kalil and located in the Lebanese enclave some 20 miles northwest of Williston, was a center for landseekers and for "itinerant businessmen." In 1907, a brother, James (Jim) Massahd, after proving up a claim, opened a Kalil store in Williston. *Wonder of Williams* said that, with a flair for languages, Jim worked at his store as a butcher, but he also moved around the countryside with little regard for ethnicity or religious differences. He "traveled to the farms and killed the animals there. There were Russian, German and Norwegian settlements in the area and no matter where James went, he could converse quite easily."[18]

Kalils were business-minded. Edward Kalil, son of David, built a grocery store in Williston while his brother Wilbur ran the country farm. Many, perhaps most, of the peddlers destined for Montana would use the Kalil stores as a base of operations.[19]

But looking elsewhere in the state, it seems every permanent farm tended to be a "halfway" station for Lebanese. The Srur farm, south of Rugby, was a center; so also the Forsley and Munyer farms of Williston. The children of almost every early-day Syrian family can recite memories of "visitors, sleeping all over the place."

In the days before movies and television, the Arab world was often known to North Dakota settlers in ways that were less than flattering; a mysterious, almost sinister world, a world of Ali Baba and the Forty Thieves. All of these preconceptions would rapidly change as they came to know the itinerant "Turk" or "Arab" or "Syrian" who came with an honest smile, struggling to express himself in English and who helped with chores. When these same "Syrian" visitors often turned out to be not only "nice" men, but Muslim as well, a major revolution of stereotypes no doubt took place.

Even after a half-century, even after three-quarters of a century, the names of certain peddlers bring smiles and happy memories to hundreds

Joe Albert and his wrestling partner, the Bear. Photo taken in Ross, ND.

Courtesy: Charlie Juma Family

of present-day North Dakotans. Memorable, for example, was Mohammad Bomrad of Walsh County. This man traveled from farm to farm with his horse and wagon through much of northeastern North Dakota. His photograph frequently appears in history books of the area. The *Walsh County History* says Mohammad apparently never married. He is said to have "retired" in Edmonton, Alberta. Mohammad's brother, Nick Bomrad, was a familiar traveling man who "worked" the rural region in and about the Turtle Mountains.[20]

Horse and buggy was one thing but Joe Albert of Belcourt was a man who could do better than that. He could use one or several of his exceptional talents. He would attract an audience by bringing along a trained bear and sometimes a pet monkey. Joe Albert, who will appear on other pages of this volume, was billed as a "strong man" who could bend steel bars, wrestle his bear, and perform "unbelievable" feats with a trained goat and with a trick rope. At the end of his show he would sometimes display his wares to his deeply impressed audience. In 1997, Ahmed Kamoni, in a Valley City, ND, interview, remembers that Joe Albert would "overnight" at his father's farm in Kidder County. On one occasion, Joe "housed" his bear and monkey in the Kamoni barn. Ahmed said that when the sun arose the Kamoni horses and cattle were "no where to be seen, they were scattered all over the county."

Less spectacular but more widely ranging in his activities was Norwegian-speaking Solomon Hodge, whose territory extended over six counties. He seemed to have centered his life in the Mountrail County region. He owned land in township 156-R92. He was buried in the Muslim cemetery at Ross.

Allen Osmunson, writing in the 1982 *Cooperstown History*, remembered a "Syrian" peddler who used to visit farms in his predominantly Norwegian part of North Dakota.

> *I remember back in the early 1930s when the Syrian peddlers would come to our place to sell their wares. One of these was a very nice, gentle and well-liked man, Tofik Ahsmel. ... How excited [we] would get when Tofik came here with his buggy, pulled by a brown horse called Ruby. And how anxious we were to see what he had for sale in his trunks, and what a nice, clean smell the various cloths, tablecloths, scarves, and other wares had when he brought them out for inspection. ... I'm proud of having known him, and I'm glad that Tofik came to our home.*

The previous paragraphs contain information concerning "noteworthy Arabic peddlers," but most memorable of all were the female peddlers. This phenomenon sets the Lebanese apart from all other national groups. On this score, for example, Syrians differed decidedly from their Jewish counterparts. No records have been found concerning Jewish women who walked from farm to farm in selling ventures. But every account of Syrian life in North Dakota or Minnesota discusses such a feminine enterprise. For example, Sherifee Hasen would leave her home in Rolla, ND, when her husband departed on a peddling trip. Mrs. Hasen (known locally as Shirley) would cover her own territory and return home in time to greet her husband as he returned from his "business" circuit."[21] The United States immigration records from 1899 to 1907 show that 4,000 of the 13,200 Syrian women, upon arrival at American seaports, declared themselves to be "merchants and dealers," which Louise Houghton says means "peddlers."[22] This is remarkable; it indicates that even before entering the American scene, women were already determined to venture in such solitary professions.

Women peddlers, leaving their family circumstances, traveling alone, keeping their own accounts, seem to be at variance with the stereotype of Arabian womanhood. Certainly it's far from the notion of women covered with veils, confined behind walls, and subject to all sorts of social restrictions. The woman as peddler presents the image of a confident person, a woman almost a century ahead of her time who moved without hesitation through the still unknown prairies of the American frontier.

The peddling trade for Syrian women in North Dakota seems to have been a reoccurring part of life everywhere in pioneer America. One elderly lady in Iowa remembers "every man and woman of her original immigrant group was involved in peddling."

Deeby Sine of Williston, a Zahle native, recalled her early years in America. Duluth, Minnesota, was the "headquarters" from which she worked. In December 1939 she said:

From about 1907 to 1910 I traveled between Havre, Montana, and Duluth, Minn. with a line of ladies dresses, fancywork and laces, and made good money which helped to finance my reunion with my children. I had a sad and lonely life on the homestead, and wished many times I had never come to Dakota, but it was partly the means of getting my children here, and I am now thankful for that and the kindness they have shown me in appreciation.

Why did the women peddle? One respected account emphasized what probably should have been obvious: "It helped the family." Remembering the early days in eastern American states, another woman said it gave them a "sense of freedom, of nature." Another said she liked the outdoors.[23] Another woman remembered that she liked to peddle because there were too many living "in one house."[24] Such a response was not implausible, given the crowded conditions found in some of America's immigrant ghetto areas.

Women were peddlers in North Dakota; that is clear. Many accounts speak of it as a part-time and sometimes a full-time vocation. And all reports say that itinerant Lebanese woman seemed to have been accepted by the non-Syrian neighbors. Only one negative statement can be found, an intriguing item which appeared in the Fargo newspaper, *Search-Light,* in 1907: "A woman peddler [was] chased out of Barton [ND]." Who? Why? We don't know.[25]

Mildred Absey of Grand Forks recalled a remarkable Lebanese lady named Mrs. Anthony who came to the United States as a widow with three children—all of whom became business people of Midwestern prominence. Mrs. Anthony first went to St. Paul, Minnesota. "There were lots of Lebanese there." She bought a big suitcase and was supplied by a Lebanese wholesale merchant. She walked, often with her three children, through the city neighborhoods selling things such as lace, ribbons, and buttons. Her speech was described as "fractured English." She always wore a flowing, long, black dress "like a nun." Mrs. Anthony eventually moved to Crookston, Minnesota, "there were Lebanese there." From Crookston the dear lady would take a train to towns in eastern North Dakota from whence she would walk from farm to farm. She did this for many years. Those who remember her said "she never owned an automobile."[26]

If not on the road with her husband, the Syrian woman was often still involved in the peddler's trade: to "stay home alone with the children," to "crochet" goods for the husband to sell on his route. Mary

Farris, whose childhood was in Zahle, remembers the sad early days in a 1939 interview:

> My husband he travel, he sell men goods, some lady goods. When I get my son, John, I sick four months. I stay home alone, my husband he gone all week, sometime two week. I cry and cry. I crochet all the time. I got three, four Syrian women live in noder [sic] room. We come together and crochet. I get up six o'clock, stay up twelve. My husband come home, he see big pile crochet. He take it 'long, sell it. Oh, dat's hard times; now it's easy for everybody.

How many peddlers, whether male or female, traversed the prairies of North Dakota in the first two decades of this century? In truth, it's impossible to tell. The authors can say this much, a good 80 percent of the Lebanese families interviewed in the course of writing this book said that their forebears engaged in peddling.

A distinction has to be made between those who were "full time" peddlers and those who left the farm to criss-cross the countryside during the summer, and perhaps in the spring and fall.

Yet, a glance at the censuses of 1900, 1910, and 1920 found in the Appendix of this book shows the number of peddlers almost unbelievably small. The three census tabulations show a total of 450 Syrian-born men, yet only about 30 could be classed as peddlers. (The nomenclature was interesting: "Peddler," "Peddler/Salesman," "Traveling Peddler," "Country Peddler," "Pack Peddler," "Traveling Salesman.") The proportion of the men who were "peddlers" in the three decades is only about six percent. Something is wrong here.

Almost every scholar who has studied Lebanese and Syrians in the early part of this century has lamented the fact that the compilations of the U.S. Census and sometimes the Commissioner General of Immigration vastly underestimated the Syrian totals. Houghton already in 1911 bemoans that fact and Hitti in 1924 says the figures are "ludicrous."[27] In trying to match the names found in the North Dakota census lists with those known to have filed either one or both of their naturalization papers, the authors find that a great number of individuals disappear.

Something is definitely wrong. But could a partial explanation be the fact that a large proportion of the men were "on the road"? The census-taker would come in April or May. Shopkeepers in those months would be at home; some farmers would be putting in the crop, but what of the rest? In a previous study, several of the present authors were trying, through a census analysis, to determine the number of "cowboys" who were everywhere present in western Dakota during the ranching period. The census number proved to be miniscule. The cowhands were with the roving herds, or on "the trail." A "head count" was impossible. What of the

Lebanese itinerant merchant? Was he (or she) not also "on the trail"? And to carry the matter further, could this not be at least a partial solution to the nationwide "under estimate" of Syrian-born American residents?

Time changed things. Suppliers in the city, backpacks, a primitive wagon, all these were part of the earliest peddler's life. The horse cart gave way to specially designed wagons, with drawers, racks, and compartments. As one would expect, the years brought gradual readjustments in the wholesale sources and the marketing procedures. Writing of the 1930s concerning her part of the northern Red River Valley, Blanche Passa wrote of the visiting peddler:

> Tom Salem made frequent trips to Bowesmont with his old pick-up. He had built a hut on the back and it had a door at the rear of the box. He sold whatever products he was able to obtain elsewhere, to sell with a margin of profit. He regularly bought calves from the local farmers and after processing, sold fresh meat. Sometimes he had Canadian fish to sell.[28]

Peddlers, like Tom Salem, began increasingly to use trucks and cars in the 1930s, '40s, and '50s. Abdo Aleck and his brother Jim Aleck (both Muslims) worked the territory around Park River. They had a "big car" and knew every Norwegian family in the area. Things like Watkins and Raleigh products came into existence. Some peddlers took advantage of this more systematic house-to-house approach. The guaranteed line of goods with name recognition, advertising, and assigned territories was appealing.

Soon small trucks rumbled across prairie back roads. The 1920 Census of McClusky village in Sheridan County lists Aisem Haykel, born in Syria, 38 years of age, "Agent, Watkins." His contemporary, Ferris Skaff, for forty years was a Watkins agent. He, too, worked out of McClusky.[29]

Sam Skaff, now well known in North Dakota's business world, said in a family history account:

> My father (Ferris Skaff) worked for the Watkins Co. travelling in the Sheriden and McLean counties. He travelled by team of horses and wagon and travelled about ten miles a day in those early years, staying at farmers overnight. ... Then again travelled the next morning, calling on farmers winter and summer. ... He travelled the ruts and rabbit tracks on the dusty dirt roads on county section lines to all the farmers he could serve and meet with a friendly visit. The buggy had wooden wheels with steel rims. The two white horses who pulled the Watkins wagon were called King and Queen. The buggy had two doors in the back to pull out the drawers that contained the Watkins products to show the display to his customer clients. He also had a sample case he took into the houses. He would display his samples and sell right out of the case. In the winter my father would replace

the wagon wheels with skids or sled runners. When the winter was extremely cold he cut his rounds to the farmers.

He sold mostly vanilla, cinnamon and pepper. People often bought two or three pounds of pepper at a time, as they used pepper for their home-made sausage. He also used to sell a lot of Watkins Baking Powder. Another hot seller was Watkins liniment which was a number one item for the farmers. They used liniment for livestock and home use. Also menthol camphor and carbolic salve was very useful to the farmer for colds, cuts and bruises.

Older people remember my father, Ferris Skaff, as the friendly Watkins man. [They ran] to meet his wagon as it turned the corner at each farm near the mail box. They watched wide-eyed as he unpacked his products in the case. He often gave the children gifts such as candy and Watkins gum. He would most always leave a gift when he left the client's farm.

In the 1920s my father traded the old Watkins wagon for a Ford car, a Model T Ford. He filled the back part of the car with Watkins. During the depression people couldn't afford to buy much, so it was good if he sold as much as $10 a day worth of Watkins products. My father received the Watkins products from Winona by railroad to McClusky, ND on the Soo Line.[30]

Ferris Skaff's peddlers wagon worked out of the Sheridan County settlement.

Courtesy: Sam Skaff

Records are scarce but here and there in the census we see other names with the word "Watkins" attached. Nassif Massad is in the census of 1920 at Fessenden in Wells County. This 39-year-old gentleman is listed as "Watkins salesman." Nassif and his wife Nellie were parents of six children. The father and mother were born in "Turkey."

Thomas Nassif of Bismarck recalled his younger years when interviewed at Bismarck in August 1939:

> *I worked as a salesman [in Iowa] for about four years, then came back here and worked a year or two on my father's farm at Keif, North Dakota. Then I got the agency for Watkins Remedies and peddled them around Drake, North Dakota, for a year or two and then changed to the Raleigh Company.*

A certain modern-day fame has come for Ferris S. Skaff, the above-mentioned peddler turned Watkins salesman, who worked out of McClusky. Photographs of Mr. Skaff and his handsome wagon with its large Watkins sign were featured on the cover of the nationally known *Aramco World Magazine* of September 1986. The *REC Magazine*, of large regional circulation, featured Ferris and his wagon in its October 1986 issue.

Unfortunately the records of the Watkins company sales men and women from early in the century do not exist. The mere list of names would be a splendid chronicle of Syrian presence in the American Midwest.

Joe Albert, "Strong Man" from Belcourt

The sketch of Joe's life is brief. He arrived in the U.S. in 1901, settled in the Turtle Mountain area, took citizenship, died in the 1950s, and is buried at Oregon City, Oregon. The date of his birth, like that of many Muslim men, is hazy. Some said at death he must have been "almost 100."

Between his arrival and his death, Joe was a very busy man. He married four times. His first wife was a French-Chippewa lady who died at a young age and left him with four children. More children were born to later wives.

At one time Joe ran a Turtle Mountain grocery store and rented out boats on Fish Lake. But his heart was in the world of entertainment; in front of the public, Joe was superb. With his own tent (sometimes outdoors in schoolyards) and sometimes as a part of a circus, Joe traveled throughout North Dakota and to nearby parts of the Midwest.

A little over five feet tall, of muscular torso and immensely strong, Joe would straighten horseshoes, bend coins, and wrap a steel bar around his thigh. (One North Dakotan still has a one-half inch bar that Joe had twisted around his own neck and through his legs.)

Joe Albert: "Strong Man" showman, business man and peddler.

Courtesy:
Charlie Juma Family

Joe had a bear (sometimes two bears) and would wrestle the unmuzzled beast, to the delight of his fans, and he would challenge men to pull (not jerk!) on a rope he wrapped around his neck and under his arms. He could pull a freight car down the track (just one car, however). He would don a special harness and stand attached to a rope between two automobiles as they spun their wheels trying to drive away from him.

Small-town merchants would put on a well-advertised kind of "crazy days" promotion and Joe would perform. His act varied; he had his bear, of course, but also a white goat that tiptoed on bottles. He had a "hairless Mexican dog" and also a

121

dog that walked back and forth on a high wire. He was often accompanied by a monkey in costume: the little "fellow" would tip his hat and would strut about in the audience with a tin cup.

One time Joe had a friend, who was billed as a "wild man," dyed some hideous color. The caged half-man, half-animal, would leap, grimace, scream and throw dirt.

Known sometimes as the "Terrible Turk," Joe would occasionally challenge the local strong men to a wrestling bout. (Joe gets paid if he wins, the opponent gets the money if he can "pin Joe to the mat.")

In his later years, Joe moved with his wife's family to Oregon and did much of the same: town events, carnivals, and schoolyards. His death closed a life filled with marvelous feats. Even a half century later, his name evokes smiles from hundreds of North Dakota's senior citizens. There's no doubt about it: in his day Joe was North Dakota's best-known "Syrian" resident.

In the Peddler's Pack

North Dakota "old timers" recall Lebanese (Syrian) peddlers supplying the following goods to their rural families:

Toiletries: perfumes, creams, lotions, soaps, powders, combs, brushes.

House supplies: thread, needles, thimbles, scissors, pins, buttons.

Spices: pepper, cinnamon, nutmeg.

Religious items: crosses, rosaries.

Fabrics: silks, lace.

Practical things: stockings, underwear, gloves, caps.

Decorative items: wall hangings, tapestries

Note: The peddler, at least in the earliest days, carried his or her sale items from farm to farm. To do this they often used two packs: a large shoulder pack (or box) with compartments or even drawers, and frequently a chest pack to balance the shoulder weight. A pack could easily exceed 100 pounds, at least during the initial portion of the journey. Needless to say, many older Syrians had eventual back and shoulder problems.

CHAPTER TEN

Homesteading: Farming

The peddler's trade had certain advantages. The traveling salesperson could see at close hand an immense part of America's rural regions: new land, good land, and often ideal farmland. The peddler's "grapevine" allowed information concerning such opportunities to flow back to Lebanese centers in Minnesota, Iowa, New York, and to the homeland in the Eastern Mediterranean.

The itinerant Lebanese in the West was well aware of the flood of European and Eastern American land seekers who came in immigrant cars, in wagons, and sometimes on foot to acquire their portion of America's bountiful domains. Not surprisingly, a great many Syrians decided to forsake the mobile life, at least for a while, and sink their roots into some available homestead acreage.

Acquisition of land through homesteading (or its companion procedures: preemption and tree-claiming) was a relatively simple process. It demanded neither an ability to speak English nor a sizable amount of funds. It was available to any individual, male or female, who had reached the age of 21 and who was either a citizen or intended to become a citizen. Homesteading therefore was within the reach of most adults, whether single or the head of a family. An initial fee of 10 dollars was required. This was followed by a stint of five years in residence, the construction of a simple house and some cultivation. (The five years could be shortened at times by commutation—a procedure in which, after two years, 18 months, or sometimes 14 months, the land could be purchased.) After fulfilling the requirements and payment of a small fee, a deed for as much as 160 acres was presented by the federal government to the land claimant.

One hundred and sixty acres, when put on the market, could mean anywhere from 300 to 2000 dollars. This was an opportunity worth considering. Indeed, the five years on the land did not preclude the possibility of making occasional sales trips to nearby settlers who might seek the usual peddlers' merchandise.

It would be no exaggeration to say that for almost all Syrians in North Dakota, survival in early days depended on two large factors: peddling and homesteading. In the background of both these enterprises, of course, was the "network" of information that spread everywhere in the Syrian world. This is clearly evident in the memories of David Kalil of Williston as he recalled his arrival in North Dakota. His 1940 WPA interview says:

> *I heard of homesteads in North Dakota and there was some Syrians who had homesteaded here before, so left Duluth and filed on land in 1903, northwest of Williston. Went back to Duluth and worked a while. I had a letter written to land office here at Williston and they told me land was still here, so I came here and went out on homestead in 1904, I think. Broke up all my homestead with horses and proved up, raised quite a few horses and cattle and had good crop.*

Dozens of other family accounts tell of the early homesteading experience. Nassif Freije married Latefie Abrous in St. Paul, Minnesota, in 1894. After a stay in Fargo, the couple moved to Walsh County where they homesteaded in 1899. Soon the family was in business in nearby Lawton and later in Edmore. Family members still own the original parcel of homestead land. One of the grandchildren, John Freije, is today the mayor of Mayville, North Dakota.[1]

Some off-the-boat immigrants knew exactly where their destination was to be in their new homeland. Bo Alley Farhart of the Muslim community of Ross, after two years in Central America (where he says he "went broke") received seventy dollars from his brother in North Dakota. Mr. Farhart recalled in November 1939: "I came directly from New York City to Ross, North Dakota, where I immediately filed on a homestead and am still residing on the same."

Rural Farm Directory: Ross Area (early 1990's)

Courtesy: John Guerrero

Sam Omar, in May 1902, left Beirut and by the fall of 1902 was homesteading in Mountrail County. He was true to the promises he made on filing for his claim; he improved his land, lived on it, and received his patent deed. Even more, he acquired his U.S. citizenship in 1921.

Joseph Abraham arrived in the United States in 1896. Looking back over the years in his new country he said in 1940: "I'm glad I came here. If I stayed there [Syria] I'd die long ago." Mr. Abraham took up a homestead in Pierce County in 1902. Mr. Abraham's first years were busy and prosperous. The drought of the 1930s, however, had disastrous consequences. The family lost their farm holdings. He summarized his successes and failures:

In springtime, 1902, I come and get land eighteen mile south Rugby. I build little shack first—eight by eight—then I build bigger ever once in while. I prove up in 1903. I raise wheat, barley, oats, corn, and got ten cattle, sometime fifteen, twenty-five and forty. I got pigs and chickens too. I got pretty good crop once in while; when we get crop we make living; when we don't, make mortgage on cattle, on farm, anything. Sometime broke, sometime got money. I raise some turkey too; once I sell pretty near two hundred dollar, but it's hilly there and turkeys get away, I can't find any more. So I don't raise turkey no more. We got best kind water; have well and wind-mill. We live all time on farm till three year ago; when we get good house, barn, chicken-coop, granary and everything. Then we lose it. I have six thousand dollar buildings on my farm; when we get rain, we get crop; no rain, no crop. The first year I get crop, I get married again—1915; that's the best crop I get.

Joe Nicholas, Cando, said his father, Nicholas Ausey, homesteaded near Bisbee. His father, he recalled, chose his land at the spot where "the wagon wheel broke and they couldn't fix it."[2]

The mention of a broken wagon wheel is a reminder to the modern reader that taking land in primitive North Dakota was not the easy task that family chronicles now seem to depict. Perhaps the years of modest success blotted out the barren, lonely landscapes that first greeted the landseekers from the dozens of countries who looked to the prairies for their future well being. Yet Lebanese, it seems, tended to be quite matter-of-fact about their experiences for most accounts dwell very little on drought, hailstorms, and primitive living conditions. One dear lady in 1939 did say this: "I don't think I'd do same if I can live again. 'Course I suffer a lot in olden days, and I wouldn't want to live over that time." Yet she said, "I never go back to my country. I remember this country better'n the Old Country."

A rare glimpse of such difficulties can be seen in a Walsh County account published by Viviane Doche in *Cedars by the Mississippi*:

Eva Absy [sic] came from Ferzoul, south of Zahle, with her family when she was two years old, in 1891. They left Lebanon to escape from Turkish rule, and settled in Grafton, North Dakota, where her father and uncles were granted a hundred and sixty acres of land in return for fourteen dollars. The land was divided into four sections, one for each brother. Jim Bill, a neighbor farmer, helped them as much as he could when they first started. Her father built a barn with stones that he dug out himself. He had to build his own house and his wife helped by baking mud bricks. Eva used to help on the farm and her sister used to go by sled to bring the needed water. Her father dug nine wells but they were all alkaline. They used primitive methods to dig the well. The land was fertile but the family could not take the severe winters on the farm. Life was too difficult; they suffered from isolation and were not used to the new farming practices. The family grew bigger every year. They finally moved to St. Paul.[3]

Farming could be cruel in early-day North Dakota; the weather, the isolation, but occupational hazards also faced the newcomer. The *Williston World* in November 1907, reported:

A. Munyer of Bonetraill had a serious accident last week while hauling grain to Williston. The horses were frightened and ran away ... passing over his legs. ... Mr. Munyer was to have made final proof on Wednesday of this week."[4]

Most of the 1939-40 interviewees were neither glowing in their recollection of their homesteading years, nor were they excessively pessimistic. Jabour Munyer of Williston recalls those days in a February 1940 interview:

Then [after peddling] I come back to Williston, live on my homestead. After I prove up I rent my land, and have pretty good crops for few year. 1912 I get 2500 bushel wheat, my share not less than eleven hundred bushel. I buy horses and machinery. One time I borrow $1248.00 from First National Bank, just my note. I raise horses—had thirteen head— and hundred fifty chickens.

Side Abdallah, of the Muslim community in Ross, recalled his first days in an October 1939 interview:

Then I started farming. I bought some horses, a plow, drill, disk, and drag. I hired a man to break my land for me and planted some flax and wheat. The crop was good. My first home was a one-room, 12 x 14 frame shack. You see, I planned to return to Syria if they gained independence from Turkey.

Side Abdallah, like so many, never returned to Lebanon. Some others, however, never thought of a return to the Old Country nor did they cherish the idea of remaining on a farm; rather they saw homesteading as a first step to something better in America. Hassin Alley Juma of Ross didn't even plow up his own land, he hired others to do the labor and worked at jobs "elsewhere." Mr. Juma said in an October 1939 interview:

When I first started homesteading, I built a frame house that measured twelve by fourteen feet. I hired a man to break and sow the land for me, and also hired someone to harvest and thresh. I have never done any of my own farm work as I have always worked elsewhere at different trades.

Attas Boutrous did much the same: he took the quite legitimate procedure of hiring the work done. (Residency, however, was required.) With the land sale money he returned, at least for a while, to Sioux City. In Bismarck, July 1939, he remembers:

I have never farmed in this country and when I had my homestead I hired a neighbor to break up what land I had to have broken up. I only lived there for fourteen months and made commutation proof on my homestead and then returned to Sioux City. I later sold the homestead and invested the money in my business.

Syrian-Lebanese Farmsteads in North Dakota 1895–1915

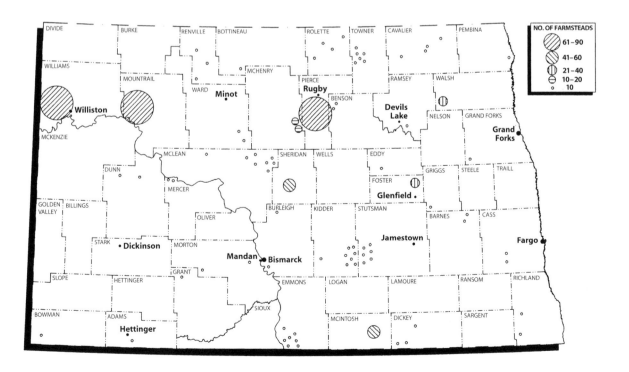

Farming was an opportunity to acquire "ready cash." Joe Albert, born "west of Damascus," described his first North Dakota days in a 1940 Williston interview:

I worked around there [Minnesota] for three years and then went to Marshall, Iowa, and worked there on a farm till 1910 when I came to Williston. I worked on railroad a while, then went up to Bonetrail and bought a relinquishment for one hundred and seventy-five dollars and filed on one hundred and sixty acres of land. This land was three miles west and one mile north of Bonetrail. There was twenty acres broke on the claim and I hired about twenty more acres broke. I did not farm this myself, but rented it out. I bought two horses but just so I could drive around. I made a fourteen months' proof and kept it three years. After I proved up I had some good crops off this land and then I sold out.

Mentioning farm difficulties subsequent to his homestead time period, Joe Seeb, an Ain Arab Christian born, in his words, "30 miles from Damascus," says in a Williston interview of April 1940:

In 1933 I have a big fire. I was coming home from field with one of boys and I say "look, there's fire by our house!" He say, "no, that's other side of barn." But when we come close we see it's right by barn, and we go try to get horses out. We get one out and he run like everything; then we get a big mare out and she run away. But I lost my barn and hay and got nine horses burned. That's awful bad. I got no horses left.

In 1934, one day my wife she go to town with boy, and Arthur he's working about three quarter mile from home with six horses. I go over to see how he's getting along 'cause he's not very big and I'm afraid he can't handle those six horses. It was getting pretty stormy and it was high wind. I tell Arthur he better come home now—it might be a bad storm. So we come home. When we get pretty near home one girl come out holler "fire, fire!" I go inside and see it's fire in house; we try to put it out, but it's in chimney and it's such a strong wind we can't get it out. We lose everything, and it's lots of clothes for eight people. Then I got nothing left; I have to start all over, and then I get no crop since long time before that.

But it would be unfair and inaccurate to portray all Syrian farm experiences as short-lived ventures or filled with disillusionment. A look at the land atlas of Williams County in 1937 found Syrian farmers flourishing throughout Bull Butte, Mont, and Cow Creek townships. Indeed, 20 or more Lebanese names are listed. Much of the three townships could be described as "Lebanese territory."

Mrs. David Kalil of Williston discussed her three, perhaps four, decades in America with a WPA interviewer in August 1940. Her first years in North Dakota are described in a few words:

I come to my sister and stay four months with her. I file on land on the Muddy, but I don't prove up. I sell my relinquishment, and after four months I get married, in 1911. My husband, Sid Zine, got farm twenty-five miles northwest [of Williston].

This brief account should alert the reader to the fact that homesteading was not just a male enterprise. We must remember that American law allowed anyone, male or female, to take land if they were 21 years old, single, or the head of a family.

H. Elaine Lindgren, in her book *Land in Her Own Name*, has extensively documented the participation of women in the North Dakota "land rush" period. She found, for example, that the proportion of women among the state's total land claimants varied from county to county; as low as six percent to as high as 18 and 20 percent. This latter figure, 18 percent, was true of Williams County, the site of a large Lebanese settlement. Indeed, Dr. Lindgren found that fourteen of the eighty identifiable Lebanese homesteaders were women. In Pierce County, the Rugby area, six of the seventy-six Lebanese who filed were women.

Barbara Wizer, a native of Zahle, when interviewed by the WPA at Williston said:

When I was eleven years old my mother [a widow] came to this country. …Four years later my mother sent me a ticket. … I came all alone. I was in Fargo about a year and a half and then went with my mother to Rugby. My mother filed on land about eleven miles from Rugby.

It's interesting to note that the above settlements were of Christian background. In Mountrail County, where most of the Lebanese settlers were of the Muslim faith, not one of the seventy-one claimants was a woman.[5]

What does this mean? Perhaps the wave of Muslim immigrants to America, at least during North Dakota's land "boom," was predominantly male. Or maybe it was a matter of time periods. The Christian Lebanese movement to the United States started earlier and was in greater numbers. It is possible that Christian women were already attuned to the larger American world and would be more likely to venture into the unknown prairies. But could the absence of Muslim women also have been due to the age-old question of "women's status"

Mary Juma and grandsons. She with her husband were the first couple to homestead in the Ross Muslim community.

Courtesy: Rosie Juma Chamley.

in an Arabic society? Yet, how does this square with the fact that Muslim women were "pioneer peddlers"? Were Muslim women really restricted to the more "safe" and more domestic roles? Quite frankly, we don't have answers to these questions.

We do have, however, some clues as to what role Muslim women played in land ownership, as contrasted with the matter of homesteading. The 1920 Census of Ross, North Dakota, lists a 43-year-old lady, Allica Juma, as a "farmer." Even earlier, Mrs. Sadie Kagella, a Syrian-born lady in the Walsh County 1910 census, is classed as a "farmer." She and her son ran the farm operation. There's no doubt that even within the first generation Muslim and Christian women would retain possession of their deceased husband's land and most likely they would continue the farm enterprises. They could, thereby, be legitimately classed as "farmers."

Seen from the end-of-the-twentieth century perspective, every agricultural survey in North Dakota indicates the dramatic decline in the total number of farmsteads in the state and the corresponding increase in the size of farm operations. Such a thing is true of North Dakota's Lebanese rural enclaves in the Christian area northwest of Williston. The number of Lebanese descendants actually living on a farm today has been reduced to a mere handful. Yet several such families now farm tracts of land that total 2000 and even 3000 acres. In the Muslim rural community near Ross, again only several families remain in residence on a farm. Here, too, the size of the acreages can be measured no longer in terms of hundreds but now into the thousands of acres.

Early Ross Area Islamic Farmers at haying time.
Courtesy: Charlie Juma Family

In the Pierce County area, only one farm is still occupied and run by a Lebanese descendant. This individual is married to a Scandinavian lady. The couple attends the Lutheran Church. In the Sheridan County enclave the last Syrian farmer left his farmstead in 1964.[6]

Ownership of the land does not necessarily mean actually *running* the farm. The two are often different enterprises. Williston, Rugby, Stanley (near Ross) and Bismarck have numerous men and women of Syrian background who still own but do not operate the farms of their forbearers. On occasion men will help in the spring and fall with planting and harvesting tasks, but for the most part they are absentee owners.

Was the decline in Lebanese residency or farm occupation within the past generation any more drastic than that of other ethnic groups? The answer has to be an educated guess because all groups have been involved in the exodus from the farm. But, in truth, Germans from Russia now farm most of the Rugby Pierce County Syrian lands. Norwegians have taken over the operation of much of the Williston and Ross lands.

This is not surprising. Many reports have indicated that the Germans from Russia and the Norwegians are the most "durable" of all major ethnic groups in North Dakota. They seem to have an affinity to large scale, highly capitalized farm enterprises.

Yet when compared to the many other national groups in the state, Syrians rank among those who did surprisingly well in coping with the vagaries of the Dakota semi-arid "Big Sky" country. A dozen other groups came, took land and left with much greater rapidity. Some lasted only a few years: Irish, British, Jews, African-Americans, Old Order Amish, Dunkers, and Danes.

Seen, therefore, in the context of time, Syrians from the rather gentle climate of the Eastern Mediterranean did remarkably well as they struggled to survive on the Great Plains of North Dakota.

Hospitality

An old Arab proverb goes like this: "A small abode will hold a thousand friends." One of the quintessential elements of Arabic culture is hospitality. The real charm of Arab traditions is their open door policy to visitors. This virtue emphasizes accessibility to people and a desire to make a guest comfortable. Arabs are hospitable worldwide, whether they are in Beirut, Sao Paulo, Sydney, New York, Paris, or Williston, North Dakota. This generous characteristic extends to not only family and friends within the intimate circle, but to total strangers as well. Arabs in strange cities are rarely alone if they find fellow countrymen.

Tavern owner Amid Hach of Wales, North Dakota, is an example. Amid farmed in the Wales area and it is said that if he had a bountiful harvest he would share the proceeds with the community. Joe Hiawatha of Rock Lake often put on a big feast of kibbi for his neighbors. Peddlers everywhere were treated as guests. Alec Hasen, a Rolette County peddler, once stayed 26 days with another family northeast of Dunseith during a winter blizzard. Alec himself, along with numerous other peddlers, would stay on the Nick Ausey farm in Bisbee between trips. Indeed, most merchandise was shipped to the Auseys from St. Paul or Crookston. The arrival of trunks was often a social event for farm families. Neighbors, with great delight, would inspect the trunks, which held shoelaces, ribbons, buttons, thread, laces, perfumes, clothing, and other merchandise.

Sometimes a symbol of Arab hospitality would be the renowned, yet bitter, black coffee served in both Christian and Muslim homes. On special occasions, Christian Arabs would toast friendships with a drink of arak, a strong liquor derived from grapes and anise. Charles Joseph of Williston had an age-old phrase, "Do not deny me the pleasure of being your host." The traditional last words to departing guests are, "You have honored us with your presence." In turn the guest replies, "It is we who have been honored."

CHAPTER ELEVEN

Shopkeepers:
The First Decade

The Fargo newspaper, *Search-Light,* on November 24, 1906, had this report: "Assyrians are opening stores in several towns in the state."[1] If the readers were knowledgeable, this little report would have been cause for special interest. Here we have immigrants who arrived in the state no earlier than ten years previous; immigrants who knew neither English, Scandinavian, nor German before they reached American shores. This is an American success story.

The 1906 news report was a little tardy in announcing the advent of Syrians in North Dakota's business scene. The *Williston Herald* of December 21, 1905, mentions the "A Bousiliman, Fair Share Store," featuring dry goods. On the same date, the newspaper says, "John Shikany, a new store," an establishment that was both a "grocery" and a "dry goods" type of business. It was called "The Fairdeal Store."

John Kassis arrived in the United States and proved up on land in Pierce County in 1902. He farmed for a while. His best crop was in 1904 when he says he "got $1.00 a bushel for wheat." Kassis reported in a 1939 WPA interview: "In 1905 I sold out and came to Williston. Me and my brother started in business right away. We put up a building on East Broadway (in Williston) and had a general store."

Again the reader will stand in admiration. The Williams County newcomer arrives in the United States, homesteads, farms, learns English, acquires a store building and operates it, and does this all within no more than three years!

And the Kassis interview account was not an exaggeration. The *Williston Herald,* in the May 7, 1905, issue, has an advertisement for "the Kassis Brothers Clothing Store." And even further: the December 21, 1905 issue of the same newspaper advertised, "A.B. Kassis, General Merchandise." The story is not complete. By 1908 the Williston World was carrying advertisements for the Paris Candy Kitchen. Abe Kassis is mentioned as an owner.

Kassis did not have an exclusive claim to the Williston business world. In 1907 a gentleman named Tom Zine was operating his own store. H. K. Saykally was advertising in the Williston paper in 1908. He ran the St. Louis Candy Store. In 1910 Tom Germanus had a general store in Williston. By the 1910s, Syrian owners could be found in additional business concerns: a meat market, a confectionery shop, and two pool halls. The Kalil clothing store was also a going concern.[2]

The roundabout way in which early Syrian merchants came to Williston can be seen in the life of Charles A. Joseph, who left Zahle at the age of 12 years in 1897. He went to the Montana mining town of Butte, then to Alder (the gold fields), where he worked in his brother Mike's store. A big man, he would journey all the way to Salt Lake City, obtaining merchandise for the firm. Later he was peddling ladies goods at Havre, Montana, and there he met his future wife, Margaret Bohamra. Margaret's parents were from Baalbek, Lebanon. She and her family lived for a while in St. Paul, then in Virginia, Minnesota, and then moved to Williams County's Cow Creek Township where they homesteaded. Charles Joseph married Margaret, and soon the couple moved to Salt Lake City and by 1918 started the Williston Joseph's Ready to Wear store. (It continued as a family-owned business until 1999.)

Was Williston a unique situation? Probably not, for as early as 1900 the U.S. Census lists B. Lian of Syrian birth as operator of a Fargo billiard hall and Mickal Assid as a "dealer in fruit" in Cass County. Already in that same year, the town of Rugby in Pierce County had Abdalla Shama and Charley Turk; both were merchants. Mr. Shama came to the United States in 1893. Mr. Turk came in 1891. Abe Mikel says, in a WPA report of 1939, that he worked in his uncle's store in Rugby in 1902. (This was within six years after the arrival of Pierce County's first Syrian homesteader.) George and Richard Assad, according to the 1900 U.S. Census, came from "Ceria" in 1890 and 1894 respectively. They were "restaurant keepers" in Wahpeton in Richland County.

By 1910, the U.S. Census lists 28 Syrian-born individuals in such categories as: "merchant," "owner, dry goods," "storekeeper." In 1990 only one of the 55 males of Syrian birth was involved in railroad work. In 1910, 17 men worked on the railroad but of that number, fourteen were part of transient railroad construction crews.[3] This observation should put to rest the oft-repeated but clearly false statement that "Syrians came to North Dakota because of railroad jobs."

Of more interest is the continued Lebanese involvement in farming. Thirty-six were "farmers" in 1900; ten years later the number was 65. The 65 included some who were still in the homestead stage, but also a number who had remained on the land even after acquiring their clear

titles. Perhaps 18 of the 54 who carried the census designation "farm laborers" were siblings or farmers' sons. A similar proportion of the "farm laborers" were newly arrived fellow countrymen or relatives. In the previous Homesteading-Farming chapter we saw the gradual drift of Syrians away from farm enterprises, but for the first decade or two, there's no question that they "gave the farm a try."

The census categories indicating private business ventures are of particular interest. In 1900, a handful of Syrian-born individuals were running their own businesses. As noted above, by 1910, twenty-eight (all men) were in that merchant classification. Another seven men worked in family firms. The trend into the business world became more evident in the 1920 Census when forty-one individuals (all men) were listed as proprietors of some type of mercantile venture. Most were town merchants. (Eight others seem to be working independently or in a family business.)

Finally, the recorded number of self-declared and apparently full-time peddlers increased from seven in 1900 to a possible ten in 1910. As seen elsewhere in this volume, these census numbers are inaccurate. Certainly there were dozens of full-time peddlers on the road and perhaps as many

Kalil Store, 1908, Williston.

Courtesy: Wilbur Kalil

as a hundred in part-time "selling ventures." This is clear from other recorded materials and interviews. There is no way of knowing exactly how many Syrians were working as peddlers in quest of a supplemental income and, at the same time, saw farming and town businesses as their primary source of livelihood.

A farm, the railroad, a business, and no doubt some peddling on the side, made up the fast-paced early life of a Zahle native, Joseph Azar, interviewed in August 1939 at Bismarck:

> *I left New York by train to Rugby Junction where I worked on farms for a while. I came to Williston in 1899 and worked around that town for some years. I also operated a pool room there. In 1914 I filed on a homestead, and after proving it up I came to Dickinson, North Dakota and worked on the railroad there. I also operated a pool room here for about two or three years. Then I came to Bismarck and went into the produce business and have been here ever since.*

As an example of the Syrian immigrant's efforts to "sort out" the various suitable occupations in the New World we have Attas Boutrous who left the port of Beirut with high expectations. After his processing in 1899 at Ellis Island, he went to Sioux City, Iowa, where he found employment in a meat-packing house. North Dakota seemed to be a land of promise, so he tried his hand at farming. Filing a claim in 1902 at Denhoff, he found the land to be very poor for agriculture. He abandoned the claim before "proving up." He then began to think of the business world. He worked here and there in North Dakota until he set up the "Corner Grocery" and entered the real estate business in Bismarck. The various enterprises prospered and his descendants still reside in that community.[4]

Attas Boutrous was not alone in Bismarck. Michael Saba owned a restaurant, the Nicola family had a bowling alley, and another Arabic family owned a fruit market. Tom Nassif ran a pool hall in that city in 1920 and William Ellis operated a barbershop.

The Turtle Mountain towns and villages received an influx of Lebanese business-minded people whose homesteading ventures had proved less than desirable. Albert Ferris homesteaded near Rock Lake and then had a bakery; he also owned a pool hall and liquor store in Belcourt and rented boats at Fish Lake. Asmael (Smiley) Allick had a cafe. Alex Albert ran a grocery and clothing store. Kade Albert had a liquor store. Sidney Harris (Siad Zahra) set up a clothing store in Rolla, which the family still operates. Alec Hasen started The Golden Rule store in that same city. Alex Abas, a well-known peddler, ran a pool hall at Bisbee. K.C. Sine owned and operated a candy and ice cream store and at one time ran a dry goods busi-

Golden Rule Store;
Rolla, Alec and
Shirley Hasen
Courtesy:
John Guerrero

ness. (K.C. is remembered as a "very generous man" who was reputed to have been "the shortest man in town.") Emil Hassen (Ahmed Houssine) started a dry goods and grocery store in Dunseith. Tom and David Haggar had a pool hall at nearby Rock Lake. Alex Kinney farmed at Edinburg, and then operated a grocery and dry goods store.[5]

In the Pierce County area, Nasif Sawaya, in 1920, owned a bowling alley at Rugby. The same year, Ole David had a general store in that town. David Hapbib, who farmed originally near Silva, moved to Rugby and went into the grocery business. Frank Munyer also owned a grocery store. The previously mentioned Shama and Turk families had stores in Rugby at one time; two of Assif Munyer's boys, Vic and Eddie, owned a tavern called appropriately "Vic and Eddie's Bar."[6]

Elsewhere in the state, Alec Hasen is still remembered at Ashley. He operated a store called James and Hasen. Remembered also are Tom, Charles, and Rose Mike who operated a grocery store in the little Benson County town of Filmore.[7]

The Tanous family was well known in the Hettinger area. Joe, Abe, and Deeb Tanous lived with the Ausey family near Cando until 1907. They had come to America in 1898. The 1910 and 1920 censuses find the three brothers in various businesses at Hettinger.[8]

There was a notable Lebanese presence in the city of Dickinson, a town halfway between Hettinger and Williston. A Syrian gentleman was known locally as "Rabbit." The name was merited by the fact that he was said to have been the "largest rabbit dealer in America." Until World War II, he was part of the Dickinson business scene. "Rabbit" would pay

$1.00 per animal (domestic or wild) and would ship the pelts to processors "by the semi truck load."

In eastern North Dakota, Shepherd Township (Walsh County) farm residents often moved to Grand Forks. Ed Absey eventually owned a major car dealership. Two sons joined the elder Absey in his business. The Deraney family likewise prospered in Grand Forks, operating both a liquor store and a car repair business. In Brocket and Edmore, and eventually in Mayville, the Shepherd Township Freije family owned implement dealerships.[9]

We've noted with particular interest that relatively large numbers of Muslim farmers and peddlers took stores in the Turtle Mountain area, but Muslims were active elsewhere in the state. Hassen Eli (originally Hassen Ali el Kadrey), for example, had a store in Sharon in the 1920s. He moved later to a farm among Muslim families near Glenfield. Albert Alley peddled near Hope and Northwood and then ran a general merchandise store for several decades in Glenfield. Alec Hach had a grocery store and later his son Amid and daughter-in-law, Annie, continued with the store and bar in Wales. Mike Saign, like the Hachs, was the sole Muslim in a non-Syrian village. Mike Saign ran a tavern at Mapes until his death in 1965.[10] Morris Osman, of Muslim background, came to the United States in 1907. After homesteading, he ran a butcher shop in Ross. (He eventually moved to Detroit, Michigan.)

Floyd Boutrous, a Bismarck businessman with roots in Sheridan County said, "Many Arab immigrants set up small businesses as railroad towns popped up beside the newly laid tracks all across the plains." With a bit of exaggeration and yet an element of truth, Boutrous said, "I'll bet you there was one Lebanese business in every one of those towns."[11] In Floyd Boutrous's own county (Sheridan), even though Lebanese left the area very quickly, several stayed long enough to set up businesses in McClusky, the county seat. George Skaff had a general store and a man named Kellel ran a grocery.

Crookston, Minnesota, so closely allied with North Dakota, also experienced a surge in Lebanese small business during the early years of the 20th century. Over a period of time Lebanese operated several dry goods stores, a confectionery store, and three, perhaps four, restaurants. (Allay Omar Sage, a Muslim, owned two.) One grocery was called The George Peter Store; a son took over and it became The Peter George Store.

In summary it could be said that something like an "explosion" of Lebanese business occurred within two decades of settlement in North Dakota. Many names are listed above, but in terms of statewide totals, the 1920 U.S. Census lists 84 people of "Syrian" background who worked in some kind of merchant endeavor. They were found in 23 counties—

almost half of the state's total counties. In that year almost fifty were private businessmen—no women! (What does that mean?) The men were listed as running "general stores" and sometimes, confectioneries; they were also in pool halls, the grocery business, and running a livery stable. One was even in photography.

Some cities during the first decades had a genuine cluster of Lebanese businesses. Williston had more than 10 such merchants. Seven were located in the Turtle Mountain villages and another seven were in Fargo.

The majority of the 50 merchants in the 1920 Census were of Christian background, yet 14 were of the Muslim faith. Muslims could be found, for example, in general merchandise stores, pool halls, saloons, and restaurants. The mercantile world seemed to appeal to everyone of Lebanese descent, regardless of religious persuasion.

A Unique Heritage

Belcourt's Kade Albert wore many hats in his lifetime, including that of businessman, church leader, veteran's official, tribal council person, and family man. Born in the late 1920s to a Lebanese peddler, Alex Albert, and a French-Chippewa mother (nee Anne Gourneau), Kade had a triple heritage: Lebanon, France, and Native America. Kade Albert's mixed heritage was not unusual to the Turtle Mountain people.

The Arabic culture mingled with the native way of life through other unions: Lebanese peddlers took root with names like Ferris, Harris, Albert, Murray, and Kadry. The mixed cultural unions affected Turtle Mountain life in political, economic, and religious ways.

Freida Hassen, a long-time businesswoman of Rolla, said that these unions shared common bonds of extended family, hospitality, and a zest for life. Kade Albert married Evelyn Haggar, whose family were Christian Arabs from Mushgara, Lebanon. He went on to found the oldest established business in Belcourt, the Tomahawk Bar.

CHAPTER TWELVE

Railroads

Without doubt, railroads, whether in their construction periods or in their operational activities, were the largest business enterprises in North Dakota during the first several generations of settlement. The previous chapters in this volume warned against overstressing the influence of the railroad jobs either in directing the flow of Syrians or in sustaining their presence on the prairies. The authors of this book are convinced that it was the peddler's trade which pointed the way to the West, and it was the peddler's trade which later proved the major supplement to land and merchant endeavors.

Nevertheless, the railroad played an important role in early Syrian prairie life; it was the major artery used by itinerant Syrian merchants as they moved to "jump off points" along their chosen routes. Further, it allowed the peddlers to resupply themselves with needed merchandise. And, when finally engaged in either farming or small business, the railroad functioned for Syrians in the same way as it did for other national groups: personal transportation, shipment of goods, and method of communication.

Syrians cannot be classified as a "railroad group," as were certain other ethnic groups that can be found in *Plains Folk: The Ethnic History of North Dakota:* Greeks, Italians, Japanese, and Armenians. These immigrants came to the prairies *because* of the railroad and some subsequently stayed and went into diverse types of non-railroad occupations.

This is not to deny that some Syrians saw railroading as an occupation; indeed, in St. Paul and Minneapolis, a number of newly arrived men worked at railroad jobs, but some were also involved in construction work, packing plants, and textile mills. All of these jobs seem to have been a matter of temporary expediency. Few Syrian men regarded railroading as a permanent type of employment.

The U.S. Census, taken every decade, gives us a glimpse of what must have happened throughout North Dakota from the moment the first iron rail was laid until the 1930s when all industrial development slowed or even stopped. *Plains Folk,* the state's ethnic history, said an estimated 10,000 Italians were employed at one time or another on seasonal work crews as main and branch lines were being constructed, or for that matter, when facilities were being erected.[1] The census picks up literally hundreds of crews at work at some railroad siding or another: Italians, Balkan men, Japanese, Greeks, Black-Americans, German-Russians, and the like. Some crews numbered 25 and even 30 men. The Lebanese component in this avalanche of men was a comparative handful. Can we say that Lebanese were individuals who didn't like a "gang situation?"

The 1910 U.S. Census shows six railroad men of "Syrian" birth at Minnewaukan in Benson County. (They were newly arrived, coming to the U.S. in either 1909 or 1910.) In that same census eight Syrian-born men were found in a similar category at Max village in McLean County. These eight workers arrived in the United States sometime between 1907 and 1910. (The majority came in 1909.) This reinforces the contention that the railroad jobs tended to be a temporary "first job" kind of employment. Where were the Syrians who came ten and twenty years previously?

Two men of Syrian birth, Marcus Marrift and Nick Lyanott, in the 1910 Census, seem to have been in year-around railroad jobs. They were at Marmarth, North Dakota, and were listed as "RR Employees." In Fargo, that same year, fellow countrymen Mike Herman and Richard Sam were classed as "section hand RR" and "laborer RR." Whether these men intended to stay in their railroad jobs is questionable. Both were only 17 years of age.

The 1920 Census shows four men who actually stayed in the state in permanent railroad employment. One each could be found in Kidder, Pierce, Ramsey, and Dunn counties. These men were classed as "laborers, RR" and "section hands." They were married and were clearly not part of the contract type of railroad "gangs."

Crookston, Minnesota, just 25 miles from Grand Forks on the North Dakota border, is a different matter. We have noted on previous pages that Crookston was a "stop over" site for many Syrians as they moved permanently to Dakota, or as they would make their "selling trips" through that state. But Crookston did see a number of what seem to have been permanent Syrian employees on the railroad. In 1910 there were eight Syrian-born Crookston men listed in the census in railroad jobs: four were "steam laborers" and three were "laborers, RR section." In the 1920 Crookston Census, five were "steam laborers," one was a "flagman," eight were "laborers." Three others were "section hands" and there was also a "roundhouse worker" and a "locomotive fireman." One lady is labeled as "wash woman/RR."

The classification of "round house worker" and particularly "locomotive fireman" indicates Syrian men who were definitely intending to stay in railroad employment for some time. It must be mentioned that a total of 26 adult Crookston individuals were Syrian-born in 1910, the number increased to 56 in 1920. Certain "original family" Crookston names, according to modern-day informants, had at one time a railroad connection: Salem, Joseph, Amon, Isaac, Anthony, and Solomon.

Charlie Joseph, of Crookston, worked on the railroad for many decades. (He lived to be 102.) Mr. Joseph was known to have taken "a swig of arak" every day. In his very elderly years, when asked the secret of his longevity, Charlie would say, "Arak and hard work."[2]

The 1920 Census contained the name John Isaac, a man who started on the railroad at Crookston, then moved further west to work at Rugby, and finished his railroad career again in Minnesota. Railroad work, for some men at least, made possible a movement back and forth between Minnesota and North Dakota.

Deraney and Srur family members of Grand Forks spent a whole generation working on the railroad at Grand Forks. The Deraney father and three sons grew up on a farm in Walsh County, moved to Grand Forks, and after military service in World War II the sons took railroad jobs. Some retired with railroad pensions. Two men from the Srur family of Rugby likewise moved to Grand Forks, another brother went to Minot. The three Srur men were long-time railroad workers from the 1950s to the 1980s.[3]

Eugene Alley, of Glenfield Muslim background, spent 41 years on the Great Northern Railroad (later Burlington Northern). He retired in the 1990s and lives at Sibley, North Dakota, where he served as mayor of the city. A dedicated worker, Alley was called to work at Minot during the blizzard of 1966. Driving over a hundred miles from his Glenfield home to the railroad yards, Mr. Alley found that few, if any, of the Minot workers had "braved" the storm to report for work. Needless to say, Alley was not popular for some days among his fellow workers.[4]

At Rock Lake, North Dakota, Joe Hiawatha was a colorful individual who appears elsewhere in this volume as he applied for citizenship on three different occasions (in three different locations). Mr. Hiawatha "worked on the railroad for many years." He retired and continued to do "odd jobs" in Rock Lake until his death in 1946.[5] Hassyn Murray also of Muslim and Turtle Mountain background, lived at Dunseith. He, too, is said to have worked for many years on the railroad.

The *Aramco World Magazine* of September-October 1986 featured Arthur Seeb, whose parents came from Ain Arab and homesteaded near Williston. Arthur Seeb retired from the Burlington Northern after "38 years, 4 months and 13 days"; he had served the railroad as a brakeman and later as a conductor.[6] Some ex-railroad men say today that Art Seeb was a key man in facilitating the North Dakota portion of the merger of the Great Northern and the Northern Pacific.

Several Syrian WPA interviewees mention the railroad as a temporary job, a means of getting personal finances under control and then moving on. Joe Salmon, remembering his early years in the United States, said in a Bismarck interview in August 1939 that he filed on land in South Dakota but it was alkali type of soil. "So I gave that up and came to North Dakota in 1916 and worked on the railroad section gang for a while and then on farms."

Joseph Azar came from Zahle to New York and arrived at Williston in 1899. He worked for some time around Williston, then ran a pool hall, and homesteaded in 1914. Selling his land he moved to Dickinson and took railroad employment. He later ran a pool hall in Dickinson and in August 1939 was operating a produce store in Bismarck.

The U.S. Census took its count only once in each decade, but what of the intervening years? There is no real way of knowing exactly how many men (and perhaps women) of Syrian background took seasonal jobs on the railroads in North Dakota as they sought to supplement their farm or small business income. Every national group in the state boasts some of its members who helped "build or repair" the railroad at some time or another. Lebanese, too, played a part, although a minor one, in North Dakota's pioneer railroad building period.

CHAPTER THIRTEEN

Syrian Enclaves

This chapter will describe the Syrian farm settlements which arose during North Dakota's early development period. The men and women will often be categorized as "Syrian," for that is the census term used in many of the earliest years but, in fact, the first arrivals everywhere were from Lebanon. It was rare, as has been noted in previous pages, that a citizen from some other Middle Eastern Arabic country came to North Dakota before the middle of the Twentieth Century.

Main North Dakota Counties of Lebanese/Syrian Immigrants Based on Major Religious Affiliation

Islamic (Sunni & Shia)	Catholic (Maronite & Melkite)	Orthodox (Greek & Syrian)
Mountrail	Williams	Williams
Rolette	Pierce	Sheridan
Foster	Towner	Pierce
McIntosh	Walsh	
Pierce	Polk (Minnesota)	
McHenry		

Before the discussion of rural Syrian settlements begins it is necessary to mention the fact that an enclave of *urban* Lebanese might have existed in North Dakota before any of their countrymen took out homestead claims. On March 18, 1893, the *Fargo Forum* reported that there were fifteen or twenty "Melchite" Catholics in that city, enough to merit the visit of a priest from Mount Lebanon in Syria. The news item reads as follows:

Rev. Basil Sowaya, a Melchite priest from Mount Lebanon in Syria, celebrated Mass at the Catholic Church last Thursday morning. He came here to look after the fifteen or twenty Syrians who live here.

The article explains the doctrinal history of the "Melchites." It begins with rejection of Roman Catholic doctrines after the Council of Chalcedon in 451 AD (a difference in the nature of Christ's humanity and divinity). Later a reunion with Rome took place. The article says further, "they retain their ancient rites … they still retain the ancient liturgies of St. Chrysostom and St. Basil and the Canon Law to which they have been accustomed." The article concludes with the statement, "the number of Melchite Catholics is about 40,000." (The figure, 40,000, is certainly a worldwide total. No such an amount existed in America. Perhaps the total would be true in the United States today.)

We know a little about Rev. Basil Sowaya. (From other sources we know his name is spelled variously as Souaya or Sawaya.) He was born in Zahle, was a priest of the Basilian Chouerite order, and arrived in Chicago in 1890 (perhaps even 1887). After 15 years in that city, he returned to Lebanon and became Superior of his religious community. Father Sowaya never shows up again in North Dakota news reports. He may have been a traveling emissary for the Melkite patriarch in Beruit. Perhaps his reports occasioned the arrival of the permanent Melkite priest, Fr. Seraphim Roumie, who lived in the Pierce County settlement. Roumie's residence in Pierce County began in 1903 (maybe in 1902).[1]

A careful look at the 1893 Fargo *City Directory* shows at least seven Lebanese "peddlers" living in three residences on Front Street. One of the names is John Chikany, who reappears as a homesteader in Twp. 156-R72 (Pierce County) in 1897. Another is Kalil Turk. This was probably Charles Turk, a pioneer settler in Pierce County, who homesteaded at the same time and was a rural neighbor of John Chikany.[2]

Walsh County

Most Lebanese homestead settlement occurred in the central or western part of North Dakota. Yet one of the earliest, perhaps the very first, sprang up in the Red River Valley in Shepherd township at the west edge of Walsh County. The year of these first arrivals was 1897. And this was a relatively early date, less than a decade after Dakota Territory was divided and the new State of North Dakota came into existence.

Families known to have acquired land in Shepherd Township include the Josef Abseys, Peter Abseys, the Moses Freijes, the John Morans, the Abraham and William Zeins, the Charles Fayettes, and the Joseph Deraneys.

Joseph and Peter Absey (their father's name was Absey Fren), along with Moses Freije, signed their naturalization first "intent" papers in Walsh County in June and July 1897. This was usually a prelude to filing

Four generations of
the Freije Family

Courtesy:
Bob and Pat Freije

for land. Most likely they chose their Shepherd County homestead in the summer or fall of that very year. Other families came within a matter of a year or two. The Joseph Deraneys purchased land after the first decade of settlement. (Lebanon has a long history: the name Deraney comes from Comte De Arient, a French officer during the Crusades.)

Located with Bohemian settlers to the east and Norwegians to the north, this small group was mostly from Zahle. Close family members would eventually (perhaps simultaneously) take land in the Rugby, Pierce County area.[3]

Most of the Walsh County, Shepherd Township settlers were what neighbors would call Syrian Catholic (Maronite, or Melkite), although one family, the Freijes, was Syrian Orthodox. The descendants of Moses Freije recall that an Orthodox priest came to the Lawton area (adjacent to Shepherd Township) and baptized "two or three" children at the family home. The priest's visit may have happened several times. (On one occasion a Freije baby was taken to St. Paul for baptism).[4]

Ed Absey, son of Peter Absey, in a 1983 interview said that he was baptized at the family home when Fr. Seraphim Roumie, the Melkite priest of Rugby, visited their Shepherd Township farm. Ed Absey recalled that when the priest performed the liturgy for local residents in their home his father took the role of what he called "Mass server."[5] (Family tradition has it that Peter Absey, in Lebanon and in Dakota, held a highly regarded position in the religious community, a "cantor-like status," which was often passed on through the family's generations.) Peter Absey probably accompanied Father Roemie to many of the nearby farm homes. Many families recall the priest's presence. The Shepherd Township Lebanese were small in number however, and within two decades most had affiliated with nearby Catholic parishes of the Latin Catholic rite.

Farming in Shepherd Township was not unpleasant. The 1920 and the 1930 censuses find Lebanese still on the land. The difficult years of the late 1930s, however, caused most to move to larger cities. Today, Grand Forks has a number of the Shepherd Township descendants who are engaged in businesses, the railroads, and the assorted construction industries.

Pierce County

In both land and numbers, the largest rural Syrian-born settlement in North Dakota came about in an area that extended up to 40 miles around the city of Rugby (Pierce and McHenry counties). The Great Northern Railroad built its tracks through the region in 1886 on its way to what was to become Minot; it continued eventually to the Pacific Coast. Nine years after the railroad's arrival, some eight miles southeast of Rugby a cluster of Lebanese men and women chose land and began building their claims shanties.

Federal Land Office Tract Books list the following individuals as filing for land in 1897 in the southern half of Meyer Township (T156-R72) and much of Reno Valley Township (T155-R72) (Note: The penmanship is often indistinct in the Land Office Records): Metree Wazer, Charley Kassis, David Bossin, Elias Wazer, Nassif Sawaya, Abraham Kassis, John Kassis, Abraham Boussad, Joseph Boussad, Risk Sawaya, John Shicany, Nicholas Shicany, and Charles Turk. (An early Pierce County historian adds George Srur and Albert Shamma to the list of earliest land claimants.)[6]

The Land Office microfilmed records, though sometimes blurred, make it almost certain that the date of the first filing was 1897 and that the above mentioned thirteen men (perhaps there were others) could be classed as the Syrian pioneers in that part of North Dakota. This was the beginning of a series of Lebanese land acquisitions which spread over seven additional neighboring townships.

In 1898, Reno Valley and Meyer townships witnessed the arrival of other homesteaders. They included Assad Kassis, Debis Numur, Mike Numar, Issif Munyer, Helen Esta, Theophlias Haman, Joseph Shicany, Kalel Younas, James Halis, Joseph Esta, Kaley Sawaya, Nassif Boysasad, Rosa Sawaya, Mary Boussad, and Frank Munyer.

The land claimants in 1897 and 1898 were all Christian in background and predominantly male. But the reader will note the names of Helen Esta, Rosa Sawaya, and Mary Boussad.

Nabal Sabia, George Sabb, Moses Sabb, Niryme Skaff, and Joseph Skaff joined the Syrians in Reno Valley and Meyer townships in 1899. Several new landseekers from Lebanon appeared in Reno Valley and nearby Elverum Township in 1900. Four more came in 1902. From sources other than the Federal Land Records, it appears that six additional names can be placed on the Pierce County landowner roster: George and Abraham Razook, Sam Wizer, Joe Saba, Sam Saloum, and Albert Dunn (Abdella Dann ?). The dates are uncertain.

On March 5, 1901, a rural post office was established in the Syrian enclave. It took the name Beyrout. The postmaster was Attas David who homesteaded on Section 2, Elverum Township. The post office was most likely in his home. Records show that the Beyrout Post Office was discontinued in 1906.[7]

It should be noted that the Syrian settlement was not taking place in isolation. Germans from Russia, by the hundreds, were flooding into Pierce County and into nearby McHenry County.

The year 1902 saw an additional half dozen Syrians taking land in Balta Township (T154-R73). At the same time at least a dozen Syrians were filing on their acreages in a scattered fashion in townships north of Rugby. (Not all were men; Mary Feyiad was on two 80-acre land parcels.) At this very time another distinct group of Lebanese immigrants began filing for land southwest of what was to become the Pierce County village of Orrin. Twenty men, almost exclusively Muslim, chose acreages throughout Elling Township (T153-R74) and spilling over into Schiller Township of McHenry County (T152-R75). Also taking place was another collection of Syrian land claims some fifteen miles to the north in McHenry County's townships T155-R76 and T155-R77. At least ten men were involved. Pierce and McHenry Muslim land seekers included names such as Mohammed Hash, Mahmud Shood, Mahmond Hasen, Allah Hasen, and Mohammed Zeer. (The records abound in misspelled names.)

Farming in central North Dakota did not appeal to these Muslim men. By 1920 not one of the thirty land applicants was listed in the census of Pierce or McHenry county.

In perspective, we know that a total of 150 Lebanese settled at least for a while in the Rugby area townships. Of that number, some 130 were in Pierce County and 20 were in McHenry.

One should also note that the above totals represent those who *filed* for land, not those who actually received their patent deeds. Many chose their acreages but left the land before fulfilling the residency or "improvement" requirements. For the Rugby area, a good guess would be that thirty percent abandoned their claims and sought their "American dream" in other climes or occupational ventures. But in this the Lebanese were no different than many, perhaps most, homestead groups. The required few years of residency on the barren Dakota plains was too great a price to pay for what the homestead publicity called "free land."

With a rare exception the non-Muslim settlers of Pierce County were of either Orthodox, Maronite or Melkite Christian affiliation. As mentioned earlier in this volume, the Maronite and Melkite Christians were affiliated with the Pope in Rome. The Orthodox situation was often confused. At various times they looked for leadership to the Patriarch of Moscow, the Patriarch of Constantinople, and eventually to the Patriarch in Antioch.

The *Minot Daily News* of March 15, 1975, published a feature story on the Pierce County Lebanese settlement. The story included a photograph of a 1914 gathering of Orthodox faithful assembled at the Reno Valley School. Two dignitaries, "a priest and archbishop from St. Paul," stand amid their local coreligionists. Among those present were two 1898 homesteaders: Frank Munyer and Assif Munyer. Other family names can be found in the photo's descriptive legend: Wazer (Wizer), Schachor, Razook, Skaff, Dann and Salome. These family names probably represent at least a portion of the pioneer Orthodox families who proved up and took permanent root in Pierce County.[8]

Some Catholic settlers—whether Maronite or Melkite, the records are unclear—are listed in O. T. Tolfsrud's *Fifty Years in Pierce County*. Their names were George Saba, Joe Boussad, Charles Turk, Nick Shickany, Albert Shamma and Joe Esta.[9] These pioneers met first in homes and then built the St. George Church, a small frame structure, on Section 24 in Meyer Township (T156-R72). Gathering the little congregation together was Fr. Elias Aaquel (Aakel) who spent several months in the Rugby area in 1902.

By 1903, Fr. Seraphim Roumie had arrived and taken charge of the St. George congregation. (Perhaps it was under Fr. Roumie's urging that the church structure was erected.) Fr. Seraphim Roumie—a sketch of his life is presented elsewhere in this volume—served Maronite and Melkite Catholics in five or six different locations all along the Great Northern Railroad main line. He would start, perhaps, in Crookston, Minnesota, and travel from Grand Forks westward toward Montana. Walsh County families in the Red River Valley would be visited, so also Pierce County, then parishioners in Williams County (where he would eventually homestead), and from there he probably spent time with Syrian Catholics in Montana.

The St. George Church Melkite congregation numbered, according to O. T. Tolfsrud, "more than fifty families." In 1906, the church building was moved to Rugby, where it continued as a Lebanese focal point.[10] In that year Fr. Roumie took residence in Chicago and another Melkite priest, Timothy Jock, became pastor. Yet tragedy struck in 1910 when the church had a fire which burned it beyond repair. The Lebanese subsequently built another smaller church within the city limits. Later accounts say it was "near the site now occupied by the Milton Berger Sales, the former East Side Grocery."

Certainly, at least in the first decade of settlement, an active Lebanese community centered around Rugby. One brief note in the ethnic history of North Dakota says, "A Syrian social club, with the picturesque name, Flower of Syrian Unity, remained active for some time."[11]

Lebanese priests continued to staff the Pierce County Lebanese community, at least intermittently, into the mid-1910s. (Fr. Roumie was known to have made occasional visits to his North Dakota parishioners until 1915.) During most of these early years, the Lebanese priest was the only Catholic priest in Rugby—he took care of both Latin rite and Syrian Catholics. The Latin priest took up permanent residence in 1908.[12]

Fire again struck the St. George congregation, destroying the "new" church in 1912. By this time the number of Melkite or Maronite Pierce County residents had declined to the point that the Syrian families felt they had no option but to affiliate with either the Rugby Latin Rite church or the rural Latin church at the Johannestal German settlement. O. T. Tolfsrud, in his 1943 book, said of the original St. George congregation, "Only three of the families are now remaining in the community."

How many of the original St. George families were of Maronite and how many were of Melkite background is difficult to determine. Certainly both groups were present for this was the case in other North Dakota Syrian Catholic areas. Yet the terms Maronite and Melkite never appear in early accounts, nor do modern descendants recall such a distinction. Fr. Seraphim Roumie was a Melkite priest, but he regularly served North Dakotans of both rites. (We are assured by authorities today that the priest would not switch from rite to rite, rather he would conduct services everywhere in the Melkite tradition.)[13] Present-day Melkite church records, furnished from the Melkite archives in West Paterson, New Jersey, indicate some Pierce County Catholics who were definitely Melkite: the Shicany and the Youness families.[14] Catholic baptismal records, transfered to the Latin Rite Rugby Church, list the following for November 6, 1901: Adam, Joseph and Mary Cassis, Salome Boussad, Saddie Chikane (Shicany) and Lilly Asta. These baptisms were probably done when a Lebanese priest made an initial visit to the Pierce County settlement. Later baptisms occurred in February and March 1903: George Kirk, Fahad Shavayre, Iddie Turk, and Joseph Shikane. The records show that a Lebanese priest was also baptizing Latin rite children. In 1901 and 1902 there were German-Russian names: Vetsch, Axtmann, Welk and Voeller. By 1909, the Latin Rite church of Rugby had a Schecanny [sic] and a Shama baptism.

Just as the number of Pierce County Catholic Syrians diminished within two decades of settlement, their Orthodox neighbors experienced a similar decline in numbers. Yet we know from the *Minot Daily News* photograph discussed previously that the Orthodox "Archbishop from St. Paul" held services in 1914 for a sizable number of fellow religionists in the Reno Valley school. It may have been that in the late 1910s word came through (correctly or incorrectly) indicating that the Archbishop wished his Orthodox faithful to join the Rugby Episcopal Church. Today, the local Episcopal congregation is inactive. Some third-generation Lebanese belong to the Rugby Lutheran Church.

Pierce County settlers still have a monument of sorts that recalls their presence. A special section of the Rugby Catholic cemetery contains graves and Arabic inscriptions. Buried side by side are members of both the Catholic and the Orthodox traditions. It has been said that this part of the cemetery at one time was called "The Cedars of Lebanon."

Ross

There seems to be general agreement that Mary and Hassin Juma, natives of Bire, Syria, were the first married couple to have settled in the Ross portion of Mountrail County. To this day, the Ross enclave is recognized as the largest and most celebrated of all North Dakota Muslim communities.

We have Mary Juma's own words to describe her arrival in Mountrail County. She told the WPA interviewer in 1939:

We were in Canada in 1900 and in Nebraska in 1901. In 1902, we came to western North Dakota where we started to peddle. It was at the time when there was such an influx of people to take homesteads, and for no reason at all, we decided to try homesteading too.

This perhaps is the story of most Ross settlers. It's not very complicated. There were no promotion schemes, no newspaper enticements. The young couple came to the New World, got a good look at some parts of America, started peddling in North Dakota, and took advantage of the homestead opportunities which were just becoming available near Ross.

As mentioned in an early portion of this book, several Muslim men were in the Ross area in 1900 and 1901. None, however, filed their first naturalization papers in Mountrail County in 1900, and "first papers" were necessary for the acquisition of land. Hassin Juma filed his first papers in October 1901. Could these earlier gentlemen have been squatters on their land and filed their claims at a later date?

The initial claim dwellings must have been the standard wood frame hip-roofed structures. (Perhaps some were of sod.) Bachelor men often built a 12 by 14 foot building to conform to homestead requirements. Bo Alley Farhart said, "My first home was a 10 x 12 feet frame shack."

Charlie Juma, in a 1977 interview, remembered the typical homestead "shanties." "They were 12 foot by 14 foot," he said, "a frame structure with external tar paper. The inside of the house was plastered with chaff and clay." With a touch of a smile he said, "In the Old Country they knew how to do this." Mr. Juma explained how they heated the first claim shanties: sometimes they burned old railroad ties, occasionally they would burn the coal that fell off the railroad coal cars. Eventually they heard that seams of coal could be found in the coulees and they either dug it themselves or purchased it from local farmers who began excavating their own private "coal mines."[15]

Mary Juma, in 1939, described her early farm home for the WPA. She said it was a "low three room structure." (Was it the original house?) Mrs. Juma said further, "the thing that sets this farm apart as a Syrian American home is that all the buildings are located close to the house and all the chickens and sheep come close, even to the doorstep of the home." The barn, according to Mrs. Juma, "is quite large."

Another Federal Writers Project report exists, one that presented a synopsis of interviews and observations concerning the Ross Syrian enclave. The Project, done in 1936 in the middle of the Depression years, was largely carried out by unemployed North Dakota schoolteachers and professionals. At that early date Muslims were certainly a curiosity: a people seldom met on the American public scene. Such things as dances, foods and religious traditions caught the outside observer's eye. The term "Mohammedan" was used often and occasionally the word Moslem. (Indeed, "Mohammedan" was the word used by the Ross neighbors in describing the Syrian farmers who lived among them.)

The Writers Project report says "their mode of dress is the same as ours with the exception of the elderly women who wore bandannas around their heads. … The occupation of these people is grain farming and stock raising. They send their own children to public schools, in Ross and Manitou." The Report said further, "we find that they have acquired a fair ability to read, write and speak our language."[16]

The first married settlers in the Ross community were the above-mentioned couple, Hassin and Mary Juma. This fact can be substantiated by Federal Land Office Tract Book records and it is well accepted by modern-day Ross residents. Hassin Juma filed for his claim in 1902 and received his patent deed in 1908. Mary Juma, in a 1939 interview, said without qualification, "We were the first Syrians to homestead in this community, but soon many people from that country came to settle here." Yet Mary Juma's son, Charlie, said in a 1983 interview that Sam Omar was the first to come.[17] Memories, perhaps, with the passing of time became vague? (The first arrival is one thing, but there's no doubt that Hassin and Mary Juma were the first married couple to settle in the Ross Muslim area.) The 1936 Writers Project report supplies some pioneer names. It said, "some of the earliest settlers" were Hassin Juma, Side Abdallah, Sam Omar, Solomon Hodge and Bo Alley Farhart.

For a more complete look at the sequence of settlement we turn to the pages of the now available Federal Land Office Tract Books for contiguous Ross, Alger and T156-R92 townships. These records indicate that at least 24 Syrian men filed for land in 1902, a further 14 did so in 1903, another eight took land in 1904-05. In the years 1906, 07, 08, another 20 filed on their claims. This makes a total of 66 in just three townships. At least a dozen others filed during that first decade on land in townships to the north and the west. (Note: Some who filed on land did not actually "prove up.")

Those who filed in 1902 were the following: Mose Hamid, Albert Mustafa, Joseph Forbite, Hassin Juma, Abdul Rahmen, Hassin Farhart, Gosman Omar, Mahmed Sadden, Albert Salem, Charles Salem, Abdula Mosfa, Hamid Hassin, Hassen Merrik, Hasian Dorosq, Side Abdallah, Abdella Adray, Fayah Iish, Abdel Allie, Amid Assem Juha, Jaja Allie Juha. (Note: indistinct handwriting and the clerks' tendency to anglicize names often introduced misspellings.)

Though some names are probably absent, the above list is as compete a roster of the earliest Ross community settlers as can be obtained today. The sequence went like this: some pioneers came (single men? Hassin and Mary Juma ?) and a wave of Syrian-born land seekers flooded into the area within the next few months, others came later. The information network—whether peddlers, word of mouth or letters, or perhaps Arabic newspapers—was highly efficient and surprisingly rapid.

No women appear to have been among the first homesteaders, yet Mary Juma, a wife, was present. Other sources—personal interviews—

indicate that others among the first land seekers were married and some were accompanied by their wives. (Some wives may have still been in "Syria.")

How many men and women were eventually part of the Ross community? U.S. Census reports for 1910 and 1920 show that living with the farm families was a collection of non-farmers with labels such as "laborers, peddlers, farmhands." Add to this the newly born (or arrived) children, and we have a good-sized and very visible collection of unique prairie people. Certainly well over a hundred Muslims were part of the Ross settlement in the first decade: men, women and children. (And children came fast and frequent; Hassin and Mary Juma's son, Charlie, the first Ross "Syrian" child, was born in 1903, a year after the couple had settled on their land.) Here in the western part of North Dakota, thousands of miles from their homeland, a viable Muslim community took root. How very unpredictable; yet it happened.

Central to the newly formed Muslim community, and certainly giving its members an internal cohesion, were their religious traditions. It is generally accepted in modern American Muslim historical circles that the first recorded organized Islamic prayer service in the United States was held, some say as early as 1900 (?), at Ross.[18] And this religious gathering probably took place in someone's home. Recalling the early days, Mary Juma told the WPA interviewer: "Before we built our church, we held services at the different homes. We have a month of fasting, after which everyone visits the home of another, and there was a lot of feasting."

The services before a mosque was built, and later in the mosque itself, were most likely led by a man in the congregation who was versed in the Koran and in Islamic traditions. The Federal Writers Project, interviewing Joe Hiawatha in 1936, said the following: "Persons are designated in the United States by the Sheik of Syria to hold rituals over their people." Hiawatha said further, "And these people … can perform marriages among their own people."

The Federal Writers reporter said that the informant, Joe Hiawatha himself, had the "ear of the Sheik in performing marriages and holding rituals." It's strange that no other name of prominence has appeared in newspapers, written materials, or recent-day interviews concerning the identity of such official local prayer leaders. (In fact, Ross residents today do not even remember Joe Hiawatha.) Of note also is the fact that the word "imam" never occurs in conversations with elderly men and women in the Ross community. They often speak of a "Sheik from Canada" who would teach and preside over funerals. Could Mr. Hiawatha have been designated as prayer leader by a "Sheik" from Canada (or Detroit?) who acted in the name of the Sheik from Syria?[19]

We know from interviews with "old timers" that for routine prayer gatherings certain respected and knowledgeable men of the community led the assembly in prayer. Among them were H. A. Juma, Amid Abdallah, and Allay Omar. None, however, seems to have received the position of special leader or group spokesman from some outside authority.[20]

In 1929 (1930 ?), the Ross Muslim community built a religious edifice: a mosque located about two miles southeast of the town. (Bo Alley Farhart's WPA interview said, "Our first church was built in 1927." To confuse things more, the deed for the land is dated 1930.) It was a half-basement building of cement with a shallow gabled roof. And it was this structure that many contend was the first mosque in America, first in the sense that it was not a converted building, but rather one constructed specifically to serve as a Muslim prayer center.

The mosque did not escape the attention of the larger American Lebanese world. The October 1929 edition of the *Syrian World* reported:

Moslem Mosque in the United States

According to an announcement in Al-Bayan, an Arabic paper published in New York, the Moslem colony of Ross, N.D., is planning the erection of a mosque in their town on which building operations will start this coming spring. A committee has been formed to prosecute the work and an appeal issued for the collection of funds from all the Arab settlements in the United States. Al-Bayan strongly supports the project and calls on its readers to contribute generously ...[21]

There were plans to build an upper level to the structure, but the hard Dust Bowl and Depression years came to the region in the ensuing 1930s. The Ross Muslim faithful, like their fellow North Dakotans everywhere in the state, put all construction "on hold." The eventual second story never came about.

The word "mosque" was seldom, if ever, used to describe the building. Local Muslims called it the "Jima," a word for gathering. Their non-Muslim neighbors called it the "Mohammadan Church."

The building itself was modest in size, perhaps 30 by 40 feet, with an entrance to the west. Four windows were on each of the longer sides; two were at the end. A few steps led down to a single room; there were no interior partitions. There were no provisions in the building for such things as foot washing, although several benches were present. Shoes were set off to the side. The faithful brought their own rugs but there was an elegant floor rug in the middle of the room. A coal stove was on the north wall, the wall surfaces were calcimined and the wood ceiling joists were clearly visible. The northeastern corner of the room was set aside as the "prayer room," but no walls separated that particular area.[22]

The congregation, as prescribed, faced east as they prayed. Arabic language services lasted one and a half hours. Men and women sat and knelt separately. Joe Hiawatha said in a 1936 interview that the participants thoroughly bathed their entire bodies before going to the "church" services. He said the faithful avoided wearing ostentatious "new" clothing and that "instead of removing their hats or caps, they wore them all through the service."[23]

No food was consumed in the building, but in the summer a sort of picnic—potluck—took place outside on the grounds.

Mary Juma, remembering the days before the mosque, said: "My husband is buried in Rose Hill Cemetery, Ross, North Dakota. We didn't have our Syrian cemetery at the time of his death, but he was buried with Muslim services.

After its construction, the Muslim "Jima" was the site of funerals and there are today more than 20 graves in the adjacent Muslim cemetery. It was on these occasions especially that the "Sheik" would come down from Canada. Edmonton, Regina, Swift Current and Calgary, all centers of Muslim life, are mentioned in conversations with present-day Ross descendants. But the "Sheik" in the earliest days would also come to spend time—as much as two months—living with families so that he could "teach and hold services." Some printed religious materials were

The "Jima" Mosque several miles southeast of Ross, ND.
Courtesy: Minot Daily News

brought from the "Old Country," but there existed also a short English-Arabic booklet that could be used for basic instructions and prayers. (The Canadian "Sheik" was said to have used this book for instructing both elders and children.)

On the other hand, today's descendants of the Ross settlers do not recall much in the way of religious instructions. How much formal Islamic instruction took place at the Mosque is vague in the minds of the grand-children and even children. Vague maybe because it was long ago? Vague maybe because very little took place? One descendant said, "I don't think there was any." Another said, "We went to meetings at the Jima. We had meetings with the parents and the kids, but I can't remember what went on at the gatherings."[24]

The drought years of the 1930s brought a population decline to every North Dakota town and neighborhood. The Ross area, being in the dry western part of the state, was especially hard hit. The World War II years changed things. Rains came and good farm prices, but by then many of the young men had left for military service and the younger women often went off to work in war industries. The Ross Muslim community continued to decline in population and soon the "Jima" was seldom in use. Funerals continued, but now they were held at the funeral home in nearby Stanley. The most recent gravestone in the Ross Muslim ceme-tery is labeled 1999 (Nazira Omar), so burials still take place. By 1979 the mosque was in serious disrepair, with water and rodent damages. The cemetery committee decided to dismantle the building. Only an open stretch of prairie marks the site today, yet marked into the soil are inden-tations which show clearly the basement wall outlines.

No organized Muslim prayer services take place in the Ross region today. A few second-generation individuals read their Koran and say their daily prayers with special diligence. A number of others keep the obser-vances in a modified form—the Ramadan fasts, the Muslim prayer beads, the food laws, the daily ritual. (Some, on occasion, attend a local Protestant service and also say their Islamic prayers in private at home.) Now and then an "old-timer" may travel to Swift Current (Saskatchewan) to take part in the full ceremonies of his or her childhood. Grandchildren and great-grandchildren still reside in the Ross-Stanley area but often attend the Sunday services at a local Lutheran congregation.

Sheridan County

Without giving any details other than in the "early 1900s," the 1936 Federal Writers Project report said, "Twenty three young Syrians made up a group which homesteaded in McLean County." Questions arise: Who? Where? Exactly when? No "Syrians" reside today in the county.

To answer the "where" question, we have to note that what the 1936 author labeled McLean County is actually, due to later county divisions, present-day Sheridan County.

The *Bismarck Tribune*, in recording the proceedings of a 1940 multi-state Attiyeh family convention in that city said:

> The Attiyeh homesteaders were the five Nicola brothers, Ferris, Salem, Salom, Salma and Solomon; A. Boutrous, Moses and Isaac Abdullah; William Ellis, Moses Haddad, Joe and Thomas Kellel, George and Nassif Massad, Sam Melham; Carl, George, Rustum and A. O. Nassif and Shaker Nassif and Mike Saba. The two friends were Ferris and Abe Skaff.[26]

We know from personal accounts that most, perhaps all of the McLean (Sheridan) County settlers had Attiyeh family connections. The *Bismarck Tribune* report specifically mentions Sheridan County. Certainly some of Writers Project "twenty three Syrians" are on the above list.

Federal Land Office Tract Books are of great help in the task of reconstructing the events of the "early 1900s." They show a collection of Syrian names in a somewhat compact area: five or six sections about ten miles northeast of the town of McClusky. In fact, we find Mistofa Shabina filing on land in 1902 in Township T148-R75. Then in May 1903 Solom Nicola and Moses Abdullah filed on Section 35, T148-R76. This land was a few miles east of the town of Lincoln Valley. In June of that year, Aisem Haykell (Hikel) and George Kellel took land in the same township, on sections 18 and 34. By July and August, two more Syrian men chose land close by. Both had the last name Nicola. In that same year Joseph Kellel and Kamel Hessie filed on section 2 of Township T147-R76. In 1904, Mike Saba also came to section 2 of the same township. Several more Syrians arrived to homestead in 1906 and 1907.

Federal Land Office records show that the Federal Writers Project report of 23 land applicants was accurate and they confirm that all the applicants were male. Twenty-three seems to have been the exact number settling in Sheridan (then McLean) County. The Attiyeh Convention list was also accurate.

As mentioned elsewhere, the Attiyeh family centers historically on the village of Ain Arab and the Sheridan County settlers were, it appears, almost exclusively from that town and were of the Syrian Orthodox faith.

Naturalization records supply more details. (Note: First papers were needed to homestead.) Looking closely at the men mentioned in the Attiyeh report, we find that Attas Boutrous filed his first naturalization "intent" papers in McLean (now Sheridan) County in July 1904; Salem Nicola did the same in May 1905. Tom Kellel's first papers are dated in November 1905. These three men were the earliest "Syrians" to make applications in McLean (Sheridan) County. They were followed by Salma Nicola in 1906 and Abe Skaff in 1907. Sam Skaff in 1995 recalled:

> *My Father, Ferris Skaff, and Grandfather, Shaker Nassif, took advantage of the Homestead Act that granted one quarter of land, 160 acres, to anyone over twenty-one or the head of a household, who would live there five years with at least seven months of each year and make certain improvements. To speed the process, homesteads could be commuted or purchased for $1.25 an acre.[27]*

Many of the original Sheridan County settlers were not "off-the-boat" immigrants. Joe Kellel had filed his first papers in 1902 in Ward County. George Massad did the same in Pierce County in 1902. (Kellel's second papers were in Sheridan County in 1907, Massad's took place there too, in 1911.)

The Syrian homesteaders were at a certain disadvantage. Germans from Russia had been claiming land in the county since 1897. Syrian settlers came late, in a virtual flood, especially in 1902. The Syrians, therefore, did not get the best of the farm locations. This may explain why they left the area so rapidly. (The last Syrian on a Sheridan farmstead left in 1964.)

As mentioned, the Sheridan families were almost entirely of the Syrian Orthodox faith. No church was built during their rather short time in residence. Yet Orthodox priests did visit and conduct religious services. Descendants remember two clergymen: Fr. Tom Skaff and Fr. Yanney. They are said to have come from Sioux City.[28]

Williams County

The Williams County Syrian community was not the first of its kind in North Dakota, nor was it the largest in total numbers, but it can be classed as the most enduring and self-conscious of all such groups. (To this day, an ethnic celebration rarely takes place in Williston, the area's major city, without Lebanese representation.)

Wonder of Williams, the remarkably complete history of Williams County, tells the story of some, but not all, of the area's first Syrian settlers. According to their family accounts, in 1903 David Kalil, Alex Aboud, Joe Albert, and Abraham Abdo arrived to take up free land. One long-time Williston resident says that David Kalil was working out of Duluth as a peddler. Traveling through, he looked over the Williston area in the later part of the 1890s and subsequently returned to take up a homestead.[30]

The date, 1903, coincides very well with the naturalization records of the State Historical Society of North Dakota. In the Williams County lists we find the following Syrian-born individuals filing their first papers—always an initial step in land acquisition—to the local court in 1903. (The spelling may vary somewhat from Land Office records, U.S. Census reports, and present-day family usage.)

April 9	Abraham Shickony (Shikany) (in the 1910 Census)
April 10	Maggie Toby, William Eattol
April 16	David Kall (Kalil) (in 1910 Census), Joseph Firoah (Farah)
April 17	Hasaba Lyon
April 18	Bertha Faroah, John Faroah, Gregory Faroah, Sara Mackay, Anise Homsey
May 2	Thomas Nehmy
July 20	Serafin Roumie
July 22	Regina Kassis
August 3	Sadwaya Aefofoe Rahal
October 19	Mary Bouslman (Bousliman), Mary Saba
October 24	Bohurae Haggar, Martha Haggar
November 2	Abdula Bohamra
November 4	Mary Slebay

The above list of citizenship applicants reveals a number of things that make the Williams County Syrians unique. (1) The rapidity with which such a great number of newcomers sought the status of full-fledged Americans. They filed first papers almost as soon as they reached the Williams County region. This hardly fits the "get rich and return home" generalization found in publications concerning other parts of the nation. (2) The presence of such a sizable number of women, eight out of the total twenty-one. Indeed, several of the women appear to be wives who applied at the same time as their husbands. Again, this does not fit the standard first arrival expectations. (3) Without exception, the 1903 applicants in Williams County were Christian. (4) The most famous of all Lebanese North Dakota religious leaders, the pastor of St. George's Church near Rugby, Fr. Seraphim Roumie, is on the list of applicants.

Syrians in Williams County had no church building to call their own, but they did have several national rallying places: a "Syrian Hall" was located in the 700 block of Williston's 3rd Avenue West. It was a small frame building, perhaps 20 by 30 feet. Old-timers say it was on the spot where the Wilbur Kalil home now exists. Out in the country another "Syrian Hall" could be found in the midst of a Syrian neighborhood, Section 28, Township T156-R102. A rural Syrian store and a blacksmith shop also existed not far from the "Hall." David Kalil operated the store in its earliest days. The St. George Syrian Cemetery, with some 30 graves, is a half-mile from the spot where the hall once stood.

Father Seraphim Roumie is said to have conducted services in "one of the two Syrian clubs built by the people." Father Seraphim's trips to the Williston area came to an end in the mid-1910s. The halls must have been built some time in the early part of that same decade.[31]

Some historians have called the two "Syrian Halls," one in the country and one in town, the first Syrian Halls in America. (The history, *Plains Folk*, mentioned that a Syrian club, but not a hall, "once flourished in North Dakota's Rugby community.") Caesar Farah, in *American Immigrant Cultures*, says the first convention of Syrian clubs was held in Williston, North Dakota, in 1918.[32] A well-published photograph of that convention seems to have been taken in the Syrian Hall in town.

The rural store, the hall, and blacksmith shop mark what might be called the center of the Williams County Lebanese enclave. The majority of the homesteads were found in three townships: Cow Creek (T156-R102), Bull Butte (T156-R103), and Mont (T155-R102). These areas exist, more or less, 15 miles northwest of the City of Williston. The Lebanese homesteaders found their neighbors in almost every direction were Norwegians, yet immediately to their south was a small cluster of Ukrainian farm families.

The Williams County Lebanese were Christian and historically they came, like their fellow countrymen elsewhere in the state, from the three Old Country religious groups: Orthodox, Melkite and Maronite.

The Orthodox Christians did have an occasional Orthodox priest who supplied their liturgical needs and also gave some individuals instruction in their faith. Two clergymen are remembered or can be found in regional history books: Father Sady (Saidi—spelling unclear) and Monsignor Abramhous from St. Paul. Most likely these men came to Williams County while making a circuit from St. Paul; possibly from Nebraska, through South Dakota, and perhaps through Sheridan County's Orthodox settlement area. But, as mentioned elsewhere in the book, given the sparseness of the population and the distances involved, the Orthodox Archbishop advised the Williams County faithful to join the local Episcopal congregation.

Melkites and Maronites found themselves together in the Williams County settlement, yet the historic differences between the two traditions are distinctions unknown to present-day descendants. Certainly Melkites were present in the Williams County area. Fr. Seraphim Roumie, a Melkite priest, labored among the early settlers. Fr. Elias Aboud, of Omaha,

Nebraska, an Orthodox? Melkite? priest, was a "visitor." Indeed, the Melkite National Archives lists the following Williams County residents as part of their membership. The names are taken from the Arabic script: Abuslimans (Bousilmans), Germanos (Jermanos ?), Makihoul, Masaad, Saikally, Hafadh, Nakaad (Naked), and Kassis. This is a partial list, the archivist says, but seems to represent a sizable Melkite presence. Parish records at Williston's St. Joseph Latin Rite Catholic Church contain the following family names in the early baptism records: Kassis, Jermanus, Basilman [sic], Kalil, Nedoff, and Aboud, Zine, Joseph Layon, Shickaney [sic], Bousilman, Joseph (Charles E. and Robert). Taken together, the above lists of names indicate that a substantial portion of the original Williams County families was either of Maronite or Melkite origin.

There must have been an amicable arrangement between Father Seraphim Roemie and the local Catholic parish priest. The recording of baptisms in the St. Joseph's Church books is one thing, but the *Williston World* reported in November 1907, "Father Saraphine [sic] Roumie, the Assyrian priest, arrived here last night from Rugby, and on Sunday will hold Mass in the Catholic Church and also baptize several children. Rev. Roumie will remain here two weeks."[33]

Like the Orthodox Church authorities, the Catholic Lebanese religious leaders finally had to terminate their trips from distant eastern cities to the far west of North Dakota. A time came (by the mid 1910s ?) that both Maronite and Melkite families permanently affiliated with St. Joseph's Catholic parish. Their descendants, if still in Williams County, can be found there today.

The Williams County settlers were overwhelmingly Christian. But just as the Christian enclave in Pierce County had a handful of Muslim land-seekers, naturalization records also provide names like Mohamid Gasson filing his first papers at Williston in 1907. Jisam Farhart, a Muslim name from Mountrail County, filed his first papers in Williams County in 1910. Did these gentleman homestead in the Cow Creek-Bull Butte area?

The Pierce County Christians and the Williams County Christians, at least during the settlement times, had close relations. The same family names appear with great frequency. Taking land in both counties were Munyers, Skaffs, Shikanys, Abrahams, Massads. Applying for citizenship in both Pierce and Williams counties were Lyons, Maloufs, Sawayas, Bouresous, Kassis, and Maloofs. Were they relatives? Certainly there was movement between the two groups. As mentioned above, Fr. Seraphim Roumie, pastor of the Pierce County Syrian Church, filed his first papers in Williams County.

Today the grandchildren of the Williams County Christians who remain in the Williston area are the most visible and most numerous of all the "survivors" of North Dakota's Syrian enclaves. Indeed, a good portion of the land settled by their pioneer American ancestors is still owned and in some cases still farmed by men or women of Syrian background. In an obvious exaggeration, one non-Lebanese interviewee mentioned a local "Syrian" who "owns half of the county."[34] Syrian descendants have been active in Williston life since the very earliest times. Some set up small businesses "in town" within two or three years after the first arrivals took land. Through the past three generations, Lebanese descendants have frequently occupied positions of prominence in Williston, as County Commissioners, as the Chief of Police, as bank owners, board of director members and business leaders.

Turtle Mountains

What is sometimes called the Turtle Mountain Syrian settlement is really a wide arc of early farmsteads spreading from the vicinity of the Rock Lake town, through the land north of Bisbee, then to the south of Rolla, Belcourt and Dunseith. In an intermittent fashion, Lebanese homesteaded and often purchased small farms (seldom large acreages) which became residences and these, in turn, often served as "headquarters" for two decades of new-comers. The farms, when plotted on county maps, fall into Towner County to the east and Bottineau and Rolette counties to the west.

The Syrian settlement apparently began when Abe Tanous and Nicholas Ausey homesteaded a few miles north of Bisbee in the spring of 1898. (Yet some records seem to indicate there were two *earlier* settlers: Joe Tanous and Deep Tanous in 1897. They were not far from the farms of the Auseys and their brother, Abe Tanous.) In 1899, Samuel Ausey arrived, a brother of Nicholas Ausey. This gentleman and a friend, Sadie Iserma, took land in the same general area. Members of this first contingent were Christian and often had family ties with the Walsh County settlers.

In 1900 Walter Romball filed in Towner County. Moses Aghaney followed him in 1901. Charles Hagger, Mary Hagger and Hammond Hash took more Towner land in 1902. Others came in subsequent years.

To the west, in Bottineau County, Hamod Abdallah and Ali Abdallah chose their land in 1902. The same year, in Rolette County, Joseph Solomon homesteaded. In 1904 Albert Ferris, Sam Alick and Joe Alick joined them in the same county. Many of the above farmers were of the Muslim faith.

There was a certain "stepping stone" kind of process at work in the Turtle Mountain area settlement. The Nicholas Ausey farm in particular was a "half-way" home for perhaps hundreds of both peddlers and land-seekers. And prior to that, Walsh County homes served the same purposes;

Tombstone: Islamic
section, Dunseith,
ND, cemetery.

Courtesy:
John Guerrero

the Walsh (Shepherd Township) Absey farms are mentioned as "first stops" on the way to the Bisbee area.

The Turtle Mountain area is unique in that relatively large numbers of Syrian migrants continued to come to the region after homesteading was complete, some as late as the 1920s, even in the 1930s, and occasionally after World War II in the 1950s. Agriculture, by that time, was of minimal concern, rather peddling and small business opportunities led them to come to Dakota's prairies.

And indeed, Syrian small businesses soon appeared in all the towns adjacent to the Turtle Mountains: Rolla, Bisbee, Belcourt, and Dunseith, of course, but also smaller towns such as Perth and Rock Lake.

Muslim settlers were so frequent in the Turtle Mountain region that one could say the area constituted the second Islamic community in North Dakota. Mrs. Kathryn Harris, a long-time resident of Rolla, said that in the early days, Christian Syrians in the Turtle Mountains were a minority. Mrs. Harris estimated that between 25 to 30 Syrian families were present, at one time or another, "between the towns of Perth and Dunseith." If one were to add the single men, the Turtle Mountain area could have contained close to one hundred first and second generation Lebanese.[35]

The years have taken their toll. Only remnants of the original families remain, several in business, a few more in terms of land ownership. Yet for the Muslims, a special portion of the Dunseith cemetery is filled almost exclusively with Arabic grave inscriptions and here and there the graves are marked with Islamic symbols.

The Turtle Mountain Christians affiliated almost from the beginning with the local Latin rite Catholic parishes. As for the Muslim residents, "sheiks" from Canada must have come down at least for Islamic burials. There are no reports, however, of public Muslim prayer services. Private prayers (family-centered ?) must have taken place as part of the daily or weekly routine for indications are that the first settlers were devout people. Muslim prayer beads and copies of the Koran are still cherished by grandchildren. They remain as reminders of the faith of their grandparents.

Many of the present-day descendants of both the Muslim and Christian settlers are the product of not only inter-religious marriages, but also inter-racial unions. Very often the Syrian men married local Metis women. And the Metis people, the majority in some of today's towns, were themselves of mixed background—an historical combination of French and Chippewa or Cree, dating from the fur trade era. One gentleman, a local businessman, when asked to describe his ethnic heritage, said "I'm Arab, Muslim, Chippewa, French, Catholic and Knights of Columbus."[36] (Chapter 19 in this volume contains a discussion of Lebanese-Native American special relations.)

One second-generation son of a Lebanese Christian father and a Metis mother was a portrait (and landscape ?) painter of some note in the Turtle Mountains. His work reflected a mixture of motifs. A family member said, "In the 1950s it was fashionable to be French, so he painted "French." In the 1960s he became Arab, and with the 1970s his works were Indian."[37]

Clearly, the Turtle Mountain Syrian enclave differed decidedly from other contemporary North Dakota Arab settlements: its dispersed char-acter, and its short-lived relationship to the land, its business accumen and its mixed racial and religious origins.

Glenfield

The land around the Foster County village of Glenfield in central North Dakota received its first homesteaders in 1885. For the next two decades a flood of landseekers, mostly Scandinavian, came to the area.

Sometime in the 1920s, Syrians of Muslim background came to the area. By the end of the 1930s, a cluster of Syrian families could be found on land a few miles northeast of Glenfield. The land was probably purchased from earlier settlers fleeing the state during the Dust Bowl years.

County plat maps for the late 1930s through the 1950s show that the northeastern corner of Glenfield Township (T146-R62) was farmed for the most part by Muslim Syrian families. The names are as follows: Jerome D. Eli, Charles Alley, Hassen Eli, William Eli, and Claments Gader. Three miles to the east of this group of families was Ernest Alley and one mile south of Glenfield was Charles Gader. This latter gentleman came to Glenfield in 1936. Hassen Eli came in 1934, after living for some time at Sharon, ND. (Coming to Glenfield at such a date, Hassen nevertheless quickly learned to speak Norwegian.)

There is a connection between the Glenfield Syrians and the earlier Ross community. Perhaps some had previously farmed near Ross and moved to what they considered a more favorable location: the land near Glenfield.

It seems the families who took land were attracted to the area by the success of early Syrians in the Glenfield business world. William Alley is said to have come to America in 1914. After a tour of duty in World War I, he returned to Lebanon, married his wife, Hasaby, and spent some time in Crookston, Minnesota. By 1924, Albert and William Alley were in Glenfield running the Alley's Cash Store. They continued at least into the 1940s. (In 1935 it included the Alley "Ice House.") Charles Alley had a store in 1928. The Abdo Kadry Pool Hall, also of Syrian ownership, was in operation in 1932.[38]

The Muslim religious traditions continued at Glenfield through the first and somewhat into the second generation. The *Fargo Forum* of July 9, 1937 reported a newsworthy event:

> [A]t Glenfield last Sunday there was a Mohammedan wedding. Ida Hadley, 17, became the bride of Hassen Eli, Jr., 18. The marriage was conducted by a Mohammedan priest from Dunseith, N.D. with 25 or 30 guests present. A few of the guests were in full Mohammadan costume and entertainment included a sword dance and a fencing match. The bride's father, playing on double pipes, provided the music for the wedding dance which followed. (Note: The Fargo Forum anglicized the name; it was Hadey, not Hadley.)[39]

Muslim funerals took place under the guidance of an imported spiritual leader. (From Dunseith? From Canada?) "Old timers" gathered periodically for prayer, and Ramadan was a regular part of their yearly life experiences. Hassen Eli was usually the leader. Young men of Muslim background served in World War II. In recent decades, Veterans of Foreign Wars burial services have taken place with flags, rifle salutes, and the customary Muslim chants and ritual.

Eli, Alley, Kadry and Gader names can be found on the school student rosters from the 1930s until the current day.

Today the descendants of the original Syrian families are still in the Glenfield agriculture and business world. In fact, more than any other North Dakota Syrian group, the Glenfield people came to their community and stayed. There occurred the usual departure of children as they graduated from school and left the area for employment, but nonetheless the original families still are part of the community life. In 1997, an Alley descendant was running the Glenfield Bar and the Gader family was regionally known for its trucking enterprises. Even more of significance, of the 36 operating farmstead photographs shown in the 1987 Glenfield anniversary history, seven were second-generation Lebanese family operations. No Lebanese enclave in the state displayed such proportionate agricultural longevity.[40]

The religious dimension of their life, however, has changed. Second and third generation Lebanese are seldom of the Muslim faith. Now they belong to the Lutheran congregations and some few are Methodist. Yet some of the more elderly Glenfield Lebanese admit to attending Christian services on Sunday, while saying Muslim prayers privately at home.

Random Homestead Clusters

Not included in the above description of North Dakota's major Syrian settlements were the occasional Lebanese individual or family that took root, sometimes in clusters, sometimes alone, in a dispersed manner throughout the state. Certainly half of the state's counties saw the arrival of adventurous Lebanese men who picked land in a predominantly Norwegian, German, or an ethnically mixed neighborhood. Northeast of Ashley, for example, nine "Syrians" filed in township T131-R69, seven in nearby T131-R68, ten in T130-R67, and a half dozen in an adjacent township. All the claims were taken between 1903 and 1908. Almost all were Muslim. Another collection (also Muslim) could be found between Tappen and Medina, on the east edge of Stutsman and the west edge of Kidder counties. At least nine names occur on land records.

These isolated clusters tended to be short-lived. Records show that some individuals filed on a claim, but "relinquished" it within a few months. Many "commuted" the claims, buying them out-right after 14? 18? months or two years. These were rapidly sold to more durable neighbors. (The 1920 Census reported only two Syrian families in all of McIntosh, Stutsman, and Kidder counties.) The homesteader left the area with a pocket full of cash and moved to more amenable surroundings.

A final note: The residents of the various Lebanese rural enclaves discussed in this chapter were certainly aware of the existence of the "other" Syrians who lived elsewhere in the state. As one would expect, an especially warm relationship existed toward other North Dakotans who were from the same Syrian villages. This was true even more if they were of the same religious tradition. Marriages were fostered, job opportunities were offered, and family celebrations were open to all such special friends or kinfolk. There was, in fact, a continued movement in the earliest days between Pierce County Lebanese and their William County counterparts. Some movement socially and, in a few cases, some marriages came about between the Pierce County residents and the more northerly Turtle Mountain Christians. Glenfield Muslims felt a special kinship to the Ross settlement people.

The traditional Lebanese hospitality toward all Arabic visitors, of whatever religious affiliation, was everywhere evident, as seen throughout this book. Muslim families stayed with Christian families as they were "getting settled." Peddlers of every religious background were welcomed as they "stopped over" on their journeys through the countryside. The divergence in beliefs, the variance in diet, feast day and fasting traditions were accommodated with surprising ease. But as the book *Plains Folk* said of North Dakota, there still remained "a polite degree of social distance." Close friends came from those who shared the same Old Country backgrounds. And though mixed faith marriages were rare, the *Plains Folk* author was correct when he observed that, at least in the earliest decades, "interfaith marriages aggravated tensions. Hard feelings arose."

From Lebanon to North Dakota

Lebanese Home Village	Major Religious Affiliation	Major ND Later Affiliation	Primary ND Towns Where They Settled	Counties of Settlement
Bire, Rafid, Kfar, Dines, Khirbet, Rouha, Karoun	Muslim	Lutheran, Muslim	Ross, Stanley, Rolla, Belcourt, Dunseith, Glenfield, Binford, Bisbee, Michigan, Crookston (MN)	Mountrail, Rolette, Foster, Griggs, Towner, Nelson, Polk (MN)
Ain Arab	Orthodox	Episcopalian and Orthodox	McCluskey, Denhoff, Bismarck, Williston, Rugby	Sheridan, Burleigh, Williams, Pierce
Zahle	Melkite Catholic and Orthodox	Roman Catholic, Episcopalian and Orthodox	Rugby, Williston, Edmore, Lawton, Bisbee	Pierce, Williams, Walsh, Ramsey
Farzol and Mushgara	Melkite Catholic and Muslim	Roman Catholic and Muslim	Williston, Rugby	Williams, Pierce
Bouhaire and Toula	Maronite Catholic	Roman Catholic	Crookston, (MN)	Polk (MN)

Lateefe Joseph

In 1913, on the eve of World War I, a young Maronite girl left the scenic mountain village of Bouhaire, Lebanon, for the port of Tripoli. She left behind the goats and sheep she had tended, as well as the grapes and lentils. As a devoutly religious girl, she prayed at the mountain shrine of St. Anthony and attended Mass at St. Maron's Church in Bouhaire. The most difficult part of emigration was thought of the family she left behind. More than 80 years later, tears came to the eyes of Lateefe Joseph as she recalled leaving behind her parents, brothers and sisters. As her boat left for America she received a priest's blessing. Her destination was Crookston, Minnesota, where she joined her older brother Charley who worked on the Great Northern Railroad. During her lifetime she learned that the Turks had kidnapped their father and killed two of her siblings. The devastating famines of World War I exacted their toll on the Ottoman Empire province of Mt. Lebanon, including the Joseph family. In Crookston, Lateefe embarked on a restaurant partnership with Joe Elbinger that spanned the years of 1921-1966. Blackie's Cafe would become one of Crookston's finest.

Many of Crookston's Maronites had to prove the legitimacy of their Eastern Rite Catholicism. She recalled one incident when as a teenage girl she was called a "Black Syrian" at church and the priest demanded the two female offenders apologize. According to Father Daniel Noah, himself of Crookston Maronite background, many non-Lebanese were jealous of the Lebanese women because "they cleaned the Church better."

When letters arrived from the Old Country they were often written in French; Lateefe would take them to the local French nuns for translation. In 1971, Lateefe was able to realize her lifelong dream of a visit to Rome to see the Pope and a five-week stay in Lebanon. She lived to be 98, five years younger than her brother Charley, who died at 103.

Rosie Juma Chamley

Rosie Chamley is amongst the last of a disappearing group. She was raised as a Muslim and attended the first mosque built in North Dakota. The place was Ross, North Dakota, a stark contrast to Bire, Lebanon, the home of her grandparents, Hassin and Mary Juma. Rosie's father, Shahati "Charlie" Juma was the first-born (1903) child born in the Ross Muslim farm community. Her mother, Sada, was from the Gader family. (Relatives settled in Glenfield, North Dakota.) Although the family in the 1940s began to attend the local Lutheran church, Rosie can still recite Arabic sections of the Quran.

Charlie Juma became a community leader in Ross and Stanley. He was known as a "troubleshooter" for Mountrail County's Lebanese settlers. The two Juma sons, Hassen and Charlie, Jr., became enterprising farmers. In 1970 Hassen died unexpectedly, leaving behind his wife and six children. Stanley's Lutheran church was overwhelmed with mourners. A few years later Rosie's rather young husband died and she and her son, Will, had to struggle to make ends meet. Will became a champion wrestler and football player at Stanley.

Rosie Chamley of Stanley, ND, daughter of Charlie and Sadie Juma, Ross pioneers.

Courtesy: John Guerrero

Today, at six feet, four inches and 260 pounds, Will, a family man, is employed on oil rigs in Williston, North Dakota. Rosie Chamley is proud of her heritage and prouder still of the grandchildren who share her Lebanese ancestry.

CHAPTER FOURTEEN

How Others Saw Them: Prejudice?

It has been frequently observed that Americans tend to assign a social rank to categories of people according to their Old Country place of origin. Such phenomena have often been studied. Social distance scales indicate that a British Isles designation is most favorable. Northern Europeans are next in acceptability; Southern and Eastern Europeans occupy a lower position in the various social rankings. The term "Arab" is definitely not a badge of honor in the minds of many Americans.

But did such a classification occur in North Dakota? No serious examination of the question has ever been made, but it is obvious in historical accounts that those original settlers who could trace their roots to the pre-revolution colonies and ultimately to the British Isles saw themselves as a more superior type of individual; they were the "true Americans" with the proper backgrounds. Scandinavians and Germans, the groups who made up the preponderance of immigrants, could never in the first two generations measure up to the social level of the early "Anglo" pioneer city or farm dwellers. These immigrant groups from northern Europe, however, moved eventually into the more esteemed categories, with the departure of many of the original "Yankee" boomers and speculators. In North Dakota, an eastern European Russian background has never been a status symbol. Indeed, census takers found early Russian-Germans and Ukrainians using various subterfuges to escape a possible stigma. Germans from the Black Sea often became Romanian; Ukrainians became Austrian.

People of Arabic background, relatively late arrivals, certainly had a problem. Dark skinned, in contrast to the Scandinavians and Britons, unfamiliar with the European language system, of nontraditional religious backgrounds—Maronite, Orthodox, or Muslim. The cards seemed to be stacked against them.

Did prejudice exist? If so, how much and where? To begin the discussion one must mention a ruling by the Chief of the United States

Department of Commerce and Labor, Richard K. Campbell, who declared in 1909 that Syrians could not acquire U.S. citizenship. They were "Asiatic" and were not "free, white persons." The Department of Commerce and Labor's decision thereby excluded Syrians on the basis of earlier court decisions, some of which dated back to the first U.S. naturalization law in 1790.[1]

This departmental decision was duly publicized at the time in North Dakota; the *Jamestown News,* for example, gave it a prominent headline in bold print. Needless to say the Department's action sent shock waves through the North Dakota Syrian community. In defense of Syrians everywhere, and certainly of the great number of "Syrians" in its local trade area, the Ross newspaper of November 19, 1909, quoted a well-informed citizen, "If Syrians are to be barred from citizenship, the government should not have accepted their first papers and allowed them to file on land." For the Arabic settlers in northwestern North Dakota, the matter was not merely a remote example of bureaucratic excesses; it was a very real threat, for almost 200 Syrian people in that part of the state had filed on land. Indeed, only four years before that decision, more than 30 Japanese not far from Ross had lost their homesteads due to a similar revised governmental policy decision. Japanese had filed on their claims, lived on their land for a certain amount of time, and then saw their claims canceled. The oriental exclusion acts were the issue.[2] (Note: To file on land one must have been a citizen or indicated intent to obtain citizenship, i.e., filed the first papers.)

The threat of losing one's claim to land loomed even more ominously for Syrian prairie homesteaders because of an event that happened in their state, North Dakota. Newspapers reported that in Stutsman County, the request for acceptance of final papers and the ultimate land title on the part of a local "Syrian" had been questioned.[3] It would be sent away to the Department of Commerce and Labor for a decision. Even more, another "Persian" elsewhere in the state had received an outright rejection as he sought his final papers.[4]

The matter was eventually put to rest and North Dakota Lebanese felt more at ease when a series of court judgments threw out the Campbell, Department of Commerce and Labor ruling. A circuit court in Georgia said, "A Syrian from Mt. Lebanon, near Beirut, is a free white person." This was followed shortly afterwards by similar decisions in other American courts.[5]

Legal status is one thing but public sentiment is another and in North Dakota attitudes toward "Arabs" may have been influenced by occasional news accounts. Reports occurred, for example, which noted that a North Dakota Arab stabbed another Arab in a land ownership fight. Another report detailed how one Arab farmer shot another Arab farmer's horse. In almost every such case the newspaper clearly identified the protagonists as "Arab" or Assyrian or some such label.

Yet newspaper accounts of such occurrences were rare in North Dakota. What seemed to strike the newspaper writers was the "strangeness" of the Arab way of life. A news account in 1937 in the *Fargo Forum* singled out the fact that a "Muhammadan" wedding in Dunseith featured "a sword dance and a fencing match."[6] The first Islamic funeral in Fargo is reported (June 13, 1907) as featuring a Muhammadan "aman" [sic] as the presiding official. The Koran was used but the newspaper said, almost in surprise, that the event "didn't differ from the ordinary funeral service."[7]

The uniqueness of Syrian customs often gave rise to a certain puzzlement, and the fascination extended not just toward Islamic people, but Christians "Arabs" too were sometimes newsworthy. The Fargo *Search-Light* newspaper on August 1, 1908, had one line: "There was an Assyrian wedding at McIntosh." But such a designation occurred repeatedly in regional newspapers: "Arab funerals," "Arab foods," "Arab dances." This in itself doesn't imply prejudice, but considering the many hundreds of weddings and funerals that took place each year it certainly indicates curiosity.[8] Syrians were "different."

An incident occurred on the Northern Pacific Railroad in 1904 that indicates the ease in which Syrians could be classified as less-than-reputable people. The news items show also the physical circumstances in which the Syrian new arrivals found themselves. The story begins with a *Jamestown Sun* report. The news caption read as follows:

Jamestown Daily Capital, Monday, February 22, 1904

TRAIN WRECKERS MADE A MURDEROUS ATTEMPT SATURDAY
TO WRECK THE N.P.'S CRACK TRAIN AT MEDINA.

WARNING GIVEN AND TRAIN SAVED.

RAILS REMOVED ON A CURVE ON A
HIGH EMBANKMENT BY THE DESPERADOES
WHO STOLE TRACK TOOLS FROM THE HAND-CAR
HOUSE AT MEDINA.

THREE DESPERADOES WITH A TEAM INVOLVED
IN THE DESPERATE DEED.

SECTION FOREMAN HANSEN'S FIGHT FOR LIFE
IN A HAND TO HAND CONFLICT ON THE TRACK. HE ESCAPED
WITH WOUNDS AND GAVE WARNING.

VILLAINS TRACED INTO WELLS COUNTY.
NORTHERN PACIFIC OFFERS $1,000 REWARD FOR CAPTURE
AND CONVICTION.

Levi Hansen, the section foreman, was featured in the newspapers at length. Many paragraphs described his "fight for life" with the assailants. Understandably the railroad detectives were on the scene to investigate.[9] The next day's report said:

ALL A FAKE?
RAILROAD OFFICIALS ABOUT COME TO THAT CONCLUSION.
HANSEN IN THE SWEAT BOX.

"It was all a fake."

That seems to be the general opinion among railroad officials regarding the alleged train wrecking attempt near Medina Saturday night. . . . Those who have been at Medina closely looking over the ground and connecting the links assert that the chain of evidence points strongly toward the section foreman.

The third day the newspaper says:

TWO SYRIANS CHARGED WITH ASSAULT ON LEVI HANSEN
ON TRACK NEAR MEDINA SATURDAY NIGHT
ARE THEY TRAIN WRECKERS?
HANSEN SAYS HE IDENTIFIED BOTH OF THE MEN
AS HIS MURDEROUS ASSAILANTS.

Section Foreman Hansen and the officials and detective force which has been at Medina since the attempted wrecking of No. 1, reached Jamestown Tuesday night and a 2-1/2 hour session was held at the office of Justice Parson where Mr. Hansen again told much of the incidents of Saturday night and swore to complaints charging Richard and Joseph Kanen [sic], two Syrians, with assault upon him with dangerous weapons. Officers left for Medina to arrest one of them, the other being at Crystal Springs.

It is said that Mr. Hansen identified one of the Syrians as his assailant of Saturday night, the larger of the two men being at Crystal Springs. According to the story told by Hansen, as reported here, his assailants that night appeared to him dark and with the features of Indians though they spoke English well. This is said to be the description of these Syrians, though Jos. Morat, said to be a relative of them, who was in Jamestown last week, spoke English imperfectly.

The defendant Syrians are said to live eight miles south of Medina where a number of them have secured claims.[10]

Levi Hansen was indignant over the suggestion that he faked the incident to receive rewards from the railroad company. News reports gave further details. Richard Kanan, the "Syrian," lived nine-and-a-half miles south of Medina. A certain Wm. Ogall, also "Syrian," was arrested with him and was soon discharged from the jail. Another news item from February 25th reported:

HANSEN GAVE BONDS FOR $500 FOR HIS APPEARANCE TO PROSECUTE. R. KANAN HELD FOR ASSAULT

Richard Kanan, who speaks English quite well but is unable to understand the "hard" words, lives in squalor in a building about 10 by 12 ft. with his wife and baby nine months old.

"Moni? I got nuttin," he said. "Owe my brotha-law $15 dolla, notha man thirty dolla, some more for masheenerie. I got nuttin. The sheriff he tell you so."

Sheriff Eddy left orders at Medina to furnish some groceries to the destitute wife and get them to her today. Kanan says he was home all day Saturday. Went eight miles south to get a load of manurefuel—had to pay $1.25 a load for it; others charge $2 a load. It is what the Russians call "mist." Sunday his brother wanted him to go with him to Crystal Springs and they went across country, reaching the Springs in the evening and remaining until Wednesday.

On February 26th, Mr. Kanan's wife and child arrived on the scene. The defendant's pitiable life circumstances soon became evident.

TERSE TOWN TALES

Mrs. Annie Kanan, wife of Richard Kanan, the Syrian in jail on complaint of Section Foreman Hansen of Medina, arrived last night with her child to see what had become of her husband. She is being cared for until the release of her husband. Sheriff Eddy and deputies are summoning witnesses at Medina for the preliminary hearing to be held March 1st.[11]

Public opinion, if evidenced by the newspaper report, seemed to be turning to sympathy for the Syrian man on trial. A February 29th report gives the reader a glimpse of what may have been the lot of many Eastern Mediterranean land claimants.

FLED THE SULTAN RICHARD KANAN'S HISTORY BRIEFLY OUTLINED. BEGAN FARM LIFE WITH PRACTICALLY NOTHING

Richard Kanan, the Syrian charged with the assault upon Section Foreman Hansen, says he was born within 50 miles of the ancient city of Damascus. But the oppression of the Sultan and his minions led him 12 years ago to emigrate to great, free America of which he had heard something. He worked as a laborer, peddled goods during the summers and two years ago filed on land nine miles south of Medina, he and his brothers taking up over a section close together. It seems that all their property was pooled and now they have about a dozen horses. Last spring 125 acres were broken up on Richard's place and 25 acres on a brother's claim and the 150 seeded to flax. Richard seems to be the best farmer among them and as they had no drill he seeded the land by hand. The crop promised an abundant yield until their hopes were dashed into the earth by a hail storm which pounded the fields black when the flax stood about two feet high. Only 240 bushels of flax was secured from the 150 acres.

Richard says he had but $100 when he filed on his land two years ago. Shortly afterwards he met a woman from his own native land who also peddled goods during the summers and they were married in the Syrian colony in Fargo. Richard says his wife has sold Turkish goods and needle work in Jamestown.

His wife was afraid to stay alone on the claim and her brothers paying fare for her she came down to be with her husband.

Kanan lived in the utmost poverty and destitution on his claim and it is believed good food, a warm place and the care of a physician will put him on his feet again.[12]

After five days the celebrated trial came to a conclusion. The newspapers on March 5 printed this closing set of paragraphs. (We see that the Syrian family was Christian; they had their child "christened.")

KANAN RELEASED
EVIDENCE NOT SUFFICIENT TO WARRANT
HIS DETENTION. THIS CHAPTER CLOSED.

The case against Richard Kanan has been dismissed the evidence not being sufficient to hold him. A strong, but not an absolute alibi, was presented for Kanan and the evidence against him was not supported by evidence other than that of Levi Hansen.

Sunday the baby of Mr. Kanan and wife will be christened and the Syrian and family will return to their home very much cheered and benefited by their stay in Jamestown.

Mr. Hansen returned to Medina today to resume his duties on the road as section foreman.

The story of Richard Kanan does not end with the distressful events mentioned above. Already in October 1903 he had filed his first papers for naturalization. He received his citizenship in Stutsman County Court in July 1908. After some time on his claim he sold the property and moved with his growing family some 200 miles west to Fryburg in Billings County. There he set up what was termed locally as the "Kanan Store." Old-timers still recall that he sold general merchandise, but also sold ice, horses, and his store served as the town's cream station. The Kanan children went to the Fryburg school.

Mr. Kanan wanted to become an American as quickly as possible. Richard was not his real name; rather it was Massad. His citizenship was received under the name Massad Kanan. (His 160 acres were given him in 1911, under the name Masood.) By 1925, Richard with his wife Annie and their children left Fryburg—a tiny settlement—and moved elsewhere in the larger American world.[13]

The authors of this volume searched early North Dakota newspapers for similar stories that might indicate anti-Arabic sentiment. But in truth, other than the Kanan episode, no such spectacular events seem to have taken place. But this does not mean that a quiet, low-keyed suspicion of the "dark skinned" neighbor did not, at times, exist. The application of the adjective "Arab" in news reports concerning personalities and incidents occurs with a frequency that seems excessive.

Yet surprisingly, when interviewed in the late 1930s, Lebanese early settlers had nothing but praise for the reception they received during their first decades in North Dakota.

"All nationalities were very friendly to me when I first came to this country and I surely can't kick about them." So said Joseph Azar at Bismarck in August 1939. At the same time another Arab contemporary said, "As far as different racial groups other than mine are concerned, they have all proved their friendliness."

Joseph Munyer of Rugby and Williston said in February 1940:

Yes, there were quite a few Syrians around Rugby, all of them emigrated here from Syria. Everybody seemed kindly and tried to help each other. I do not think anyone around Rugby were prejudiced against me because I was a Syrian, or at least they did not show it.

Joe Albert of Williston is almost glowing in his comments about relations with other national groups. In February 1940 he reported:

I had the best kind of neighbors while around Bonetrail; there were quite a few Syrians, Russians and Norwegians around there, but they were all good neighbors. Ever since I came over from Syria everybody has been friendly with me, and when I first came everybody helped me all they could—more friendly here than in the Old Country.

Scandinavians seemed the most friendly to Samuel Nicola who lived near Denhoff and was interviewed at Bismarck in July 1939:

The Norwegians and Swedes were the most friendly people when I first came to America. I also have some friends among the Germans.

Something of the same was said by George Saba in a 1939 Bismarck interview:

I think my people get along with the Scandinavians the best, but all the nationalities have been very friendly toward us, however all have seemed friendly, and it is hard to tell the difference in their attitude toward us.

Yet Thomas Nassif, of Sheridan County and of Bismarck, said in August 1939: "The Germans were the most friendly." But he also said, "They were all friendly enough."

Mrs. David Kalil of Williston was a little more nuanced as she replied to the August 1939 interviewer. Religion seemed an issue:

I never have no trouble with nobody, only one woman she call us black, but that's just one. She don't like Catholic, and it's funny—she's black, more black as us. But I don't care. I go to Catholic church and I work for ladies aid.

The language problem seemed a minor one. (We must note that every one of their neighboring immigrant groups was struggling at the same time to master the intricacies of the English vocabulary and usages.) Allay Omar of the Ross Muslim community, said in 1939:

I am a member of the Farmers Union … I had very little trouble because of a lack of knowledge of the English language as my brother always accompanied me wherever I went. All the people in my neighborhood were very friendly and they helped me whenever they could.

Assisting the Lebanese immigrants as they adjusted to the fabric of the newly developing rural and village neighborhoods were several factors which, to use a modern phrase, created a "positive image." Lebanese worked hard! And on the Dakota frontier, that quality was highly esteemed. But also they took care of their own! An old-time, non-Lebanese attorney in Williston said of the dry 1930s: "No Syrians were on welfare."[14]

The heroism and tragic death of a young man from Syria elicited both admiration and sympathy in early southeastern North Dakota. (He left a widow and children in his homeland.) The occasion was a hotel fire in October 1919 at Hettinger. The *Adams County Register* of November 12, 2001, has this report:

> *Nick Lyons, the young Syrian cook, was at first reported safe as he had been seen going down the long hallway from his west end room toward the front office. At daybreak, however, his charred remains were found where the office had been. It was believed that in his heroic endeavors to arouse other occupants, he was overcome as he reached the last door. His wife and several small children had planned to join him in America in a few months.*

A perusal of the "around town" items in the *Ross Valley News* and the *Ross Promoter* shows a surprisingly gentle attitude towards the Muslim farmers in the Ross area. During the first three decades of settlement the references to Islamic religious life are "softened" by terminology which emphasized the similarity, not the differences, between the local Muslims and Christians. The Mosque was called the "Mohammedan Church," the sheik who came for special events was referred to as "the Reverend ..." Ramadan was the "Mohammedan Lent," the Koran was the "Mohammedan Bible." The news media of Ross, at least, was striving to avoid abrasive elements which might disrupt Mountrail County community harmony.

The above paragraphs give the impression that the Lebanese were "accepted" by their North Dakota neighbors. And this is probably true for the most part. But when local present-day non-Syrians were asked to remember the past, reports of at least some discrimination appear. Neighbors will say that indeed the Syrians were "looked down upon." "Woe to the young lady who dated one of those dark ones." Williston residents of Lebanese background today remember the phrase "black Syrians." In fact, some relate that there was aversion on two scores: they were Syrians and they were Catholic. (In truth, many of the Williston Lebanese were Catholic and in those days in that predominantly Protestant city being a Catholic did not enhance one's social status.)

One present-day Williston businessman said he was the first Lebanese boy who was a "starting athlete" at the local high school. This was in the 1940s. He said, "Some animosity arose because I was on the teams."

When pressed by a contemporary interviewer, other modern-day Lebanese descendants do say that there were, indeed, "some problems." One elderly gentleman said that at the age of nine and ten he heard playground comments about his Syrian origins.[15] Another Williston man remembers being taunted as a youth for being a "black Syrian." This resulted in verbal altercations and sometimes involved a physical tussle.[16]

The term "black" occurred frequently in the Ross area: the "black ones," "Black Syrian," or just "Blackie." Such phrases are still remembered from childhood days, yet present-day Lebanese say, "we're now good friends" with those who were their teen-aged adversaries. But one second-generation man recalled, "I had to fight regularly."

The olive-toned complexion of the early Lebanese settler must have, at times, contrasted quite conspicuously with the "blonde" Nordic populations which are so prominent in much of the American Upper Midwest. This may well have been the source of the reoccurring word "black." In 1995, at Crookston, an elderly resident was asked, "How was the work performance of Syrians on the railroad crews?" The gentleman responded that they "worked every bit as good as white people."

At the University of North Dakota in Grand Forks as late as 1953, one Williston Lebanese student, of Christian background, was denied membership in a fraternity because of his heritage. He was accepted in another fraternity. (Yet at the same time two Williston Lebanese boys, excellent athletes, were admitted to the very same offending fraternity.) During the same period a young lady of Lebanese origins, who had been a homecoming queen in her nearby Minnesota town, was not accepted by a UND sorority because some thought she was Jewish. Two girls said in her defense that she was not Jewish. The sorority decided that they still did not want her.[17]

Nonetheless, wherever they resided in North Dakota, Syrians never seem to have felt sorry for themselves; they never saw themselves as "victims." Floyd Boutrous of Bismarck said there were some adolescent comments and even fistfights but "We were working too hard [in the 1930s] to get involved with such foolishness."[18] A well-known Turtle Mountain Muslim lady of considerable civic prestige, when asked in 1982 if there were ethnic slurs directed toward local "Syrian" people, said, "No! And there had better not be any such smart remarks!" There never was, nor is there today, an effort to excite pity or guilt from the non-Syrian community in retribution for "past failures." On the contrary, the Syrians, whether of Christian or Muslim background, imply in their comments that they made it on their own, that obstacles to progress, if such things were present, proved to be little or no deterrent to acceptance in the American scene.

Often the very item that singled them out as a distinct group was played up, rather than hidden. In Hettinger a Lebanese-owned tavern was called the "Mecca Bar." In Williston a Lebanese owner placed a camel on the point of the gable over his popular downtown store. A camel statue graced the front yard of a leading merchant in Grand Forks. A Syrian flag and photo of an Arab leader was displayed on the wall of a small town liquor establishment. Indeed, some refer to themselves, even today, as an "old Arab."

One thing that would lead the present-day observer to believe that prejudice toward early Arabic people, though present, was minimal is the remarkable rapidity with which they plunged into the American world of business. As can be seen elsewhere in this volume, "Syrians," along with Jews, immediately became small-scale merchants (peddlers) and within a decade had already established stores in the various Dakota towns. Few other off-the-boat immigrants displayed such self-confidence.

It may also be observed that the prairie world into which the Lebanese "business" man (woman ?) entered was not filled with serious social or economic roadblocks. That world seems to have been, for the most part, ready to welcome the Lebanese presence. Already in her 1911 report, Louise Houghton said, "A North Dakota postmaster writes, with evident approval, of the wonderful industry of the Syrian peddlers who travel with teams from city to city, making a house-to-house canvass of the towns, and visiting every farmer on the way."[19] As if to reiterate that observation, North Dakota Governor John Moses, in the 1920s, is quoted by Adele Younis as describing Lebanese as "hard workers on a land adverse both in climate and soil."[20]

South Dakota, a state much like North Dakota, saw within recent years two United States Senators, James G. Abourezk, a Democrat, and James Abdnor, a Republican. (Both had relatives in North Dakota.) Neither of these individuals tried to hide their "Arab" background. Rather they, at times, became spokesmen for Middle Eastern peoples as they sought fair treatment in American foreign policy. There were no signs of an inferior attitude in their years of public service.

"We Must Prove Ourselves"

In response to a remark by Senator David Reed (Penn.) labeling Syrian immigrants as the "trash of the Mediterranean," the Syrian World of May 1929, published the following:

"America will not appreciate fully who we are and what we are until she is shown. We must prove ourselves. We cannot dwell on our past, but look to our future – being Americans, loyal always and showing it, while retaining the best of our Syrian heritage.

We have faith in our Youth and must do all we can to keep our Youth worthy and proud of his Syrian heritage as he proves himself a real American."

Kary Kelly

Kary Aggie Kelly recalled the Fargo of a half-century ago as a nice city with a minimum of diversity. Fargo was populated by people of Northern European background, Kary was Lebanese. Her father, Sam Aggie, had arrived in Fargo after World War I to join his brother Solomon in business. The clan came from Zahle, Lebanon, had somehow ended up becoming Aggie from the original Hegerie. Fargo, in the mid-1920s, was not always a friendly town. One time Kary's father was told to park his car several blocks away from his Fargo business. The advice was given him by Ku Klux Klan members who liked neither Syrians nor Catholics. Sam complied reluctantly, fearing violence. By the time World War II arrived, Sam had married a Syrian lady from Chicago. They raised two daughters and one son in Fargo. Kary fondly recalled the Lebanese families in town: Nassifs, Kallods, and Skaffs. She attended local Catholic schools and graduated from Shanley High School. As a female entering the world of real estate and property management, she knew there would be barriers. Her work ethic and determination would serve her well when her father died in 1968. She and her sister today manage Aggie Investment firm. Kary married Bill Kelly, and they have one son. Fargo now is a much more diverse city with a variety of newly arrived immigrants. Her advice is to work hard, be respectful, and stay close to one's family.

Floyd Boutrous:
An Active and Loyal American

Born in 1917, just as the United States was entering World War I, Floyd Boutrous, over 85 years later, would reflect on his life and say with enthusiasm, "God bless America." The son of Attas and Della Nassif-Boutrous, Floyd is aware of how different his life would have been if his parents had not migrated from the village of Ain Arab in Lebanon.

Floyd Boutrous, logtime Bismarck businessman and community leader. North Dakota's "Mr. Constitution."

Indeed, life has been happy in North Dakota. In his long career, Floyd ran a grocery store, a dance hall, and was involved in real estate in Bismarck. He helped Lawrence Welk in the 1940s, at the same time his older brother Dr. Tom Boutrous helped fund Danny Thomas in his early days in Michigan.

Floyd mingled with America's "greats" while on the board of Radio Free Europe. He would eventually help bring Presidents Kennedy and Johnson to Bismarck, and was at Truman's inauguration (yet he's been a lifelong Republican). His patriotism led him to found the North Dakota Heritage Group, dedicated to educating students about their rights as citizens. For this he is widely known as "Mr. Constitution." His friend, Supreme Court Chief Justice Warren Burger honored Floyd's contributions.

While promoting Miss North Dakota beauty pageants he met his future wife, Dian, in 1959. They married that same year and raised five sons. (Dian's untimely death at age 50 occurred in 1990.) Attas is a Bismarck physician. Nick, Allen and Steve are all in West Coast enterprises. Michael, the youngest, learned Arabic and is the only family member who has visited Lebanon. The sons have diverse interests. (Steve was a class A wrestling state champion and went on to become a "Mr. North Dakota" bodybuilder.) Floyd Boutrous's options in life do not include "retirement"; there's too much to do.

184

CHAPTER FIFTEEN

Naturalization

Hundreds of North Dakota foreign-born Lebanese, like thousands of immigrants from other national backgrounds, sought citizenship in the American Republic. This legal status, of course, became more worthwhile after the newcomer made the decision to remain in the United States, after the "streets of gold" ideas had dissipated and the New World became comfortable and even attractive.

The desire to return home must have faded quickly, for one author using US Census totals, says the following:

An impressive number of Syrians became naturalized Americans by 1920. Of the recorded 55,102 foreign-born Syrians and Palestinians, about 41 percent, or 22,583, were naturalized or had received their first papers. In the next decade, the figure rose to 61.8 percent of 63,362, or 39,129.[1]

As can be seen in the Appendix to this volume, a rather large number of individuals appear in the North Dakota 1900, 1910 and 1920 census under the classification of "born in Syria" and "born in Turkey." A much larger list of men and women can be found in the Naturalization portion of the Appendix.

Perhaps this is the place to discuss the question of how many Syrian-Lebanese ever resided in early-day North Dakota. Unfortunately the published totals in the official census volumes are of limited value. They represent a "snapshot" look at populations during the census years. What of the intervening years? What of the confusing national origins: Turkey? Syria? Arabia? Lebanon? What of the Lebanese who were "on the road" in peddling ventures?

Census publication totals for Syria-born individuals in North Dakota are confusing. The 1920 report in one place, for example, says 289 adults were present (195 nationalized). A few pages later the same volume says there were 483 (170 naturalized) Syrians in the state.

Whatever the census figures might be, the authors of this book will pursue a different course, hoping to catch at least some sense of the longer, multi-year size of the Lebanese influx in and out of North Dakota.

The number of Syria-Turkey-Lebanon born adults found in the extractions from the census printed in the Appendix is as follows: 119 in 1900, 330 in 1910, 316 in 1920. (The Appendix material was obtained through a careful, line-by-line, review of the microfilmed census manuscripts for the above years—over three million entries.) Eliminating the duplicates, 62 in all, through those different time periods, a total of 727 names can be found. The Appendix also presents the naturalization lists for all the years from 1895 to the 1930s. Some 800 separate individuals— these were not listed in the census reports—filed either their first or second paper in North Dakota. The combined total of individuals found in both the census and the naturalization compilations comes to approximately 1,550. This figure does not include children born in the Old Country, nor does it include the many peddlers who traversed the state and who were uninterested in citizenship or were never within the reach of census takers. We might also add the sizable number of men and women who homesteaded in North Dakota between census counts and had filed their naturalization papers somewhere other than in North Dakota.

Taking into consideration all the above factors, one can easily say that over 2000 Syria-Lebanon born individuals lived at one time or another in North Dakota during its earliest decades.

This chapter will focus particularly on the naturalization experience of Syrian-born men and women who came and left, but also of those who stayed. What will be said about Syrians is certainly not unique, for every immigrant American went through much the same procedures.

The acquisition of that hoped-for citizenship status required a passage through two official stages. The initial step required the applicant to supply some basic biographical information and to officially declare his or her desire to take citizenship status—this was commonly called the "first papers."

The so-called second papers, the actual application for citizenship, could be filed after five years of residence in the country. This too could be done in any court of record (district, state, or federal) with a clerk of court assisting the applicant. The court official would subsequently witness the required oath of allegiance and thereby certify that citizenship was granted and with that action the applicant received the rights of the American way of life and undertook the accompanying responsibilities.

North Dakota residents, of course, had a special reason for acquiring their citizenship status, or at least beginning the process, for homesteading involved citizenship. To acquire land one must have been a citizen or have indicated the intention of becoming a citizen (the first papers). An itinerant peddler who wished to make his or her fortune in the merchandising business and return to Syria, accordingly, would have no need to be concerned about such things as first papers or second papers.

Census tabulations are of limited value, as already noted, because the count happened only once every ten years and often missed the peddlers who were inaccessible "on the trail." But they are limited also because individuals may have deliberately avoided the census-taker for various personal reasons: illegal entry? intent to remain alien and someday return to their homelands? and, for some, a fear of any governmental officials. Making the tracing of "Syrian-born" names even more difficult was a homestead provision that allowed the land occupants to "commute" their acreages, a process by which they could purchase the property after a short period of residence—14 months? 18 months? two years? With this procedure, the individual could acquire land, sell it and leave North Dakota, all within two or three years. In a rather rapid fashion an individual could arrive in the state, make a few dollars, and depart.

Citizenship records were another matter. The documents were open to public scrutiny. Small town newspapers regularly published the names of those who filed their second papers. An example can be found in a May 1914, issue of the *Mountrail County Promoter,* the newspaper that served the Ross area.

Petitions for Citizenship

Mohamid Allie Gossum

Rasmus Ona

Bo Ally Farhart

Jiana Farhart

Morris Osman

Salem Caled Juma

What is interesting above is that this is the third mention of Rasmus Ona and Mohamid Allie Gossum. From other records we know they had both filled out petitions for citizenship, initially on May 23, 1913, and again on October 17, 1913. Apparently the first petitions were not accepted. Clearly there was nothing automatic about the citizenship acquisition. Often the "paperwork" was rechecked and sometimes the official verdict was "denied."[2]

The complete list of North Dakota's early-day "first papers" and "second papers" applicants is available today, thanks to the State Historical Society of North Dakota (see the Appendix). Even a casual look at the naturalization records will show that some courts at certain locations had an unexpectedly large number of Syrians who submitted their various "papers." Understandably such towns as Rugby, Williston, and Stanley appear, for these were central to large "Syrian" rural enclaves. So also Bismarck and Minot, which were major railroad dispersal points.

One curious court in Ashley, North Dakota, was the District Court for a region that included McIntosh County. Scattered "Syrian-born" home-steaders were in the area, but no large contiguous settlement was present. The Ashley court's records deserve a particularly close look. The results will be indicative of other portions of the state and will show, perhaps, some of the "behind-the-scene" factors that occasionally arose, not just in terms of Syrians but of other national groups as they sought citizenship status.

McIntosh County can be characterized as the "private preserve" of John Wishek, a local banker, a land promoter, a political force, and the namesake of the area's largest city: Wishek, North Dakota. John Wishek, who took land himself under the Homestead provisions at the early date of 1884, is remembered today as the great patron of the Germans from Russia. These pioneer people flooded the region after leaving (actually fleeing) their century-old villages in the Ukraine. In McIntosh County and its environs they found an American steppe which resembled their wheat-country steppe in the Old World.

The entire procedure by which a newcomer became a citizen in North Dakota and the rest of America was a fairly simple thing (at least during the turn-of-the-century decades). The process actually began when the new arrival disembarked from a ship at a seaport or stepped off a Canadian railroad. If the immigrant came legally, the name would be on the ship's manifest and proof could thereby be established concerning the arrival circumstances. By 1906, an official document, a "certificate of arrival," was given the new-comer. This provided the name of the vessel, the exact date and the port of entry and the name the immigrant used on the ship. The certificate was to be presented to the "court of record" at the time of the filing of their first papers (the intent to acquire citizenship). [3]

A certain amount of not-so-legal activity occasionally took place. Some Syrians, as mentioned before, came over the Mexican border wearing sombreros and were considered Hispanic in origin. Some came through the Canadian border on foot or by way of backwoods roads. As will be noted later in this chapter, some certificates of arrival must have been passed along to illegal immigrants, for naturalization records in North Dakota show the same person applying for first papers on two or three separate occasions.

No. *383*

188

ORIGINAL

UNITED STATES OF AMERICA

Department of Commerce and Labor
BUREAU OF IMMIGRATION AND NATURALIZATION
DIVISION OF NATURALIZATION

DECLARATION OF INTENTION
(Invalid for all purposes seven years after the date hereof)

State of North Dakota
County of McIntosh } ss:
In the *District* Court
of *Third Judicial District*

3. *Side Howard* , aged *41* years,

occupation *Pool Hall Manager* , do declare on oath that my personal
affirm
description is: Color *White* , complexion *Dark* , height *5* feet *7* inches,

weight *165* pounds, color of hair *Black* , color of eyes *Brown*

other visible distinctive marks *none*

; I was born in *Betronia, Asyrkay*

, on the *1st* day of *June* , anno

Domini 1 *879* ; I now reside at *Ashley, North Dakota*

I emigrated to the United States of America from *Marseilles, France*

on the vessel *Do not know the name* ; my last
[If the alien arrived otherwise than by vessel, the character of conveyance or name of transportation company should be given.]

foreign residence was *Betronia, Turkey; I am married; the name of*
my wife is Christina; she was born in Russia, and now resides at Ashley, North Dakota.
It is my bona fide intention to renounce forever all allegiance and fidelity to any foreign

prince, potentate, state, or sovereignty, and particularly to *Mohammed VI*

Sultan of Turkey , of which I am now a citizen ; I
subject

arrived at the port of *New York* , in the
State
Territory of *New York* on or about the *15th* day
District

of *July* , anno Domini 1 *905* ; I am not an anarchist; I am not a

polygamist nor a believer in the practice of polygamy; and it is my intention in good faith

to become a citizen of the United States of America and to permanently reside therein:

SO HELP ME GOD. *Witness to mark*
Otto F. King
John Stabler
his
Side ✕ Howard
mark
(Original signature of declarant.)

Subscribed and sworn to before me this *9th*
affirmed

[SEAL.] day of *February* , anno Domini 19 *22*

H D Piper

Clerk of the *District* Court.

By , Clerk.

11—2626

First Papers;
Naturalization
Process: Side
Howard, at Ashley,
ND, born in
Betronia, Asyrlay

Courtesy:
Minot Daily News

The "first paper" process was not complicated. The applicant appeared before the court and indicated his or her intent to acquire citizenship on an official form (usually with the aid of a clerk). Recorded thereon was the name, place of birth and country of origin, date and place of arrival in the United States. The concluding statement, under oath, said that the individual intended to become a citizen and "renounced forever all allegiance and fidelity" to the current ruler of his or her former country. The oath included a promise to "support the Constitution and the government of the United States." A signature or a witnessed personal "mark" concluded the document. (Not surprisingly a "mark" appears on the forms completed by many North Dakota Lebanese applicants, for writing a name in English script was not yet part of their American experience.) This constituted the "first papers," the "intent" papers. After five years, the applicant, any place in America, could apply for the actual acquisition of citizenship, the so-called "second papers."

The calendar of the District Court in Ashley, McIntosh County, was busy with citizenship matters in the first two decades of the 20th Century. Printed below is a sample from portions of the years 1903 to 1905. The following men, all born in Syria, appeared in the Ashley court on the various dates to make known their declaration of intent to become a United States citizen. In every case they solemnly swore that they would "renounce forever" the "Sultan of Turkey."

March 10, 1903	Mickal Cadry, arrived in New York, November 1897
March 30, 1903	Sahid Cadry, arrived in New York, June 1901
April 4, 1903	Assaf Haggar, arrived in New York, July 1897
April 4, 1903	Joseph Haggar, arrived in New York, July 1899
April 4, 1903	Albert Haggar, arrived in New York, April 1897?
April 27, 1903	Abraham Albert, arrived in New York, November 1901
April 27, 1903	Albert Sakeen, arrived in New York, November 1901
May 29, 1903	Sam Haggar, arrived in New York, September 1899
September 7, 1903	Salamon Haggar, arrived in Detroit, January 1901
December 17, 1903	Alex Hash, arrived in Detroit, January 1901
January 16, 1904	Albert Salamon, arrived in New York, December 1901
May 6, 1904	Albert Bumrad, arrived in New York, January 1902
May 16, 1904	Albert Jones, arrived in Detroit, July 1901
June 10, 1904	Alex Hamway, arrived in Detroit, June 1901
July 15, 1904	Ally Seioin, arrived in Detroit, December 1901
July 15, 1904	John Joe, arrived in New York, December 1903

July 16, 1904	Ali Albert, arrived in New York, July 1899
July 18, 1904	Alli Katry, arrived in New York, December 1898
July 18, 1904	Mike Calid, arrived in New York, December 1898
July 18, 1904	Sam Wase, arrived in New York, December 1898
July 21, 1904	Frank Johnson (born Syria), arrived in New York, November 1901
July 21, 1904	Ule George, arrived in New York, November 1901
July 23, 1904	Albert Junio, arrived in New York, December 1902
August 29, 1904	Joe Assat, arrived in New York, June 1904
October 31, 1904	Albert Alec, arrived in New York, December 1902
November 2, 1904	Sahid Abraham, arrived in New York, November 1898
November 2, 1904	Salma Abraham, arrived in New York, April 1902
November 2, 1904	Mohamad Hammad, arrived in New York, October 1898
December 21, 1904	Frank Kacem, arrived in New York, July 1898
December 21, 1904	Albert Kacem, arrived port of Pembina, ND, December 1901
January 7, 1905	Sam Bahy, arrived in New York, July 1889
January 10, 1905	Albert A. B. Hassen, arrived in New York, February 1899
January 13, 1905	Joe Saly, arrived port of St. Vincent (Minn.), August 1901
January 16, 1905	Monstaf Osman, arrived in Boston, October 19, 1903
January 21, 1905	Albert Abraham, arrived in New York, September 1900
January 27, 1905	Sahil Hamray, arrived in New York, July 19, 1903
February 4, 1905	Albert Hatch, arrived in New York, July 1901
February 11, 1905	Elli Halt, arrived in New York, December 1901
February 11, 1905	Ed Zear, arrived in New York, December 1901
May 3, 1905	Joseph Siamn, arrived in Quebeck (sic), December 1902
May 15, 1905	Sam Hatch, arrived in New York, month (?) 1900
February 9, 1906	George Alleck, arrived in New York, July 1901

The above names and accompanying information, all from a relatively short time period, reveal something of "what was going on in McIntosh County." (1) Both Christians and Muslims were applying in the same time period. (Names like Mohamed are mixed with Joseph and John.) (2) All the McIntosh names were male. (3) The three-year time period, the busiest in the court's history, coincides with the years when that south-central part of the state was "opening up" for settlement. The desire for land therefore must have influenced at least some of the applications. (4) Syrians who came to North Dakota included some new arrivals. (Joe Assat arrived in New York in June 1904 and by August was filing his "intent" in McIntosh County.) But "old-timers" were also appearing on the Dakota frontier; many arrived in 1898 and 1899. (Assaf Haggar came via New York. He arrived in 1897.) This means that many had experienced the temper and mood of the New World and ultimately decided to try their hand in the newly developing prairie world.

The question of "why McIntosh" comes up. This county was truly in the hinterlands, located on a branch line of the Soo Railroad far from major Syrian settlements and far from the rapidly expanding Dakota commercial centers.

Could the presence of the wheeler-dealer John Wishek have made the difference? John Wishek is recognized as a promoter who had few peers in his day. How many favors did he dispense? How many corners did he cut as he brought people into his part of the state? Indeed, the name John Wishek or the name of his associates can be found frequently as a witness on many "Syria" citizenship applications. How many seaport "arrival papers" were overlooked or considered in perfunctory fashion? Did the word go out, via the "peddler grapevine" or through letters that Wishek could, with a certain ease, guide the newcomer through the pathways of official red tape?

As an aside, it might be noted that Ashley and the nearby town of Wishek were centers of a surprisingly large eastern European Jewish homestead development. (At one time there were synagogues in both towns.) Was John Wishek a "friend" also of Jewish immigrants?

John Wishek was not the only "patron" in the state who gave special assistance to "Syrian-born" immigrants. In 1940 the *Bismarck Tribune* printed an extensive report of an Attiyeh convention held in that city. Four hundred members of the Attiyeh clan met from July 13 to 15. The Bismarck host families were primarily first- or second-generation descendants of homesteaders who took land near McClusky in what was called McLean County and is now Sheridan County. A featured part of the convention was a salute to North Dakota's then current Chief Justice, W. L. Nuessle. The *Tribune* reported:

It was Justice Nuessle, who as a young state's attorney of McLean County, helped members of the Attiyeh family, fresh from their native Syria, to obtain homesteads and prove up on the same.[4]

There were 23 young Syrians in that first party of homesteaders, 21 of them being descendants of Attiyeh, the other two family friends. They all settled near Denhoff, and they recall that Justice Nuessle would often drive in his horse and buggy from Washburn to help them in their struggles to get a start in the new world.

The young attorney, W. L. Nuessle—himself a 1913 Sheridan County homesteader— was a patron, a friend of Syrians, a person who knew the intricacies of American law. Most likely the word went out that Sheridan County was a favorable location for new settlers. Attorney Nuessle was not in the self-promoting business. There is no evidence that he wrongfully "cut corners." Those who knew him at the time said he was merely a conscientious citizen with a concern for people with special needs. But there's no doubt that he too shared in the "boom" and promotion mood of his era. Lebanese were a new and hard-working group of immigrants who deserved to become a permanent part of the relatively new State of North Dakota. Lebanese of Sheridan County background even today remember Justice Nuessle as "our patriarch."

It may well be that other parts of the state had leaders like John Wishek and W. L. Nuessle who gained a reputation for looking kindly on Syrian immigrants. If such were the case, the Lebanese information "network" would spread the word and newcomers would look to the Dakota prairies for a possible home.

The patronage of key individuals was a factor in bringing newcomers to the state, but of even more significance was the development of an initial cluster of permanent settlers. Every study of American immigration indicates that the shock of entering the New World was so intense that the newcomer, whether in the city or in the countryside, would seek the relative security of settling with others of their national backgrounds. An initial collection of Syrians took land near Ross, North Dakota. Others then came. So also Pierce County and Williams County. Something of the same took place in John Wishek's McIntosh County. Mike Abdallah, a Muslim who later moved to Ross, said this in a 1939 interview: "I was assisted to my first American residence by other Syrians living in that community, and an opportunity to make a living. That was at Ashley, ND [McIntosh County]. Hassyn Murray and Frank Osman lived there in a Russian settlement."

McIntosh County, as noted earlier in this volume, never saw a permanent Lebanese enclave develop. It was a temporary place of residence.

Federal land records do indeed indicate that nine Syrian-born individuals filed for land in Township T131-R69, ten filed in township T130-R67 and at least ten other Syrians were elsewhere in McIntosh County, but seldom were their land claims immediately adjacent to each other. No compact and permanent enclave ever developed. The land records also show that few spent the full five years in residence. Most commuted (approximately one-and-one-half or two years) and then purchased their land. Many actually gave up—"relinquished" is the official term.

That McIntosh County was a "temporary" stop in the Syrian-born immigrant's search for a permanent American home can be seen through a close look at the Naturalization Record Index at the State Historical Society of North Dakota at Bismarck. (See Appendix, this volume) Seventy-five "Syrians" filed either their first or second papers at Ashley in McIntosh County. And for the most part these were first paper applications, the prelude to homesteading. The individuals did not stay long for only 17 percent of that total were applying for their final citizenship status (or second papers). In Williams County, 140 filed either first or second papers. Second paper applications accounted for twenty-six percent of that number. Pierce County had 155 applications, of which 34 percent were seeking final citizenship. In contrast, Mountrail County, the Muslim Ross community, lists only 50 applicants, yet 60 percent of these individuals were seeking their ultimate citizenship status.[5]

The proportions of final applications for citizenship as seen above show that McIntosh County was just a "first step" toward something better in America; no one seems to have stayed. In Pierce and Williams counties, most first applicants moved away. Yet some (thirty-four percent) did stay, at least for a while. In contrast, the Muslims in the Ross-Mountrail area seemed to like North Dakota for sixty percent sought full citizenship while in the Ross community; the broader horizons of America were not as attractive. In the first decades Muslims of Ross were more willing to "tough it out" on the prairies.

The first paper, the declaration of intent, came out in a revised form in June 1906. Subsequently, not only date and port of entry were required, but the conveyance (steamship or railroad) used at the time of arrival was to be indicated. Not just the place of birth was to be listed, but also the port from which the vessel left for its immediate trip to America (e.g., Marseilles, Bremen, Liverpool). Also required was the "last foreign residence," the town in their former homeland.

A physical description was entered into the "intention" document: color, complexion, height, weight, color of hair and eyes and distinctive marks. Of particular interest in this description paragraph was the fact that in North Dakota Syrians were universally identified as of "white" color and "dark" complexion. (The adjective "Oriental" never occurs.) The phrase "distinctive marks" is also of interest. One of the first chapters in this book quotes a New York reporter who observed that tattoos were frequent among Syrian newcomers. A perusal of declaration forms filed in North Dakota shows such things to be infrequent. On rare occasions one finds the following: one man had "three tattoo marks on each temple." Two intent forms said "tattoo marks on back of left hand," two noted the presence of a "cross on right arm." One said, "tattoo on both right and left temple." (Bishop Nicholas Samra, Melkite archivist, notes that a cross, a tatoo and date on the hand or arm could signify a visit to Jerusalem, a "Hajj.")[6] Seen in perspective, it seems the tattoo marks were probably no more frequent among Syrians than most other national groups.

The "last foreign residence" line provides an array of names which reflected the shifting and often-confused national categories in which the Dakota Lebanese immigrants found themselves. They include: Beirut Turkey, Beirut Syria, Damascus Syria, Constantinople Turkey, Zahle Assyria, Byrouth Syria.

The rejection of a "foreign prince or potentate" statement also gave rise to a variety of answers: the "Emperor of the Ottomans," the "King of Turkey," the "Sultan of Syria" and most often the "Sultan of Turkey." The "potentate's" name was usually correct. Most in North Dakota mentioned Mohammed V and sometimes Abdul Hamid II.

The Declarations of Intent after September 1906 contained an additional sentence. "I am not an anarchist; I am not a polygamist nor a believer in the practice of polygamy." Why were such phrases inserted? Were the American officials responding to stereotypical but current reports that southern and eastern Europe was a hot bed of wild-eyed anti-government zealots? Was the polygamy phrase added because of an influx of Muslims? It seems unlikely, for Arab country immigrants were minimal in contrast to the millions who were arriving from northern and western Europe. Were there overtones of the Mormon experience in the early American west or from a wave of Mormon immigration from Europe?

The revised 1906 "intent" paper required the applicant to list his or her "occupation." A variety of terms appear in the North Dakota Lebanese declarations such as "salesman," "cook," "laborer," "farmer," and "peddler." The latter three were the most frequent in North Dakota.

The second papers, the actual petition for naturalization, understandably demanded more information. Once again the renunciation of the foreign prince, potentate or state were required. So also the rejection of polygamy. The anarchy issue was spelled out in more descriptive language. The petition of 1908, for example, says this: "I am not a disbeliever in or opposed to organized government or a member of or affiliated with any organization or body of persons teaching disbelief in organized government."

The second papers contained this statement. "I am able to speak the English language" and "I have resided continually in the United States of America for a term of five years at least immediately preceding the date of this petition." If married, the applicant listed the name of his or her spouse, the spouse's place of residence. Included also was the name, date and place of birth and place of residence of each child.

Two witnesses were required. These individuals indicated under oath that they were American citizens and personally knew the petitioners. They swore that the person had lived in the United States for at least the five previous years. They testified that the applicant was "of good moral character, attached to the principles of the constitution" and "the petitioner is in every way qualified" for citizenship.

In McIntosh County, the witnesses for Syrians seem very often to be merchants, lawyers, or bankers. The names included "John Wishek, banker"; "Thomas Johnstone, postmaster"; Albert Jones, merchant." Perhaps it was that way elsewhere in North Dakota. The new immigrant, surrounded by his or her neighbors who were of alien status, would have their most frequent contacts with "Americans" who were in the professional categories: merchants, lawyers, bankers, postmasters.

It was these very individuals who were the town promoters, the "boomers," of early-day North Dakota. It would be only natural for members of this gentry class to help the newcomers, and sometimes, perhaps, to be "overeager" in assisting them on the road to permanent citizenship. Of no small significance is the fact that the clerks received a fee for each set of naturalization papers filed in their court.

It is known that in some of America's eastern cities, the acquisition of citizenship papers was done illegally as a voter registration device for corrupt politicians. There were instances in which the five-year wait was overlooked—sometimes even without first papers—and the court precipitously validated the "second papers." Within days the grateful batch of new citizens voted according to the dictates of a particular political party.[7]

In their review of North Dakota Syrian naturalization records the authors have found no clear-cut examples of such illegalities. (Nor do historical accounts report such things.) Nonetheless, here and there hints of what might be called "laxity" among court officials do occur. In McIntosh a number of rather vague arrival vessels are listed: French Line, Fiber Line, or "do not know." It's obvious that certificates of arrival were not required of every applicant. In fact there exists, amid the naturalization papers, official letters (from the US Department of Labor's

Examiners Office in St. Paul) calling the court's attention to discrepancies as to certain dates and locations indicated on the various forms. Indeed, a number of second paper petitions are labeled with the phrase "denied."

Yet North Dakota court officials, in their eagerness to bring settlement to their respective counties, certainly allowed the entry of many "hazy" and unverifiable dates, locations and other data. The whole matter of the individual's actual name must have been the occasion of the utmost confusion. The petitioners usually were unlettered in English and wrote in Arabic. WPA interviewee, Sam Omar of Ross, said, "My surname is not Sam, but Husein, but as I could not spell well when I came to this country, I took the name Sam." Allay Omar of Ross told the WPA, "upon my entrance into the United States, I was unable to spell my name, so someone took the liberty of writing it for me and misspelled my surname." For example, where do McIntosh County "first-paper" names (found earlier in this chapter) come from, names such as Frank Johnson, "born in Syria" and John Joe, "born in Syria"? The Kallod family in Fargo today jokes about the fact that their grandfather (Ibrahim Sheban) took "Kallod" because he saw it as a label on a wagon and thought it would be appropriate.

Date of birth could be equally perplexing. As seen in earlier chapters, many Syrian men did not know their actual age because their families concealed their age out of fear of the Turkish draft.

Compounding the confusion was the matter of the "arrival paper," the official form that the immigrant received as he or she left the boat or crossed the border. This document indicated the date of arrival, port or place of arrival, name of the vessel, and departure location. There's no doubt that some newcomers to the United States crossed the borders illegally. And it is clear from published accounts concerning immigration elsewhere in America that "arrival papers" were passed around, thus enabling the "illegal" immigrant to apply for naturalization under an assumed name. The lists of "first paper" applicants now on file in North Dakota does, in fact, contain a number of instances in which the same person filed his first paper two and even three times in separate county courts. There could be several explanations for this, but it is possible that even in North Dakota arrival papers were "passed around."

When the WPA interviewer, in 1939, approached one of North Dakota's "Syrian" early settlers he refused to answer any questions whatsoever. The notes on the interview form are as follows:

Note: This subject is very difficult to interview. His attitude indicates fear of giving information about himself, but what the cause of that fear is, I am unable to say. He absolutely refused to answer any questions. At first he was going to tell me something about the customs and usages in his home country, but upon me producing the questionnaire, he glanced at the first page and read one or two of the questions, and absolutely closed up, and refused to say anything in answer to any questions I asked him.

The inexactness noted by the present authors in the review of historical records presented here and there in this volume mirrors the problems that faced researchers elsewhere in America. Alixa Naff says in her *Becoming American: The Early Arab Immigrant Experience*:

Syrian craftsmen, for example, were told to say they were farmers on the assumption that America preferred immigrants with a farming background. Furthermore, true ages were exaggerated or lowered and single women entered as married or divorced. Untold numbers, as has been noted, slipped undetected across Canadian and Mexican borders for decades. Sometimes they entered as immigrants from these countries; frequently they smuggled friends and relatives with them. Many of those who were mistakenly left in Australia, South America, and the Caribbean later entered the United States listed on ships' manifests as immigrants from those regions. And, how many entered on relatives' passports and naturalization papers is another question mark.[8]

The above paragraphs are not an indictment of Lebanese as such. These "happenings" were taking place throughout America and were present in one way or another among every national group. In fact, looking through the various records it is safe to say that in North Dakota there was probably a minimum of outright fraud in the filling out of the various petitions, but there must have been a lot of "don't ask too many questions."

By 1918 probably two-thirds of the Syrian-born North Dakota settlers who wished citizenship had filed at least their first papers, and very often their second. It was at this time that a law was passed which speeded up (and perhaps simplified) the naturalization process for aliens who were members of the Armed Forces. Some North Dakota residents took advantage of this "short cut" to citizenship. Joseph Munyer when interviewed at Williston in 1940 said this:

I was drafted in the army and went overseas. I had my first citizen papers before I was drafted and got my final citizenship papers at Camp Dodge, Iowa. I served in the war until June 15th, 1919, just lacked ten days of being a year.

Kassam Ramadan, of Muslim background, after homesteading in Montana, joined the Army in 1917, and served in France. In a 1939 interview at his farm home near Lignite, ND, he said: "I was honorably discharged in 1919 and given my citizenship papers." (In the same interview he proudly remarked that he still received his American Legion

Magazine.)

One episode in the story of North Dakota Syrians and their quest for citizenship must be mentioned. (It is dealt with briefly in the discussion of prejudice in Chapter 14.) There occurred in 1909 a series of events that caused consternation to many Syrian-born individuals who might seek naturalization. Officials in several states declared that Syrians were not Europeans but were, in fact, "Asiatic," (or at least were not in the "free white" category) and therefore were prohibited under the various limitation statutes from becoming citizens. The U.S. Department of Commerce and Labor accordingly advised its various agencies to refuse any further request from Arabic peoples. For many men and women who had already filed their first papers, this meant they would have no chance of fulfilling their dream of becoming a full-fledged American and for many, the acquisition of their homesteaded land claim would be forfeit.

Such legal action against North Dakota's Syrian-born settlers was no trifling matter. They were much aware of the fact that only a few miles west of the Ross community, over thirty Japanese had summarily been struck from the Federal Land Office records on that very "Oriental" score. The Syrians probably knew also that in Minnesota a lawsuit had reached the court which claimed that Finlanders were "oriental" and thus could not become citizens.

The Finlanders were ultimately vindicated. The Japanese were refused any redress. But luckily the Syrian status was clarified. The "Asiatic" claim was discarded by legal action in several American courts and the Department of Commerce and Labor reversed its decision. E. S. Oderkirk, writing for the Federal Writers Project summarizing interviews with early North Dakota Lebanese reported on October 24, 1936: "In 1909, the United States government withdrew its objection to their naturalization and as a result the majority of the people are citizens of this country."

The 1936 Oderkirk statement was correct. The U.S. Census of 1920 corroborates this observation. Of the 289 men and women of Syrian birth in the state, 195 were citizens and 28 others had filed first papers. Those Lebanese who wished to return to their homeland had already done so. The remaining group was committed to staying in their New World. They had been pioneers in their parts of the state. They had earned a permanent place in their state's history.

What's in a Name?

Joe Hay of "Syria," took first papers in Williams County, 1909.

Edward Vangstad of "Arabia," first papers in Ward County, 1902.

Frank Johnson of "Syria," first papers in McIntosh County, 1904.

Lillie Rory of "Syria," first papers in McIntosh County, 1907.

Asad Experience Wilson, inducted into the Army at Stanley, 1918.

Mohomed Ali of "Turkey," second papers in Grand Forks County, 1927.

Mary Forsley of "Turkey," first papers in Pierce County, 1902.

Albert Jones of "Syria," first papers in McIntosh County, 1904.

Lizzie May of "Turkey," first papers in Foster County, 1898.

Mohamrad B. O'Sine of "Turkey," first papers in Towner County, 1913.

Joe Hiawatha of "Syria," first papers in McIntosh County, 1905.

Albert Birs of "Syria," first papers in Sargeant County, 1927.

The Annual "Picnic"

Ann Hach vividly recalled the almost yearly Arabic gatherings at Roosevelt Park in Devils Lake. While the picnic's origins were in Bisbee, ND, it gradually grew to over 100 people. Ann, along with Kay Harris and several other women, would bake as many as 300 loaves of Syrian flatbread. They would prepare grains, spices, oils, and lamb to make kibbi. The result of this massive labor of love was what Ann's husband, Amid, called "something to die for." Whole families would come from across the Upper Midwest to eat, dance, and socialize. The Lebanese women of towns like Wales, Rolla, Binford, Glenfield, Michigan, Ross, Belcourt, Edmore, Dunseith, and Williston would offer their additional cooking specialties to the throng.

Both Muslim and Christian Lebanese would partake in this unique celebration. Names like Abdallah, Abraham, Ausey, Alley, Albert, Eli, Freije, Gader, Harris, Hasen, Jaha, Juma, and Nicholas were on the roster. Ann Hach said it was "good medicine for all." Looking back at those events, Don Nicholas of Harwood says that as a young person he was astounded for it seemed like half the Middle East came to North Dakota for a picnic. The last picnic was held in the early 1980s.

Lebanese "picnic" at Roosevelt Park in Devils Lake, 1967.
Courtesy: Lori Nicholas Kennedy.

CHAPTER SIXTEEN

Cohesion: Strengths and Weakness

Since settlement times, Lebanese have been almost an invisible group in North Dakota. This was understandable, perhaps, in the earliest decades for the state was after all a swirl of new arrivals from several dozen foreign cultures. The Lebanese presence was highlighted in a limited way for the farm family who was visited by the "very foreign-looking peddler" and certainly the neighbors who lived near the various rural "Syrian" farm clusters were aware of the Arabic people who lived in their midst.

An Invisible People

This seemingly "invisible" condition can be partly explained by the fact that the numbers of Syrians in the state have been small. Yet Syrians were not the smallest of North Dakota's groups. Their numbers probably equaled that of the Finns in the state, and Finlanders were not an unknown group. It can be argued that Syrian totals equaled, and even exceeded, that of the Jews. And certainly the Jewish presence was well known.

Clearly, certain factors were at work making the Lebanese an overlooked group. And in this regard the mere location of their settlements would cause them to be ignored by history and the media. With the exception of the dozen families who settled in Shepherd township in Walsh County, the Syrian immigrant clusters were located outside of the Red River Valley, and at least until recently, the "Valley" has set the tone for the rest of the state. It's the Red River Valley that supplied the preponderance of leadership in terms of academic interests and the direction of public concerns. It is unfortunate, but it's true, that Syrians were out in the "West," the hinterlands.

Lebanese were, at least initially, rural people, living on homesteads or in smaller towns: Ashley, Rugby, Hettinger, Bisbee, and Williston. Rural people are not headline people. Furthermore, Lebanese were quiet people; not the type that would often appear in any news headline kind of activities. Certainly the more newsworthy political type of activity was not a Lebanese trademark. Coming from Old Country villages which had been subject to a bewildering number of national jurisdictions — Ottoman, Turkish, French, Syrian — involvement in extra-village politics was unthinkable. In this they resembled North Dakota's Germans from Russia. Though sizable in numbers, this particular group of Germans avoided any sort of political limelight. They had been "islands" in a Russian empire that threatened to swallow up any aspiring political ambitions.

But the invisibility of Arabic people may also have been a matter of choice. Maybe they sensed they were "from the other side of the tracks" culturally. Speaking and writing in a language that had no parallels amid the European languages that were current in early Dakota, the Lebanese perhaps preferred to keep a low profile. Added to the language problem was the popular stereotype of the "Arab": swarthy, unfathomable, with veils and camels in their background. The public perception was far from complimentary. To be highly visible, and yet too obviously foreign, could invite animosity. Frontier physical conditions were difficult enough without adding the burden of social "troubles."

The Lebanese in North Dakota had, therefore, a number of strikes against them. Certainly they would have to overcome these considerable obstacles if they were to survive as a recognizable and accepted group. But every one of America's ethnic groups had difficulty preserving their national heritage after two or three generations of American life. They were surrounded by other nationalities and submerged in a basically Anglo-American world. They were beset by a myriad of forces that demanded their allegiance: standardized American schools, an omnipresent media, captivating recreational forces, and necessary economic, political and legal forms. Indeed few groups have managed to stay "visible" for long.

Power in the Community

Some American minorities have seen the emergence of a strong spokesman, a power figure, who galvanizes the community and represents to the larger world the uniqueness and potential strength of their special group. These figures may flourish on a regional or even national scale. For the Lebanese there was no Martin Luther King, nor Ceasar Chavez. There was no Mayor Daley, Ignatius Donnelly, or Governor Floyd B. Olson who would raise the group from their "invisible" status.

"Of all the immigrant races, the Syrians seem to be most jealous of those of their number who aspire to leadership and are consequently the most leaderless." So writes Philip K. Hitti, author of the 1924 pioneer study entitled *The Syrians in America*. Hitti, educated at the American University of Beirut, spent much of his life as a scholar at New York's Columbia University. He continues, perhaps a bit unfairly, "leaderless in many ways, yet deluged with petty and self-made leaders, the Syrian in this country presents a lamentable sight."[1]

Hitti writes that in the initial moments after the arrival in the United States, some leaders assumed their position on the basis of Old Country status; "blood superiority," he called it. This was particularly true of the Druze and Muslim communities. Hitti implies that with the dispersal to far-flung parts of the nation and with the passage of time, such traditional authority patterns dissipated.[2]

Mitigating against a "Syrian leader" was the fact that most people from Lebanon did not see themselves as "Syrian," rather they were Muslims, Maronites, Melkites or Orthodox. In addition, they had been citizens of separate communities in the Old World; nationalism in those early days was a European phenomenon. Accordingly, even though they sometimes lived adjacent to each other in a city, they were the traditionally "individualists."[3]

But was Philip Hitti entirely correct in diagnosing the Syrian-American community as being lamentably leaderless? Certainly the mobile peddler conditions were not amenable to any sort of centralized power. Yet some sort of internal influence must have been present. The suppliers, for instance, had power and financial means. They could dictate both the credit limits and, to some extent, the trade territories. Dwelling in the stable Syrian enclaves of the larger cities, they certainly had some control of the lives of others, at least the newcomers.

But, after all this has been said, it would be surprising if key figures did not emerge in the local Syrian communities, leaders who were more or less comfortable with the officials in "City Hall," with the police department and other leading non-Syrian figures.

Such a leader is implied in a Department of Justice report concerning a rather large town in Iowa. Irregularities occurred in naturalization papers. The document alleges that, at times, when a naturalized Syrian died, his papers were returned to the "King" of the colony who then sent them back to the Old Country. These papers allowed another Syrian to illegally come to the U.S.[4] Whether the charge was true is not clear, but the reference to a "King" is highly plausible.

Many national groups had a "King" man. (In North Dakota such a personage was found among early Greeks, African-Americans, and

German-Russians, to name only a few.) This gentleman emerged as an unofficial liaison between members of the ethnic community and the police, the civic government, and court officials. When an issue arose which was beyond the ability of the new immigrant to comprehend, the "King" would contact the "right people." In some cultures the "King" had the task of "running out of town" individuals who were of unsavory character. In return the "King" received special favors. His task sometimes was "to turn out the vote" at election times.

North Dakota had its unofficial Syrian "kings." Mr. Harris in the Turtle Mountains was known to have had political "contacts" with government officials. Sometimes he interceded in naturalization processes. Mr. Harris was a veteran and his wife was prominent in American Legion circles. David Kalil of Williston, a very early homesteader and owner of a grocery store, often was a go-between in issues that involved civil authorities and delinquent debts among local Syrians. One elderly non-Lebanese lawyer said, "If there ever was trouble with a Syrian, I would go to Dave Kalil. He would straighten it out."[5] Others of Williston background describe Charles Owan as a key figure in some Lebanese-oriented community issues. Nicholas Ausey was a kind of titular head of "Syrians" in the early Cando-Turtle Mountain days. When one Syrian died as a result of a fight with a fellow countryman, Mr. Ausey served as court translator. The perpetrator got off without a sentence. Attas Boutrous of Bismarck was revered among Lebanese because he knew prominent state government leaders and could be of assistance when there was a need.

A *Gackle Republican* newspaper account of February 18, 1910 (quoting the *Jamestown Sun*), specifically mentions a "King" among local Syrians. Several of the news paragraphs are of interest:

> *The Pecular [sic] Marriage Custom Brok [sic] Out in a Row Among the Syrians Residents*

> *Young Steve Adams, son of Joe Adams, one of the Syrian residents of this county, was taken in charge by the sheriffs, Thursday and afterwards released by the states attorney, there being insufficient grounds to hold him on the charge of assault and battery upon his wife …*

> *The parties were released by the states attorney after paying the costs of the proceeding and seven of them left for Council Bluffs and Omaha, for a trip among them the wife of Steve Adams and her father, the King. It is not known whether they expect to remain or not.*[6]

Cultural Maintenance

We know from the consideration of other ethnic experiences that other conditions, if present, can assist a group as it struggles to maintain a sense of national allegiance. One is certainly the size of the national enclave. On this score the Lebanese Christians in the Williston area were numerous enough to reinforce each other for a generation, perhaps two, if they had the will. The same is true of the Muslim settlement near Ross. Such a continuance of tradition for any great length of time would be difficult, but it could be possible because, unlike their counterparts in congested urban circumstances, the Dakota Syrian enclaves were isolated by the geographical prairie distances. German-Russians and Norwegians in the state had settlement areas that often stretched over 40 and 50 miles of territory. They could and, in fact, did, maintain their ethnic integrity. The Williston and Ross Lebanese areas were perhaps ten miles in width. Being that close to the non-Lebanese neighbors inevitably brought problems: schools of mixed nationalities, inter-group marriages, mixed political and social groups. Nonetheless, they, too, maintained some sense of solidarity.

Helpful also in promoting ethnic adhesion was prior experience as a minority group. Jewish settlers certainly could draw from the struggles and the grandeur of their past difficulties. Likewise, North Dakota's Germans from Russia had lived, previous to America, for a century as a minority in a sometimes-hostile Russian environment. German-Russians had a language, a religious stance, an attitude toward marital choice, parental control and a work ethnic that was geared toward defense against outside forces. In contrast, Lebanese came to America from a land in which everyone was of a basically similar Arabic culture. To survive as a minority in their new country demanded the development, almost immediately, of maintenance procedures. If they failed, the next generations would be swallowed up in the mainstream American world.

Of great advantage in carrying forward an ethnic tradition was a continued contact with the Old Country, a taproot to the parent culture. The vibrancy of the present-day Great Plains Mexican-American populations, with their roots below the Rio Grande, is a classic example. Norwegians in North Dakota never lost their lines of communication to Norway. Nostalgic second- and third-generation descendants were (and still are) crossing the Atlantic for home country visits. In addition, new immigrants from Norway continued to arrive in the state into the 1930s. A Norwegian brogue can still be heard on the streets of many North Dakota hamlets and towns.

Apart from a trip to a native village in search of a wife, Lebanese in North Dakota have witnessed comparatively few nostalgic visits back to the homeland. The "late" Syrian-Lebanese migrations (since 1960) have focused on the East Coast or at least on America's larger cities. With the exception of those in professional positions—graduate students, professors, and physicians—few recent Middle East people have come to North Dakota. And often these "professionals" move within a few years to more amenable locales.

A common religious affiliation was everywhere of enormous help in the continuance of a national tradition. In fact, some argue that without religious bonds any culture will rapidly dissipate. And in North Dakota, Polish communities had their Polish Catholic parishes; Norwegians had the Lutheran churches, so also the Finns, the Danes, the Ukrainians, and a dozen others. Churches were rallying points for every group. Unfortunately, as this volume amply demonstrates, Lebanese were religiously fragmented: Muslim, Orthodox, Melkite, Maronite. Yet, when Melkite priest Father Roemie arrived in Rugby or Williston on one of his occasional visits, a gathering of all Syrian Christian groups took place. The same was true when the Orthodox Archbishop came to Pierce County in 1914. So even a divided religious situation could still have its moments of unity.

Helpful also to cultural survival were nationality-oriented societies. From their earliest days in America the Norwegians had the Sons of Norway, Czechs and Finns had their various lodges, Irish had the Ancient Order of Hibernians. Lebanese never did have a formal pan-Syrian organization. The Attiyeh group existed for a small percentage, namely the Ain Arab people of Orthodox background. Attiyeh was somewhat effective, but no other group arose to represent the rest of the Great Plains Lebanese.

A partial explanation for the presence or absence of ethnic rallying points—organizations or public display—may be found in the degree of public acceptance that a group might have received from the rank and file Americans that surrounded them, particularly the acceptance of the Anglo Americans who controlled much of early public sentiment. Norwegians, while not particularly welcomed by the "Anglos," were nonetheless among the most favored of European immigrants. They were not WASPs but were northern European and Protestant and were at least second class WASPs. Irish, too, were accepted, at least reluctantly, for they spoke English, knew the Yankee ways, and had been in America for one or two generations before the Dakota land settlement. Germans from Russia were the last of the large groups to be admitted into the Dakota "real American" category (and this has taken place only within the past 20 or 30 years). These people arrived in massive numbers about the same time as the Lebanese, just before and after the turn of the century. They carried the stigma of being Russian ("Roosians," they were called) and also German. America fought two wars with Germany and was fearful of Bolshevism in the 1920s and 1950s. Only in the 1960s did the German-Russians raise their heads and organize formal societies that trumpeted their unique background and their special place in Great Plains history. Lebanese, of Arabic origin, small in number, fragmented by religion and carrying a mysterious past like the German-Russians, kept a low profile. The Yankee gentry tolerated them, but certainly did nothing to enhance their status.

Many North Dakota groups had celebratory moments which captured the attention of their neighbors, invited others to participate in their special brand of "fun," and perhaps elicited some degree of admiration: St. Patrick's Day for the Irish, Syttende Mai for the Norwegians, "August the Deuce" for Icelanders. In frustration, some modern American Finns, aware of their lack of a special day, recently invented St. Urho's Day, a mythical gentleman who chased the grasshoppers out of Finland. No such a day highlights the Lebanese-American calendar (although in Quartzite, Arizona, Hadji Ali [the "Hi Jolly" of camel fame] is memorialized in an annual citywide celebration).

During the past century there occurred in North Dakota only one event in which the Lebanese presence and culture was set forward for general public appraisal. The occasion was a well-heralded display of photographs at the University of North Dakota Art Gallery, which took place for a few weeks in October 1981. Thanks to the assistance of organizations such as the Attiyeh Foundation and the Harvard Semetic Museum, the works of photographer Felix Bonfils were presented. Portrayed with a degree of excellence were scenes from Lebanon which, according to the accompanying literature, "captures the haunting remembrances of lands and customs known to the first Syrian and Lebanese immigrants to the Dakotas."

Central to the maintenance of cultural unity on the scattered Dakota prairies were the activities of a professional clergy, trained often in national seminaries and well versed in the group's traditions. Jews in North Dakota, though few in number, at one time had as many as six rabbis, located in both the west, the middle, and eastern parts of the state. German pastors served German groups, making possible services and youth instruction in the native language. The relatively few Ukrainians in the state had Ukrainian priests, services and catechisms. Norwegians had Norwegian Lutheran pastors. So also Polish, Czech, and Irish priests were in their respective ethnic congregations.

With the exception of Fr. Seraphim Roumie's half-decade stay at Rugby, no Syrian clergy were permanent in the state. All were a "circuit rider" type of clergy. Muslims without a "professional" set of clerics were at an even greater disadvantage. Charlie Juma, of Muslim background and prominent in the Ross-Stanley area, said in 1977: "We couldn't keep a 'minister.' They were family men and we couldn't support them."[7]

Compounding the Syrian-Lebanese problem of tradition continuance was the ease in which the Orthodox Syrians moved into the English-speaking Episcopal congregations. The rather gentle transfer of Maronite and Melkite Lebanese into the Latin-speaking Catholic rites also did little to enhance the survival of Syrian cultural ways. For most groups religion was a cement holding traditions in place, but among Syrians it could, at times, become a divisive force in the New World.

The lack of a permanent professional clergy presented a set of difficulties to North Dakota's Muslims, but there was another more subtle problem: the lack of literacy among the Muslim women. Mothers have traditionally been the carriers of values from one generation to the next. If the mother had limited reading skills, and this seems often to have been the case from testimony earlier in this volume, cultural traditions would have to be presented to the children orally. The prayer books and catechisms which assisted Christian mothers were seldom available in the Muslim world.

There was one way in which the Muslim faith could have been passed from one generation to the next, and that was the establishment and encouragement of procedures by which a Muslim son or daughter could meet their counterparts in another North American Muslim community. And this did happen. In the Ross community, a number of second-generation girls married Muslim men in Canada. (They remained in that country and some Ross descendants say this departure helped lead the North Dakota Ross settlement into decline.) So also, if the young person attended a large American university which contained a sizable Muslim student population, there was a good chance that an Islamic marriage would take place. This was an option used by other small religious groups in North Dakota. Mennonites enrolled their young people in Mennonite colleges. Jewish couples tried to send their offspring to university settings that offered a good-sized Jewish population. In every case, it meant sending the younger folk to institutions that were not in North Dakota. A lady of North Dakota Muslim parentage was one of six Muslims at the University of Minnesota who, in 1969, established a Muslim prayer group. This became the nucleus of an Islamic center whose membership now numbers in the thousands. Marian Kadrie, of Muslim background, grew up in the Sterling-Driscoll area and for decades she has been the leader of the Baha'i organization in Fargo.

There were variations of this theme. Sometimes just visiting a Muslim community in Canada? in Detroit? might lead to a successful courtship.

Ramiz "Ron" Hasen of Rolla, ND, met his prospective wife, Freida Ayad, of Michigan City, Indiana, at a Muslim youth convention. Knowledgeable members of the Cedar Rapids, Iowa, Muslim community say these events took place in the past and continue even today.[8]

It would be unfair if comments in previous pages should give the impression that Syrian new arrivals were burdened with a serious problem of illiteracy. Earlier in the volume tallies of newly arrived Syrians indicated that in 1903, 62 percent of the men and 32 percent of the women could read and write Syrian. The description of the home villages as presented in the WPA interviews in an earlier chapter, almost always contain a reference to school days in a Lebanese childhood. We can assume, therefore, that a goodly proportion of the newly arrived Dakota Lebanese were literate.

Native language newspapers were central to the eventual preservation of almost every minority group in America and we know from the WPA reports that a number of Syrian-language newspapers were received in the Dakota prairie homes. For example, WPA interviewees, speaking in 1939-1940, mentioned several publications: Bo Alley Farhart, of the Ross Muslim community, said: "We get one newspaper, the *Al-Bayan*, a Syrian paper published in New York." Sam Omar from the same community said, "We subscribe for the *Literary Digest*, *The Minot Daily News*, and get some Syrian papers which are published at Damascus and Cario [sic] Egypt." Mary Juma, also of Ross, said her family received *Al-Bayan*. Others in the Ross area, when interviewed in 1992, recalled the old-timers reading *Al Bayan* because it gave them "news of the Old Country and also of religion."

Al Bayan was a newspaper of Muslim origin, yet Joe Nicholas, a Christian from Cando, in 1995 listed it as being part of his family's reading materials. For some reason, present-day Lebanese descendants remember explicitly only one Christian-oriented Syrian newspaper, the *Al Hoda*. We know that others were circulating in the early days. Ed Nedoff, a native of Zahle, said in a 1939 interview at Williston:

> I picked up the English language from newspapers and magazines. All I had was couple months night school in Lawrence, Massachusetts. I was maybe about 18 years old.
>
> We get the Williston Herald and buy some others once in a while. I used to take Syrian papers, but don't get it any more. I like to read, but can't see very well and can't afford to buy glasses.

Samuel Nicola of Bismarck said in July 1939, "We used to take the *Lebanese Gazette*." Perhaps this was a Christian newspaper. Another Christian, Joseph Salmon of Zahle origin and a Bismarck resident, in the

Joe Nicholas, son of Nicholas Ausey, very early Perth-Dunseith homesteader.

Courtesy: John Guerrero

same year said: "I take the *Daily Worker* and also a daily paper. The only foreign paper I take is the *Maltan Libnan* which is published in Zahle, Syria, and I get it every two weeks."

We can be certain, therefore, that a small array of Arabic newspapers were arriving in the mailboxes of many North Dakota Lebanese farm and city dwellers in the first and second decades of this century. The peddlers' grapevine would alert them to the existence of these papers and Arab people, as immigrant people elsewhere in America, understandably desired a vehicle by which they could follow in their native language the news of their homeland and pertinent events in their adopted American homeland. In addition, an Arabic newspaper might allow the immigrant to locate families and friends who had spread throughout the American countryside.

We know something of the many Arabic newspapers which once existed in the United States. Though the names may not strike a note of recognition among today's Lebanese descendants, some must have circulated at one time or another on the Dakota prairies.[9] By 1912, Louise Houghton says the relatively small Syrian population in the United States supported 10 Arabic newspapers and magazines. She lists the *Star of America*, the *Muraat-Ul-Gharb (Mirror of the West)*, *Al Jamyat (The Sower)*. Houghton says the *Al Jamyat* "encourages farming and goes out to over 500 towns and villages." Listed in her account were also *Al Hoda*, *Al Dalil*, and *El Mohet*. These weekly or semi-weekly publications were printed in New York. There were others: a semi-monthly publication of the Orthodox Church bore the name *Al Kalimat (The Word)*[10] and in the mid-1920s the now-famous Khalil Gibran edited the publication *Al Fanoon (The Arts)*, which featured his drawings as well as his literary pieces.[11]

In 1924, Philip Hitti reports that the largest of all daily newspapers was the *Al Hoda*, which had a Maronite affiliation.[12] Its daily production seldom, if ever, exceeded a 5,000 press run. (Joe Nicholas of Cando in central North Dakota, remembers his parents regularly reading the *Al Hoda* in the 1920s.)[13] *Meraat-Ul Gharb* was a periodical published by the Orthodox Church and its readership, too, numbered something around four or five thousand. The newspaper *Al Omma* was also part of Midwestern life.[14]

Yet it seems that Arabic newspapers were not of paramount importance in the preservation of the North Dakota settlers' Arabic traditions. Whatever the newspapers might have portrayed, they certainly didn't give rise to concerns about Old Country politics. Modern-day descendants never mention debates or even serious discussions concerning civic affairs in Lebanon. The New World became the old-timers' focus of attention almost from their first moment in North Dakota. Attas Boutrous, who was born in Ain Arab in 1867 and came to America at the turn of the century, remembered in 1939: "I used to read the daily papers and I never subscribed to any foreign language papers or magazines — I joined the Elks — I became affiliated with the Republican Party."

As one could expect, America's foreign-language newspapers begin to suffer circulation difficulties as the second and third generation descendants came into their own. Among North Dakota people of Syrian background, with few classroom opportunities to systematically study their language, the second and third generation transition could lead to a rather rapid demise of interest in various Arabic publications. Abdo A. Elkholy, Arab scholar, reports that only 20 percent of the second generation immigrants in Chicago was able to read Arabic. In fact, he said 71 percent of the third generation Arabs could not understand their ancestral languages.[15]

Second-generation difficulties are clearly seen in the interview of Mrs. Mary Juma at Ross in 1939:

We always speak in our native tongue at home, except my grandchildren who won't speak Syrian to their parents. They do speak in Syrian to me because I cannot speak nor understand English. My grandchildren range from fourteen months of age to eight years, and there are four of them.

I can't read at all, neither in English nor Syrian. My son and daughter-in-law tell me the news they think might interest me.

The Williams County history, *The Wonder of Williams*, has this paragraph, which illustrates the corrosive effect of school attendance:

The children of these Syrian immigrants had the same problems starting school as did the Norwegians or any other immigrants — they did not speak English. To save their children the embarrassment of not being understood in school, the parents spoke English only.[16]

The Lebanese children in the village of Hettinger were insulated from the shock of entering school without some knowledge of English. Abe Tanous, a community leader, would gather them together before they began the first grade. He gave them an informal course in basic English.

The deleterious effect of American school attendance in maintaining language can be detected in the words of Mrs. Barbar Wizer of Williston who said, almost with sadness in 1940, "My children all talk Syrian, but can't read or write it. They start to talk English when they went to school, and that's all they talk now. We can't afford to take no papers."

David Kalil, a Christian of Williston who was born in Syria in 1880, with a certain pride yet perhaps regret, told an interviewer in a 1940 WPA report:

The children are Wilbur, age 31, farms and works in pool-room winter time; Rosalie, age 29, works in office in Montgomery Ward's store; Edward, age 28, lives in California, office work; Sam, age 26, stays at home, works State Highway Department part time; Adele, age 24, at home; Leona, age 20, California going to school; Marian, age twelve, at home going to school; and Charles, he's age ten and at home going to school. They all went through high school but Adele. We talked Syrian at home till the children went to school; Edward and Wilbur can talk Syrian, but the others don't know anything but English. I take the Al Hada [sic], a Syrian paper published in New York, and the Williston Herald and Farmers Press. We still prepare some of our foods like we did in Syria.

The sentiments expressed by Lebanese families as they viewed their traditional culture slipping away with the second and third generation were no doubt shared by parents of many other North Dakota national groups. To hold to the past seemed an almost impossible task.

Time and outside influences steadily eroded language and the more obvious of Lebanese traditions in North Dakota. There were, however, a number of forces that did bind the Syrian immigrants together in a neighborly fashion and sometimes in a statewide manner. The first was, of course, the gathering of the family or, as they say in the modern world, the "extended" family. Side Abdallah of Ross said in 1939, "In the early days we Syrians used to gather at each others' homesteads and we feasted, danced and played games." But Mr. Abdallah, a Muslim, added the comment, "Social life was never centered around our church [the mosque]." Sam Omar, also of the Ross Muslim community, told the WPA interviewer "In the old days we used to have parties and baseball was the favorite pastime for many." Speaking also of the Ross community was Mary Juma, "Our home has always been a gathering place for Syrian folk."

Certainly there were hundreds of occasions in which families and friends came together in festive moments with Old World food and fun, often with a sprinkling of the Lebanese language, dancing, and humor. Their neighbors were doing the same thing with Norwegian or German customs as centerpieces or, as time went on, as delightful additions to social gatherings.

In 1996, Vernon Owan recalled an Easter custom that was popular in early Williston days. It was called, at least in English, "egg cracking." Owan's father would carefully carry his favorite "unbreakable" egg to a neighbor's home—Munyers, Bousilmans, and Josephs were mentioned. The men would challenge each other to an egg-hitting contest. The owner of the egg that cracked was obliged to serve a toast of Arak. (The trick was to grasp the egg tightly and strike the opponent's egg with one's "pointed end.")[17]

1st SYRIAN CONVENTION WEST WILLISTON-N.D.
دلوّتمر السوري الدول في المغرب

America's first convention of Syrian Clubs, Williston probably in 1918.

Courtesy:
Wilbur Kalil Family

Today the memories of elderly North Dakotans of Lebanese origin reveal small, informal "arrangements" that showed the desire of the first settlers to maintain their connections to their fellow countrymen. There was, for example, the tendency to trade with other Lebanese. Some rivalry existed, but generally the early individuals "helped each other out." Even the present generation, on occasion, will send business to what they laughingly call a fellow "Kibbi." It may also be noted that in the past there was a "handful of Syrian homes" together on the edge of Belcourt. Williston, too, saw a collection of Syrian homes, not necessarily adjacent to each other but in the same part of town.[18]

Earlier in this volume, the presence of one, perhaps two, Syrian halls in Williams County was mentioned: one in Williston and one in the country. A Syrian club was noted in the discussion of the Rugby community. Reports do say that the first gathering of representatives of American "Syrian clubs" took place in Williston in 1918. So at least for the Lebanese in the northwestern and north central part of North Dakota, Lebanese fellowship and traditions were kept alive for some decades in a formal way. It is not clear when the "clubs" became inactive. Most likely the advent of the Great Depression caused their demise.

Lebanese, or Syrians as they were called throughout the first half of this century, did have more ambitious statewide gatherings in the form of nationality-centered "picnics." Unfortunately these reunions were almost spontaneous; invitations went out by "word-of-mouth" and news reports are hard to find. Summertime picnics took place periodically from the 1930s until the 1980s. Many were at Devils Lake, some at Rugby, at Fish Lake in the Turtle Mountains, even at Grand Forks and Fargo. Orthodox, Catholics, and Muslims participated. (The Fish Lake gathering drew some of its participants from Canada.) Floyd Fayette remembers gatherings at his Walsh County family farm which drew participants from as far as Williston, the Turtle Mountains, and Winnipeg. Joe Nicholas of Cando, Al Srur of Grand Forks, and the Hach family of Wales were among those who put on what might have been the last, a gathering at Devils Lake in 1982.[19] Few, if any, formal speeches were made. Rather it was food, stories of the past, and a great chance to use the old language. Recalling the earliest of these "reunions," one gentleman said the men would dance and party for "three days without sleep."

Of special note were the descendants of the Attiyeh family which found their cohesiveness especially in the fact that they had a common origin and could very often claim Ain Arab as their home village. The Attiyeh gatherings were not just the expected fun and frolic. They had a formal convention-like format and they gathered for some rather clear-cut purposes. Although the dates vary, 1930?, one authority says the Attiyeh Society was formally organized on March 15, 1935, in Cedar Rapids and Sioux City, Iowa. Within a year it was incorporated. The official aims were to "keep the members and their children together." Record keeping, aid to needy members, and advancement of younger members in "higher education" were among its first stated goals.

An informal history of the Attiyeh organization says that it was made up of the descendants of "an ancient and honorable Arabian tribe" that existed during the early part of the eighth century in the "Southern Syrian" Desert. Some families converted to Islam, the Christian portion of the family migrated to central Syria. Some eventually settled in eastern Lebanon on a site that had Roman ruins and "three springs," the present-day town of Ain Arab.

The Attiyeh gatherings were of great importance to Ain Arab settlers. In 1939, George Saba told the interviewer:

> There are not so many Old Country customs that the Syrian people observe in Bismarck, but when we meet at the Society of the Attiyehs' convention once a year we follow many of the Old Country customs, such as barbecued mutton, arrac and other Syrian foods served during this celebration. We also have some Old Country dancing and Old Country music.

Pioneer members of the Attiyeh Family Society, Bismarck Convention 1960. Seated: Mrs. Salem Nicola, Mrs. Salma Nicola, Salma Nicola, Della Boutrous. Standing: Tom Kellel, Tom Nassif.

George Saba gives more information concerning the Attiyeh gatherings. In his 1939 WPA interview he said:

I joined the Attiyeh Society which is an organization of my relatives here in the United States; brothers, cousins (1st, 2nd, 3rd), uncles and so on. They number now some over a thousand. We have a convention once a year when we meet some place and have quite a celebration for several days. Next year this celebration will be held in Bismarck. The Attiyeh is the original family name of our tribe.

The 1940 Bismarck Attiyeh convention (as mentioned earlier in the volume) took place in mid-July. On that occasion the *Bismarck Tribune* reported:

Chief Justice W. L. Nuessle of the North Dakota Supreme Court and former Gov. George F. Shafer will be the principal speakers when the Attiyeh society, composed of descendants of a Syrian patriarch of that name, convene in Bismarck July 13-15.

More than 400 descendants of Attiyeh and his seven sons, some of whom emigrated to America in 1895, are expected to come principally from the Dakotas, Iowa and Minnesota. A number will come from as far east as New York City and as far west as California, according to Floyd Boutrous of Bismarck, general chairman of the family reunion.

Rev. M. M. Yanney, pastor of the Greek Orthodox Catholic church of Cedar Rapids, Iowa; Sam Nassif, president of the Cedar Rapids unit of the family, and Carl Nassif, president of the Sioux City, Iowa unit, will be other principal speakers.

Highlights of Saturday's sessions of the reunion will be an hour devoted to exposition of the old dances of Syria with Syrian music as an accompaniment. Dancers and musicians will be in native costume and use native instruments.[20]

Attiyeh gatherings, at least in North Dakota, continued into the 1970s. Each occasion featured the age-old dances and music of Lebanon. Each emphasized the foods of the past. The old-timers, certainly, saw it as a chance to introduce the "young folks" into their unique Middle Eastern heritage.

Mike Saba, a third generation Lebanese-American, remembering what he called "a convention" in the 1970s (probably Attiyeh) said:

The drum beat started and many people got out on the dance floor and started to do this wonderful line dance, with everyone joining hands in the front, and the dancer putting his hands above his head, bouncing up and down, dancing to the beat of the music.[21]

Twenty years have passed since the last North Dakota "Lebanese picnic." The Attiyeh Society, if it still meets, does so in a local or less spectacular manner. (The last National Attiyeh convention took place in 1996 at Las Vegas.) The first generation, the old patriarchs and matriarchs are dead. They no longer provide the young with the legends and lore of the Old Country. Lebanese, like almost every national group that settled the Dakota farms and villages, are now third- and fourth-generation Americans, a generation for whom the Old Country is just a small part of their family heritage. Events of the present have engulfed the heritage of the past.

Only a smattering of Lebanese farmers still remains in the various homestead settlement enclaves. Melkite and Maronite grandchildren are members of Latin Rite Catholic churches. Third-generation Orthodox Christians play key roles in several Episcopal congregations, especially in Williston and Bismarck. Muslims who remain, second-generation men and women, still say their prayers five times a day, still avoid pork, and revere the Koran, but the Ross mosque has long since disappeared. Many of the grandchildren of the Muslim families in the Ross-Stanley-Glenfield areas consider themselves to be Lutheran.

One second-generation Stanley resident who attended the Ross mosque as a young man still senses regret that the building no longer exists. "It doesn't feel good, because it was a good congregation."

He now attends the Lutheran church. Yet he's philosophical about the matter. He says, "The only thing is that there is a little different beliefs, but we're all humans."[22]

Grandchildren of Muslims in the Turtle Mountain area often have Metis (French-Indian) mothers and they are of Catholic affiliation. Already mentioned is the Belcourt man who declares his ancestry to be "Arab, Muslim, French, Chippewa, Catholic, and Knights of Columbus." One Fargo resident, a twenty-year-old son of a second-generation Lebanese father and a Swedish mother, when recently asked if his Arabic ancestry made any difference in his life, replied: "Yes, I get a sun tan very easily."

Yet memory of Lebanon with its dramatic history and rich culture lingers into the ensuing generations. Of that we have a certain statistical evidence. The U.S. Census for the first time in 1980 asked the question, "What is your ancestry?" In North Dakota, totals of particular interest are the following:

Single Ancestry		**Multiple Ancestry**	
(only one national designation given)		(two or more designations given)	
Arabian	57	Arabian	28
Lebanese	464	Lebanese	221
Syrian	263	Syrian	169
Turkish	54	Turkish	24

The number of recent immigrants (students, professors) in North Dakota was miniscule in 1980. The above figures show the self-definition of the state's long-term residents. It is clear that Lebanon is a part of the life of many North Dakotans, even in the case of mixed nationality children.

Many of the 1980 respondents identified themselves by the original classification: Arab or Turk (Ottoman). Increasingly the "new" term Lebanon was gaining prominence. Yet many still called themselves "Syrian."

The external signs of Lebanon, the festivals, the language, the dress, no longer exist. Yet that is not the end of the story. There are scholars who insist that, while the most noticeable signs of the various ethnic cultures have disappeared here and elsewhere in America, ethnicity everywhere still persists in something more fundamental: a basic set of personal values. In fact, some experts contend that the residue of ethnicity, in many parts of the United States, exceeds all other factors in directing the life of individuals and whole communities. Values remain as a heritage: attitudes toward work, toward family and friends, toward success, toward politics, and toward God. Today's Lebanese descendants are decidedly different from their Norwegian, American Indian, and German counterparts. In a very real way, Lebanon, that delightful and sometimes war-torn land in the far distant Eastern Mediterranean, still is present throughout much of the Northern Plains.

In fact, there are signs of a renewed interest in some of the more visible—some would say more superficial— elements of the past. The third and fourth generations become romantic about "roots." One third-generation Lutheran mother leads her children in a prayer before meals that is half Islamic and half Christian in its format. Throughout the state Lebanese grandmothers and often grandfathers teach their children the delight that can be found in traditional foods. Seen very frequently today are kibbi (from boiled durum wheat and meat, vegetables and oils); cabbage rolls (from chopped meat and rice); flatbread (sometimes like the Scandinavian lefse), and koch (an Easter doughnut flavored with anisette). Chapter 19, "Food and Drink," will present a more complete discussion of this topic.

Raymond Atol

In a law enforcement career spanning over 50 years in North Dakota, Ray Atol didn't take a lot of guff. But he always said there were two sides to an argument. Born in 1930, of Lebanese immigrant parents in Bull Butte Township in Williams County, Ray would make northwest North Dakota his home for 67 years.

After service during the Korean War, Atol began his career as a Tioga, ND police chief. He was soon serving as a Williams County Deputy Sheriff and as a Williston city motorcycle policeman. Then from 1964 to 1991, he served as Williston's chief of police. During those years he rode Harley Davidsons, smoked cigars, arrested hardened criminals, and occasionally engaged in fisticuff events. His unlimited energy saw him undertake many responsible jobs: local and state American Legion positions, hospital boards, school PTA tasks, Republican Party leadership.

Although proud of his heritage, he saw himself first as an American. Upon his "retirement," Ray served as a Williams County Commissioner until his death in 1997. Fellow commissioner Dan Kalil, himself of Lebanese ancestry, said that Ray "made things go and got things done." His view of life was to make a community a better place for the children of the next generation. Jackie Williams of the local Republican district stated, "He can only be described as one of God's miracles."

CHAPTER SEVENTEEN

Into the Mainstream

Sixty-three North Dakota men of Syrian parentage are known to have served in the United States Armed Forces in the First World War. The four-volume *Official Roster of North Dakota Soldiers, Sailors and Marines, World War, 1917-1918* indicates that seven of that number were American-born. This means that 56 men of Syrian birth served between 1917 and 1918 in America's war endeavor.[1] The US Census total of Syrian-born men and women in the state in 1920 was 289. Does this mean that seventeen percent of North Dakota Syrian men and women were in the military? (This seems unlikely; we know the census missed large numbers of Syrian residents.) Whatever the answer, it is clear that Syrian men did not shirk their duty. Even though many intended, perhaps at least initially, to return to their homeland, they were nonetheless loyal to the United States. (The Appendix of this volume contains a synopsis of each North Dakota serviceman's military record.)

Veterans-Patriotism

William Alley, a long-time Muslim merchant in Glenfield, Foster County, came to America in 1914. A Cooperstown history said he joined the U.S. Army in 1917, "not because he had to but because this country had been so good to him. That was his way of saying thank you."[2]

A closer look at the *Official Roster* shows that 14 men enlisted and the remaining were drafted. Twenty-six of their number served overseas. Four were killed in action. Four received the Silver Star for gallantry. (One received the French Fourragere Award.) Three men were discharged as sergeants, four as corporals, and the rest as privates. Such far-above-the-average performance of duty makes Syrian patriotism very apparent. It is obvious that Syrians served as front-line troops, the ones who bore the brunt of the hard and unheralded campaign assignments.

Of curious note, however, are the *Roster* notations indicating that three men were discharged within a month after the Armistice, "by reason of being a subject of Turkey." These individuals were stationed in the continental United States and had no overseas service. What does this mean? Perhaps it was a quick method of "downsizing" the post-war military. Certainly it did not mean that aliens could not serve in the United States forces for Albert Kalad of Pembina County, one of the decorated war casualties, was listed as an "alien."

The total number of North Dakota men and women of Syrian ancestry who participated in the Second World War will always be an unknown. (Mixed parentage clouds the calculations.) If the totals follow the precedent of the First World War, the proportions were probably well above the state average. One indication, however, of their allegiance to the American homeland is the fact that since the Second World War, two State Commanders of the Veterans of Foreign Wars (Phil Srur and Edward Haykel) could claim Syrian background. In addition, Ray Atol, long-time chief of police in Williston, served in the 1990s as State Commander of the American Legion. Chuck Joseph was the Legion's 40 and 8 Grande Chef de Gare du North Dakota in 1987.

A thought-provoking symbol of Lebanese loyalty to their adopted country is the grave of a Muslim man who died in 1941. It lies in the prairie cemetery located next to what was once the Ross community mosque. The modest inscription informs the passerby that the deceased was a member of the 158 Regiment, America's 40th Division.

Wherever the descendants of North Dakota's pioneer Lebanese settlers may abide today, they will be found active in veterans' circles. In the Veterans of Foreign Wars and the American Legion organizations, stories of the Arab world will sometimes arise. Phil Srur of the US Navy in the Mediterranean in World War II was an interpreter between North African natives and American servicemen. Bill Nassif of Strasburg, North Dakota background was shot down on a bombing mission over Poland. In the initial interrogations, the German officer said he was Jewish of Middle Eastern origin. Nassif said, "No! I'm Syrian from the United States and I'm Catholic." Eventually the Germans found a Catholic priest who checked Nassif's knowledge of the catechism and ritual gestures. "He's Catholic," the priest said. With apologies, the officer sent him to a regular camp for Air Corps prisoners.[3] (In 1999, the Polish government honored Bill Nassif for his contribution to the "liberation" of the Polish homeland.) Sam Skaff of Sheridan County background spent one and a half years in the Middle East Theater during World War II. His Arab-North Dakota background served him and his nation well for his tour of duty took him to places which geography books call "Arab country" nations.[4]

America was number one. An immense gratitude was present in the North Dakota Syrian community. As mentioned before, this is surprising when we remember that the many first generation immigrants initially hoped to acquire a modest fortune and return to their home villages. But perhaps it's not surprising when we realize that, in fact, most *did not* return home. America was not a place to "get rich quick," but it did provide a decent income, an array of rights and freedoms, and an opportunity for their children to become "successful." When these advantages became apparent, they fell in love with their American homeland.

Speaking of Williston Syrians, Jesse Joseph recalled, "You never said anything against America in their [the Lebanese] presence." As if to exemplify that Lebanese character trait, Floyd Boutrous of the Sheridan County colony and later of Bismarck, devoted much of his life to the advancement of loyalty on a state and even national level. In 1990 he received an award "for patriotism" from Chief Justice Warren Berger. Boutrous was involved in Radio Free Europe, in the Crusade for Freedom Campaign, and The American Freedom Documents Program. (The *Fargo Forum* in September 1995, called Floyd Boutrous "Mister Constitution.") Mr. Boutrous often said, "We are Americans of Syrian descent, not Syrians in America."[5]

Loyalty to America was not just a North Dakota phenomenon. Philip Hitti, in his volume *Syrians in America,* says Syrians far exceeded other national groups as they participated in the military in the First World War.[6] Michael Sulliman, writing in *Crossing the Water,* said military documents from that war show that "No less than 13,956 or about 7% of the whole Syrian community served in the United States Army."[7]

Politics

Louise Houghton, the authority on early Syrian American life, wrote that "Syrians avoided politics; they would sometimes vote but never assume public office."[8] If this generalization were correct for American Lebanese, we might assume that at least that some other immigrant groups saw politics in the same way. Politics was someone else's concern. And North Dakota records show that there were a number of immigrant groups which were underrepresented, or even absent from the political scene: Germans from Russia, Poles, Ukrainians. Some reasons can be suggested: one is the fact that democratic processes in the United States were new and confusing; second, the village or the clan in their former homeland was the focus of their loyalty, not the nation; finally, early American life had to be concerned first of all with earning a living and this allowed little time for the luxury of political action.

And there is evidence that in much of America the Syrian-Lebanese people did, in fact, avoid political office, at least during their initial period in this country. The highly respected *Harvard Encyclopedia of American Ethnic Groups* has a discussion of Arabic education, religious life, literary endeavors, and the like. It contains nothing of political involvement in the New World. Such a discussion is also absent from the Syrian portion of the Minnesota ethnic history, *They Chose Minnesota.*

Political life and Arabic origin on the Great Plains presents a somewhat different picture. North Dakota, unlike several other states, has had no Arabic "native sons" in the U.S. Congress, but there have been an array of political figures on a local level. Syrian-born Aisem Haykel, already in the 1930s, was county auditor at McClusky in Sheridan County. Abe Tanous of Hettinger County was federal marshal in Hettinger County in the 1930s. Charlie Juma, of Muslim background, held county offices at Stanley, North Dakota, in the 1940s and 50s.

Lebanese second and third generation men were prominent in North Dakota's Williams County's political scene. Raymond Atol was Chief of Police in Williston for 20 years, and today two of the five county commissioners in Williams County are of Lebanese background. Robert Freije is a county commissioner in Ramsey County and his brother John is mayor in the predominantly Norwegian town of Mayville. Abe Tanous, in his earlier years, was mayor of Hettinger. The same can be said concerning Lewis Masad of Mott, and Eugene Alley of the village of Sibley. Hasson Murhey was mayor of Davenport for twenty years. Kade Albert served on the Turtle Mountain Tribal Council. John Noah of Fargo was head U.S. probation officer for North Dakota. In Cando, Gene Nicholas has been a legislator of statewide influence for the over 20 years—perhaps the longest tenure of any in today's state legislature. In Pierce County, Alex Munyer was county commissioner for at least a dozen years.

In no instance has a North Dakota public official of Arabic background downplayed his or her Syrian origins. Indeed, they often boast of being "an old Arab" or even a Lebanese "camel jockey." Kibbi is a food that is often featured when guests are present on festive occasions.

Higher Education

A Directory of Foreign Students in 1919 records the names of 35 students of Syrian background in America's colleges and universities. (Some were at Harvard and Columbia.) Philip Hitti estimates the number in 1919 was close to 50, "of whom only two are girls."[9] Louise Houghton, writing a little earlier, in 1911, says, "40 Syrian young men and five girls in 14 towns and cities are known to be pursuing a university education." She admits the list was not exhaustive. Yet she decries the fact that only one university student could be found for every 1800 American residents of Syrian ancestry[10].

A Lebanese scholar of some note was part of North Dakota's higher education circles in the 1920s. The gentleman, Jabir Shibli, born in Btighreen, Lebanon, came to America in 1908. Trained in a Presbyterian seminary, he served as pastor, among other places, in McIntosh, South Dakota. He received a master's degree from the University of North Dakota in 1918. He subsequently was on the faculty of a short-lived but respected institution called the Fargo College. Later, after acquiring a doctorate, he taught for nearly 30 years at Pennsylvania State University. While there he wrote a number of books including one, a standard text-book on trigonometry, which was in use for many years in American institutions of higher learning. Loyal to his homeland, he is buried in Lebanon.

For several decades the University of North Dakota at Grand Forks asked students in the first semester of each academic year to answer a number of questions concerning their backgrounds. One highly interesting question dealt with national origins. In 1930-31, two students listed "Syrian." Sixteen hundred and forty-eight men and women were attending the university in that year. (Curiously, Syrians fell under what University registrar called the "Slav" category.) In 1934-35, one student among the 1543 enrolled called him/herself "Arabian." In 1938-39, two Syrian students could be found among the 1769 general enrollment figures. (Again, Syrians were listed in the "Slavic" general category.) In 1939-40, three Syrian students were present (1828 total enrollment). The next year, 1940-41, three out of 1865 were Syrians. In 1941-42, two of the 1507 students were Syrian. In 1942-43, two of the 1238 were of Syrian background.

The number of University of North Dakota students of Arabic background rose considerably after the completion of World War II. No official records are available, but personal interviews brought forth the names of dozens of young men and women. By the late 1940s, life on the farm or in a small town business became less attractive and the GI Bill was in place. The University was an avenue to success in the larger American world.

Three sons of the Arabic-speaking Ahmed Ferris family, which ran the Kon Tiki Corner "convenience store" at Rolla, attended North Dakota colleges in the post-World War II years and are now active in the international business world. The young men, all tri-lingual, live in Brazil, Texas, and the middle eastern country of Dubai.

Today in North Dakota a sizable list of professionals—physicians and attorneys—can be compiled whose grandparents were from some Syrian Muslim or Christian village.

Yet a list of "successful" present-day Lebanese men and women in North Dakota would point not to the more academically inclined occupations, but particularly to those in the mercantile world. Hard work, an affinity to business, a basic honesty, these qualities and not advanced education stand behind their reputation for excellence.

The Wider Business World

The first two decades of Syrian settlement in North Dakota were characterized earlier in this volume as a time that saw an "explosion" of merchant activity. If nothing else set the Lebanese apart from other arriving national groups, their surprising business acumen makes them unusual. Only two other groups showed such an aggressive business attitude: the British Isles people with Eastern American roots and the Jewish settlers who came during the homestead period.

The "shopkeeper period" is perhaps the phrase that can best describe the earliest two decades of Syrian life in North Dakota. Even as farmers, most men spent time on the road peddling, and they were frequently doing this with the hope of acquiring a small store in one of Dakota's newly founded towns. The Lebanese were certainly at a disadvantage because they had not only to master the language but also to grasp the essentials of the American wholesale, retail, and financial procedures. They had to do all this while at the same time having little access to working capital. No wonder they had to "start small."

The Shepherd Township, Walsh County, settlement can probably be considered the earliest of the state's Arab settlements. By 1931, Ed Absey (son of Peter Absey) and his wife Mildred, moved from Shepherd Township to Grand Forks. Working first in the trenches of a power company, Ed earned extra cash by being a pugilist in local carnivals. The pitch probably went like this: "Ten dollars if you can beat Ed, come one, come all." Soon, as a side job, Ed was working for Salem Motors (a Lebanese Crookston car dealer). By 1938 he was a full time car dealer in Grand Forks. With his two sons, returning war veterans, he eventually built a lavish auto showroom and repair shop on the south edge of the city. The internationally acclaimed Ramada Inn of Grand Forks is the product of his son Bob's entrepreneurial endeavors.

Coming also from the Walsh County settlement was the Freije family. The elder Freije (Moses) came to the United States and worked as a peddler before homesteading in 1897. He soon proved up on his land, even buying an additional full section (in 1908). Moses' brother Nassif

Joe and Loretta
Nicholas of Cando
with sons Don, Gene,
and daughter Lori.

Courtesy:
Nicholas Family

arrived in North Dakota and within a few years the two men moved to
Lawton where they ran a pool hall and battery store. The building burned
and in 1944 the Freije family moved to Edmore in adjacent Ramsey
County. There Shabel, son of Nassif, acquired an implement dealership.
The family ran a tavern as a side venture. Shabel's children grew up, for
the most part, in Lawton, which had a heavy Bohemian population. The
language of the children on the street was Czech so some Freije children
spoke Czech before they learned English. With the move to Edmore, the
family was surrounded by Norwegians. Not surprisingly, Nassif became
known as "Nels" Freije. The present generation of Freijes continues in
the implement business at Edmore and also at Mayville.[11]

The Deraneys were another Shepherd township family that moved to
Grand Forks in the 1930s. The parents ran a neighborhood grocery store.
Three of the sons worked for the railroad. Today one is a liquor dealer.
Another is in the auto repair business.

The more central part of the state is home to Eugene Nicholas, son of
Joe Nicholas and grandson of Nicholas Ausey of the Cando-Perth area.
Gene, a prominent local farmer, is a state legislator and a Cando promoter
who has been influential in bringing sizable businesses to that community. On the side, he runs a 600-acre jalapeno farm in Arizona.[12]

Abdallah (Abe) Tanous filed his first naturalization papers in Towner
County in 1906. He had taken land near the farm of his cousin, Nicholas

Ausey. Soon he moved to Hettinger in Adams County. Abe's two brothers also came to Hettinger and all three spent time on the road as peddlers. In the 1920 Census at least three Tanouses (brothers and nephews) operated businesses of one kind or another. (One had a tavern called the Mecca Bar.) Abe himself was active in bringing Lebanese to America, even journeying to the Old Country to assist them in the process.[13]

The Sheridan County Lebanese community contributed a number of families who achieved a degree of prominence. Ferris Skaff left the farm and moved to Bismarck, then back to McClusky (Sheridan County) where he traveled, first with a wagon, and later a truck, selling Watkins products throughout Sheridan and McLean counties. Ferris Skaff had five children, all of whom graduated from the McClusky high school. The family farm and the Watkins business were kept until his retirement. He died in 1975. Sam Skaff, one of Ferris' sons, sold papers on the streets of Bismarck, and later, while still in grade school, helped his father sell Watkins products on the road. In 1942 he was drafted into the Army and spent one and one-half years in the Near East.[14] Sam Skaff is a well-recognized North Dakota entrepreneurial figure. He developed an extensive series of restaurants and, in recent years, has built apartment complexes in Fargo and Moorhead.

Among the Sheridan County settlers who chose Bismarck as a step in the ladder to American success was the Boutrous family. Attas Boutrous brought his family to that city and started the Corner Grocery. One of Attas' sons, Floyd, became a city realtor and has been mentioned on previous pages as a national leader in promotion of patriotism and loyalty. Floyd's loyalty was also to his state. He was a key person in setting up trade missions to the Near East in promotion of North Dakota grain. Floyd's brother, Thomas, became a well-known Detroit physician. (He was a friend and supporter of Danny Thomas in the early days of his entertainment career.) Boutrous family descendants in present-day North Dakota are often numbered in the lists of physicians and attorneys.[15]

Also from the Sheridan County community was Naif Saba, son of Michael Saba, who homesteaded in 1904. Naif established a restaurant in Bismarck. His son, Michael, has been involved, like Floyd Boutrous, in the worldwide promotion of Great Plains agricultural products. He has held responsible positions in organizations focusing on Arab-American affairs and was a key person in the fund-raising arm of the Danny Thomas St. Jude's Children's Hospital in Memphis, Tennessee. Bill Shalhoob, of Ain Arab background, owns two motels in the Bismarck-Mandan community and was the head of the Regional Economic Development Committee. Gary Anderson of the Bismarck Nicola family (a Sheridan County descendant) owns a Fargo- and Bismarck-based liquor distributing company.

Williston, as seen in an earlier chapter, was a hot bed of Lebanese mercantile activities. (Within ten years after settlement almost a dozen small firms existed in the area under Lebanese ownership.) The Kalils homesteaded in Bull Butte Township. Soon one family was running a township grocery store and very quickly another Kalil brother was in the grocery business in the City of Williston. As time went on, a Kalil family member established a furniture store and played a major role in the operation of a local bank and a large restaurant/tavern. One of the descendants, Charles (Bud), became a vice-president of the Metropolitan Bank in Fargo.[16]

The Owan family, of Bull Butte origin, was also in banking and real estate. Abe Owan, at one time, was considered head of one of the largest farm conglomerates in the state. The Joseph family, descendants of Charles Joseph, can be found in commercial positions throughout Williston. Joseph's "Ready to Wear Clothing Store" has been called "one of the oldest businesses in town." The owner, Charles (Chuck) Joseph, is also a gaming equipment distributor and has a Williston lounge.

Fargo has its Lebanese men and women of prominence. The Kallod family, originally from Tokio, North Dakota, has for years operated a carpet business. Until recently, the Nassif family (from Sheridan County) ran the same type of firm, and a descendant of the family was a Fargo attorney. Fargo also became home to Sam Aggie who came from Chicago in the 1920s. Starting with a fruit stand, he became a large-scale real estate owner and manager. The enterprise is still in family hands.

The Turtle Mountain Syrian enclave is still represented in the city of Rolla. Side Zahra, of Muslim background, arrived in America and took the name Sidney Harris. After working as a peddler out of Perth, North Dakota, he moved to Rolla and established the Harris Clothing Store. Sidney and his wife Kathryn became pillars of the Rolla community. Their leadership extended into such diverse things as local American Legion, Chamber of Commerce, and Legion Auxiliary enterprises. The Harris store is still run by Quentin Harris, a son of Sidney and Kathryn.[17] Across the street in Rolla, Ron Hasen, son of Alec Hasen (originally Debaji) runs a rival clothing store, one established by his father called The Golden Rule. Alec, like so many of his contemporaries, started selling merchandise from farm to farm before taking up permanent residence in the town.

We see in this chapter a remarkable "success" story. Starting from the most humble of occupations—peddling—Syrians, whether Muslims or Christians, have risen to prominence in large numbers and in a surprisingly short period of time.

Najla (Ghazi) Amundson

An example of the recent Syrian cultural additions to North Dakota life is Najla Amundson, who, until recently, was co-anchor of evening news programs at WDAY-TV in Fargo. Najla was born in Akron, Ohio, of Syrian immigrant parents (her father has a doctorate in thermodynamics and her mother has a Ph.D. in plant sciences). At Brookings, South Dakota, Najla completed high school and attended South Dakota State University. In 1987 she won the Miss South Dakota title and sampled life in front of a camera. With a master's degree in journalism from Northwestern University, she took a newsroom job at WDAZ in Grand Forks. By 1992 she was an assistant professor at the University of North Dakota School of Communications. After a stint in private advertising, she married Paul Amundson, also of TV and newspaper background, in 1993.

Najla's life combines many elements: the role of wife and mother, the task of being a news writer and TV celebrity, a commitment to her Muslim faith, an allegiance to a husband of Minnesota Scandinavian background, a Midwestern up-bringing, and a great respect for her Middle-Eastern roots.

Two Sisters

When President Bill Clinton was elected President in 1992, one of his first cabinet appointments was for Health and Human Services. The appointee was an American of Lebanese descent named Donna Shalala. In doing their background check, the F.B.I. placed a call to Diane Fritel of Wolford, ND. They asked Diane what her relationship was to Donna Shalala. Diane replied that they were "wombmates" who grew up together in Ohio. The startled F.B.I. asked for clarification, and Diane quickly explained they were actually twin sisters. The next day Bill Clinton called Diane, stating that he and the F.B.I. had taken it in good humor. Donna continues to visit Diane and Bob Fritel on the farm once or twice a year. Family members still have a good laugh about the President's remark.

CHAPTER EIGHTEEN

Food and Drink

Affter almost forty years in America, Samuel Nicola, reminiscing about his ancestral village in Lebanon, recalled vividly the food that marked his youthful days. Speaking at his home in Bismarck in July 1938, he said:

> *The Old Country meals consisted of mutton and goat meat, all kinds of vegetables, corn on the cob, all kinds of fruit, Kibby, Jabia and roasted green peas. When anyone was invited to the home they received all the same treatment, except there is much more respect shown for the older people than are shown the older folks in this country.*

Good food and a warm welcome for guests. This theme occurs again and again in the pictures of the "Old Country" that lingered in the minds of Syrian-Lebanese old-timers. The authors of this volume have written elsewhere about many national groups that took root on the Northern Plains and they can say, from personal experience, that no group can surpass the Lebanese in the degree of hospitality and the abundance of food that is laid before visiting strangers. Certainly it is true today and all signs seem to say that it was true in the past.

Thomas Nassif, a Bismarck resident in August 1939, when remembering his turn-of-the-century home in Ain Arab, referred (almost predictably) to the food and the treatment of guests:

> *The Old Country meals consisted of vegetables, fruits of all kinds including dates and figs, mutton and goat meat, hallwah [sic] which is a food made out of different kinds of seeds, with butter and seasoning, kibby, which is a favorite Syrian dish and is made of meat and grain boiled and ground. We also serve jabia which is another Syrian food and is made with cabbage leaves rolled around ground meat and meal, something on the order of hot tamales. We also served cheese at the table made from goat milk. We had lots of fruits on the table in the Old Country because there*

The food tradition
still lives, Baklava.

*are large orchards of every kind of fruit everywhere and a person could
live there almost indefinitely on nothing but fruit picked as he went along.
We were all treated the same at the table except when there was guests
and they were treated with the usual politeness.*

Needless to say, Thomas Nassif's early years on a barren Dakota
prairie homestead must have had some nostalgic and even sad moments;
there were little of the dates and figs and "large orchards" filled with
fruits. Absent also were the "different kinds of seeds" and various condi-
ments that would give the meager pioneer foods the sparkle of Middle
Eastern flavors.

Joseph Azar, like Thomas Nassif, recalled his youth in Lebanon after
almost 40 years in Dakota. Speaking in 1939 at Bismarck, his attention
focused on the local cuisine:

*The Old Country meals consisted of goat meat, mutton, potatoes, beets,
carrots, rutabagas, fruits of all kinds and dark bread, and wine. The
cooking was done with olive oil and the dishes were very rich. They made
some Old Country dishes that haven't been seen in this country which
are made of ground wheat and meat. Plenty of grapes are served. Then
there was a kind of a bread made of wheat flour and rolled thin and baked
and was something like a pancake. Then another food was made by
pressing and rolling thin cooked fruit like apricots and drying them. There
were many other kinds of food made from wheat meal and meat which I
cannot describe and are not found in this country. Potatoes are eaten very
seldom and usually a sack of potatoes last a family one year. Eggplant is
an important food and is used the year around.*

Phrases like "dishes that haven't been seen in this country" and "potatoes are eaten very seldom" remind the reader that the homesteader, already burdened with primitive housing problems, new farming methods, and the isolated location of the farmstead, was forced also to make some radical food adjustments.

The North Dakota Lebanese newcomer was inevitably surrounded by homesteaders from Scandinavia, Germany, and the British Isles. The food contrasts were often quite startling. It is not an exaggeration to say that the Germans loved pork, the British tended toward beef, and the Norwegians, when they could get it, liked fish. In contrast, Mary Saliba, an Ain Arab native, when recalling her "native land" in an August 1939 interview at Bismarck said:

> The people in my native land are not great meat eaters, however, mutton and goat meat were served on the table quite frequently. The people rely mostly on vegetables, fruits and foods prepared from wheat, rye and oats. Cheese made from goat milk was always on the table, along with roasted peas and beans. We also raised quite a few chickens as did the other neighbors and eggs would be a regular food on the table.

Gleaned from conversations and interviews with dozens of first and second generation Christian and Muslim Lebanese, all with roots in the Dakota homestead and peddler period, a number of food items emerge. The reader will notice the absence of both pork and fish.

Yubrak: (The *Jabra* or *Jabia* mentioned in a previous paragraph.) This consisted of cabbage leaves around meat and rice and various flavorings.

Kibbi: Ground lamb or beef, with a special cracked wheat (bulghor) and onions and spices. When cooked it is *Kibbi Sineey.* If raw it is *Kibbi Neeyi.* (Spelling variations abound in various cookbooks: *Kibbeh, Kibbeh bil sanien, Kibbeh Naye.*)

Kusa (Kousa): A unique Middle Eastern squash that is picked when about four inches long and when stuffed with meat and rice becomes *Kusa Mahshi.*

Khobaz (Khubz) Arabee: A flat bread, kneaded, stretched, and in Lebanon, baked on a dome-shaped hot grill.

Tabbouli: A salad of tomatoes, onions, parsley, crushed bulghor, wheat, with olive oil and lemons.

Fasouliyya: Green or white beans with onions and scrambled eggs.

Rishta: Lentils with noodles; also *Megadarra* (lentils with rice).

Zlabyi: A ball of dough, kneaded, flattened and fried in oil, then sprinkled with sugar.

Ftayir: Small triangular meat pies, with onions and flavorings.

Telaibe: Round soft bread, often spread with a sharp-tasting seasoning called *Zartar (Zahtar).*

Hummus: A favorite Lebanese bean. "Garbanzo bean?" "chick peas?" These are American names which may be the same or at least similar to the Old Country originals.

The above list, of course, is limited. It has been noted that Lebanese politics was seldom mentioned in North Dakota "Syrian" family circles, but food is different. The topic immediately provokes long discussions on basic food items: the names, the preparations, and the seasonings. These are part of prairie Lebanese lore. Yet no compilation of North Dakota recipes has been made. (Is it too late?)

The very sound of the names set the Lebanese food apart from the "meat, potatoes and gravy" of many of their neighbors. The use of lamb and even mutton emphasized the different types of culinary staples. Many Germans and Scandinavians would "eat horse meat before they would eat a sheep." And goat meat! This too was a food item that many non-Lebanese neighbors regarded with aversion.

Yet the neighbors often looked at Syrian food with a certain fascination; cooking methods were also admired at times. The book *Tales of Mighty Mountrail,* a county history, when describing the local Lebanese families, most of whom were Muslim, has this to say:

> *One aspect of the Syrian culture which is enjoyed by people of different ethnic backgrounds is their culinary art. Much of their cooking is done with oils, and is generally very tasty. They use durum wheat in many of their dishes—or flour made from durum wheat—usually mixed with meat. They bake a delicious bread which resembles the Norwegian lefse but it is more bread-like in taste. When they came to America they brought with them some vegetables not common to this country such as different varieties of beans, peas and tomatoes.*

The Mountrail County history goes on to describe the flatbread, which along with Kibbi was found in every Lebanese home.

> *A favourite bread still made by Syrian women today is their "Flat Bread"; although with the passing of the coal range with its large flat cooking surface, they have had to adapt their methods to the modern electric and gas stoves.*[1]

Adaptation to early prairie circumstances gave rise to a certain ingenuity. As mentioned above, American stoves had to be used instead of the dome-shaped "saj" which was placed on an open fire in Lebanon. The Mountrail County women placed a sheet of quarter-inch flat iron on top of the wood stove.[2] (A modern woman of Lebanese lineage uses a Norwegian lefse hot plate.) All sorts of adjustments were demanded in the pioneer period: cracked durum wheat, grown in North Dakota, replaced the bulghur wheat that was the standard Old Country ingredient. Olive oil was replaced by local "store-bought" oil. Lentils gave way to an American pea. Kousa squash found a temporary North Dakota squash substitute. Hummus beans became chickpeas in the United States. Domestic grape leaves were unobtainable, but Williston Lebanese found wild grapes "along the river." (In eastern North Dakota children gathered wild grapes for their parents along the Red River.) Mint was plentiful; it grew like a weed when planted on the prairie. Wild onions could, if needed, replace the garden varieties. Beef became more popular. Lamb and goat meat were rare on the prairies. Antelope at times was a substitute.

Some food items had to be temporarily forgotten: dates, figs, quince, pomegranates, artichokes, okra and pistachios. In time, of course, as money became more plentiful, mail order catalogs and grocery chains made some hard-to-get Old Country items available. Specialty food stores in larger cities were soon discovered and what Americans called "exotic" spices and rare types of nuts became obtainable. The Lebanese peddler helped the very early settler, at times, for some spices were part of his or her trade inventory. Today, even though the prices are high, one can, with a certain diligence, purchase pine nuts, anise, sesame seeds, saffron, mahleb and zatar.

Liquid refreshments were part of every Lebanese festive gathering, but the special blend of "Turkish coffee" was hard to get and the *raqwi*, an Old Country coffee pot, was especially difficult to obtain. Neighbors, when they tasted the coffee, had one invariable description: "very strong."

For non-Muslims, wines of various sorts could be acquired at even the most unsophisticated small-town tavern. Louis Nassif, remembering Ain Arab in a Bismarck interview in August 1939, spoke of Old Country meals and the wine which seemed to have a special significance:

> *The Old Country meals consisted of vegetables, fruit, goat and mutton, a little beef and some wine. Wine was usually served with meals and as a rule everyone had a plentiful supply on hand. Each farmer made his own wine or had it made in the distilleries or wineries from the grapes they raised themselves.*

In North Dakota another popular Old Country liquid refreshment was not easily obtainable: *Arak,* a liquor, which has been called the "Lebanese national drink." The residue of pressed grapes, it was flavored with anise and gum mastic. Non-Lebanese were warned that it had a "kick like a mule" and they were cautioned to try just a "snifter" the first time around.

Lebanese immigrants were not concerned about the supposedly debilitating effects of *arak.* George Saba, formerly of Ain Arab, referred to it as "punch" when speaking in 1939 at his Bismarck home:

We raised wheat, rye, lots of peas, olives, grapes, from which we made Arrac [sic] punch, and some years we had close to a million pounds of grapes which were made into Arrac and wine. There was some Anise raised in the vicinity but we did not raise any of this.

Lebanese men in various parts of North Dakota were known to have manufactured "home brew" beer and wine. Certainly they tried to fabricate liquor that resembled arak. One "old-timer," recalling the 1930s in the Williston area, said the men would go to a particular farmstead, sleep in the barn, even on cold winter days, and brew up a batch. "For two weeks they would gather; in ten days it would brew, in 14 days it would be ready. In the meantime, the men would butcher a lamb, chop it up with onions, and serve it with flat bread and black Greek olives. Then a big party would take place."

These were Depression years; in fact, some of the years were during the Prohibition period. Yet Lebanese and knowledgeable non-Lebanese asserted that the "Syrians never made booze to ship out; it was for personal use." This is not to say that "Syrians" in every case refused to participate in the distribution of illegal liquor. Some, on occasion, did get involved. Canada was "wet" and North Dakota—along with the rest of the United States—was "dry." All that was necessary was a "fast big car" and a little imagination. One older Lebanese gentleman admitted his youthful participation in that particular kind of "international trade." The enterprise could be risky. One wintry day the "agents" had blocked the roads out of a little border supply town and the gentleman in question had to drive all the way to a large and "more friendly" North Dakota city on the snow-filled railroad tracks. Nonetheless, after detailing his experiences, the man quickly added, "But I never sold any bad booze." He was an honest businessman.

Lebanese may have become intoxicated at times but the culture, at least as it was manifested in North Dakota, did not see "getting drunk" and "acting drunk" as a particularly admirable condition. Attas Boutrous, an Ain Arab Christian, saw alcohol as a part of Old Country life, but within certain restraints. At Bismarck in July 1939 he said:

There are no saloons in Ain Arab and every family makes their own liquor and wines. They have three distilleries or wineries and they make their own wine from the grapes they raise. Each family rents the distillery for two or three days and make their own supply. They are still doing this in Syria I understand, and a married man cannot go out and spend his money in the saloons and let the family go hungry as they do here.

Continuing his discussion of Old Country attitudes toward liquor, Mr. Boutrous said:

America is superior in every way to the Old Country except in the way they handle the liquor. The Old Country is superior in this to America.

Looking with disdain at the American excesses in drinking, Joe Albert, a Christian from a village he described as being "twenty five miles from Damascus," said in Williston in February 1940:

I never knew what whiskey tasted like till I came to America, and although I tended bar and been around saloons ever since I have been here, I have never drank any to speak of—a glass of beer or one drink of whiskey is all I take at one time. Maybe it is because of tending bar that I don't. I have seen men make such fools of themselves that it kind of disgusted me.

The use of wine or *arak* was one definite line that separated Christian Lebanese from their North Dakota fellow countrymen, the Muslims. The authors of this book cannot find any significant food differences between the pioneer Muslims and Christians, except this matter of intoxicating beverages and, of course, the consumption of pork.

Muslim prairie settlers were known, in some cases, to take an occasional sip of *arak* "for medicinal purposes," but habitual consumption was rare, almost non-existent. This, however, did not prevent some Muslim families from having a bottle in the home for use by non-Muslim guests. And the personal avoidance of alcohol did not stop several Muslim men from setting up small-town taverns. Alex Hach, for example, came to America as a young man and by the 1930s and 1940s was operating a bar and general store at Wales, ND. Amid Hach, the son, and his wife Annie, made the tavern a flourishing enterprise. The couple played an active part in every facet of the Wales community. In fact, the Catholic priest was often a guest at the Hach table. Amid Hach's funeral contained Muslim prayers, but was essentially a non-denominational service. Albert el Tassis, a prayer leader from Winnipeg, presided but two Catholic priests participated in the event.[3]

In the little town of Mapes, a Muslim gentleman named Mike Saign also ran a tavern. The establishment operated at least through the 1940s and 1950s. The owner, an impressive man with a "big mustache" was said to have displayed two pictures behind the bar: one was Franklin D. Roosevelt and the other was an imposing Arab dignitary. A tipsy traveler one day stopped at the tavern to quench his thirst. Afterwards he swore that the owner stood between the two pictures, had a handlebar mustache, a gold tooth and wore a turban. He reported that he gulped his drink and departed in haste. Whether there ever was such a thing as the "gold tooth" and the turban is questionable, for Mike was seen by his neighbors as anything but sinister.[4] His house, like that of Amid Hach, was a frequent stopping place for local Catholic priests. Mike Saign's wife was Catholic. Often Mike would accompany her to Mass. Mike would tell the priest, "I can say three Muslim rosaries in the time it takes you to say one Mass."[5]

Liquor was one thing, but pork especially divided the Muslims from the fellow Lebanese Christians. Muslims, of course, would not eat pig meat. One report said if a pig were being butchered while Muslims were visiting a farm, they would "turn away" rather than take part even remotely in the process.

Butchering practices differed in some ways between the two Syrian religious categories. Mike Abdallah, a Muslim, after some 30 years in America, speaking at Ross in 1939 said:

We have a religious belief concerning the butchering of meat. We believe that an animal should not be shot or hit in the head to kill it, it should be bled to death. We think that when an animal is shot or hit in the head, the evil and sins remain in the meat and it is a sin to eat this meat. We also know that when an animal is butchered our way the blood drains from the meat better and in this way the meat is a lighter color and it will keep much longer.

Mike Abdallah's concern for the proper slaughtering of an animal was shared by all of his Muslim neighbors. The animal was not to be shot or struck with a mallet; rather a knife thrust was to be made, accompanied by a prayer which included the phrase, "In the name of Allah, the Great." Additional words could be added as the animal was designated for home consumption or for the poor. Afterwards the blood was drained completely. Dietary restrictions which insist on the avoidance of pork and also the use of properly slaughtered meat, certainly brought into play all sorts of conscience problems in frontier America (as it does, of course, even today). Each individual and each family was faced with the problem whenever they visited their non-Muslim neighbors for a festive meal. How the Muslim family handled the matter of grocery store canned goods—pork? slaughter methods?—was also something that demanded a solution, and it probably varied from individual to individual. Yet the Muslim food problem had its frontier parallels: Catholics with no meat on Friday, Jews with kosher regulations.

Indeed, there were parallels with other ethnic groups at every turn. Syrian-Arabic foods were not always "different" or "exotic." One estimate has it that perhaps 30 percent of North Dakota's homesteaders were also, at least broadly speaking, from the Middle East: Germans from Russia were particularly present where most Lebanese took farm homes. The Pierce and Sheridan County Syrian settlements were literally modest sized islands in counties that were, in effect, German-Russian seas. (German-Russians, of course, had lived for almost a century just north of

Turkey near the Black Sea.) In addition, the Williston Lebanese found themselves neighbors to a settlement of native Ukrainians.

George Saba, of Bismarck, recalling foods from his home village, Ain Arab, says this:

Jabia is another favorite dish in our country. It is steamed cabbage leaves which is wrapped around coarsely ground meat, rice, salt, pepper and other spices; sometimes tomatoes are added in the center of the leaves. The whole mass is then put in a kettle and in layers, covered with water and cooked.

Any Ukrainian, any German from the Ukraine, in fact many people of Slavic background, will immediately recognize George Saba's culinary specialty. For the Ukrainian it was golubtsi. The Germans pronounced it "halupsie" and Polish and Jews, with somewhat similar names, had it as part of their ethnic fare. (Today, on the prairies, it's commonly called "cabbage rolls.")

Not at all strange to these same non-Syrian "Middle Eastern" people was a popular Lebanese dessert, a sweetmeat called *halawa*, known to Germans, Jews and Ukrainians as *halvah*. Grocery stores throughout the central part of North Dakota carried *halvah*, especially during holiday times. They also featured the dried bean-like, flavorful treat called *rashyi*, known in German as "Johannsbrot," and in English as St. John's bread. *Ftayir*, the small triangular meat and rice-filled dough envelope will be seen as *Kase Knoephla* (German) or *pierogi* or *vareniki* (Ukrainian) and *pierogy* (Polish). (Both Ukrainians and Germans often filled it with cottage cheese.)

But even the famous Syrian flat bread (called *khobaz arabee* and a variety of other names) would be recognizable. Norwegian neighbors would compare it to their own "flat bread," thin sheets of a potato-based delicacy called *lefse.*

Germans from the Ukraine were well acquainted with the salty black olives which graced the table at "almost every meal." "Greek olives" they were called. And the occasional North Dakota neighbor of Greek ancestry would declare that Lebanese *salata kuthra* bore a resemblance to what they would consider their own national salad, the *horiatiki salata.*

Publications detailing life in turn-of-the-century villages in Syria sometimes mention the common tobacco burner called a *narghile,* a pot-like vessel by which several individuals at leisure could inhale a cooled smoke through flexible tubes. Such a device occurred in North Dakota, but infrequently. Did cigarettes and roll-your-own tobacco (Bull Durham ?) spell the end of this a sociable custom?

Ingenuity, as seen on previous pages, allowed the homesteading Syrian to overcome many dietary obstacles. One example is bulghor wheat, which was a frequent Lebanese staple. It was unattainable on the prairies, but North Dakota was one of the world's leading producers of durum wheat. The Federal Writers Project files from 1942, without any reference to the author, has this interview concerning Syrian practices:

> *Each year they take a quantity of [durum] wheat, boil it, then allow it to dry in the sun; it is then crushed in a machine similar to a coffee-mill of gigantic size. The machine is operated by horse-power, in a manner similar to a well-digging machine. The crushed wheat is then screened to free it from hulls. It is stewed with meat and vegetables, or with sweet oils, and used much as we use rice.*[6]

Today, well-illustrated Lebanese cookbooks are found in the homes of every "Syrian" descendant. As one would expect, holidays are occasions for an array of the early-day foods. The names, passed on orally, sometimes vary from the modern cookbook (as can be seen in the above paragraphs) but the foods retain the delightful Eastern Mediterranean flavors. Some items have become almost a symbol of Lebanese ancestry. Kibbi would be first on that list. Joe Hiawatha at Rock Lake, North Dakota, would sometimes mix up a "big batch" of kibbi and put on a big feed for his neighbors. The delighted participants called it "Syrian hamburger."

Other food items are shared with non-Lebanese neighbors, especially at holidays; a good example is mahleb flavored *kak,* now often called an Easter doughnut. Non-Lebanese also have experienced well-known *Khoba Arabee* or flat bread. Arak, too, is sometimes shared, amid smiles and humorous stories of the past. And we must not forget the Pan-Arabic *shish kebabs,* a delicacy which, with a bewildering number of ingredients, occupies the center of many American backyard summer festivities.

Anthropologists have long noted that American ethnic groups, with the passage of the generations and perhaps unwittingly, begin to emphasize and invest with special symbolism certain national foods. The foods represent to themselves and their neighbors the traditions of their ancestors. In their former land, the food might have been incidental to their regular diet, but in the United States the delicacy (often not so delicate) assumes an almost sacred meaning. Almost like the national flag, the food represents an "Old Country," which most have seen only in their imaginations. Lefse and lutefisk are honored Norwegian symbols. Haggis is Scot; kielbasa is Polish; kolach is Czech. Kibbi is the Lebanese symbolic food. In fact sometimes Lebanese in America refer to a fellow countryman as a "kibbi."*

---

* For some foods used in early Mid America see: Lee S. Tesdell et al. (ed.), *The Way We Were: Arab Americans in Central Iowa* (Iowa City: Grand View College, 1993), pp. 3, 12, 14, 17-19, and Deborah L. Miller, "Middle Easterners," *They Chose Minnesota,* June D. Holmquist (ed.) (St. Paul: Minnesota Historical Society Press, 1981), p. 518.

Kibbi: Syria's National Dish

2 pounds of lean ground beef or lamb
1 cup of Burghol wheat, cracked, fine
1 onion, large, grated
Salt and pepper (to personal preference)

Soak wheat in cold water. Drain by cupping and squeezing in hands. Add meat, onions, and spices. Grind one or two times. Add water (1/2 cup, cold, or use wet hands) to soften. Knead, then serve.

Note: Most cookbooks have a half-dozen Kibbi variations: with special spices, with walnuts, with yogurt? Baked? Patties?

A parallel delicacy sometimes found in America, especially at "men's" gatherings, is called "tiger meat." In more sophisticated surroundings it's called "steak tartare."

Arak

Arak is spelled variously as Arak, Arrac, Arrack, and Arraici. Although the liqueur is almost a symbol of Lebanon and Syria, it is also common in Iran, Jordan, and Egypt. In Jordan, for example, more "Arrack" is consumed than wine. In Iran, over two million gallons of "Arak" are consumed each year.

The Bekaa Valley of Lebanon is the source of three-quarters of the nation's grape production. Most is used for table consumption, some for dried raisins and some for grape juice. And, in truth, the inferior grapes are used for the making of wine and Arak.

Arak, according to the label on the bottle, is "made of distilled grape juice, flavored with Anis." (Gum mastic is also a component.) The brand name found very often in Midwestern American liquor stores is Rozzouk, "a product of Lebanon's Arak Rozzouk Distillery." (Razook is the name of several Lebanese families who settled in the Pierce County area at the turn of the Twentieth Century ... is there a family connection?)

CHAPTER NINETEEN

Different and the Same

Syrian-Lebanese, like every national group, carried to the American shores their own unique cultural background. There were elements of that culture which would prove to be beneficial as the people took root in their new homeland. There would also be features of their traditional way of life that could cause them difficulties. Through the decades of adjustment the new Americans would be forced to strike a balance between the Old World and the New. They would have to decide which traditions could be sacrificed and which might be too precious to discard.

The Woman's Role

The status and rights of women were perplexing issues for Lebanese in Dakota and elsewhere in the United States. An outsider might approach the matter with the stereotype of a recessive female, bound by Old Country customs that relegated her to the sidelines in education, politics, and economic endeavors. A closer look should warn the observer that such a perception must contain a great deal of inaccuracy. As we have seen on earlier pages, a North Dakota Lebanese woman would dwell all by herself in her solitary homestead shanty; the Lebanese woman peddler would traverse the prairie trails alone, going from farm to farm without the protections of village life. That same woman would single-handedly "run the farm" during the long absences of her peddler husband. We see here an independent, able woman, almost modern in her self-assurance.

Such a woman must have had a childhood and adolescence in Lebanon that made her capable of such feats. Certain aspects of her home life and education must have equipped her to be "modern" in her new

American setting. We are not exactly sure, as we look back over the generations, what family life was like in Lebanon but we do know something of the education. We know that in almost every case the early North Dakota Lebanese women had some Old Country education, perhaps formal and certainly home-centered. We are aware that many girls did attend village schools. We know, for example, that foreign missionaries erected girls' schools almost at the same time as those that were assigned to males. The 1910 US Immigration Department, according to Louise Houghton, put the illiteracy rate for all Syrian arrivals at 56 percent. She also said the illiteracy level for both women and men between the years of fourteen and forty-five was 43 percent. As seen in the WPA reminiscences of this volume, available education facilities probably varied from village to village. Tutors? Town schools? Church schools? Yet Ms. Houghton, in her 1911 research, does say that it would be "difficult to find half a dozen illiterates in any one of the 107 villages where American schools exist." (Can this be true?) Yet Ms. Houghton does not qualify her observation nor does she differentiate between boys and girls in her statement.[1]

One must be careful in generalizing about the level of education among North Dakota's pioneer Lebanese women. We possess no statistics concerning such things. As if by way of a warning, we have the words of Adele Younis, one of America's foremost students of the American Lebanese experience. She says in her book, *The Coming of Arabic-speaking People to the United States:* "About 100 Syrian homesteaders settled around Williston, North Dakota. A few were graduates of the Syrian Protestant College. Included were their wives, many of whom were cultured and knowledgeable."[2]

Nonetheless, it is clear from all sources that in the Old Country women attended school less frequently than men. And, as seen often in this volume, the illiteracy rate among women as they arrived on America's shores was higher than their male counterparts. The figures taken from Ms. Houghton's work, however, concern the early migrations, before 1910. All reports say that these earliest decades of migration were primarily among Christians. The Muslim migrations to this country began in the decade before World War I and continued, under the quota system, until the 1950s. There is probably no way in which we can determine the exact proportion of Muslim women settlers in North Dakota who could read or write; their number was probably quite low.

Mary Juma, in 1939, spoke disparagingly about her childhood education. She was from "Byria, Bushia" and was of Muslim background. She migrated after the turn of the century to Ross, North Dakota.

*I received no education as our people figured that it was a waste of time
and money to teach a girl to read and write. There were no schools in our
village, and those that were taught to read and write were taught by a tutor.*

On the other hand, Blanche Abdallah, reflecting on her childhood in Ross,
ND, remembers clearly the Arabic newspapers in the home of her
Muslim grandparents, both of whom were immigrants from Lebanon.
Ms. Abdallah says that although her grandmother was illiterate, some
women in the Ross community could read. They were sometimes self-
taught or instructed by family members.

A look at homestead federal land office books may tell us something
of the status of the early Lebanese women. An analysis of land claim
records in Mountrail County gives the researcher a surprise: not one of
the 71 Muslims who took land in Mountrail County was a woman! On
the other hand in Williams County, 100 miles west of Mountrail, 14 of
the 80 Christian Syrians who filed for land were women. The 14 women
(18 percent of the total) compares very favorably with other ethnic groups
in that part of North Dakota.[3]

What does this mean? Did the Muslim background make it difficult
for women to strike out on their own in farming ventures? There could
be another reason. When homesteading was taking place in western
North Dakota, the flow of Lebanese to America tended to be Christian
and women were part of it. The Muslim stream to America came later
and was disproportionately male. Women were a rarity.

Women's Work

North Dakota during settlement times was a raw frontier; hard, physical labor was the foundation of all enterprises. Women everywhere were
forced to toil in the farmyards, the barns and the fields. For women, life
provided a double burden, accompanying their husbands in agricultural
work during the daylight hours and laboring in the home with domestic
tasks during the early morning and late evening hours.

Mrs. Libbie Layon of Williston in 1940 assessed her early years in
North Dakota. "I have hard time on farm. I never farm before. I get
married. I live on farm all my life. But that's better for kids, then you don't
worry about them. In town they get into something. I like farm for that."

The U.S. Census classifications are of little help in delineating the
farm woman's place in the early North Dakota settlement decades. The
occupation category for the wife is usually left blank (no job of significance?), or occasionally it is listed as "homemaker." Memories of children and grandchildren tell us otherwise. Life for the farm wife meant

years of back- breaking physical toil. Unquestionably women of all national origins (except for the privileged few who were wives of large farm managers), regardless of upbringing or preferences, performed tasks that in more gentle circumstances would be classed as resoundingly masculine. In America, Lebanese women worked in the barns and fields alongside their "men folk."

For women of the second generation, it may have been a different matter. A woman who mastered the art of peddling could, or at least her daughter could, with little difficulty apply those same skills to the procedures of a small business operation. In Crookston, for example, we find Sadie George running a family grocery store in the 1930s. Such a thing must have taken place in Williston, perhaps even in Rolla.

But whatever happened in terms of store ownership, there's no doubt that women worked in the stores. In the 1910 Census of Williams County, Mrs. Debe and Mrs. Jennie John are listed as "own income." The same was said of Julie Skaff and Mary Skaff. What does "own income" mean? Ramie Farrah of Mont Township near Williston in 1910 had the same census classification. In 1920 the Census of Rock Lake village in Towner County has Mrs. Rachel Soloman classed as a "day laborer." In that same year, Rachel Bahme was a bookkeeper and Martha Bahme was a telephone operator. Both were in Williams County, and both were daughters of Syrian-born parents.

Personal Adornment

When arriving in the United States, fresh off the boat at Eastern seaports, each national group understandably wore something of their native garb and displayed elements of their home culture. In 1895 New York, a writer remarks, "The women are usually decorated in Syrian style with tattooed ornaments, sometimes covering large surfaces of the body and the back of the hand."[4] Nothing of this sort was described on North Dakota applications for citizenship.

The more visual signs of Old Country Syrian life disappeared rather rapidly in North Dakota, certainly at a faster pace as the Syrian residents moved away from the "Little Syrias" of Eastern cities. In Iowa, for example, a report said that the fez was seldom worn, and then only in the intimacy of the home. A time came when Old Country costumes emerged only on the occasion of family or civic celebrations.

Head coverings for women, whether winter or summer, were common customs in Syria for both Muslims and Christians. Face veils, if they ever were part of the Lebanese home culture, are never mentioned in North Dakota accounts. An east coast writer said drastic changes in women's garb might bring forth conscience problems for Muslims. One person was quoted as saying clothing changes could be "contrary to [her] religion."[5] Yet in North Dakota, early day women's clothing forms among all ethnic groups seemed to be a matter of minor significance. Small variations occurred in style—color preference, skirt length—in the earliest days from village to village, the residue of Old Country traditions, but such things were expected in the sometimes isolated atmosphere of the new prairie towns.

Nonetheless, early indoor and outdoor photographs of Syrian women on the Dakota prairies, of whatever religious background, showed a shawl type of head covering. Indeed, Mrs. Anthony, a Christian lady peddler who worked out of Crookston, Minnesota, and later out of Lawton, North Dakota, always wore a loose-fitting long dress and a scarf, "like a nun," her daughter related.[6] The history of Cooperstown, a predominantly Norwegian city, describes the Muslim neighbors (Glenfield): "The women wore long sleeves and covered their heads."[7]

In perspective, however, head coverings were almost universal among middle-aged and older women on the Dakota prairies. The Anglo-American wore bonnets; some nationalities wore kerchiefs or even stocking caps. But a distinctive scarf-shawl (babushka) was everywhere present among women whose origins were from Eastern Europe. Ukrainian women and German women from the Black Sea villages wore the dark scarves regularly in North Dakota when outdoors. Such a practice continued into the second generation of American life.

There might have been something other than tradition at work in these circumstances. North Dakota seasons dictated, in the past and even today, a certain head covering. The cold winds of winter and the hot sun of summer make such a headdress a very reasonable accommodation.

As a side comment we may note that early photographs show men adopting the standard American farm overalls from the first days of settlement. Work circumstances certainly dictated the practical Great Plains garb. Apparently for winter chores the men, too, would wear the traditional Dakota sheepskin coats. On religious festival days, in fact at all formal gatherings, the early-day Syrian men wore contemporary American suits. One does, however, get the impression that owners were not comfortable in their formal suit wear: the collars look tight; the shoulders seem slightly hunched under the burden of the fancy garb.

Marriage: The Wife, The Husband

A glance through the U.S. Census for Williams County in 1920 shows Charles Youness coming to America in 1896, his wife, Anna, arrived in 1901. Charles Albert came in 1899, his wife, Irene, came in 1902. Charles

Zien arrived in 1900, his wife, Esther, in 1903. James Kalil and his wife, Sophie, came in 1899 and 1911 respectively. Joe Boussad came in 1893 and his wife, Lillie, arrived in 1899. The variations in the arrival dates show, without doubt, that the men came first. Did a wife remain in the Old Country till the husband got "established" and was able to send travel fare, or did the man come as a solitary migrant and subsidize the journey of a prospective wife to America at a later date? How many men journeyed back to Syria on a matrimonial quest? How many might have been arranged marriages? How many single women came to the United States and met their mates subsequent to their arrival times? Answering the above questions can be just a matter of guesswork. Perhaps all of the above possibilities occurred at one time or another.

For some marriages the records are clear. Sam Allick, for example, homesteaded in Bull Butte Township of Williams County in 1910. In 1926 he returned to Lebanon and married his wife Massade. The couple farmed until 1964 when they moved into Williston. George Barkie came to America in 1902. He took land in Bull Butte Township in 1905. His account in *Wonder of Williams* says he later sent to Lebanon for his wife Mary and their three children.[8]

Alec Hasen, after some 20 years in North Dakota, went back to Lebanon with marriage in mind. He didn't believe in arranged marriages so he spent a year renewing old acquaintances. He fell in love with a young lady, married her in 1922, and returned to America. Alec was forty-two and his wife Shirley was twenty-two.[9]

Marriage did not always survive the departure of the husband to America in search of prosperity. As seen earlier in this volume, Side Abdallah returned to Lebanon and built a house for his family. He came back to North Dakota alone, continued farming, and died in America at an advanced age.

The return to the "Old Country" to acquire a wife was not unique to Syrians. It was common to most immigrant groups. "The mail order brides" phenomena occurred with many variations: a random group arrives? a matchmaker dispatches a bride? a letter writing arrangement? All these were a well-recorded part of western pioneer experience. The discomforts of the frontier were such that many men preferred the single life until they could acquire the amenities of gracious living. With a degree of prosperity they could set up a union through Old Country contacts or even return to their native lands and choose a prospective mate. Indeed, the returnee might be particularly attractive if he, perhaps, paraded his accumulation of American wealth and experience.

"I lived on my homestead (in Sheridan County) for eight years and then went to the Old Country to get married. When I returned, I lived on my homestead … until 1916." So said Samuel Nicola of Bismarck in 1939.[10]

In 1952, two Lebanese women became the brides of older Lebanese-American men from North Dakota. Dehebie "Debbie" Kadrie, at age 19, of Rafid, Lebanon, became the bride of Hassen Eli of Glenfield, North Dakota. Unfortunately her husband died shortly into the marriage. Eventually Debbie remarried (a man named Jack Dorrance) and became an American citizen. At Binford, North Dakota, Ghalie "Gayle" Salberie, at age 21, of Kfar Dines, Lebanon, arrived to become the wife of Albert Abraham. She too became an American citizen and still resides in Binford.[11]

A Turtle Mountain widower merchant named George Albert journeyed to Lebanon and brought his new wife, Fatima Heymour, to North Dakota. The couple spent the rest of their lives on the prairies. Alley Omar Sage of Crookston did it differently. He went back to Lebanon, married, and never returned to the New World.

There is one "problem" which could have risen in America, but was certainly rare in North Dakota: the matter of multiple wives. A particularly Muslim issue, this situation could have exploded and besmirched the image of Lebanese everywhere in the United States.

When a newcomer to America applied for citizenship, the process included the rejection of a foreign king, or the Kaiser or, in the case of many Lebanese, the Sultan of Turkey. The application said further that the perspective citizen declared that he or she "disavowed polygamy and anarchy." Very prominent in the applicants' citizenship was a phrase that went something like this: "I am [not] married and my wife's name is _____." The place and date of birth and the name of each child was listed.

This rejection of polygamy and the listing of a wife (or husband) and children were certainly aimed at applicants who might have come from countries in which multiple spouses were an accepted custom. (The issue was a sensitive one in the United States; Utah had been granted statehood in 1896 after an extensive discussion of the polygamy question.)

Whatever the American political scene might have dictated, it is clear that for Muslims coming to North Dakota, there was an unequivocal message: two wives would be illegal. And once and for all the applicant was on record. This information could be used against a person if he were married and sought to acquire a second marital spouse on either side of the Atlantic.

The great majority of Muslims who decided to remain in North Dakota honored such a provision. No court case involving polygamy can be found in any state judicial record.

Yet, stories do surface as old-time residents of Lebanese background reminisce. No names are mentioned, but North Dakota was a long way from Syria and official reports did not always travel efficiently across the Atlantic in the early decades of the century. Some pioneers did, without fanfare, have a wife in each of two different widely separated worlds.

There was no religious obstacle that stood in the way of a Muslim man taking a second wife. Such a thing is permitted in the Koran. But for those immigrants who wished to remain in America, a polygamous arrangement would involve a degree of subterfuge and perhaps expulsion from the country. Perhaps an even greater deterrent to polygamy was the fact that the public opinion in the United States was decidedly against such a thing—and Muslims in North Dakota, quite understandably, did not want to be ostracized in their small American communities.

Making the past cloudier, in some cases, was the fact that divorce in Syria was a less cumbersome matter than in the United States. (For Muslims, divorce was a civil action and was certainly easier to obtain than for Christians, who viewed marriage as a religious sacrament.) An occasional grandchild wonders whether grandfather had a former wife in Syria, one which family accounts do not mention. In several cases such embarrassing information does become known and the specifics are presented to the "outsider," but only in hushed tones. Again, it's very rare but present-day Lebanese have met others of Syrian-Muslim origins and in the discussion find they have the same great-grandfather, a gentleman who had a wife in the United States and another in Syria. Needless to say, "cool feelings" sometimes exist between the various modern branches of grandfather's families.

Syrian men in North Dakota sometimes had to look no further than St. Paul, Minnesota, or Sioux City, Iowa, to find a wife. As seen elsewhere in the volume, a large number of single Lebanese women began arriving in America after the turn of the century. The early arrivals tended to be Christian, but Muslim women began arriving in the United States in substantial numbers a decade or so later. Muslim men in North Dakota looked perhaps to settlements farther east. Several Ross Muslim men found their prospective spouses in Canada.

The age of the wife who found her mate in America was very young by contemporary standards. If we can believe the census dates of birth and the age of the first child, some women were married at 14. But, given the family reluctance to record ages—the Turkish draft problem— perhaps the "early" age was not the true age. And the census records show frequently the ten, fifteen, or twenty-year difference between the ages of North Dakota couples.

What do we make of the early age of the bride or the age discrepancies of the husband and wife? Were these marriage traditions unique to Lebanese men? Probably not. Italian and Balkan men often returned with very young wives as they sought "helpmates" in their adopted American homeland. In addition, maturity came early in the stressful frontier circumstances. Regardless of national group, wives on the Great Plains were often 16 years of age. Almost every modern-day family, as it uncovers its genealogical record, is surprised at the youthful marriage ages of some of their maternal ancestors.

A dowry, a gift exchanged between the families of a prospective marriage couple, was a frequent part of life among some of North Dakota's first-generation national groups: Germans from Russia and Polish, for example. Something of the same was true of the Lebanese Old Country world. Sam Omar, of Ross Muslim heritage, recalled it in a 1939 interview. "In asking for a bride, a Syrian boy approaches the mother of the girl ... if the two parties can agree, a stated amount of money is set aside, so in case of separation ... caused through the fault of the man, the bride receives the money."

In an incident already mentioned on a previous page, we see that the *Gackle Republican* of February 18, 1910, reported an inter-family altercation. A young man was arrested for "assault and battery":

> *The husband of the girl claimed to have purchased her for $1625. They have been married about a year. The girl's parents finally induced her to leave him on the grounds of cruelty, and took her home with them. The husband claimed to have the right to his wife, as according to the custom of their race her price had been duly paid and she belonged to the person who bought her.*

The issue was settled through negotiations between both families. The newspaper item concluded with this note: "The parties were released by the state's attorney after paying the cost of the proceeding."

Muslim Adjustment

As indicated in the previous pages, Muslims brought to America some unique cultural and religious traditions that gave rise to special difficulties as they adjusted to what might be called the Great Plains "diaspora." The estimated five hundred Muslims who once lived in North Dakota were surrounded by other, often very different, Christian groups. In the Ross-Stanley area they found themselves in the midst of Norwegian Lutherans. In the Turtle Mountains, the majority of their neighbors were of French or French-Indian (Metis) Catholic peoples.

Three generations have passed since the early settlement days. Such a time period provides a "laboratory" of sorts in which various influences and adjustments can be put in perspective.

To begin, as has been often noted, we must admit that Syrians (Lebanese) "looked" different when compared to many of their Dakota neighbors. They were dark-skinned, in contrast to their Norwegian and British Isles counterparts. Their language had no relationship to those of their English, Scandinavian, or Germanic fellow settlers. Their religious ceremonies, whether Muslim, Orthodox, or Melkite-Maronite, resonated with chants and rituals that, at first sight, had no counterpart in the usual American religious format.

There were elements of the Muslim life that in the Old Country proved to be routine, but were sometimes serious problems as they adjusted to the prairie environment. The Muslim culture, on one hand, had great respect for women, but their traditions often seemed to relegate women to roles that, by American standards, could be considered inferior. Such initial problems as socializing with non-Muslim neighbors on a couple-to-couple basis might present problems. Even a handshake between a man and a woman could be a matter of concern. Yet one could mention other national groups in which the man and woman, at least in public, did not seem to be "equal." In several early non-Syrian groups the man would always walk on the street ahead of the woman. In several other groups, men would never be seen in public with women engaged in card games or similar leisure-type activities. And, to put the matter into a larger context, women in early America were denied many of the "privileges" that were part of the masculine world. The list is long: to vote, to enter certain professions, to smoke in public, to frequent taverns, to engage in certain sports.

Several very obvious difficulties were discussed on earlier pages; one was the matter of dietary laws: no pork, ritual slaughter. These could give rise to problems of conscience; was it necessary to read the label on every soup can? (See the chapter on Food and Drink.)

The question of food was just a symptom of the more fundamental and pervasive issue of how to maintain their unique Muslim culture in this new and almost overwhelming American world. Two sets of difficulties emerged. (They have been discussed briefly on earlier pages.) The first was the religious education of children. Islam, like Christianity and Judaism, is a "religion of the book." If the mother, the usual religious instructor, had difficulty reading—and many did—how could the faith of the parents be transferred to the next generation? If a "catechism" type of material was not readily available, or if knowledgeable "instructors" were few in number, a basic knowledge of the religious tradition would escape the minds of the children and grandchildren. The heart might grasp the essentials, but what of the head?

A related problem arose when a young Muslim offspring reached marriageable age. Sons or daughters attended grade and high school with friends who were of Christian religious orientation and some would, quite naturally, contemplate a "mixed marriage." This latter problem could well have been the most fundamental difficulty. Mixed marriages, wherever they take place throughout the world, may become a cultural hemorrhage that can often prove to be fatal. (See Muslim portions of Chapter 13: Syrian Enclaves)

Muslim Advantages

Certainly there were problems of adjustment in the New World, yet the Muslim way of life contained specific cultural features that proved to be beneficial as they faced the stresses of the prairie environment. (Some of these "advantages" were discussed on previous pages.) The Muslim religious tradition, for example, did not require a mosque for worship; Muslim prayer was considered an individual matter. Prayers, therefore, could be said anywhere: in a home setting, at work in the fields, or "on the road." Further, the Muslim tradition had no ordained priesthood. A prayer leader could arise from the ranks of believers at any time or circumstance. Only knowledge of the Koran and an appreciation of the traditions were needed. Works of charity, concern for the homeless and the poor, were cardinal principles in the Muslim way of life. The wayfarer was respected. Of particular importance was the fact that weddings need not take place in a church setting, nor did funerals require a formal religious environment.

It's easy to see how the Muslim religious traditions were appropriate to the life of a peddler, a solitary itinerant person, often away from home and often dependent on the hospitality of strangers and fellow countrymen for housing and nourishment. The Muslim had a "portable" religion, one that the peddler could carry along in a private fashion as he or she ventured into the unknown.

The American political system caused difficulties, at times, to some of the other immigrants who took land alongside Muslims in central North Dakota. Taxes, conscription in the military, allegiance to the government, were upsetting to Mennonites and Amish, but these caused no crisis of conscience to the Muslim. The newly arrived Muslim found American draft laws to be less harsh but much the same as those of their prior Syrian homeland.

Observing Syrian Muslim (or Syrian Christian) differences from a larger perspective, one must remember that North Dakota, during settlement times, was a garden in which several dozen separate cultures blossomed. Only the relatively few Yankees, the Old Americans, along with some second-generation Germans and Irish, embodied what was perceived as a truly American way of life. For the most part, everyone was "strange." Arabic people were just one more fragment in an already colorful mosaic of exotic, newly arriving peoples.

Looking even more closely, one sees parallels that perhaps made the Arabic life understandable and even acceptable. Arabic people, whether Christian or Muslim, prayed when an animal was butchered, the same was also true of Jews. Muslims would not drink alcohol. This was not out of line with the state's widely favored prohibitionist sentiments. (North Dakota was a "dry state," both by state and federal law, for much of its first forty years of existence.) Muslims had prayer beads, so did Catholics of a dozen ethnic backgrounds. Muslims had the Koran; Christians and Jews had the Bible. Muslims covered the dead in a shroud of white cloth, but so did the Jews at funeral times. Ramadan was seen, in fact, as the Muslim Lent. Fasting was commonplace in most Christian traditions. Holy days might vary, but such a thing as sacred time was not unknown: Fridays for Muslims, Saturdays for Jews, and Sundays for Christians. The Syrian flatbread looked remarkably similar to the Norwegian lefse which graced the tables of thousands of North Dakota homes. Christmas was no problem for the Muslims; Jesus was a great prophet and worthy of special honor. Shoes were removed at Muslim worship, but again, almost all families removed their work shoes when entering the early farm homes. Facing the east at prayer should not have been strange to the Christian, for, where possible, many buried their dead and oriented their churches toward the rising sun.

Syrian-Lebanese were different from their contemporaries a century ago, but, looking back over the past generations, perhaps not as different as one would imagine.

As others have pointed out, however, to be regarded as different does not necessarily mean one becomes an object of bigotry. Solitary black farmers, as seen in the volume *African-Americans in North Dakota*, were generally accepted in their communities. They were the first to admit, in retrospect, that on first encounter their immigrant neighbors studied them with a certain degree of apprehension. After the initial "getting-to-know-you" period, they were eventually received as full-fledged members of the rural community. Studies of early Jewish settlements on the prairies often quote early residents as saying much the same. Prejudice and discrimination was minimal.

Compatibility: Arab and American Indian

One does not have to look long at the distribution of Lebanese households across North and South Dakota before being struck by the frequency of Arab businesses located on Indian reservations. These were not business firms that flitted in and out of Indian areas, but were establishments that existed for at least a generation. Whether dry goods, retail clothing, or groceries, Arabic merchants often supplied the needs of local Native Americans. Interviews of old-time reservation dwellers say the Lebanese storeowner had a reputation for honesty and amiability. As a result, the storekeepers were able to turn a modest profit and raise their families in rather permanent circumstances. The Lebanese merchant displayed a sense of equality; he did not view the native culture as inferior. Speaking in terms of North Dakota's Turtle Mountains, second generation Rolla businessmen Ron Hasen and Quentin Harris mention a special affinity, a sense of trust that existed between the Arabic merchants and local French-Chippewa people.[12] Indeed, the dark-complected and black-haired Lebanese might have had an advantage over other European ethnic groups in dealing with native peoples. To the Indian people, the Lebanese, who appeared to be a group apart from "whites," were perhaps less intimidating than their more aggressive Anglo-American counterparts.

Reports say that something similar happened in Crookston. The George and Peter stores, both Lebanese-owned, were favorite shopping centers during the 1950s and 1960s for Mexican migrant workers who came "north" each summer season.

Not surprisingly, some Lebanese men married native women, and traditional Lebanese Muslim or Christian community attitudes seldom discouraged such unions. The fact is that many such marriages were very successful; it can almost be said that on the Turtle Mountain Reservation in Rolette County, mixed ancestry marriages were the norm, not the exception. For centuries, unions between French fur traders and Indian women had occurred, creating a new and unique culture called today either the Metis or the "Mitchif" people. Former North Dakota State Representative Les Lafountain of Belcourt, who was well acquainted with a number of mixed Lebanese-Chippewa families, insisted that the couples were well-accepted and played an integral role in the reservation life.

When Lebanese immigrant Alex Albert opened a general store in the Turtle Mountain Reservation town of Belcourt in the early 1920s there was a huge demand for groceries, meat, and clothing. His French-Chippewa bride, Ann Gourneau, bore him two sons, Fayes and Kade. Both sons ran businesses in Belcourt. Later Fayes, for 28 years, held the job of Belcourt postmaster, and Kade ran the oldest continuously operating business in Belcourt, the Tomahawk Bar.[13]

The wife of Joe Albert, famed as the "Syrian bear wrestler," was a Chippewa lady from Belcourt. Albert's Turtle Mountain friend, Albert Ferris, also married a Metis girl. Born in Lebanon, the last part of Ferris'

life was devoted to peddling in North Dakota. Albert's son, Sam Ferris, became a highly rated Golden Gloves boxer and eventually ran a dry goods store and farmed. Grandson Albert Lee Ferris became a well-known artist. The great-grandson of Albert Ferris is today a radio announcer in Rolla named Kade Ferris.[14]

Selma Kennedy of Grand Forks recalls her dual Lebanese-Chippewa background with pride. Her father, Joe Allick, came from Damascus, Syria, to escape the Turkish army. Living in the Turtle Mountain area, in a short time he took a Chippewa-French wife and shortly afterwards joined the First World War U.S. Army. Returning from France, he spent many years in janitorial work. His descendants still treasure a series of letters, in Arabic, in which he and his family members kept each other abreast of both the successes and the hardships of life on both sides of the Atlantic.

Quentin Harris, son of Sidney and Kathryn (Ausey) Harris, married Jeanette Grant of Belcourt and raised their family of five girls and one boy in Rolla. The family owns and operates Rolla's Harris Clothing Store.

Ibrahim Sheban (James Kallod) was originally from Batrounie, Syria, and settled on the Sioux Reservation near Devils Lake with his French-Canadian wife in the early 1920s. For forty years, James Kallod ran a general merchandise store that served the local Sioux Indian families. The Lebanese gentleman could speak Sioux and even sing their songs. His Sioux name was Wa Kee Ona (meaning appropriately, "carrying

The Tokio Store, run by the Jim Kallod family for 40 years on the Devils Lake Sioux Reservation.

Courtesy: John Guerrero

things"). He couldn't read or write but was accomplished in arithmetic. He would total up the various purchase prices on an adding machine and have the patron sign the slip. James' son, Jim, was born at Tokio, ND, on the reservation. He became a respected businessman in Fargo. Another son was killed in the Second World War. In all, four Kallod sons served in that same war. Jim Kallod (Jr.) retired in Fargo and died in 1999. He is buried there, but his memory is revered throughout the Tokio area. Each year Jim would bring thousands of Christmas gifts to reservations throughout Minnesota and the Dakotas.[15]

Illness and Death

Life at the beginning of the twentieth century, as one can imagine, was not always a matter of health, safety, and longevity. Medicine was primitive, farming could be dangerous, sanitation was sometimes non-existent, and transportation was often hazardous.

Life was filled with uncertainties, but neighbors were everywhere of assistance. When Hassin Farhart of Ross was badly hurt, a physician and "many willing hands" were at his side. The *Ross Valley News* of September 17, 1909, reported:

> *Last Tuesday afternoon, a Seryian [sic] by the name of Hassin Farhart, who was hauling grain to town, was knocked down and run over by a run-away team. It seems that Farhart had drove into the elevator with a load of grain, and after the grain was unloaded, the team became frightened and started to run, and Farhart became very excited and ran out the opposite door in an effort to stop his team, and ran directly in front of the wild animals, and was knocked down and run over.*

> *He received many serious wounds about the head and face, and possibly a fractured skull.*

> *The news that a man was injured was no sooner given out, when many willing hands were giveing [sic] assistance to the injured man. He at once was giving [sic] medical attention from Dr. John J. Whyte of this place. At this writing the injured man is resting nicely.[16]*

The early moments in North Dakota history could be stressful in not just physical ways. Before the Lebanese homesteading period ever began, a peddler was hospitalized for emotional problems. (Peddling, unlike farming, could be an exceedingly lonely life.) The *Dickinson Press* in 1894, reported:

> *A full-blooded Arabian is the latest patient to be sent to the North Dakota insane asylum.[17]*

Death, of course, was part of the early North Dakota scene. The *Stanley Sun* of November 10, 1905, gives a tragic moment involving a Ross Muslim resident.

Death came swift and sudden last Sunday morning to Albert Taha, an Assyrian living near Ross. He was walking along a side track of the Great Northern when a freight train came along.

The article says he was heavily bundled in a big overcoat. The gentleman stepped out of the way for a freight and didn't see an on-coming passenger train.

"Taha was well known and stood well in the estimation of his friends and neighbors." "The remains were buried in Fairview Cemetery here on Wednesday."[18]

Death meant the problem of finding both a suitable service for the deceased, and also a place of burial. For a Muslim in the first settlement decades, it was a serious problem. For Christian Maronites and Melkites the process could be relatively easy, a Latin Rite priest would be at hand if a priest of their own rite was absent. For Orthodox, an Episcopal priest was readily available. The Catholic cemetery in Rugby has the "Cedars of Lebanon" Syrian section, with both Catholic and Orthodox graves side by side.

For the early Muslim settlers, the proper ceremony for the dead was dictated by Old Country practices. A Muslim mosque was built west of Ross in 1929. At the same time a plot of land was acquired to serve as the final resting place for Muslim dead. (Very early Muslims had to be buried in predominantly Christian cemeteries.) This Muslim cemetery exists today and the crescent and star are affixed to an arch-like entry to the holy ground. (See Chapter 13 on Syrian Enclaves)

A Muslim funeral was a thing of special interest to non-Muslim neighbors. This can be seen in a news account of a Fargo funeral. *The Leeds News* of June 13, 1907, reports:

Attorney Kodrey Buried Yesterday in Riverside Cemetery—Fargo Amon Conducted the Services.

With the solemn chanting and singing and the reading of passages from the Koran, the first Mohammedan funeral service which ever took place in Fargo was held Monday afternoon in Riverside cemetery over the body of Attorney Kodrey, who died Friday evening. The services were attended by a large number of the local colony of Syrians, who followed the body to the cemetery from Luger's undertaking parlors. Albert Kodrey, the local amen, or priest, officiated. The service was in English and except for the fact that the Koran was used it didn't differ from the ordinary funeral service.[19]

One may note the unfamiliar figure of an "amen." This man was, in fact, an imam, a prayer leader, who was never considered a "priest" in the Muslim tradition. Also noteworthy is the deceased gentleman's name: Attorney was not his profession, rather it was an Anglicized version of an Arabic name. His name: Atty Kodrey.

Joe Hiawatha, labeled as a "Syrian-Mohammedan" when interviewed at Rock Lake, ND by the Federal Writers Project in October 1936, made a statement which may or may not have been accurate. He said, "The Syrians bury their dead before sunset of the same day that the person died, or if the person dies after sunset, he is buried before the next sunset."

In the Ross community the body was prepared before burial by men and sometimes women—a white wrapping enveloped the corpse and a religious leader called a "sheik" recited a long series of chant-like prayers. (The word imam was never used at Ross, at least in the memory of Muslim modern-day descendants.)

An undertaker from Stanley, a nearby town, assisted in the ceremonies. Sometimes the service was held in the funeral home's chapel, but on occasion it was in the Ross Mosque. Local men dug the grave. Regularly a ceremonial shovel of earth was shaken into the grave. If non-Muslim family members were present, they, too, would place a token amount of earth into the grave. Certainly the prayers and moaning of the family members, especially elderly ladies, caught the attention of non-Muslim funeral guests, but no one can recall the use of "professional mourners." The sheik that presided at the funeral ceremony was often from Canada: Edmonton, Calgary, Swift Current.[20]

Gravestones at the Ross Muslim cemetery display Arabic symbols; some graves were covered completely with a slab of concrete. Tombstones, especially in the earliest days, were made of concrete with hand-inscribed names and dates. One grave is a type of concrete house with bottom, sides and top. (A semi-obscure notation in one historical account said that a house for a grave goes back to certain regions in the Old Country, where shifting sands almost demanded a house structure. Could this be true?)

The Ross Muslim Cemetery today contains twenty-two grave markers, of which two are Christian graves. One is the Christian wife of a Muslim man; the other is their Christian grandson. (A Christian infant is said to have also been buried on the premises.) There is a rural cemetery south of Ross filled with Christian graves; yet two Muslims in 1917 were buried among them. The 1905 burial mentioned in previous paragraphs was in the "Fairview Cemetery." These are funerals which took place before the establishment of the Ross Muslim Cemetery. (The Muslim cemetery's first marker is dated 1920.) Two other "Syrians" are said to have been buried in a lot across from the Ross elevator.

Muslims in the Turtle Mountain area buried their dead, not in a separate cemetery, but in a special portion of the Dunseith Cemetery. Today, at least 20 Muslim graves are present, with star and crescent emblems and Arabic inscriptions on tombstones. Several "little house" kind of grave structures are also evident.

Strange funeral combinations of east and west, Muslim and Christian, occurred on the North Dakota plains. The Congregational Church history of Michigan, ND, for example, notes the burial of a local Muslim gentleman.[21] One North Dakota tombstone has both the star and crescent and the cross inscribed in a very obvious fashion: a Muslim husband, a Christian wife. A grandson says, "Grandmother wanted to make sure that as a couple they were doubly safe. She wanted to cover all the bases."

Ghalie Abraham, a long-time resident of Binford, North Dakota, went to a great amount of effort to fulfill her husband's final request. The old man wanted to be buried on the land of his childhood, Bire, Lebanon, and not Binford, America. Mrs. Abraham struggled through a maze of 1970-era legal and transportation difficulties, but she was successful. Mr. Abraham now rests in peace at the place of his birth[22].

Along U.S. Highway 2

When Hussein "Sam" Sheronick in 1949 undertook a trip from Cedar Rapids, Iowa to Edmonton, Alberta, he stopped along U.S. Highway 2 for dinner at a restaurant in Stanley, ND. Fluent in Arabic, he was surprised to hear men at the next table talking in his native tongue. One of the men introduced himself as Charlie Juma, gave him an Arabic greeting, and asked him to join the conversation. Sam learned that there was a mosque at Ross, right down the road, which was built by some of the first Muslims in North America. Sam, in turn, informed the men that the Cedar Rapids Mosque was built in 1935. He himself often taught young Muslims in its facilities. Sam Sheronick, as late as 1997, would still regale his Iowa friends with the story of strong coffee and warm Lebanese hospitality "way out there" on Highway 2 in North Dakota.

Sidney Harris

Said Zahra was born in Khirbet Rouha, Lebanon in 1896. By 1906, his father, Mohammad, had immigrated to Crookston, Minnesota, where he became a salesman. His father's name became George Harris and his son was named Sidney Harris. During World War I, Sidney enlisted in the U.S. Army and returned a disabled veteran. He later married a Christian Arab wife, Kathryn Ausey of Perth, ND, against his father's wishes. They moved to St. Paul, MN, where he worked for Ford Motor and eventually returned to North Dakota to farm near Perth. Two Harris sons had been born, Norman and Quentin. The depression years hit farming hard so the family moved to Fish Lake, north of Belcourt, where Sidney peddled and operated a dairy farm. By the 1950s they had established a clothing store business in Rolla, which the son, Quentin, operates to the present day. Sidney, who died in 1973, believed strongly in patriotism. He and his wife were prominent in American Legion affairs. His grandson, Dr. Scott Harris, is a heart surgeon in Fargo.

CHAPTER TWENTY

An Overview

Hundreds of thousands of settlers were attracted to the northern prairies in the last decades of the 19th century and early 20th century. It was an unknown land, harsh and remote in many ways. Yet records show that in North Dakota alone they came from over forty different ethnic backgrounds.

Why and How

Two questions arise: why did they come and how did they come? As to why they came, the obvious and almost universal answer is free land. There were several exceptions. Some few came for employment in North Dakota's only large industry, the railroads (Greeks, Armenians, Japanese), but for Syrians and every other group it was the acquisition of free homestead land that enticed them to come to this particular part of America. Millions of acres of government-owned prairie were "opening up" at the time of their arrival in the United States (or, at least, shortly afterwards) and the word went out that people with minimal financial assets could get an inexpensive start, acquire a degree of property and perhaps even adopt farming as a way of life. At the least, on a homestead they could survive until they mastered the essentials of America's economic and social customs. How did they come? What stirred their interest and pointed the way to the prairies? The answer varies from group to group. For the Germans from Russia (the *Volksdeutsche*), it was railroad and state advertising that first alerted them to the Dakotas. Scouts traveled on ahead, word went back and in large groups they came to the new and free land. For Norwegians, it was also railroad and state advertising, plus letters from earlier settlers in Minnesota that caused them to look to the new prairies. For Czechs, it was glowing reports in Czech language newspapers that brought them from earlier settlements in Iowa and

Wisconsin. The same could be said for the *Reichsdeutsche,* the German-Germans: good reports and, at times, church immigration endeavors. For Jewish settlers it was often philanthropic agencies that suggested the Dakotas and sometimes gave financial assistance to the migrant who wanted to get away from the eastern seaboard congestion.

For Lebanese, the lure of free land was the key factor. Behind their movement to the prairies was not railroad advertising, not Arabic newspapers, but the word going out either to eastern American states or to the home villages by way of the peddlers' network and, perhaps, in later decades, letters from America.

In this, Lebanese were unique. Traveling men (sometimes women) could look over the land, assess its possibilities, and send word to relatives and friends that Syrians, too, could join the hoards of newcomers as they chose their own personal part of the American landscape.

Part of the message sent back by the grapevine may also have been about the receptivity of the northern prairie people. Indeed, the peddler had visited hundreds of farmsteads, had helped with the chores, sat at the table and been welcomed as a fellow American. The fact that the whole Dakota countryside seemed to be populated by "newcomers" to the United States may have figured into the peddlers' favorable assessment of the Dakotas. Everyone was foreign, so a new arrival with an Arabic background did not stand dramatically apart as an "outsider."

In one way, the Lebanese newcomer to the Dakota prairies differed from many homesteading groups. For the most part, the Lebanese man or woman tended to look at farming as a stepping-stone to life in the New World. In this, Lebanese resembled the Old Yankees (English), the Irish, and the Jews. Farming was a way to get started, to master the American system and eventually to start a business or perhaps go elsewhere for more congenial jobs and climates.

All the records indicate that for Lebanese the acquisition of land was generally regarded as a speculative venture in which land was a commodity. For some, initially, it was a chance to pick up a bundle of money and return with a degree of affluence to Syria. For many it was the entryway into the larger world of American commerce. Yet in time some few did come to see the farm as a permanent family multi-generational enterprise.

Some General Impressions

The preparation of this volume required the accumulation of hundreds of family histories, newspaper accounts, and personal reminiscences. Looking through the collection of early Lebanese materials, the authors observed certain attributes that are especially noteworthy. On the next few pages the reader will find a summary of these characteristics, a set of patterns or themes that made the early Lebanese life worthy of admiration. This is a risky undertaking. Many of the observations may fit well in a description of other national groups. Yet taken together they will show something of the uniqueness of North Dakota's first two generations of Syrian settlers.

Group loyalty was a theme that became apparent in almost every discussion of Lebanese settlement days. It was first to the family, to parents and children, but also to the extended family of aunts and uncles and cousins. It extended beyond that. Often the special relationship embraced an extensive collection of individuals, half-brothers, and step-sisters, half-cousins. Perhaps some of this loyalty occurred because they had been friends and fellow-citizens in the same village in the Old World. In America it is clear that kinship obligations demanded a great amount of personal sacrifice as individuals and whole families under difficult circumstances assisted in farming operations, job seeking, and in business ventures. Even in the "Dirty Thirties," Lebanese managed to survive, thanks to mutual family and perhaps community assistance. One outside observer in Williams County said, "Syrians were never on the county or government dole."[1]

Present also was a loyalty toward their fellow religionists: Muslim to Muslim, Christian Maronite to Melkite, Orthodox to Orthodox, and often a surprising concern of non-Orthodox Christians toward Orthodox and in return of Orthodox for fellow Lebanese Christian neighbors. Indeed, it appears that sometimes priests from the separate religious traditions would supply the holy ceremonies for all three Christian groups, disregarding the ancient church boundaries.

Religious loyalties in Western America had a certain flexibility. Maronites and Melkites, though their religious roots extend back through centuries of diverse experiences, soon found a sense of community in the New World. A relatively easy transition was made to the Latin Catholic parish life in villages and cities. Orthodox Christians often found a permanent home among the doctrines and ceremonies of the Episcopal Church. Distinctions between Shi'a and Sunni Muslims blurred. In every case, it must be remembered that for all groups bishops and religious authorities were far away. It wasn't difficult to ignore the niceties of ecclesiastical law.

In the Old Country, very little, if any, loyalty extended to governmental entity; to the village or its environs, yes, but not to a particular political authority. In this, Lebanese were different from most Dakota immigrant groups whose kings or national shrines, or even battlefields were still held in high regard. As mentioned elsewhere in this volume, Lebanese were, in a sense, men and women without a national rallying point. There were no common heroes or feast days like St. Patrick's for the Irish, Syttende Mai for the Norwegians, or Columbus Day for Italians. There arose no Pan-Arabic movement. Little public outrage arose in reaction to the wars and oppressions that have taken place in the Near East in recent decades.

Hospitality was everywhere a trademark of Lebanese life. Perhaps such a thing can be seen as an attribute of loyalty. The early Lebanese home and farmstead was, with rare exceptions, a haven for newly arrived and not-so-new traveling Arabic peoples. Fellow villagers, fellow religionists, were particularly welcome but even the Muslim and Christian differences were set aside and assistance was given: for a day, for a week or more. Non-Arabic neighbors, friends, and even travelers often comment on the "table brim with food" that greeted them at even the most brief of visits. Indeed, it is said that a visitor, when stopping at a Lebanese large or small business, became the center of attention. Customers could wait as the guest was escorted to a back room table with its incredible sweets, liquid refreshments, and conversations.

The *mobility* of the early Lebanese migrants highlights every early-day account. A move from Syria to Canada, on to American industrial cities, perhaps to Minnesota, and then to a farm in North Dakota. Sometimes the route was Europe, then Latin America, on to the factories of eastern America, then to the Dakotas. To carry a pack or ride a wagon to a thousand farms and a hundred villages, was standard practice. No single group in America can match that kind of mobile lifestyle. "A man without a country," "a citizen of many villages." These comments rang true in the Midwestern American countryside.

Mastering the American Ways

Unlike most groups, the Arabic language background provided few if any advantages to the new Syrian immigrant. To start with a non-European language, a Mediterranean lifestyle, a minimum of "modern type" education, and then suddenly to find themselves on the great expanses of mid-American plains, most people would shy away from such a collection of obstacles. Yet the Syrian-Lebanese survived, devising self-help ventures, untangling the American retail-wholesale systems, understanding advertising and marketing. Often all these skills were acquired within a matter of three or four years! In contrast to many other national groups, one seldom found an immigrant from Syria who lived for long in America who did not know some English. Again, unlike several other Eastern European groups in North Dakota, the authors have found no court record of Syrian truancy. Work for the young was important among the Lebanese, but at least minimal education in the American ways was even more important.

A deep and abiding *allegiance to America as a nation* characterized the attitudes and deeds of Lebanese men and women everywhere in North Dakota, an allegiance that arose rapidly once the idea of "returning home" was set aside. If it is true that Lebanese lacked a sense of nationhood, they quickly developed one for their adopted country. "You never spoke adversely about America in our presence," so said an early Williston resident. As seen in an early chapter, the proportion of Syrian-born men who entered the armed services from North Dakota in World War I is without equal. And they tended to be front-line troops. Six percent were killed in action. The Silver Star, the army's third highest award, was given to four Syrians from the state. Veterans groups could boast of a disproportionate number of active Lebanese members through the past generations; many of whom held the highest offices in state veterans' affairs.

Gratitude to the nation for supplying both freedom and opportunity was a theme that reoccurred in memories and reports of every one of the state's Lebanese communities. Even if they at times suffered discrimination, their first response, if asked about the matter, was to downplay its extent or even deny its existence. Resentment towards its perpetrators seemed to be singularly absent.

Law Abiding

Louise Houghton, in 1912, writing concerning New York, says the Syrian citizens "are quiet, peaceful, and law-abiding." She admits there were a few cases of assault—quarrels often on religious grounds. She reports that there were also "a certain number of smuggling cases."[2] With minor exceptions, therefore, Syrians were considered law-abiding citizens in the earliest eastern city settlements. Ms. Houghton could just as well have been writing about the North Dakota Lebanese scene at that same moment in time. Telmar Rolfstad, an elderly non-Syrian lawyer and public official in Williston said, without qualifications, "there were no crimes" among the Lebanese of that city.[3]

Mr. Rolfstad would have introduced some qualifications if he could have seen the entire span of "Syrian" North Dakota life throughout the first several decades of settlement. In some counties there were episodes involving horse theft, fist fights, even weapons discharged. Yet, in most cases, it was a matter of inter-group altercations: Lebanese versus

Lebanese. Certainly the "king man," mentioned earlier in this volume, would sometimes be involved in resolving the various mishaps. This man would moderate disputes between individuals and, perhaps, between a Lebanese individual and public officials.

In all honesty, however, it should be noted that there were Lebanese actions that seemed to fall somewhat outside of the law. "Syrians" were known to have manufactured their own "arak," but for "personal use," they would quickly say. At least one prominent Lebanese family got its financial start through the grandfather's commerce during prohibition days. He transported Canadian whiskey to thirsty North Dakotans. Yet in later years he insisted: "I never sold bad booze." It was quality stuff.

Odd Ways

Some Lebanese customs were, to say the least, "odd" to their fellow landseekers of European background. Earlier in this volume a February 18, 1910 news report in *The Gackle Republican* told of a bride who had purportedly been purchased by her husband for $1,695.00 and now wanted to leave the man. The gentleman was angry. He claimed "to have the right to his wife. Her price had been paid ..." The newspaper termed it a "peculiar marriage custom."

An "odd" incident occurred in Crookston, Minnesota, which involved North Dakota state laws. The *Fargo Forum* of August 1908 introduced the report in bold print: ASSYRIANS HAVE SOME ODD WAYS. The incident started at Crookston. The Chief of Police, a man named Eck, was trying, at the date of the news report, to understand what had happened. The newspaper item contains the following:

> *Tool* sold a horse to his cousin, Kool,* who paid the cash, $180, for it. Tool pocketed the money stating that he would leave the horse in the livery barn. Instead he loaded his wagon with goods and left the city with the horse and the money he had received for it. Kool swore out a warrant charging Tool with stealing his horse, which he bought and paid for. Chief Eck took up the warrant, hired a livery gig and apprehended Tool several miles west of the city making for North Dakota as fast as he could drive, and brought him back to the city. Both are Assyrian peddlers and local Assyrians acted as mediators, and after Tool had been brought back to the city he turned over the money to Kool again, paid all costs and was let off.* [4](* pseudonyms)

Lebanese were a *practical* people. Everywhere we get the impression that they were not happy with delays; they wanted to get on with the business of making a living and carving out their little niche in the New

World. Hard work was valued (and this attribute may have contributed much to their acceptance by non-Syrian neighbors). Education was desired for their children, but education for the sake of education was never fostered. The humanities were not valued; practical subjects were. Yet some second generation did attend college and the third generation often did very well in academic studies.

Politics at first was someone else's endeavor. Some first-generation Lebanese voted, but many ignored the voting booth. For subsequent generations it was a different matter. Not only did they vote, some ran for public office. And when elected they often excelled. Williams County, the location of what is probably North Dakota's most enduring collection of citizens of Syrian background, has seen many Lebanese in prominent political positions. The same can be said for the Walsh and Sheridan county second and third generation Lebanese. South Dakota's two U.S. Senators of Lebanese background should provide evidence that political aspirations do, at times, have a place in the lives of Syrian immigrants' descendants.

Father Sharbel Maroun

When Father Sharbel Maroun came to the United States in 1976, the Lebanese Civil War had been raging for one year. Lands were confiscated, cars were bombed, business transactions came to a halt, and overseas travel was curtailed. Lebanon's national identity was at stake in this long, bitter war rooted in religious and economic rivalry.

Father Maroun had left his home village of Kafarselwan to become a Maronite priest. He eventually came to St. Maron's Church in Minneapolis in the early 1990s. The rest of his family immigrated to New Jersey. His father's retirement money of 200,000 lira became worth about $110.00, due to inflation. Even worse, his brother was critically wounded during the war.

To bring lasting peace and stability to his homeland, Father Maroun offers a simple solution. He states, "No church teaches bad and all teach faith and family values." To restore dignity to Lebanon, Father Maroun believes in "praying hard, working hard, and respecting life."

Omer Sage

To Omer Sage, the recipe for a successful life was simple. Treat people with respect, earn your keep with an honest day's work, and be grateful for what you have. Born in 1919 at Moorhead, Minnesota, to a Rafid, Lebanon immigrant father (Alley Omar Sage) and a Scandinavian mother (Molly), he spent most of his life in Crookston, Minnesota. His father ran restaurants and Molly raised the family. Crookston had a unique blend of citizens from many ethnic backgrounds, but to Omer they were all good people.

During World War II Omer served in the U.S. Army in the European and Asiatic theatres. Other than his family, he was proudest of the military service. Humble and of good-nature, Omer spent most of his life as a house painter and his reputation for good work was impeccable. Upon retirement, Omer's time was devoted to volunteer work at Crookston's Golden Link Senior Center, in addition he was a frequent visitor at hospitals and nursing homes. When Omer died in May of 2002, his son David said he had lost his best friend. Many Crookston citizens could say the same.

Sarah Sharpel

Sarah Sharpel was born in Medina, ND, in 1914, just as the First World War had begun. Her father and mother had earlier left Rafid, Lebanon to escape the cruelty of the Ottoman Turks. "They would clean out all you had and force the young men into the military," Sarah remembers her parents saying. Sarah's father, Abraham Alley, had married Lila Juma and took the surname of Abraham. When he died in 1918 his widow was left to raise five children. Sarah's mother remarried Mike Abdallah of Ross, ND, thus blending her children with an eventual seven more. The entire family would learn Arabic in order to recite the Koran. Sarah still recalls the sounds of waking up to the daily prayer rituals. By 1929, the able-bodied men had poured cement and put a roof on Ross's half-basement-like mosque. She remembered it well for it was the year of her marriage and her husband, Alley Omar, helped with the roof project. Sarah and Alley raised their children through the difficult Dust Bowl and World War II years. Many of the Muslim neighbors left for Canada and Michigan during those tough times. Those who stayed survived by "cooperation, thrift, and strong family ties." Sarah's youngest child, David Omar, was handicapped and homebound. She enrolled in school herself and accompanied him to class. He eventually graduated from Ross High School. The recent 100-year all-school reunion gave Sarah special recognition. Sarah lives today in Menard, Texas.

CHAPTER TWENTY-ONE

Nostalgia: Returns and Modern Tourism

Hassin Alley Juma of Muslim background and a Ross, North Dakota, resident, reminisced in 1939:

While moving from one place to another, I worked at different trades. I peddled some places and worked in an automobile factory for some time. What I wanted to do was to get rich in a hurry and return to Syria.

Mr. Juma lived the majority of his adult years on a North Dakota farm, and he is buried in a wind-swept prairie cemetery. Yet his first hope was to return to the place of his birth.

Almost every observer of the American Syrian experience mentions the immigrant's initial hope of acquiring some wealth in the United States and eventually returning home. These same observers quickly add that the majority stayed in their adopted country.

Such a hope was not unique to the Syrians. Oscar Hadlin, the most renowned scholar on American immigration, wrote in *The Atlantic* that in one particular year, 1956, perhaps 3,000,000 people lived in Europe who had spent some time in the United States.[1] They came to the New World and subsequently returned to their original homelands. North Dakota early family accounts are replete with stories of people going back to their home village with a bit of American wealth. *Plains Folk: North Dakota's Ethnic History*, quotes a report in 1912 that, "at least a hundred Greek homesteaders left North Dakota to return to their countryland to fight in the war with Turkey." The author concludes that Greeks were either "extremely patriotic" or they were in America for a "temporary" period of time.[2]

But it was not just Greeks who wished to return. Relatively prosperous and well-acclimated Norwegians went back to Norway. Even Germans from Russia returned to the Ukraine, aware, perhaps, of impending revolution or other social distress. Indeed, it was the experience of American GIs in World War II that almost any village they entered in Italy or the Balkans had a resident who would come forth and say he once lived in Chicago or Pittsburgh or some such part of America.

Looking closely at the Ross-Mountrail enclave, an area in which a large proportion of Muslim immigrants filed their second citizenship papers and intended to stay in America, we find from land records that many other Muslim settlers began to leave the area very rapidly, some without even acquiring their desired plot of land. They were not happy with the region, and went elsewhere; a few, according to "old-timers," settled in Alberta and Saskatchewan in Canada (some into farming, some into the business world). And there is no doubt that Detroit, Michigan, with its auto industry, drew many away from early North Dakota.

Yet, how many of the original land-claimants actually went home to "Syria" to stay? A study of the Mountrail County history would give the impression that perhaps one-fourth of the early Muslim settlers listed on its pages ultimately returned to their home districts in Lebanon. (This seems a remarkably high number of returnees—estimates of "returns" in America's east coast suggest 20 percent or less.) Was the sight of America as seen in Dakota too harsh? Was it profitable enough to allow at least some degree of affluence so that the nostalgic ones could "go home"?

We know that such early departures also took place in every North Dakota Syrian Christian enclave. All over the state many left even without proving up their initial land claims. In Pierce and McHenry County, for example, many land records are labeled "canceled" or "relinquished." Did the prospective owners eventually return to Syria or did they settle permanently elsewhere in America?

How many would have returned to Syria if they could have afforded to make the trip home? Again, it's not infrequent to read in the accounts of pioneers among many national groups a phrase that says "I would have gone home if I could."

Joseph Salmon of Bismarck, a Christian from Zahle, as he considered his situation in America, said in August 1939, that he would not like to go back to Lebanon, and yet he was objective about things:

America is not much superior to the Old Country, as they do not have any war scares there now. The Old Country is superior in that they raise more fruit and vegetables and are assured of a crop every year. Food is not so high there and living is cheaper. We could rent a house there for $10.00 a year and it would be a large one too. In fact I think living conditions are better for the poor man than they are here in this country.

Earlier in this volume a 1904 Fargo news report was printed: "Atty Kodrey, an Arabian, passed away in the county hospital." The sadness and loneliness of life in America shows through the terse news account's lines. The young man, 23 years of age, "has no relatives living in Fargo but leaves a wife and two daughters, a mother and a sister, all of whom are in Asia."

For most immigrants in North Dakota and elsewhere in America, the prospect of returning to Syria began to dim with the passage of the years. Various forces influenced the decision to stay in this country: economic, political freedoms, and even family ties. Thomas Nassif of Bismarck said in 1939:

> I don't believe that I ever got a foothold here, I am still even, because I started with nothing, and I got nothing now. I had intended to return to the Old Country, but my father wanted to live here and I did not want to leave him. Father sent for my mother to come over, but my brother took sick over there and they couldn't come. My brother and mother are still in Syria and have never been to America. Now that I like America I don't believe that I will ever go back.

For some the lure of familiar places and faces never diminished, but the attraction of America, even the difficult America of North Dakota, was too strong to dictate a "return home." Yet, there was always the hope of a visit to the Old World village and countryside. Ed Nedoff of Williston, in 1939, said:

> I like Syria—that's my birthplace. You know a fellow can't very well forget his birthplace, but I wouldn't want to go back and live in Syria. I like the climate and everything there, but this country is better for labor conditions. I have four sisters and one brother there. I like to live in this country. One thing, I do hope that I make a trip some of those days and have plenty money to go and visit.

Jabour Munyer, who had lived in America for several decades, said in a Williston interview (February 1940): "Sometimes I think I should like to go back to visit my native land; but not to live. America is much better to live in than the Old Country in many ways. It is more freedom and easier to make a living."

Nostalgia and realism colored the memories of many "old-timers" as they thought of their homeland in "Syria." Mike Abdallah, a Muslim at Ross, told the WPA interviewer in 1939:

> In the Old Country the climate is much better than here and it seemed to make old people feel young. You could work hard all day and go to bed real tired and when you wake up in the morning you feel as if you had never worked, while here a night's sleep don't make you feel that good. It some-

times snows a foot or more over there but still the people go bare-footed and the water under the snow feels as warm as though it had been warmed on the stove for about fifteen minutes. The water on the top of the ground is always too warm to drink and be good. I think that is the only way that the Old Country is better.

The economic hardship of the Dust Bowl decade, plus the turmoil of the mid-century war years, meant that few, if any, Syrian North Dakotans could make their sentimental journey to see their beloved country.

Yet the end of the Second World War and the relatively peaceful few decades that followed gave an opportunity to an occasional adventurous young North Dakota man to visit the Near East. In fact, even before the war's end, Sam Skaff, who was in the US Army's Middle East Signal Corps, through "connections" received a month's leave to visit such places as Ain Arab and Zahle, the homes of his ancestors. "Lebanon is gorgeous," he remarked. Bill Nassif, a survivor of a German prisoner of war camp in post war years, went back to Ain Arab, Zgharta, and Aitou, his ancestral villages, in search of relatives. In Zgharta, he saw a statue of his grandfather, a celebrated warrior in local inter-group warfare. (Nassif even made a trip to Venezuela where one cousin was a Vice President, another was an army general, and, believe it or not, a third was a guerilla leader.)

Mike Abdallah, mentioned in previous paragraphs, was able to visit the place of his birth on several occasions in post-World War II years. Amid and Annie Hach visited Lebanon in 1964 to see the scenes of their parents' childhood.

Several Lebanese settler descendants visited Lebanon as part of North Dakota trade commissions; Mike Saba and Gene Nicholas accompanied Governor Art Link to the Mideast in the 1970s.

The few second and third generation Lebanese who went to the Old Country in the 1960s and 1970s were the courageous ones. Lebanon's problems in those decades cooled any serious desire on the part of most Lebanese-Americans to go back to the land of their forbearers. The news media dramatized the various national and religious disputes; photos of bombed villages, wounded civilians, and rocket attacks frequently appeared on the American evening news.

For some, the decline of interest in the homeland came about through personal experience. One North Dakota family sent money regularly to Lebanese relatives in the 1950s and 1960s and later found the family in Lebanon was "better off financially than we were." Another family scraped and saved to sponsor some kinfolk to America and, once they arrived, they seemed to ignore and even forget their North Dakota benefactors.

Lebanese "patriotism – Williston style – Vern Owan, Vicki Joseph, Chuck Joseph, Ray Atol.

Courtesy: John Guerrero

Some in the 1990s attempted a return visit. Hap Farhart (Fairhart) went to Lebanon but, because of political conditions, was unable to get to his father's hometown of Rafid. Jim Kallod and his son flew to Damascus and entered Lebanon. Once in the country, visa problems arose and they were forced to spend a few hours in jail, but through a series of bribes they got safely back to the Syrian border. Nonetheless they were thrilled to be standing on land filled with the traditions of their ancestors.

Some would have gone back to Lebanon, not just out of nostalgia, but also for economic reasons. An occasional North Dakotan insists that he or she owns land in Lebanon through family ties.[3] Fear of Syrian military activity and of political unrest has kept them from any attempt to investigate the matter of inheritance and of possible financial gain.

Yet times have changed with the beginning of the 21st Century. The wounds inflicted by war are healing at a surprisingly rapid pace. Lebanon recuperates rapidly, for after all it is a land that has seen strife on a hundred occasions over several thousands of years. Beirut is already on the list of places to visit. The Internet (lebanon.com) mentions restaurants, Pizza Huts, discos, museums, and shopping areas. Once again the "Paris of Eastern Mediterranean" is featured for the gaiety of its people, its unique cuisine, and its fabled shore line.

Perhaps the time has come, or at least is fast approaching, when a grandchild in the now relatively affluent America will seriously consider "taking the family" to Lebanon to discover what some people call "roots": to Ain Arab and the Bekaa Valley; to Zahle, the "Venice of Lebanon"; to the waterfalls and orchards of Bire, Rafid, or Bouhaire, and to the legendary cedars of Lebanon.

In fact some already have made the trip "back home." Richard Omar, of Ross, for example, has made two nostalgic journeys to Lebanon in the past few years. So also Vernon and Karma Deane Owan of Williston and Ron and Freida Hasen of Rolla.

Such a thing is not as venturesome as it may seem. If hundreds of contemporary North Dakotans make trips to Israel, the "Holy Land," why not Lebanon, a relative few miles to the north? (There's a flight each day from London!)

Lebanon has not been forgotten; it's part of the flesh and blood of hundreds of thousands of Americans. In the 1980 Census, 367 North Dakota residents listed Lebanon, Syria or Turkey as their "ancestry." Another 414 indicated that these three countries made up part of their family heritage.

A modern day "sentimental journey" to Lebanon, so ancient and probably so very new, may give the pilgrim an insight into the strength of character displayed by America's pioneer generations of Syrian-Lebanese. It has been, after all, a century since the first waves of new citizens arrived. What an admirable people! Men and women who said goodbye to their loved ones, braved the Atlantic passage, struggled through the confusion of seaports and Eastern American cities, journeyed by rail—sometimes by foot—to the Great Plains and within a few decades established themselves as respected citizens in their new nation's Middle West.

My Father is a Mayor, Too

When Kathy Freije went to Israel she visited the holy city of Bethlehem. She noticed great numbers of the Arabs were Christian. (And it's true, several million Arabic people belong to the various Eastern Rite Christian faiths.) Upon meeting the Christian Mayor of Bethlehem, she found that his name was Elias Freije. During the introduction she informed him that her father, John Freije, was a mayor, too, the mayor of a rather good-sized North Dakota town called Mayville.

Bill Nassif

Bill Nassif of Emmons County, ND: decorated war veteran, merchant and hollywood actor (often played Mexican and Indian roles).

Courtesy: William Nassif

When Bill Nassif was 15 years old the Standing Rock Sioux Nation "adopted" him into the tribe in a ceremony at Ft. Yates, North Dakota. Little did Bill know that he would be playing Native American roles in Hollywood during the 1950s. In the late 1880s Bill's maternal grandparents had come from Lebanon to ranch in Emmons County across the Missouri from the reservation. Friends of the Indians, Bill said Lebanese were frequently mistaken for Indians. Bill attended schools in Pollack, South Dakota, prior to World War II. After high school, Bill experienced the hazards of war and a German prison camp. Back to civilian life he would find work in Fargo (Nassif Rug Company) but also in Cedar Rapids, Minneapolis, and Los Angeles. In this latter city he tried acting, playing many roles in 1950s era movies. They included *Veracruz, Cattle Queen of Montana, To Hell and Back, Chief Crazy Horse, Thunder Road, The Last Hunt*, and *Strange Lady in Town*. His biggest role came in 1956 when he landed the part of Joshua in The Ten Commandments, but he broke his nose in Mexico and John Derek got the part. He knew Danny Thomas and Michael Ansara well. Bill never forgot his ranching roots in Emmons County. In 2002, Bill turned 80 years old and said, "Every day has been an adventure in my life."

Notes

Chapter 1. The Geography of Lebanon

1. Philip K. Hitti, *History of Syria* (New York: MacMillan, 1951), p. 32.
2. William S. Ellis, Lebanon, "Little Bible Land in the Crossfire of History," *National Geographic* (February 1970, vol. 137, no. 2), p. 250.
3."The Middle East," *Congressional Quarterly* (sixth edition, 1986), p. 106.
4. Philip K. Hitti, *History of Syria,* p. 41.
5. "The Middle East," *Congressional Quarterly,* p. 166.
6. Philip K. Hitti, *History of Syria,* p. 48.
7. Ibid., p. 51.
8. Thomas J. Abercrombie, "Young-Old Lebanon Lives by Trade," *National Geographic* (April, 1958, vol. 133, no. 4), p. 488.
9. Philip K. Hitti, *History of Syria,* p. 44.
10. Viviane, Doche, *Cedars by the Mississippi: The Lebanese Americans in the Twin Cities* (San Francisco: R and E Research Associates, 1978), p. 16.

Chapter 2. History

1. "The Middle East," *Congressional Quarterly* (sixth edition, 1986), p. 166.
2. William Ellis, "Lebanon—Little Bible Land in the Crossfire of History," *National Geographic* (February, 1970, vol.137, no. 2), p. 257.
3. Thomas Collelo, Ed., *Lebanon: A Country Study*, Washington, DC, Federal Research Library of Congress (May, 1989), pp. 29-32.
4. Don Peretz, *The Middle East Today* (New York: Praeger, 1988), p. 357.
5. Thomas Collelo, Ed. *Lebanon: A Country Study*, pp. 29-32.
6. Will Herberg, *Protestant, Catholic and Jew* (Garden City: Anchor Books, 1960), p. 11.
7. Philip K. Hitti, *History of Syria* (New York: MacMillan, 1951), p.
8. Convention Booklet, Attiyeh, Bismarck, N.D., July 4, 1961, no pagination.
9. Convention Booklet, Attiyeh.
10. Thomas Abercrombie, "Young-Old Lebanon Lives by Trade," *National Geographic* (April, 1958, vol. 113, no. 4), p.503.
11. Interview, Fr. Sharbel Maroun, Minneapolis, August 1993.
12. Interview, Daniel Noah, Crookston, June 1993.
13. Ibid.

Chapter 3. Religion

1. Philip M. Kayal and Joseph M. Kayal, *The Syrian-Lebanese in America* (Boston: Twayne Publishers, 1975), p. 27.

2. Ibid., p. 55.

3. Philip M. Kayal, "Religion and Assimilation: Catholic Syrians in America," *International Migration Review*, (Winter,1973, vol. 7), p. 409.

4. Ibid., p. 441, and Philip K. Hitti, *The Syrians in America* (New York: George H. Doran, 1924), p.25.

5. Monroe Berger, "A Profile of a Minority," *Commentary* (1958), p. 318.

6. Marilyn Raschka, Á Profile of Lebanon's Maronites," *Catholic Near East* (July, August, 1994, vol. 20, no. 4), p. 19.

7. Philip K. Hitti, *The Syrians in America*, p. 106.

8. Ibid., pp. 125-127.

9. Marilyn Raschka, "A Profile of Lebanon's Maronites," p. 19.

10. Alixa Naff, *Becoming American: The Early Arab Immigrant Experience* (Carbondale: Southern Illinois University Press, 1985), p. 42.

11. Letter, Nicholas Samra, October 21, 1999.

12. Ibid.

13. Philip K. Hitti, *The Syrians in America*, pp. 128-129.

14. Carol Jean Landis, "Lebanese Immigration to the United States and the Twin Cities, 1890 to 1924" (Unpublished M.A. Thesis, University of Minnesota, 1967), p. 58.

15. Deborah L. Miller, Middle Easterners" in June Drenning Holmquist, ed., *They Chose Minnesota* (St. Paul: Minnesota State Historical Society, 1985), pp. 516-517.

16. Ibid., p. 517.

17. Philip K. Hitti, *The Syrians in America*, p. 107 and pp. 130-133.

18. Alixa Naff, *Becoming American: The Early Arab Immigrant Experience, p. 42.

19. *Minot Daily News*, March 15, 1975.

20. *The Wonder of Williams* (Williston, N.D., Williams County Historical Society, 1975), vol. 1, p. 443.

21. William Sherman and Playford Thorson, Eds., *Plainsfolk: North Dakota's Ethnic History* (Fargo: North Dakota Institute for Regional Studies, 1988), p.358.

22. Ibid., p. 359.

23. Sara Elizabeth John, "Trade Will Lead a Man Far: Syrian Immigration to the El Paso Area, 1900-1936" (unpublished M.A. Thesis, University of Texas at El Paso, 1982), p. 65, and Philip K. Hitti, *The Syrians in America* (New York: George M. Doran, 1925), pp. 111-112.

24. *Federal Land Office Homestead Tract Book* (Pierce County Ledger), Microfilm, University of North Dakota.

25. Alixa Naff, *Becoming American: The Early Arab Immigrant Experience*, pp.43-44.

26. Ibid., pp. 44-45.

27. Deborah L. Miller, "Middle Easterners" p. 517.

28. Interview of Lateefe Joseph, August, 1993, Crookston.

Chapter 4. The Village Life: Marriage and Family Life

1. William Ellis, "Lebanon—Little Bible Land in the Cross Fire of History," *National Geographic* (February, 1970, vol. 137, no. 2), p. 250 ff.

2. Viviane Doche, *Cedars By the Mississippi: The Lebanese Americans in the Twin Cities* (San Francisco: R and E Research Associates, 1978), pp. 12, 23.

3. Philip K. Hitti, *The Syrians in America* (New York: George Doran, 1924), p. 25.

4. Alixa Naff, "Arabs," *Harvard Encyclopedia of American Ethnic Groups,* Stephan Thernstrom, ed. (Cambridge: Harvard University Press, 1981), p. 130.

5. Philip K. Hitti, *The Syrians in America*, p. 34.

6. Carol Jean Landis, "Lebanese Immigration to the United States and the Twin Cities, 1890-1924" (unpublished M.A. Thesis, University of Minnesota, 1967), p. 15.

7. Interview, Sam Eli, Moorhead, MN, July 1993.

8. *Gackle Republican*, February 18, 1910, p. 1.

9. Safia H. Haddad, "Women's Role in Socialization of Syrian-Americans in Chicago," in *The Arab Americans, Studies in Assimilation*, Elaine C. Hagoplan and Ann Paden, eds. (Wilmette, Illinois: Medina University Press, 1969), pp. 87, 88.

10. Abdo A. Elkholy, "The Arab American Family," in *Ethnic Families in America*, Charles M.Mandel and Robert W. Haberstein, eds. (New York: Elsevier, 1976), p. 160.

Chapter 5. Schools

1. Alixa Naff, *Becoming American* (Carbondale: Southern Illinois University Press, 1985), p. 37.

2. Philip K. Hitti, *The Syrians in America* (New York: George Doran, 1924), p. 28.

3. Ibid., p. 55.

4. Samir Khalaf, "The Background and Causes of Lebanese/Syrian Immigration to the United States Before World War I," in *Crossing the Waters*, Eric J. Hooglund, ed. (Washington, DC: Smithsonian Institute Press, 1987), p. 22.

5. Louise Seymour Houghton, "Syrians in the United States," *The Survey XXVI (1911) to XXVII (1912)*, p. 787.

6. Ibid., p. 788.

7. Samir Khalaf, "The Background and Causes of Lebanese/Syrian Immigration to the United States Before World War I," p. 23.

Chapter 6. Unrest and Departure

1. Sara Elizabeth John, "Trade Will Lead a Man Far; Syrian Immigration to the El Paso Area, 1906-1935" (Unpublished M.A. Thesis, University of Texas at El Paso, 1982), p. 8.

2. *Aramco Magazine*, September-October, 1986, p. 12.

3. Samir Khalaf, "The Background and Causes of Lebanese/Syrian Immigration to the United States Before World War I," *Crossing the Waters*, Eric J. Hooglund, ed. (Washington, DC: Smithsonian Institute Press, 1987), p. 18.

4. Louise Seymour Houghton, "Syrians in the United States," *The Survey*, XXVI (1911) to XXVII (1912), p. 483.

5. Carol Jean Landis, "Lebanese Immigration to the United States and the Twin Cities, 1890 to 1924" (Unpublished M.A. Thesis, University of Minnesota, 1967), p.30.

6. Sara Elizabeth John, "Trade Will Lead a Man Far," pp. 9, 10. Also: Adele L. Younis, "The Growth of Arabic-speaking Settlements in the United States," *The Arab Americans*, Elaine C. Hagoppian and Ann Paden, eds. (Wilmette, Illinois: Medina University Press, 1969), p. 103. See also: Adele L. Young, *The Coming of Arabic-speaking People to the United States* (Staten Island: Center for Migration Studies, 1995), p. 90.

7. Adele L. Younis, "The Growth of Arabic-speaking Settlements in the United States," p. 105.

8. Viviane Doche, *Cedars of Lebanon by the Mississippi, The Lebanese Americans in the Twin Cities* (San Francisco: R and E Research Associates, 1978), p. 38. See also, Ibid., p. 54.

9. Philip M. Kayal and Joseph M. Kayal, *The Syrian-Americans in America* (Boston: Twayne Publishers, 1975), p. 68.

10. Samir Khalaf, "The Background and Causes of Lebanese/Syrian Immigrations," pp. 18, 19.

11. Carol Jean Landis, "Lebanese Immigration to the United States and the Twin Cities, 1890 to 1924," p. 24.

12. Samir Khalaf, "The Background and Causes of Lebanese/Syrian Immigrations," p.21.

13. Alixa Naff, "Arabs," *Harvard Encyclopedia of American Ethnic Groups*, Stephan Thornstrom, ed. (Harvard University Press: Cambridge, 1981), p. 130.

14. Ibid.

15.Samir Khalaf, "The Background and Causes of Lebanese/Syrian Immigrations," p. 21.

16.Ibid., p. 22.

17. Alixa Naff, "Arabs," *Harvard Encyclopedia of American Ethnic Groups*, p. 30.

18.Samir Khalaf, "The Background and Causes of Lebanese/Syrian Immigrations," p. 22.

19. Ibid.

20. *Holy Family Church: Golden Jubilee Book* (St.Paul, MN, 1968), no pagination.

21. Philip M. Kayal and Joseph M. Kayal, *The Syrian-Lebanese in America* (Boston: Twayne Publishers, 1975), p. 52.

22. Samir Khalaf, "The Background and Causes of Lebanese/Syrian Immigrations," p. 28.

23. Ibid.

24. Ibid., p. 20.

25. Thomas Nassif, WPA Interview, Bismarck, ND.

26. Francie Berg, *Ethnic Heritage of North Dakota* (Hettinger, ND: Flying Diamond Books, 1983), p. 140.

Chapter 7. Passage to the New World

1. Alixa Naff, *Becoming American: The Early Arab Immigrant Experience* (Carbondale: Southern Illinois University Press, 1985), pp. 95-99.

2. Vernon Owan, Interview, Williston, July 1, 1990.

3. Viviane Doche, *Cedars By the Mississippi: The Lebanese Americans in the Twin Cities* (San Francisco: R and E Research Associates, 1978), p. 38.

4. Sarah Elizabeth John, "Trade Will Lead a Man Far: Syrian Immigration to the El Paso Area, 1900-1935" (Unpublished M.A. Thesis, University of Texas at El Paso, 1982), pp. 26, 27.

5. Viviane Doche, *Cedars By the Mississippi: The Lebanese Americans in the Twin Cities*, p. 49.

6. *Search-Light* (Fargo), October 13, 1906.

7. Edward Wakin, *The Immigrant Experience* (Huntington: Our Sunday Visitor, Inc., 1977), pp. 14, 15.

Chapter 8. Lebanese Dispersal: America and North Dakota

1. Carol Jean Landis, "Lebanese: Immigration to the United States and the Twin Cities, 1890 to 1924" (Unpublished M.A. Thesis, University of Minnesota, 1967), p. 19.

2. Interview, Daniel Noah, Crookston, MN, August 1993, and Richard Omar, Stanley, ND, May 1999.

3. Philip M. Kayal and Joseph M. Kayal, *The Syrian-Lebanese in America* (Boston: Twayne Publishers, 1975), pp. 63-64.

4. Viviane Doche, *Cedars By the Mississippi: The Lebanese Americans in the Twin Cities* (San Francisco: R and E Research Associates, 1978), p. 27.

5. Philip K. Hitti, *The Syrians in America* (New York: George Doran, 1924), "Syrians in the United States," p. 62, and Louise Seymour Houghton, *The Survey*, 1911-1912, pp. 488.

6. William Sherman, *Prairie Mosaic: An Ethnic Atlas on Rural North Dakota* (Fargo: North Dakota Institute for Regional Studies, 1983), p. 137; see also *Plains Folk: North Dakota's Ethnic History* (Fargo: North Dakota Institute for Regional Studies, 1988), pp. 355, 358.

7. Ibid., p. 115.

8. Ibid., p. 23.

9. Ibid., p. 115.

10. Ibid., pp. 38-39.

11. Louise Seymour Houghton, "Syrians in the United States," p. 486.

12. Ibid., p. 490.

13. Ibid., p. 495.

14. Ibid.

15. Ibid., p. 968.

16. Philip M. Kayal and Joseph M. Kayal, *The Syrians in America*, p. 68.

17. H. Elaine Lindgren, *Land in Her Own Name* (Fargo: North Dakota Institute for Regional Studies, 1991), p. 23.

18. Samir Khalaf, "The Background and Causes of Lebanese/Syrian Immigration to the United States Before World War I," *Crossing the Waters*, Eric J. Hooglund, ed. (Washington, DC: Smithsonian Institute Press, 1987), p. 11.

19. Linda S. Walbridge, "Lebanese Christians," *American Immigrant Cultures*, David Levinson and Melvin Ember, eds. (New York: MacMillan Reference, 1997), p. 384.

20. "Arabs," *Harvard Encyclopedia of American Ethnic Groups*, Stephen Thornstrom, ed. (Cambridge: Harvard University Press, 1981), p. 130.

Chapter 9. Peddling

1. David Jaffee, "Peddlers of Progress and the Transportation of the Rural North, 1760-1860," *The Journal of American History*, September, 1991, pp. 511-513.

2. William Sherman, *Prairie Mosaic: An Ethnic Atlas of Rural North Dakota* (Fargo: North Dakota Institute for Regional Studies, 1983), p. 398 and throughout.

3. Alixa Naff, *Becoming American: The Early Arab Immigrant Experience* (Carbondale: Southern Illinois University Press, 1985), pp. 132-133.

4. Philip M. Kayal and Joseph M. Kayal, *The Syrian-Lebanese in America* (Boston: Twayne, 1975), p. 99.

5. Afif I. Tannous, "Acculturation of an Arab-Syrian Community in the Deep South," *American Sociological Review*, vol. 8, no. 1-6 (1943), p. 266.

6. Alixa Naff, *Becoming American*, pp.146-148.

7. Ibid., p. 165.

8. "Program Notes," Attiyeh National Arabic-American Convention, Fargo, ND, July 2-5, 1976, p. 1.

9. *The Wonder of Williams* (Williston, ND: Williams County Historical Society, 1975), Vol. 1, p. 442.

10. Interview, Pat Freije, Edmore, ND, March 1996; also Eugene Alley, Sibley, ND, June 1996.

11. *Dickinson Press*, March 30, 1901.

12. *The Search-Light*, Fargo, January 16, 1909.

13. Carol Jean Landis, "Lebanese Immigration to the United States and the Twin Cities, 1890 to 1924" (Unpublished M.A. Thesis, University of Minnesota, 1967), p. 49.

14. Interview, Chuck Joseph and Vernon Owan, Williston, ND, June 1995.

15. Interview, Art Deraney, Grand Forks, ND, January 25, 1997.

16. Interview, Ed Absey, Grand Forks, ND, October 23, 1983.

17. Interview, Joe Nicholas, Cando, ND, August 1992 and August 1994.

18. *The Wonder of Williams*, vol. 1, p. 458.

19. Interview, Wilbur Kalil, Williston, ND, August 1954.

20. *Walsh County History*, Vol. I (Grafton, ND: Centennial Book Committee, 1976), p. 564.

21. Interview, Shirley Hassen, Rolla, ND, August 1992.

22. Louise Seymour Houghton, "Syrians in the United States," The Survey, XXVI (1911) to XXVII (1912), p. 650.

23. Ibid., p. 648.

24. Lee S. Tesdall et al., *The Way We Were: Arab Americans in Central Iowa* (Iowa City: Grand View College, 1993), p. 5.

25. *Search-Light*, Fargo, June 15, 1907.

26. Interview, Mildred Absey, Grand Forks, ND, June 1990.

27. Louise Seymour Houghton, "Syrians in the United States," *The Survey*, XXVII (1912), p. 488, and Philip K. Hitti, *The Syrians in America* (New York: George M. Doran, 1924), p. 62.

28. Blanche Passa, *Once Upon a Little Town* (Grafton, ND: Morgan Publishing, 1996), p. 99.

29. *REC Magazine*, Bismarck, ND, October 19, 1986, p. 40.

30. Sam Skaff, "My Early Life," Handwritten manuscript, Moorhead, MN, May 1995, p.19.

Chapter 10. Homesteading–Farming

1. Interview, John Freije, March 1995.

2. Interview, Joe Nicholas, Cando, ND, August 1993.

3. Viviane Doche, *Cedars By the Mississippi: The Lebanese-Americans in the Twin Cities* (San Francisco: R and E Research Associates, 1978), p. 36.

4. *Williston World*, November 1, 1907, p. 1.

5. H. Elaine Lindgren, *Land in Her Own Name* (Fargo: North Dakota Institute for Regional Studies, 1991), p. 23.

6. William Sherman and Playford Thorson, *Plains Folk: North Dakota's Ethnic History* (Fargo: North Dakota Institute for Regional Studies, 1988), p. 359.

Chapter 11. Shopkeepers: The First Decade

1. *Search-Light*, Fargo, November 26, 1906.

2. Interview, Jesse Joseph, Chuck Joseph, and Wilbur Kalil, Williston, ND, July 1985.

3. U.S. Census, 1910, Benson and McLean counties.

4. Francie Berg, *Ethnic Heritage of North Dakota* (Hettinger, ND: Flying Diamond Books, 1983), p. 138.

5. Interview, Kathryn Harris, Rolla, ND, July 1986.

6. *A Century of Area History, Pierce County and Rugby, North Dakota* (Rugby: Centennial Committee, 1986), p. 151.

7. Ibid.

8. Interview, Joe Nicholas, Cando, ND, August 1992.

9. Interview, Phil Deraney, Grand Forks, ND, August 1995.

10. Interviews, Kathryn Harris, Rolla, ND, November 1982 and Shirley Hasen and Quentin Harris, August 1992.

11. Francis Berg, *Ethnic Heritage of North Dakota*, p. 136.

Chapter 12. Railroads

1. William Sherman and Playford Thorson, eds., *Plains Folk: North Dakota's Ethnic History* (Fargo: North Dakota Institute for Regional Studies, 1988), p. 345. See also Viviane Doche, *Cedars By the Mississippi: The Lebanese-Americans in the Twin Cities* (San Francisco: R and E Research Associates, 1978), p. 42.

2. Interview, Daniel Noah, Crookston, August 1993.

3. Interview, Art Deraney and Al Srur, Grand Forks, ND, June 1996.

4. Interview, Eugene Alley, Sibley, ND, June 1985.

5. Interview, Kathryn Harris, Rolla, ND, November 1982.

6. *Aramco World Magazine*, September-October, 1968, p. 25.

Chapter 13. Syrian Enclaves

1. *Fargo Forum*, March 18, 1893; also a letter, Nicholas Samra, October 22, 1999.

2. *Fargo City Directory*, 1893.

3. William C. Sherman, *Prairie Mosaic: An Ethnic Atlas of Rural North Dakota* (Fargo: North Dakota Institute for Regional Studies, 1983), pp. 97, 115, 116.

4. Interview, Robert and Pat Freije, Edmore, ND, April 1995, and John Freije, Mayville, March 1995.

5. Interview, Ed Absey, Grand Forks, ND, March 1983.

6. O. T. Tofsrud, *Fifty Years in Pierce County* (Rugby, ND: Privately published, 1943), p. 71.

7. William Sherman and Playford Thorson, eds., *Plains Folk: North Dakota's Ethnic History* (Fargo: North Dakota Institute for Regional Studies, 1988), p. 356.

8. *Minot Daily News*, March 15, 1975.

9. O. T. Tofsrud, *Fifty Years in Pierce County*, p. 71.

10. Ibid.

11. William Sherman and Playford Thorson, eds., *Plains Folk: North Dakota's Ethnic History*, p. 357, and Nicholas Samra, Letter, May 9, 1990.

12. *Little Flower Church, 75 Years of Progress and Growth* (Rugby, ND, privately published, 1985), p. 4.

13. Nicholas Samra, Manuscript Annotations, October 21, 1999.

14. Letter, Nicholas Samra, May 9, 1999.

15. Interview, Charlie Juma to Larry Sprunk, Stanley, ND, March 15, 1977.

16. Federal Writers Project, under the name, "Joe Hiawatha," Bismarck, ND, State Historical Society of North Dakota, pp. 3, 4.

17. Interview, Charlie Juma, Stanley, June 1983.

18. Earle Waugh et al., *Muslim Communities in North America* (Alberta: University of Alberta Press, 1983), p. 98, and Adele Younis, *The Coming of Arabic-Speaking People to the United States* (Staten Island: Center for Migration Studies, 1995), p. 183.

19. Federal Writers Project, under the name, "Joe Hiawatha," Bismarck, ND, State Historical Society of North Dakota, p. 1.

20. Interview, Hassen Abdullah, Stanley, ND, February 1999.

21. *The Syrian World* (New York), October 29, 1929, p. 56.

22. Interview, Hassen Abdullah, Stanley, ND, February 1999.

23. Federal Writers Project, under the name, "Joe Hiawatha," Bismarck, ND, State Historical Society of North Dakota.

24. Interview, Rosie Chamley, Richard Omar, Hassen Abdallah, and Omar Hamden, Stanley, ND, August 1992.

25. Federal Writers Project, Syrians in North Dakota, 1936, Bismarck, ND, State Historical Society of North Dakota.

26. *Bismarck Tribune*, July 15, 1940.

27. Sam Skaff, "My Early Life," handwritten manuscript, Moorhead, MN, May 1995, p. 2.

28. Interview, Floyd Boutrous, Bismarck, ND, June 1983.

29. *The Wonder of Williams* (Williston, ND: Williams County Historical Society, 1975), pp. 1261, 1269, 2218.

30. Interview, Wilbur Kalil and Charles (Bud) Kalil, Williston, ND, July 1983.

31. Nicholas Samra, Letter, November 9, 1983.

32. Caesar Farah, "Syrians," *American Immigrant Cultures*, David Levinson and Melvin Ember, eds. (New York: MacMillan Reference, 1997, vol. 2), p. 863.

33. *Williston World*, November 1, 1907, p. 1.

34. Interview, Telmar Rolfsrud, Williston, August 1993.

35. Interview, Kathryn Harris, Rolla, September 20, 1991.

36. Interview, Kade Albert, Belcourt, August 1992.

37. Interview, Christine Ferris, Moorhead, MN, November 1997.

38. *Cooperstown, North Dakota 1882-1982* (Cooperstown: Centennial Committee, 1982), pp. 52, 60, 48.

39. *Fargo Forum*, July 9, 1930.

40. *Glenfield Anniversary History* (Glenfield, ND: Two Rivers Printing, 1987), throughout.

41. William Sherman and Playford Thorson, eds., *Plains Folk: North Dakota's Ethnic History*, p. 363.

Chapter 14. How Others Saw Them: Prejudice?

1. *Ross Valley News*, November 19, 1909, p. 1.
2. William Sherman and Playford Thorson, eds., *Plains Folk: North Dakota's Ethnic History* (Fargo: North Dakota Institute for Regional Studies, 1988), pp. 361-363.
3. *Jamestown Daily Alert*, September 23,1909.
4. *Ross Valley News*, November 19, 1909, and *Jamestown Daily Alert*, September 23,1909.
5. Federal Reporter: 1909-1910 Cases, C.C.GA1909 (Najour, 174 F 735 and C.C.Mass. 1910 Mudarri 176 F 465). For a full treatment of the issue see, Sarah Gualtieri, "Becoming White: Race, Religion and the Foundations of Syrian/Lebanese Ethnicity in the United States," *Journal of American Ethnic History*, Summer 2001, pp. 29-58.
6. *Fargo Forum*, July 9, 1937.
7. *Fargo Forum*, June 13, 1907.
8. *Search-Light* (Fargo), August 1, 1908.
9. *Jamestown Daily Capital*, February 22, 1904.
10. *Jamestown Daily Capital*, February 23, 1904.
11. *Jamestown Daily Capital*, February 26, 1904.
12. *Jamestown Sun*, February 29,1904.
13. Interview, Ellen Logan, Moorhead, June 1998.
14. Interview, Telmar Rolsrud, Williston, August 1994.
15. Interview, Charles Kalil, Jesse Joseph, Williston, July 15, 1983.
16. Interview, Don Albert, Williston, June 1995.
17. Interview, Ferial Abraham, Minneapolis, July 1998.
18. Interview, Floyd Boutrous, Bismarck, May 1992.
19. Louise Seymour Houghton, "Syrians in the United States," *The Survey, XXVI (1911) and XXVII (1912)*, p. 652.
20. Adele Younis, *The Coming of Arabic-speaking People to the United States* (Staten Island: Center for Migration Studies, 1995), p. 224.

Chapter 15. Naturalization

1. Alixa Naff, *Becoming American: The Early Arab Immigrant Experience* (Carbondale: Southern Illinois University Press, 1985), p. 255.
2. *Mountrail County Promotor*, May 15, 1914.
3. John J. Newman, *American Naturalization Records, 1790-1990* (Bountiful, Utah: Heritage Quest, 1998), p. 37.
4. *Bismarck Tribune*, July 15, 1940.
5. Naturalization Records Inventory. The State Historical Society of the State of North Dakota, Bismarck, has an impressive index of the naturalization process names and documents. The holdings begin in the late 1800s and continue until recent times.
6. Nicholas Samra, Manuscript Annotations, October 21, 1999.
7. Alixa Naff, *Becoming American, The Early Arab Immigrant Experience*, pp. 254-255.
8. Ibid., p. 109.

Chapter 16. Cohesion: Strengths and Weakness

1. Philip K. Hitti, *The Syrians in America* (New York: George M. Doran, 1924), p. 94.
2. Ibid.
3. Philip M. Kayal and Joseph M. Kayal, *The Syrian-Lebanese in America* (Boston: Twayne Publishers, 1975), p. 89-ff.
4. Alixa Naff, *Becoming American, The Early Arab Immigrant Experience* (Carbondale: Southern Illinois University Press, 1985), p. 96.
5. Interview, Telmar Rolfsrud,Williston, August 1994.

6. *Gackle Republican*, February 18, 1910.

7. Interview, Charlie Juma to Larry Sprunk, Stanley, ND, March 15, 1977. Tapes at Historical Society of North Dakota, Bismarck.

8. Interview, Joe and Liala Aossey, Cedar Rapids, October, 1997.

9. The Syrian Colony," *Harpers Weekly* (1895), p. 746.

10. Louise Seymour Houghton, "Syrians in the United States," *The Survey*, XXVI (1911) to XXVII (1912), p. 702.

11. Konrad Bercovici, "Around the World in New York," *Century Magazine*, 1924, p. 354.

12. Philip K. Hitti, *The Syrians in America*, p. 93.

13. Interview, Joe Nicholas, Cando, ND, August 16, 1992.

14. Carol Jean Landis, "Lebanese Immigration to the United States and the Twin Cities, 1890 to 1924" (unpublished M.A. Thesis, University of Minnesota, 1967), pp. 59-60.

15. Abdo A. Elkholy, *The Arab Americans, Studies in Assimilation*, Elaine C. Hagopian and Ann Paden, eds. (Wilmette: Medina University Press, l969), p.12.

16. *The Wonder of Williams* (Williston,ND: Williams County Historical Society, 1975), p. 443.

17. Interview, Vernon Owan, Williston, August 1996.

18. Interview, Selma Kennedy, Grand Forks, November 1997.

19. Interview, Ed Absey, Grand Forks, July 1982.

20. *Bismarck Tribune*, July 15, 1940.

21. Francie Berg, *Ethnic Heritage of North Dakota* (Hettinger, ND: Flying Diamond Books, 1983), p. 30.

22. Ibid., p. 138.

23. U.S. Census, Bureau of Census, 1980, Supplementary Report, PC 80-51-10, pp. 25, 61.

Chapter 17. Into the Mainstream

1. *Official Roster of North Dakota Soldiers, Sailors and Marines, World War, 1917-1918* (Bismarck: Bismarck Tribune Company, 1931), four volumes.

2. *Cooperstown, North Dakota* (Cooperstown, ND: Centennial Committee, 1982), p. 52.

3. Interview, Bill Nassif, Moorhead, MN, May 1995.

4. Interview, Sam Skaff, Moorhead, MN, May 1995.

5. Interview, Jesse Joseph, Williston, ND, July 1983.

6. Philip K. Hitti, *The Syrians in America* (New York: George Doran Co., 1924), p. 102.

7. Michael Sulliman, "Early Arab-Americans," *Crossing the Waters* (Washington, DC: Smithsonian Institute, 1987), p. 48.

8. Louise Seymour Houghton, "Syrians in the United States," *The Survey*, Volume XXVII, October 1911 to March 1912, p. 962.

9. Philip K. Hitti, *The Syrians in America* (New York: George Doran Co., 1924), p. 92.

10. Louise Seymour Houghton, "Syrians in the United States," p. 790.

11. Interview, John Freije, Mayville, ND, March 1995 and Pat Freije, Edmore, ND, April 1997.

12. Interview, Eugene Nicholas, Fargo, ND, August 1999.

13. Interview, Joe Nicholas, Cando, ND, August 1992 and August 1994.

14. Interview, Sam Skaff, Moorhead, MN, May 1995.

15. Interview, Floyd Boutrous, Bismarck, ND, April 1992.

16. Interview, Charles Kalil, Jesse Joseph, Ray Atol, Williston, ND, June 1996.

17. Interviews, Kathryn Harris, Rolla, ND, November 1982 and August 1992 and Ron Hasen, Rolla, ND, March 7, 2000.

Chapter 18. Food and Drink

1. *Tales of Mighty Mountrail* (Stanley, ND: Centennial Committee, 1978), p. 26.
2. Ibid., p. 27.
3. Interview, Alvin Kartes, Grand Forks, September 1987.
4. Interview, Arthur Monroe, Grand Forks, April 1985.
5. Interview, Frank X. Miller, Grand Forks, November 1984.
6. Federal Writers Project, 1942, in Archives of State Historical Society of North Dakota, Bismarck.

Chapter 19. Different and the Same

1. Louise Seymour Houghton, "Syrian in the United States," *The Survey*, August 11, 1911, p. 787, 788.
2. Adele Younis, *The Coming of Arabic-speaking People to the United States* (Staten Island: Center for Migration Studies, 1995), p. 196.
3. H. Elaine Lindgren, *Land in Her Own Name* (Fargo: North Dakota Institute for Regional Studies, 1993), p. 23.
4. *Harpers Weekly*, "The Syrian Colony" (1895), p. 746.
5. Alixa Naff, *Becoming Americans: The Early Arab Immigrant Experience* (Carbondale: Southern Illinois University Press, 1985), p. 286.
6. Interview, Mildred Absey, Grand Forks, ND, April 7, 1990.
7. *Cooperstown North Dakota History* (Cooperstown, ND: Cooperstown Centennial Committee, 1982), p. 52.
8. *The Wonder of Williams* (Williston, ND: Williams County Historical Society, 1975), p. 447.
9. Interview, Shirley Hasen, Rolla, ND.
10. Samuel Nicola, WPA Interview, Bismarck, July 25, 1939.
11. Interview, Sam Eli, Moorhead, MN, July 1993.
12. Interview, Ron Hasen and Quentin Harris, Rolla, August 1992.
13. Interview, Kade Albert, Rolla, August 1992.
14. Interview, Christine Ferris, Moorhead, MN, November 1997.
15. Interview, Jim Kallod, Fargo, June 1999.
16. *Ross Valley News*, September 17, 1909.
17. *Dickinson Press*, June 6, 1894.
18. *The Stanley Sun*, November 10, 1905.
19. *The Leeds News*, June 13, 1907.
20. Interviews, Rosie Chamley, Richard Omar, Hassin Abdallah, Omar Hamden, Stanley, ND, August 1992.
21. *Fargo Forum*, November 6, 1998, p. BI.
22. Interview, Ghalie Abraham, Binford, ND, June 1995.

Chapter 20. An Overview

1. Interview, Telmar Rolfstad, Williston, August 1994.
2. Louise Seymour Houghton, "Syrians in the United States, " *The Survey*, Volume XXVI, October 1911 to March 1912, p. 796.
3. Interview, Telmar Rolfstad, Williston, August 1994.
4. *Fargo Forum*, August 8, 1908.

Chapter 21. Nostalgia: Returns and Modern Tourism

1. Oscar Hadlin, *The Atlantic*, "Emigration and Disenchantment," 1956, p. 6.
2. William Sherman and Playford Thorson (eds.), *Plains Folk: North Dakota's Ethnic History* (Fargo: North Dakota Institute for Regional Studies, 1988), p. 350.
3. Interview, Sam Aggie, Fargo, June 1997.

Appendices

An Initial Observation

English-speaking appointees, as one would expect, were the individuals who took up the census in early North Dakota times. They were also the clerks in Federal Land Offices and courthouses. When immigrants applied for citizenship or land ownership, no doubt these men and women tussled with the transfer of foreign names into an English spelling on a day-to-day basis. There are letters and symbols in the Scandinavian and German language that have no exact equivalent in English. Slavic names must have been a particular headache. Certainly Arabic family names provided the officials with an especially difficult set of tasks.

And there is some question as to whether some of these individuals—census takers especially—even though they spoke English, had anything more than the most rudimentary education. Syria, for example, is listed sometimes as Cera and Seria and Ceria. And family names undergo a series of distortions. The Absey family of Walsh County is spelled in the Census of 1900, 1910, and 1920 as Asabey, Absey, and Absy. The Barkie family in Williston is listed in official documents as Burke, Barkie, Barky, and Barkey. William Atol of Williston is at times William Aettol. Bo Alley Farhart is sometimes Boaley Farhart, Bolley Farhart, and Bo Alli Farhart. (In recent years a Farhart descendant legally changed the name to Fairhart. "I would often spend 20 minutes explaining the spelling so I simplified it.") So the reader must beware.

A Side Note:

The authors made a survey of immigrant steamships' arrival manifests. The Anglicized spelling made the search an impossible task. For example, the *SS Rotterdam* arrived in New York carrying, according to its compilations, 15 individuals from Syria. Yet not one of its 934 names was recognizably of Arabic origin.

Appendix A

Arab-Americans in United States Census Reports: State of North Dakota, 1900, 1910, 1920

Introductory Note

The pages that follow contain information concerning the men, women, and children who were listed in the various censuses of early North Dakota. These are taken from microfilm copies of the census takers' schedule sheets. The microfilm "Soundex" cards for 1900 and 1920 were also used for verification purposes.

To obtain the following list, some three million entries were visually studied. The authors are the first to admit that human error will certainly have occurred.

Anyone who has worked with these film copies will know that difficulties arise when making such a tabulation. These include a problem of faint images from faded manuscript sheets and the indistinct nature of the enumerator's handwriting. The materials presented on these pages are taken from notations indicating place of birth. (The race column indicates white (W) although in several instances the symbol "B" [black] was used.) The reader will notice a wide variety of places of birth: Turkey, Turkey in Asia, Syria, Arabia, etc. These correspond to the census takers' "guess" as to political boundaries.

The census taker was often interviewing individuals who were illiterate. Sometimes the census person had only a minimal education. The census information, errors and all, is presented as found in the manuscript pages.

The authors present these lists for several reasons: (l) that the general reader may see the panorama of occupations, locations, conditions, and time frames which formed the backgrounds of life in the earliest decades; and (2) that researchers may have a handy guide in determining the identity and location of specific Dakota residents. In this latter instance, however, we recommend that the research person refer personally to the manuscript schedules. With additional background information, what is sometimes an indistinct entry may be clarified.

CENSUS—ARABIC PEOPLE

W	Wife	B	Brother	AD	Adopted Daughter	BD	Boarder
S	Son	SIS	Sister	AS	Adopted Son	P	Partner
D	Daughter	N	Niece	MIL	Mother-in-Law	HM	Hired Man
F	Female	NE	Nephew	BIL	Brother-in-Law	L	Lodger
M	Male	GD	Granddaughter	SIL	Sister-in-Law		
SS	Stepson	GS	Grandson	A	Aunt		
SD	Stepdaughter	GM	Grandmother	C	Cousin		

1900

Name	Age	Occupation	Place of Birth	Date of Arrival
BENSON COUNTY—1900 CENSUS				
Leeds Township				
Tovel, S. (Farrell ?)	25	RR Man	Aseria[sic]	USA-1892
BURLEIGH COUNTY—1900 CENSUS				
Bismarck City				
Willem, Joseph (Williams ?)	30	Peddler	Arabia	USA-1897
Willem, Mary	30(W)		Arabia	
Willem, Annie	5(D)		Arabia	
Willem, Elsie	2(D)		Arabia	
Willem, Abraham	1(S)		North Dakota	
CASS COUNTY—1900 CENSUS				
Fargo				
Turck, Anton (Artor ?)	35	Boarding House	Syria	USA-1897
Turck, Rachal	27(W)		Syria	USA-1894
Turck, Joseph	5(S)		New York	
Turck, Mary	2(D)		Tennessee	
Turck, Sophia (Coffie ?)	3(D)		North Dakota	
Lion, S.B.	35 Billiard Hall Syria USA-1888			
Lion, Helena	25(W) Syria			
Lion, Sam	8(S) Minnesota			
Fia, Charles	22(P) Syria USA-1896			
Porostum, Joseph	23 Peddler Syria USA-1896			
Velish, Joseph	35 Boarding House Syria USA-1888			
Velish, Mary	23(W) Syria USA-1896			
Velish, Aly	2(S) North Dakota			
Sade, Sara	55(M) Syria USA-1896			
Assid, Mickal	48	Dealer in Fruit	Syria	USA-1890
Assid, Marta	38(W)		Syria USA-1893	
Assid, Telma	4(D)		North Dakota	
Assid, Joseph	3(S)		North Dakota	
Assid, Alie	4 $1/2$(D)		North Dakota	
Hadad, Jakob	34		Cook Syria USA-1877	
Toboy, George	17		Syria	

Name	Age	Occupation	Place of Birth	Date of Arrival
GRAND FORKS COUNTY—1900 CENSUS				
Arvilla Twp.				
Franklin, Ammie	22(BD)	County Hospital Poor Farm	Turkey	USA-1895
McHENRY COUNTY—1900 CENSUS				
Barclay, Joseph	32		Palestine	
Barclay, Agatha	30		England	
Barclay, Ellen E.	27(SIL)		England	
Barclay, Bryan	26(B)		England	
Barclay, Joseph	9(S)		England	
Barclay, Bryan T.	8(S)		England	
PIERCE COUNTY—1900 CENSUS				
Rugby Village				
Shama, Abdalla	24	Merchant	Turkey	USA-1893
Shama, Sophia	18(W)		Turkey	
Fedul, Carlile	24(B)		Turkey	
Habeetz, Dave (Habeele?)	24		Turkey	USA-1895
Habeetz, Fahata (Habeele?)	19(W)		Turkey	
Turk, Charley	29	Merchant	Turkey	USA-1891
Turk, Fannie	23(W)		Turkey	
Turk, Sophia	5(D)		North Dakota	
Turk, Joseph	4(S)		North Dakota	
Turk, Lizzie	3(D)		North Dakota	
Lion, Salama	15(SIL)		Turkey	
Lion, Fad	18(BIL)		Turkey	
Twp. 154-R14 (Ness)				
Shacker, Alec G.	37	Farmer	Syria	USA-1889
Shacker, Mary	29(W)		Syria	
Shacker, George	7(S)		North Dakota	
Shacker, Heinay	6(S)		North Dakota	
Shacker, Emma	3(D)		North Dakota	
Shacker, Loretta	1(D)		North Dakota	
Lyady, John	50	Farmer	Syria	USA-1892
Lyady, Mary J.	35(W)			USA-1896
Twp. 156-R72(Meyer)				
Boussad, James	29	Farmer	Turkey	USA-1891
Boussad, Rachel	20(W)		Turkey	USA-1891
Boussad, Saddie	3(D)		Turkey	USA-1899
Boussad, Joseph	54(F)	Shoemaker	Turkey	USA-1896
Boussad, Nessie	52(M)		Turkey	USA-1896
Sawaya, Charlie	29	Farmer	Turkey	USA-1886
Sawaya, Nasif	25(B)	Farmer	Turkey	USA-1894
Sawaya, Jessie	17(S)	Housekeeper	Turkey	USA-1894
Boussad, Nassiff	31	Farmer	Turkey	USA-1893
Boussad, Minnie	26(W)		Turkey	USA-1897
Boussad, Lillie	4(D)		Turkey	USA-1897
Boussad, Shappel	3 $1/2$(S)		North Dakota	

Name	Age	Occupation	Place of Birth	Date of Arrival
Boussad, Aberham [sic]	29	Farmer	Turkey	USA-1888
Boussad, Mary	55(M)	Housekeeper	Turkey	USA-1889
Boussad, Richard	27(B)	Farm Laborer	Turkey	USA-1891
Boussad, Joseph	25(B)	Farmer	Turkey	USA-1891
Cassis, Aberham	28	Farmer	Turkey	USA-1890
Cassis, Freddie	22		Turkey	USA-1896
Cassis, Julia	3(D)		North Dakota	
Cassis, Mary	$0\,^1/_2$(D)		North Dakota	
Cassis, Charlie	27(B)	Farmer	Turkey	USA-1890
Cassis, Sophie	20(SIL)		Turkey	USA-1897
Cassis, John	25(B)	Farmer	Turkey	USA-1890
Cassis, Asset	23(B)	Farmer	Turkey	USA-1895
Chakanay, John	32	Farmer	Turkey	USA-1890
Chakanay, Fannie	24(W)		Turkey	USA-1890
Chakanay, Blanch	6(D)		At Sea	USA-1896
Chakanay, Shaker	4(DS)		Turkey	USA-1896
Chakanay, Batituf	2(D)		North Dakota	
Chakanay, Ferris	11/12(S)		North Dakota	
Sawaya, Rusk	29	Farmer	Turkey	USA-1899
Sawaya, Attalf	25(W)		Turkey	USA-1891
Sawaya, George	7(S)	At School	Minnesota	
Sawaya, Ole	2(S)		North Dakota	
Munyer, Ossaf	28	Farmer	Turkey	USA-1889
Munyer, Luan	18(W)		Turkey	USA-1896
Munyer, Martha	7/12(D)		North Dakota	
Munyer, Frank	23(B)	Farmer	Turkey	USA-1895
Chakany, Joseph	23		Turkey	
Kary, Alexander	24		Turkey	

Twp. 155-R72 (Reno Valley)

Name	Age	Occupation	Place of Birth	Date of Arrival
Boustes, Aberham (Bruster?)	25	Farmer	Turkey	USA-1893
Boustes, Salema	21(W)		Turkey	USA-1896
Boustes, Sophia	4(D)		Minnesota	
Boustes, Ella	2(D)		Minnesota	
Boustes, May	7/12(D)		North Dakota	
Karry, Alexander	24(BIL)	Peddler	Turkey	USA-1898
Wazer, Matthew	25	Farmer	Turkey	USA-1895
Wazer, Elias	28(B)	Farmer	Turkey	USA-1891
Wazer, Barbara	23(SIL)		Turkey	USA-1897
Wazer, Samuel	1(N)		North Dakota	
Uncle, Charlie (Unice?)	40(C)	Peddler	Turkey	USA-1891
Maroloaf, Mary	50(BD)		Turkey	USA-1891
Halaway, George	27	Farmer	Turkey	USA-1895
Sekif, Joseph	32	Farmer	Turkey	USA-1890
Sakif, Chmis	30(W)		Turkey	USA-1890
Sakif, Maggie	5(D)		Minnesota	
Sakif, Nettie	3(D)		North Dakota	
Sakif, Esper	11/12(S)		North Dakota	
Sekif, Aunie	60(M)		Turkey	USA-1897

Name	Age	Occupation	Place of Birth	Date of Arrival
Zyady, John (Zeddy?)	32	Servant/Farm Labor	Turkey	USA-1890
Kirk, Richard	26	Farmer	Turkey	USA-1891
Kirk, Nellie	18(W)		Turkey	USA-1890
Kirk, George	0/12(S)		North Dakota	
Dowalebee, Mary	45(A)		Turkey	USA-1891
Boujien, David (Bougler?)	38	Farmer	Turkey	USA-1891
Boujien, Eva	23(W)		Turkey	USA-1895
Boujien, Niba	3(D)		North Dakota	
Boujien, Ferris	1(S)		North Dakota	
Saba, Kahlil	30	Farmer	Turkey	USA-1892
Saba, Jessie	20(W)		Turkey	USA-1899

RANSOM COUNTY-1900 CENSUS

Name	Age	Occupation	Place of Birth	Date of Arrival
Jacob, Charles	19	Color listed as "black"	Turkey	

RICHLAND COUNTY—1900 CENSUS

Wahpeton

Name	Age	Occupation	Place of Birth	Date of Arrival
Assad, George	45	Restaurant Keeper	Ceria[sic]	USA-1890
Assad, Sadie	30(W)		Syria	
Assad, Assif	6(S)		Minnesota	
Assad, Nicholas	2(S)		North Dakota	
Assad, Mary	2/12(D)		North Dakota	
Assad, Richard	40	Restaurant Keeper	Ceria[sic]	USA-1894
Assad, Mary	30(W)		Ceria[sic]	USA-1894
Assad, Assed	6(S)		Minnesota	
Assad, Minna	1(D)		North Dakota	
Assad, Martha	2/12(D)		North Dakota	

Abercrombie Twp.

Name	Age	Occupation	Place of Birth	Date of Arrival
Crom, Albert	26		Turkey	

Viking Twp.

Name	Age	Occupation	Place of Birth	Date of Arrival
Abrass, Azees	26		Syria	

TOWNER COUNTY—1900 CENSUS

Twp. 160-R67

Name	Age	Occupation	Place of Birth	Date of Arrival
Assay, Nicholas	28	Farmer	Turkey	USA-1892
Assay, Mary	24(W)		Turkey	USA-1891
Assay, James A.	2(S)		North Dakota	
Assay, Joseph A.	1(S)		North Dakota	

Twp. 160-R68

Name	Age	Occupation	Place of Birth	Date of Arrival
Tanous, Deeb	31	Farmer	Turkey	USA-1891
Tanous, Annie	22(W)		Turkey	
Tanous, Thomas	4(S)		North Dakota	
Tanous, Sady	2(D)		North Dakota	
Tanous, Michael	9/12(S)		North Dakota	
Tanous, Abdallah	23	Farmer	Turkey	USA-1892

Name	Age	Occupation	Place of Birth	Date of Arrival
Twp. 161-R67				
Iserma, Sadie	43	Farmer	Turkey	USA-1891
Iserma, Mosas	20(B)	Farm Laborer	Turkey	USA-1898

STARK COUNTY—1900 CENSUS

Stark County				
Fields, George	28		Palestine	
Rumbell, Walter	32		Turkey	

TRAILL COUNTY—1900 CENSUS

Erwin Twp.				
Abraham, Thom	28		Syria	
Roseville Twp.				
Abdalla, Abrahem	25		Syria	

WALSH COUNTY—1900 CENSUS

156-59				
Absey, Joseph	34	Farmer	Aribia[sic]	USA-1891
Absey, Rinia	32(W)		Aribia[sic]	USA-1892
Absey, Eva	9(D)		Aribia[sic]	
Absey, Mina	6(D)		Minnesota	
Absey, Mike	2(S)		North Dakota	
Absey, George	8/12(S)		North Dakota	
Friar, Fred	45	Farmer	Arabia	USA-1892
Friar, Nellie	40(W)		Arabia	USA-1892
Friar, Blanch	13(D)	Servant	Arabia	USA-1892
Friar, George	11(S)		Arabia	
Friar, Bedy	5(D)		North Dakota	
Friar, Mary	2(D)		North Dakota	
Friar, James	10/12(S)		North Dakota	
Freije, Moses	24	Farmer	Arabia	USA-1889
Freije, Nels	36(B)	Dealer in Notions	Arabia	USA-1889
Freije, Latte	20(SIL)		Arabia	
Freije, Shebre	3(N)		North Dakota	
Freije, Freije	9/12(N)		North Dakota	
Zein, William	25	Farmer	Arabia	USA-1892
Zein, Rockma	19(W)		Arabia	USA-1896
Zein, Abraham(head)	43	Farmer	Arabia	USA-1895
Zein, Minnie	23(W)		Arabia	USA-1899
Zein, William	5(S)		Arabia	USA-1899
Zein, Maggie	10/12(D)		North Dakota	
Abcy, Peter	30	Farmer	Arabia	USA-1891
Abcy, Rosia	18(W)		Arabia	USA-1892
Abcy, Abcy	1(S)		North Dakota	
Frien, William	28	Farmer	Arabia	USA-1892
Frien, Frida	16(W)		Arabia	USA-1898
Frien, Abraham	53(F)	Farm Laborer	Arabia	USA-1892
Moran, John	45	Farmer	Arabia	USA-1890

Name	Age	Occupation	Place of Birth	Date of Arrival
WILLIAMS COUNTY—1900 CENSUS				
Williams County				
Moor, David	31		Asia Minor	
POLK COUNTY (MINNESOTA)—1900 CENSUS				
Crookston City				
Anthony, John	29	Carpenter	Syria	USA-1888
Abraham, Deep	34	Farm Laborer	Syria	USA-1889
Slimman, Elias	34	Farm Laborer	Syria	USA-1889
Soloman, Dick	28	Farm Laborer	Syria	USA-1887
Soloman, Saber	42	Farm Laborer	Syria	USA-1887
Soloman, Mary	49		Syria	USA-1897

1910

Name	Age	Occupation	Place of Birth	Date of Arrival
ADAMS COUNTY—1910 CENSUS				
Hettinger				
Tanous, Joe	35	Storekeeper	Turkey (Asia)	
Tanous, Cara	27(W)		Syria	
Tanous, Edward	(S)		United States	
Tanous, Harry	(S)		United States	
Deeb, Tanus	42	Storekeeper	Syria	
Deeb, Annie	35(W)		Syria	
Deeb, Tone	(S)		United States	
Deeb, Mike	(S)		United States	
Deeb, Cebhame	(S)		United States	
Deeb, Geo.	(S)		United States	
Deeb, Jim	(S)		United States	
Deeb, Sada	(D)		United States	
Deeb, Mre	(D)		United States	
Tanous, Abe	32	Storekeeper	Syria	
BENSON COUNTY—1910 CENSUS				
Minnewauken				
Joseph, Jim	38	Laborer, RR	Turkey	USA-1909
Arhab, Aliet	35	Laborer, RR	Turkey	USA-1909
Goon, Darener	32	Laborer, RR	Turkey	USA-1910
Demilnor, George	19	Laborer, RR	Turkey	USA-1910
Jonus, George	15	Laborer, RR	Turkey	USA-1910
Marmath				
Macrift, Marcus	19	Laborer, RR	Turkey	USA-1907
Lyanott, Nick	25	RR Employee	Turkey	USA-1909
CASS COUNTY—1910 CENSUS				
Gardner Twp.				
George, Mike	24	Hired Man	Turkey	USA-1908
John, Jouie	21	Hired Man	Turkey	USA-1908
Aslau, Alle	25	Hired Man	Turkey	USA-1908

Name	Age	Occupation	Place of Birth	Date of Arrival
Fourier, Shau	24	Hired Man	Turkey	USA-1908
Aslau, Auel	20	Hired Man	Turkey	USA-1908
Hadie, Adie	20	Hired Man	Turkey	USA-1907
Apdue, Yseu	20	Hired Man	Turkey	USA-1907
Salaulou, Mauddaly	20	Hired Man	Turkey	USA-1907
Fair, Nejir	28	Hired Man	Turkey	USA-1908

Fargo

Ferris, Mirril	35		Syria	
Ferris, George	10(S)		Indiana	
Ferris, Sistue	8(S)		Minnesota`	
Ferris, Rosie	5(D)		North Dakota	
Ferris, Sophiea	3(D)		North Dakota	
Ferris, Charley	40(B)		Syria	
Zahar, Mohammad	27	Owner, Pool Hall	Syria	USA-1900
Herman, Sam	59	Farm Hand	Syria	USA-1892
Herman, Ashly	50(W)		Syria	
Herman, Mike	17(S)	Section Hand, RR	Syria	
Sam, Richard	27	Laborer, RR	Syria	
Hodge, Soloman	33	Merchant, Dry Goods	Syria	USA-1897
Zahbera, Asma	50		Syria	
Sam, Abela	28	Farm Hand	Syria	USA-1906
Alie, Charley	26	Farm Hand	Syria	USA-1902
Merhiy, Houssyn	27		Syria	USA-1898
Merhiy, Elizabeth	23(W)	German Parents	North Dakota	

EDDY COUNTY—1910 CENSUS

New Rockford Twp.

Saad, Elias N.	36	Merchant, General Store	Syria	USA-1904
Saad, Solicy	28(W)		Syria	
Saad, Jimmie	6(S)		Syria	
Saad, Orphesia	4(D)		North Dakota	

EMMONS COUNTY—1910 CENSUS

Union School Twp.

Williams, Joseph	40	Farmer	Syria	USA-1896
Williams, Mary	33(W)		Syria	
Williams, Annie	15(D)		Syria	
Williams, Bessie	12(D)		South Dakota	
Williams, Edward	11(S)		South Dakota	
Williams, Alice	3(D)		Minnesota	
Williams, Alexander	3/12(S)		Minnesota	

Twp. 130-R78

William, Mike	45	Farmer	Syria	USA-1887
William, Katherina	32(W)		Syria	USA-1887
William, Willie	13(S)		Minnesota	
William, Thomas	11(S)		South Dakota	
William, Eddie	8(S)		Minnesota	
William, George	7(S)		Minnesota	
William, Joseph	7(S)		Minnesota	

Name	Age	Occupation	Place of Birth	Date of Arrival
Abraham, George	35	Farmer	Syria	USA-1903
Abraham, Annie	28(W)		Syria	USA-1903
Abraham, Sadie	4(D)		North Dakota	
Abraham, Katie	3(D)		North Dakota	
Abraham, Julia	7/12(D)		North Dakota	
William, David	28	Farmer	Syria	USA-1893

GRAND FORKS COUNTY—1910 CENSUS

Grand Forks

Allen, Charley	21	Cook, Hotel	Asyria	USA-1900
Lowis, John	30	Laborer	Syria	USA-1900
Lowis, Frydg	25(W)		Syria	
Lowis, Sarah	9(D)		North Dakota	
Lowis, Martha	5(D)		North Dakota	
Lowis, Josyh	2(S)		North Dakota	

GRIGGS COUNTY—1910 CENSUS

Hannaford

Hassan, Alfred	25	General Laborer	Syria	USA-1901
Hassan, Emma	25(W)	Swedish Parents	Sweden	USA-1901
Hassan, Adeliue	2(D)		North Dakota	

KIDDER COUNTY—1910 CENSUS

Pleasant Hill Twp.

Hansey, Nany	47	Farmer	Turkey/Asia Syria	USA-1894
Hansey, Litth	35(W)		Turkey/Asia Syria	USA-1901
Hansey, Mable	5(D)		North Dakota	
Hansey, Toyfal	3(S)		North Dakota	
Hansey, Hagel	2(S)		North Dakota	
Hansey, Nels	3/12(S)		North Dakota	
Hansey, Albert	29(B)	Farmer	Turkey/Asia Syria	USA-1901
Hansey, Asid	29	Farmer	Turkey/Asia Syria	USA-1896

Kickapoo Twp.

Amein, George	35	Farmer	Turkey/Asia Syria	USA-1896

Farmer Twp.

Ali, William	24	Farmer	Syria	USA-1905
Amad, Allie	25	Servant/Farm Labor	Syria	USA-1906
Ali, Amael	27(B)	Farm Laborer	Syria	USA-1899
Alia, Hasan	25	Farmer	Syria	USA-1899
Alia, Mohammit	30(B)	Farm Laborer	Syria	USA-1904

LAMOURE COUNTY—1910 CENSUS

Russell Twp.

Joship, Ali	30	Farm Labor	Turkey	USA-1909

Edgeley

Asker, Oscar	28	Laborer/Odd Jobs	Turkey	"Traveler"
Amit, Katib	19	Laborer/Odd Jobs	Turkey	"Traveler"
Moory, Alfred	21	Laborer/Odd Jobs	Turkey	"Traveler"
Salun, Alie	21	Laborer/Odd Jobs	Turkey	"Traveler"
Mklaid, Joe	21	Laborer/Odd Jobs	Turkey	"Traveler

Name	Age	Occupation	Place of Birth	Date of Arrival
McINTOSH COUNTY—1910 CENSUS				
Ashley				
Side, Abraham	29	Prop./Billiard Hall	Syria	USA-1903
Side, Johnna	27(W)	Parents Swedish	Sweden	
Side, Fatmey	8/12(D)		North Dakota	
Side, Alek	8/12(S)		North Dakota	
Alex, Hazen	26	Retail Merchant	Syria	
Jones, Albert	27(F)	Retail Merchant	Syria	
Twp. 130-R69				
Dell, Albert A.	22	Farmer	Syria	USA-1902
McLEAN COUNTY—1910 CENSUS				
Max Village				
Ally, John	32	Laborer, RR	Turkey/Asia	USA-1908
Hisson, Surrenan	60	Laborer, RR	Turkey/Asia	USA-1909
Carum, John	38	Laborer, RR	Turkey/Asia	USA-1909
Soloman, George	24	Laborer, RR	Turkey/Asia	USA-1909
Soloman, Esson	50	Laborer, RR	Turkey/Asia	USA-1909
Mamoth, Sussy	28	Laborer, RR	Turkey/Asia	USA-1909
Ebrin, Ally	38	Laborer, RR	Turkey/Asia	USA-1907
Mistfa, Abes	36	Laborer, RR	Turkey/Asia	USA-1909
MORTON COUNTY—1910 CENSUS				
Twp. 138-R82				
Samuel, Benjamin	36(BD)	Minister	Turkey/Europe	USA-1895
MOUNTRAIL COUNTY—1910 CENSUS				
Alger Twp.				
Juha, Alex R.	29	Laborer/Odd Jobs	Turkey/Asia Syria	USA-1900
Abella, Adie	30(BD)	Laborer/Odd Jobs	Turkey/Asia Syria	
Omer, Sam	29	Farmer	Turkey/Asia Syria	USA-1902
Omer, Allay	24	Farmer	Turkey/Asia Syria	USA-1907
Ross Twp. 156-92				
Bahne, Salem J.	45	Photographer	Syria	USA-1894
Bahne, Sullaua	45(W)		Syria	USA-1894
Bahne, Rachel B.	11(D)		Nebraska	
Bahne, Martha B.	10(D)		Nebraska	
Bahne, Ruth B.	7(D)		North Dakota	
Alley, George J.	27	Farmer	Turkey/Asia Syria	USA-1902
Alley, Hamid	25(B)	Farm Laborer	Turkey/Asia Syria	USA-1907
Caled, Ally	24	Farmer	Turkey/Asia Syria	USA-1902
Abdella, Side	45	Farmer	Turkey/Asia Syria	USA-1898
Ally, Abdul	38	Farmer	Turkey/Asia Syria	USA-1898
Ally, Fatma	25(W)			
Ally, Hamway	1(D)		North Dakota	
Ally, Side	28(B)	Farm Laborer	Turkey/Asia Syria	USA-1901
Ally, Mohammed	2(N)		North Dakota	
Ally, Latel	1(N)		North Dakota	

Name	Age	Occupation	Place of Birth	Date of Arrival
Abdalla, Omer	25	Farmer	Turkey/Asia Syria	USA-1906
Salem, Omer	35	Farmer	Turkey/Asia Syria	USA-1900
Salem, Albert	28(B)	Farmer	Turkey/Asia Syria	USA-1899

NELSON COUNTY—1910 CENSUS

Rush Twp.

Gady, Abdo	22(BD)	Peddler/Dry Goods	Asia	USA-1908

PIERCE COUNTY—1910 CENSUS

Twp. 154-R73

Abraham, Joseph	53		Syria	USA-1892

Reno Valley Twp.

Wazer, Metre	35	Farmer	Syria	USA-1892
Wazer, Tolgy	26(W)		Turkey/Asia Syria	
Wazer, Jauiss	6(S)		North Dakota	
Wazer, Sophia	5(D)		North Dakota	
Wazer, Mathilda	3(D)		North Dakota	
Wazer, George	7/12(S)		North Dakota	
Wazer, Eli	38	Farmer	Syria	USA-1890
Wazer, Barbara	30(W)		Syria	
Wazer, Solomon	11(S)		North Dakota	
Wazer, Mabel	8(D)		North Dakota	
Wazer, Hazel	6(D)		North Dakota	
Wazer, Hafri	4(D)		North Dakota	
Wazer, Olga	7/12(D)		North Dakota	
Berthad, Asia	68	Hired Man, Farm	Syria	USA-1905
Wazer, Debolia (Widow)	72(M)		Syria	
Skaff, Joseph	45	Farmer	Syria	USA-1891
Skaff, Sanas	35(W)		Syria	
Skaff, Jennie	18(D)		Minnesota	
Skaff, Annie	12(D)		North Dakota	
Skaff, George	8(S)		North Dakota	
Skaff, Nasam (Widow)	80(M)		Syria	
Malza, Joseph	32	Farm Laborer	Syria	
Saba, Joseph G.	31	Farmer	Syria	USA-1892
Dann, Abdella	32	Farmer	Syria	USA-1898
Dann, Mary	22(W)		Syria	
Dann, George	6(S)		North Dakota	
Dann, Lizzida	3(D)		North Dakota	
Dann, Adale	6/12(D)		North Dakota	
Dann, Thomas	26(B)	Farm Laborer	Syria	USA-1901

Rugby City

Esta, Joe	32	Hired Farmer	Syria	USA-1891
Esta, Uczie	37(W)		Syria	USA-1891
Esta, Albert	10(S)		North Dakota	
Saba, Charlie	35	Peddler/Notions	Syria	USA-1900
Saba, Cassi	33(W)		Syria	USA-1900
Saba, Rosie	8(D)		North Dakota	
Saba, Lauda	6(D)		North Dakota	
Saba, George	2(S)		North Dakota	

Name	Age	Occupation	Place of Birth	Date of Arrival
Razook, Abraham	40	Peddler	Syria	USA-1900
Razook, Ruzinia	40(W)		Syria	USA-1909
Razook, George	13(S)		Syria	USA-1909
Razook, Zimmiud	10(D)		Syria	USA-1909
Razook, Zimmiud	60(M)	Peddler	Syria	USA-1892
Kirk, Mike	43	Laborer/Odd Jobs	Syria	USA-1905
Kirk, Sehma	38(W)		Syria	USA-1905
Kirk, Sophia	15(D)		Syria	USA-1905
Kirk, Victoria	8(D)		Syria	USA-1905
David, Alexander	43	Farmer	Syria	USA-1893
David, Mary	31(W)		Syria	USA-1895
David, Victoria	13(D)		North Dakota	
David, Sophia	11(D)		North Dakota	
David, Habbib	9(S)		North Dakota	
David, Louie	7(S)		North Dakota	
David, Eddie	5(S)		North Dakota	
David, Samuel	3(S)		North Dakota	
David, William	4/12(S)		North Dakota	
Assid, Mike	38	Farm Labor/Odd Jobs	Syria	USA-1891
Assid, Martha	35(W)		Syria	USA-1891
Assid, Selma	13(D)		North Dakota	
Assid, Joe	12(S)		North Dakota	
Assid, James	5(S)		North Dakota	
Assid, John	8/12(S)		North Dakota	
Kouray, Charley	35	Odd Jobs	Syria	USA-1900
Kouray, Magnie	18(W)		Minnesota	
Kouray, Debi	1-7/12(D)		North Dakota	
Kouray, Albert	37	Peddler	Syria	USA-1898
Kouray, Lena	27(W)		Syria	USA-1906
Kouray, Gera C.	8(D)		North Dakota	
Kouray, George	4(S)		North Dakota	
Kouray, Philip	2(S)		North Dakota	
Liba, Neglie	32(M)	Labor/Housework	Syria	USA-1909
Liba, Lyila	15(D)		Syria	USA-1909
Liba, Gok	13(D)		Syria	USA-1909
Baba, Joseph	29	Pack Peddler	Syria	USA-1897
Baba, Irma	20(W)		Syria	USA-1906
Baba, Carry	2(D)		North Dakota	
Baba, Jennie	11/12(D)		North Dakota	
Turk, Charles	39	Department Store	Syria	USA-1891
Turk, Fanny	34(W)		Syria	USA-1891
Turk, Sasy	15(D)		North Dakota	
Turk, Lizzie	12(D)		North Dakota	
Turk, Mike	10(S)		North Dakota	
Turk, Abill	7(S)		North Dakota	
Turk, John	6(S)		North Dakota	
Turk, Fred	3(S)		North Dakota	
Turk, Frida	6/12(D)		North Dakota	

Name	Age	Occupation	Place of Birth	Date of Arrival
Shikaney, Nicholas	40	Farmer	Syria	USA-1896
Shikaney, Jismily	31(W)		Syria	USA-1896
Shikaney, Lizzie	13(D)		North Dakota	
Shikaney, James	11(S)		North Dakota	
Shikaney, Sadie	9(D)		North Dakota	
Shikaney, Rosie	7(D)		North Dakota	
Shikaney, Missy	5(D)		North Dakota	
Shikaney, Joseph	3(S)		North Dakota	
Shikaney, Amilia	1-3/12(D)		North Dakota	
Nami, Joe	50(BD)	Odd Jobs	Syria	USA-1894
Nami, Charly	13(BD)		North Dakota	
David, Atta	35	Store Clerk	Syria	USA-1892
David, Mary	23(W)		Syria	
David, James	4(S)		North Dakota	
David, Michael	3(S)		North Dakota	
David, Fred	7/12(S)		North Dakota	
Srur, George	30(BD)	Laborer/Odd Jobs	Syria	USA-1904
Srur, Blanche	25(W)		Syria	
David, Tanous K.	28(BD)	Physician-Surgeon	Syria	USA-1900
Shama, Abdalla	36	Dry Goods Merchant	Syria	USA-1893
Shama, Shafaca	32(W)		Syria	USA-1893
Shama, Deeba	9(D)		North Dakota	
Shama, Amda	5(D)		North Dakota	
Shama, Frada	3(D)		North Dakota	
Shama, Joseph	1-10/12(S)		North Dakota	
Shama, Frada	79(M)	Housework	Syria	USA-1893
Yonas,	27	Shoemaker Shop	Syria	USA-1900
Yonas, Jessie	26(W)		Syria	USA-1895
Yonas, John	6(S)		North Dakota	
Yonas, Jimmie	5(S)		North Dakota	
Yonas, Violet	3(D)		North Dakota	
Yonas, Charley	1(S)		North Dakota	
Hallaway, Joseph	31	Laborer/Odd Jobs	Syria	USA-1892
Hallaway, Jemsis	25(W)		Syria	USA-1892
Hallaway, Della	7(D)		North Dakota	
Hallaway, Edna	5(D)		North Dakota	
Hallaway, Charley	2(S)		North Dakota	
Hallaway, George	33	Laborer/Odd Jobs	Syria	USA-1892
Hallaway, Nellie	30(W)		Syria	USA-1892
Hallaway, Fina	20(D)		North Dakota	
Hallaway, Alma	8(D)		North Dakota	
Boussad, Joseph	65	Laborer/Odd Jobs	Syria	USA-1906
Boussad, Annie	55(W)		Syria	USA-1906
Boussad, Charley	6(GS)		North Dakota	

Twp. 158-R72

Name	Age	Occupation	Place of Birth	Date of Arrival
Feyatt, Charley	35	Farmer	Syria	USA-1885

Name	Age	Occupation	Place of Birth	Date of Arrival
Balish, Joe	40(P)	Farmer	Syria	USA-1880[sic]
Balish, Marybellis	33(W)		Syria	
Balish, Ollie	13(D)		North Dakota	
Balish, Annie	9(D)		North Dakota	
Balish, Nisma	6(D)		North Dakota	
Balish, Johnny	4(S)		North Dakota	
Fayatt, Anna	20		Syria	USA-1900
Fayatt, Eva	5(D)		North Dakota	
Fayatt, Fred	3(S)		North Dakota	
Fayatt, Mike	6/12(S)		North Dakota	
Fayatt, Mary	60(GM)		Syria	
Kurry (Kouray?), George	20	Farm Laborer, Working Out	Syria	USA-1902

RAMSEY COUNTY—1910 CENSUS

Lawton Twp.

Name	Age	Occupation	Place of Birth	Date of Arrival
Anthony, Joe S.	33	Retail Merchant, Dry Goods, Farm Equipment	Syria	USA-1889
Anthony, Eva	26(W)		Syria	
Anthony, Tom	11(S)		Minnesota	
Anthony, Mildred	2(D)		Minnesota	
Anthony, Morie	3/12(S)		Minnesota	

RICHLAND COUNTY—1910 CENSUS

Wahpeton

Name	Age	Occupation	Place of Birth	Date of Arrival
Assad, George	56	Restaurant Owner	Turkey/Syria	USA-1898
Assad, Sadie	35(W)		Turkey/Syria	
Assad, Ossit	16(S)		Minnesota	
Assad, Nicholas	11(S)		North Dakota	
Assad, Mary	9(D)		North Dakota	
Assad, Bridgit	8(D)		North Dakota	
Assad, Sykia	4(D)		North Dakota	
Assad, Michael	2(S)		North Dakota	

SARGENT COUNTY—1910 CENSUS

Tewaukon Twp.

Name	Age	Occupation	Place of Birth	Date of Arrival
Union, Joseph	4(GS)		North Dakota	Father, Arabia
Mother, Germany				

SHERIDAN COUNTY—1910 CENSUS

Martin Twp.

Name	Age	Occupation	Place of Birth	Date of Arrival
Nikolaus, Alexander	48	Hardware Merchant	Turkey (F/M Russia)	USA-1896
Nikolaus, Mary	46(W)		Turkey	
Nikolaus, Mary	25(D)		Turkey	
Nikolaus, Sophia	14(D)		Canada	
Nikolaus, Frederick	20(S)		Canada	
Nikolaus, Bertha	12(D)		Canada	
Nikolaus, Ella	10(D)		North Dakota	
Nikolaus, Emma	8(D)		North Dakota	
Nikolaus, William	6(S)		North Dakota	
Nikolaus, Virginia	6/12(D)		North Dakota	

Name	Age	Occupation	Place of Birth	Date of Arrival
Twp. 147-R76				
Massit, Nassif	32	Farmer	Syria	USA-1895
Massit, Nellie	27(W)		Syria	
Massit, Wade	3(S)		North Dakota	
Massit, Jounas	4/12(S)		North Dakota	
Ellis, William	32	Farmer	Syria	USA-1891
Ellis, Yuia	27(W)		Syria	USA-1900
Ellis, Yester	5(S)		Iowa	
Ellis, Sarah	1-7/12(D)		North Dakota	
Nassif, Shaker	51	Traveling Peddler	Syria	USA-1896
Twp. 148-R77				
Skaff, Farris	31	Farmer	Syria	USA-1899
Skaff, Mary	18(W)		Syria	USA-1899
Skaft, Abraham	27	Laborer/Work Out	Syria	USA-1905
Nicola, Sam	33	Farmer	Syria	USA-1905
Nicola, Lotwan	20(W)		Syria	
Nicola, Badale	2(S)		North Dakota	
Twp. 148-R76				
Nicola, Salem	30	Farmer	Syria	USA-1894
Nicola, Nellie	20(W)		Syria	
Nicola, Nicola	3(S)		North Dakota	
Nicola, Solomon	20	Farm Laborer, Work Out	Syria	USA-1905
Nicola, Sofia	19(W)		Syria	
Nicola, Salma	29	Farmer	Syria	USA-1889
Nicola, Stella	20(W)		Syria	
Allay, Amet	27	Farm Laborer	Syria	
Allay, Lizzy	27(W)	German Parents	Russia/German	
Allay, Lizzy	1/12(D)		North Dakota	
Abdella, Moses	30	Country Peddler	Syria	US-1904
Abdella, Isace	18(B)	Farm Laborer, Work Out	Syria	USA-1904

TOWNER COUNTY—1910 CENSUS

Name	Age	Occupation	Place of Birth	Date of Arrival
Armordale Twp.				
Solomon, Joseph	28	Farmer	Syria	USA-1896
Solomon, Rachel	19(W)		Syria	
Solomon, Abraham	2(S)		North Dakota	
Solomon, Jamil	6/12(D)		North Dakota	
Solomon, Edward	30(B)	Farm Laborer	Syria	USA-1900
Howell Twp.				
Hager, Mary	46	Farmer	Syria	USA-1896
Hager, David	17(S)	Home Farm Laborer	Syria	USA-1896
Alce, Joseph	25(HM)	Farm Laborer	Syria	USA-1905
Soder, Sam	35(HM)	Farm Laborer	Syria	USA-1893

Name	Age	Occupation	Place of Birth	Date of Arrival
Assy, Nicholas	36	Farmer	Syria	USA-1891
Assy, Mary	35(W)		Syria	USA-1890
Assy, Joe	12(S)		North Dakota	
Assy, John	9(S)		North Dakota	
Assy, William	6(S)		North Dakota	
Assy, Agnes	3(D)		North Dakota	
Assy, Rose	6/12(D)		North Dakota	
Albert, George	24(HM)	Farm Laborer	North Dakota	

Perth

Lyon, Frank	26	Laborer/Odd Jobs	Syria	USA-1900
Lyon, Anaba	35(W)		Syria	
Busard, Shelbe	10(SS)		North Dakota	
Busard, Lillian	14(SD)		North Dakota	
Busard, Mary	7(SD)		North Dakota	
Busard, Charley	6(SS)		North Dakota	
Busard, Albah E.	4(SS)		North Dakota	

Grainfield Twp.

Aboud, M.	31	Farmer	Syria	USA-1901
Aboud, Lusie	30(W)		Syria	
Aboud, Ania	2(D)		North Dakota	
Aboud, Sophia	1(D)		North Dakota	
Hagger, Charles	38	Farmer	Syria	USA-1901
Hagger, Abila	20(W)		Syria	
Oman, Soloman	39	Farm Laborer	Syria	USA-1904
Oman, Lurida	26(W)		Syria	
Oman, Mary	4(D)		Pennsylvania	
Oman, Lika	2(D)		Massachusetts	
Oman, George	4/12(S)		North Dakota	
Assye, Samuel	30	Farmer, Own Farm	Syria	USA-1897
Assye, Martha	27(W)		Syria	
Assye, Kathrine	6(D)		North Dakota	
Assye, Sophia	4(D)		North Dakota	
Assye, Jimmie	1(S)		North Dakota	

WALSH COUNTY—1910 CENSUS

Shepherd Twp.

Moran, John	48	Farmer	Turkey/Asia Syria	USA-1887
Moran, Mary G.	48(W)		Turkey/Asia Syria	USA-1907
Moran, Polas	20(S)	Farm Laborer	Turkey/Asia Syria	USA-1907
Kagella, Mrs. Sadie	55	Farmer	Turkey/Asia Syria	USA-1892
Kagella, Moses	30(S)	Farm Laborer	Turkey/Asia Syria	USA-1892
Faiad, Fred	55	Farmer	Turkey/Asia Syria	USA-1892
Faiad, Annie	50(W)		Turkey/Asia Syria	
Faiad, Sababy	14(D)		North Dakota	
Faiad, George	11(S)		North Dakota	
Faiad, Joseph	9(S)		North Dakota	
Fraeje, Nareef	47	Farmer	Turkey/Asia Syria	USA-1885
Fraeje, Shabel	13(S)		North Dakota	
Fraeje, Elias	7(S)		North Dakota	
Fraeje, Moses	35(B)	Farmer	Turkey/Asia Syria	USA-1889

Name	Age	Occupation	Place of Birth	Date of Arrival
Eli, Joe	26	Farm Laborer	Turkey/Asia Syria	USA-1902
Anthony, John	29(BD)	House Carpenter	Turkey/Asia Syria	USA-1894
Absey, Peter	40	Farmer	Turkey/Asia Syria	USA-1892
Absey, Rosie	27(W)		Turkey/Asia Syria	USA-1897
Absey, Absey	11(S)		North Dakota	
Absey, Kahle	9(D)		North Dakota	
Absey, Jesie	6(D)		North Dakota	
Absey, Jimmie	4(S)		North Dakota	
Absey, Mabel	1(D)		North Dakota	
Frien, Abraham	71	Farmer	Turkey/Asia Syria	USA-1891
Frien, Susan	60(W)		Turkey/Asia Syria	USA-1891
Frien, Richard	25(S)	Farm Laborer	Turkey/AsiaSyria	USA-1891
Haidd, Samuel	25(HM)	Farm Laborer	Turkey/Asia Syria	USA-1907

WILLIAMS COUNTY—1910 CENSUS

Bull Butte Twp.

Name	Age	Occupation	Place of Birth	Date of Arrival
Bousliman, Charlie	26	Farmer	Syria	USA-1900
Bousliman, Lizzie	22(W)		Syria	
Bousliman, Josephine	2(D)		North Dakota	
Bousliman, Viven	7/10(D)		North Dakota	
Samrua, Nick	21	Servant/Farm Laborer	Syria	USA-1905
Aboud, Nicholas	29	Farmer	Syria	USA-1905
Aboud, Sieg	24(W)		Syria	
Aboud, Charlie	6(S)		Syria	
Aboud, Agnes	2(D)		North Dakota	
Aboud, Victoria	1-4/12(D)		North Dakota	
Aboud, Abram	33	Farmer	Syria	USA-1902
Aboud, Jennie	24(W)		Syria	
Aboud, Sadie	2(D)		North Dakota	
Aboud, Rose	1(D)		North Dakota	
Aboud, Tom	22(B)	Farm Laborer	Syria	USA-1906
Aboud, John	32(B)	Farm Laborer	Syria	USA-1901
Polis, Seig	23	Farm Laborer	Syria	USA-1904
Barkie, George	34	Farmer	Syria	USA-1900
Barkie, Mary	30(W)		Syria	
Barkie, Effie	12(D)		Syria	
Barkie, Aesoph	10(S)		Syria	
Barkie, Rose	9(D)		Syria	
Barkie, Mike	2(S)		North Dakota	
Barkie, Rumsey	4/12(D)		North Dakota	
Munyer, Jahour	42	Dry Goods Merchant	Syria	
Munyer, Edward	21(N)	Clerk	Illinois	

Twp. 156-R102

Name	Age	Occupation	Place of Birth	Date of Arrival
Zine, Lottie	45		Syria	
Zine, Fred	22	Grocery Merchant	Syria	USA-1899
St. _____, Mrs. Debe	40	Own Income	Syria	

Name	Age	Occupation	Place of Birth	Date of Arrival
John, Mrs. Jennie	22	Own Income		
Skaff, Abram C.	25	Bookeeper, Store	Syria	USA-1900
Skaff, Nellie	22(W)		Syria	
Skaff, Charlie	2(S)		North Dakota	
Skaff, Alfred	3/12(S)		North Dakota	
Skaff, Julia	52(M)	Own Income	Syria	
Skaff, Mary	22(S)	Own Income	Syria	
Skaff, Irene	25(S)	Servant at Home	Syria	
Skaff, Eva	12(S)		Syria	
Atol, William	27	Farmer	Syria	USA-1898
Atol, Abrah	54(F)	Farm Laborer	Syria	USA-1899
Atol, Anna	38(M)		Syria	
Albit, Joseph	22	Farm Laborer	Syria	USA-1908
Abdo, Abrah	28	Farmer	Syria	USA-1888
Guzel, Owad	38	Farm Laborer	Syria	UDA-1895
Seeb, Joseph	36	Farmer	Syria	USA-1905
Zine, Charlie	45	Farmer	Syria	USA-1905
Zine, Ester	40(W)		Syria	
Zine, Charlie	15(S)		Syria	
Zine, Gorge	12(S)		Syria	
Zine, Mary	5(D)		Minnesota	
Zine, Jennie	7(D)		Minnesota	
Albert, Charlie	26	Farmer	Syria	USA-1898
Rehal, Charlie	33	Farmer	Syria	USA-1898
Rehal, Rose	26(W)		Syria	
Rehal, Julia	1-10/12(D)		North Dakota	
Younes, Joseph	28(BIL)	Farm Laborer	Syria	
Bohamra, Abdula	55	Farmer, Own Income	Syria	USA-1900
Bohamra, Saddie	50(W)		Syria	
Bohamra, Margueta	15(D)		Minnesota	
Bohamra, Joe	30	Farmer	Syria	USA-1900
Bohamra, Anna	25(W)		Syria	
Bohamra, Gwnia	1-8/12(D)		Minnesota	
Zein, Charlie A.	29	Farmer	Syria	USA-1896
Zein, Anna	28(W)		Syria	
Zein, Amlee	6/12(D)		North Dakota	
Farzle, Abrah	38	Rug/Carpet Salesman	Syria	USA-1891
Farzle, Martha	35(W)		Syria	
Farzle, Victor	7(S)		Minnesota	
Farzle, Freda	5(D)		Minnesota	
Farzle, Rosie	3(D)		Minnesota	
Farzle, George	1-8/12(S)		North Dakota	
Azar, Joseph	25	Servant/Farm Laborer	Syria	USA-1900
Mont Twp.				
Abaod, Elex	45	Farmer	Syria	USA-1903
Abaod, Anna	35(W)		Syria	

Name	Age	Occupation	Place of Birth	Date of Arrival
Magie, Sadie	65(M)		Syria	
Shikany, Elias	33	House Carpenter	Syria	USA-1896
Shikany, Effiefe	33(W)		Syria	
Shikany, Ole	12(S)		North Dakota	
Shikany, Charlie	10(S)		North Dakota	
Shikany, Abraham	5(S)		North Dakota	
Shikany, Lottie	2(D)		North Dakota	
Shikany, Philip	9/12(S)		North Dakota	
Naked, Joseph	28	Farmer	Syria	USA-1900
Naked, Susie	18(W)		Syria	
Farrah, Ramie	60(M)	Own Income	Syria	
Farrah, John	32(B)	Farmer at Home	Syria	

Williston Twp.

Name	Age	Occupation	Place of Birth	Date of Arrival
Ferris, Rashad A.	54	Farmer	Syria	USA-1893
Ferris, Mary	45(W)		Syria	USA-1893
Ferris, Asad	23(S)	Farm Laborer	Syria	USA-1903
Ferris, Johnnie	16(S)		Minnesota	
Ferris, Mamie	10(D)		North Dakota	
Ferris, Isac	7(S)		North Dakota	
Ferris, Peter	5(S)		North Dakota	
Ferris, Aunie	1-6/12(D)		North Dakota	

156-101

Name	Age	Occupation	Place of Birth	Date of Arrival
Yunoess, Charlie	52	Farmer	Syria	USA-1896
Yunoess, Aussie	40(W)		Syria	USA-1901
Yunoess, John	16(S)	Farm Laborer/Home	Syria	USA-1901
Yunoess, Mike	14(S)	Farm Laborer/Home	Syria	USA-1901
Yunoess, Frederick	6(S)		North Dakota	
Yunoess, Mary	2(D)		North Dakota	

Williston

Name	Age	Occupation	Place of Birth	Date of Arrival
Zien, Shamas	36	Farmer	Syria	USA-1891
Zien, Mary	32(W)		Syria	USA-1891
Zien, Harry	14(S)		Minnesota	
Zien, Rose	12(D)		Minnesota	
Zien, Eva	10(D)		Minnesota	
Zien, John	8(S)		Minnesota	
Zien, Victor	7(S)		Minnesota	
Zien, May	5(D)		Minnesota	
Kalil, David	29	Grocery Store	Syria	USA-1901
Kalil, Sadie	24(W)		Syria	USA-1907
Kalil, Wilbur	3(S)		North Dakota	
Kalil, Rosaline	4/12(D)		North Dakota	
Kalil, James	26(B)	Partner in Store	Syria	USA-1902
Germanus, Thomas	37	General Store Mdse.	Syria	USA-1890
Germanus, Julia	35(W)		Syria	USA-1892
Germanus, George	6(S)		Minnesota	
Germanus, Charles	3(S)		North Dakota	
Germanus, John	1(S)		North Dakota	

Name	Age	Occupation	Place of Birth	Date of Arrival
Munyer, Osaf	40	Billiard Parlor	Syria	USA-1888
Munyer, Norra M.	40(W)		Syria	USA-1898
Munyer, Nellie	14(D)		Illinois	
Munyer, Lilly	12(D)		Illinois	
Munyer, Sophia	10(D)		Iowa	
Munyer, Mary	60(M)		Syria	USA-1891
Munyer, Elias	58(B)		Syria	
Bousliman, Assad	46	Dry Goods Store	Syria	USA-1892
Bousliman, Debe	36(W)		Syria	USA-1905
Bousliman, Robert	23(S)	Sales, Dry Goods	Syria	USA-1905
Bousliman, Abraham	12(S)		Syria	USA-1905
Bousliman, Lillie	2(D)		North Dakota	
Bousliman, Moses	1(S)		North Dakota	
Taykally, Kalil	29	Candy Store	Syria	USA-1892
Taykally, Myrtle	26(W)		South Dakota	
F/Ohio, M/Missouri				
Taykally, Delsworth	1(S)		Wisconsin	
Lyon, Farris	39	Laborer/Odd Jobs	Turkey/Asia	USA-1896
Lyon, Emma	38(W)		Turkey/Asia	USA-1896
Lyon, Mike	21(S)	Confectionary Sales	Turkey/Asia	USA-1897
Lyon, James	14(S)		Turkey/Asia	USA-1897
Feris, F. N. (Lodger)	22	General Store, Sales	Turkey/Asia	USA-1905
Kassis, John	33	General Store	Syria	USA-1888
Kassis, Efaffe	26(W)		Syria	USA-1906
Kassis, Josephine	3(D)		North Dakota	
Kassis, Fred	10/12(S)		North Dakota	
Hapip, Frank	29	Farmer	Syria	USA-1888
Hapip, Thelma	29(W)		Syria	USA-1888
Hapip, Katy	4(D)		North Dakota	
Hapip, Knave	3(S)		North Dakota	
Hapip, Jim	2(S)		North Dakota	
Shikaney, John	41	General Store	Syria	USA-1890
Shikaney, Fanny R.	35(W)		Syria	USA-1890
Shikaney, Blanche	16(D)		At Sea	
Shikaney, Shaker	13(S)		North Dakota	
Shikaney, Walter	12(S)		North Dakota	
Shikaney, Mike	8(S)		North Dakota	
Shikaney, Joe	6(S)		North Dakota	
Shikaney, George	5(S)		North Dakota	
Shikaney, Bertha	1(D)		North Dakota	
Shikaney, Mary	21(C)		Syria	
Nesoes, Lotta (Lodger)	16	Dressmaker	Syria	USA-1904
Abram, William (Lodger)	26	Dry Goods Salesman, Traveling	Syria	USA-1896
Hapip, Deb	26	Pool Room/ Billiards	Syria	USA-1895
Hapip, Fanny	28(W)		Syria	USA-1895

Name	Age	Occupation	Place of Birth	Date of Arrival
Kassis, Abe	37	Grocery Store	Syria	USA-1892
Kassis, Freda	21(W)		Syria	USA-1896
Kassis, Julia	13(D)		Syria	
Kassis, Mary	10(D)		Syria ?	
Kassis, Edna	8(D)		Syria ?	
Kassis, Victoria	7(D)		Syria ?	
Kassis, Blanche	5(D)		Syria ?	
Kassis, Thomas	3(S)		Syria ?	
Kassis, Asad	28	General Store	Syria	USA-1896
Kassis, Maggie	23(W)		Syria	USA-1906
Kassis, George	0/12(S)		North Dakota	
Kassis, Lotie	17	Servant-Housework	Syria	USA-1906

POLK COUNTY (MINNESOTA)—1910 CENSUS

Crookston City

Name	Age	Occupation	Place of Birth	Date of Arrival
Thomas, Joseph	50	Laborer, Steam Machine	Seria	USA-1897
Thomas, Mary	40(W)		Seria	USA-1892
Thomas, Joseph Jr.	20(S)		Seria	USA-1897
Thomas, George	14(S)	Peddler	Seria	USA-1897
Thomas, Fathama	26(D)	Hotel	Seria	USA-1897
Thomas, Rosa	23(D)	Hotel	Seria	USA-1897
Issac, Jacob	27(B)	Laborer, Steam RR	Seria	USA-1892
Issac, Amie	1(D)		Minnesota	
Issac, Monsnun	27	Laborer, Steam RR	Seria	USA-1910
Issac, Fathama	22(W)		Seria	USA-1910
Issac, Moran	6(S)		Seria	USA-1910
Issac, James	3(S)		Seria	USA-1910
Issac, William	1(S)		Seria	USA-1910
Simm, Mike	35	Laborer, Steam RR	Seria	USA-1902
Simm, Messar	30	Laborer, Steam RR	Seria	USA-1902
Saiyer, Alley	47	Peddler, Dry Goods	Turkey/Syria	USA-
Saiyer, Viola	18(W)		Minnesota	F/Penn; M/Minn.
Noah, Martha	50	Peddler/Dry Goods	Turkey/Europe/Syria	USA-
Noah, Martha	7(D)		Minnesota	
Gibrail, Aman	35	Peddler/Dry Goods	Turkey/Europe/Syria	USA-1907
Mike, Thos	30	Laborer/RR Section	Turkey/Europe/Syria	USA-1907
Mike, Borget	60(M)		Turkey/Europe/Syria	USA-1907
Soloman, Thos	28	Laborer/RR Section	Turkey/Europe/Syria	USA-1907
Soloman, Mealy	26(W)		Turkey/Europe/Syria	USA-1907
Soloman, George	(S)		Minnesota	
Soloman, John	(S)		Minnesota	
Gibrail, Mary	46(MIL)		Turkey/Europe/Syria	USA-1907
Solomon, Marshall	45(B)	Laborer/RR Section	Turkey/Europe/Syria	USA-1907
Charles, Mary	40(MIL)		Turkey/Europe/Syria	USA-1907
Thomas, Charley	26	Laborer/RR Section	Turkey/Europe/Syria	USA-1907
Thomas, Eva	25(S)		Turkey/Europe/Syria	USA-1907
Noah, Tonas	46	Owner/Dry Goods	Turkey/Europe/Syria	USA-1890
Noah, Mary M.	40(W)	Farmer ?	Turkey/Europe/Syria	USA-1896
Noah, Michael	22(S)		Turkey/Europe/Syria	
Noah, Gibrail	8(S)		Minnesota	

Name	Age	Occupation	Place of Birth	Date of Arrival

1920

ADAMS COUNTY—1920 CENSUS

Haynes

Name	Age	Occupation	Place of Birth	Date of Arrival
Rashid, W. M.	36	Merchant, General Store	Syria	USA-1902
Rashid, Rose	32(W)		Syria	USA-1909
Rashid, Ethel	4-3/12(D)		South Dakota	
Rashid, Alfred	1-11/12(S)		South Dakota	
Rashid, Eyline Mary Anne	0/12(D)		North Dakota	

Hettinger

Name	Age	Occupation	Place of Birth	Date of Arrival
Tanous, Joe	45	Salesman/Grocery	Syria	USA-1891
Tanous, Sarah	30(W)		Syria	
Tanous, Eddie	12(S)		North Dakota	
Tanous, Henry	11(S)		North Dakota	
Tanous, Alfred	9(S)		North Dakota	
Tanous, Florence	7(D)		North Dakota	
Tanous, Leo	5(S)		North Dakota	
Tanous, Josephine	3(D)		North Dakota	
Tanous, Rose	7/12(D)		North Dakota	
Tanous, Abe	41(B)	Salesman/Grocery Store	Syria	USA-1892
Tanous, Thomas	24(N)	Salesman/Grocery Store	North Dakota	
Tanous, Mike	21(N)	Proprietor, Grocery Store	North Dakota	
Zamata, Charles	41	Proprietor, Confectionary Store	Syria	USA-1904
Zamata, Rachel	24(W)		New York	M/F Syria
Zamata, Viola	7(D)		North Dakota	
Zamata, Hazel	3(D)		North Dakota	
Zamata, Mary	7/12(D)		North Dakota	
Tanous, Deep	53	Farmer	Syria	USA-1891
Tanous, Annie J.	42(W)		Syria	
Tanous, Sadie	21(D)		North Dakota	
Tanous, Abraham	18(S)		North Dakota	
Tanous, George	16(S)		North Dakota	
Tanous, James	12(S)		North Dakota	
Tanous, Marie	10(D)		North Dakota	
Tanous, Harry	8(S)		North Dakota	
Tanous, Bob	7(S)		North Dakota	
Tanous, Margaret	5(D)		North Dakota	
Tanous, John	3-6/12(S)		North Dakota	
Tanous, Walter	1-6/12(S)		North Dakota	

BARNES COUNTY-1920 CENSUS

Name	Age	Occupation	Place of Birth	Date of Arrival
Matzek, Fred	58		Persia	
Matzek, Ernestina	52(W)		Russia	
Matzek, Otto	14(S)		North Dakota	
Matzek, Julius	12(S)		North Dakota	
Matzek, Benjamin	7(S)		North Dakota	
Rais, George	34		Turkey	
Rais, Mike George	24		Turkey	

Name	Age	Occupation	Place of Birth	Date of Arrival
Rogers Twp.				
Williams, Joseph	20(HM)	Farm Laborer	Turkey/Asia	
Joseph, Albert	30(HM)	Farm Laborer	Turkey/Asia	USA-1905

BENSON COUNTY-1920 CENSUS

Impark Twp.				
Hussein, Ali	55		Turkey	
Mike, Tom	47	Merchant/		
General Store	Syria	USA-1900		
Mike, Charley	11(S)		Minnesota	
Mike, Rosa	8(D)		Minnesota	
Sady, Mary	55(SIL)	Housekeeper	Syria	
Wood Lake				
Kallad, James	36	Retail Merchant	Syria	USA-1905
Kallad, Mary	38(W)		Canada	M/F Canada
Kallad, Fabian	16(S)		Canada	
Kallad, Alphonse	14(S)		Canada	
Kallad, Alfred	4(S)		Canada	
Kallad, Alice	3/12(D)		North Dakota	
Leeds Village				
Emo, George	43		Turkey	

BILLINGS COUNTY—1920 CENSUS

Fryburg				
Kanan, Richard	53	Merchant	Syria	USA-1895
Kanan, Annie	34(W)		Syria	
Kanan, Delia	15(D)		North Dakota	
Kanan, Sadie	14(D)		North Dakota	
Kanan, Cereanen	11(S)		North Dakota	
Kanan, Catherine	8(D)		North Dakota	
Kanan, Liman	5(S)		North Dakota	
Kanan, Ginne	1-1/12(D)		North Dakota	

BURKE COUNTY-1920 CENSUS

Mike, Joseph	60		Syria	
Portal (City)				
Abraham, James	37	City Drayman	Syria	USA-1900
Abraham, Helen	30(W)		Syria	
Abraham, Salem	10(S)		Canada	
Abraham, Josiphine	7(D)		Canada	
Abraham, Victoria	5(D)		Canada	
Abraham, George	3-4/12(S)		Canada	
Abraham, James	4/12(S)		North Dakota	
Shain, Mike	44		Syria	

Name	Age	Occupation	Place of Birth	Date of Arrival
BURLEIGH COUNTY—1920 CENSUS				
Bismarck				
Nassy, Tom S.	27	Manager, Pool Hall	Syria	USA-1908
Nassy, Lulie	25(W)		Syria	
Nassy, Hazel	4(D)		North Dakota	
Bashara, Nick	33		Syria	
Bashara, Selma	28(W)		Syria	
Bashara, Nick	2-10/12(S)		North Dakota	
Bashara, Lester	2 days(S)		North Dakota	
Boutrous, George	36		Syria	
Boutrous, Della	27(W)		Syria	
Boutrous, Thomas	8(S)		Iowa	
Boutrous, George	5-10/12(S)		Iowa	
Boutrous, Floyd	2-11/12(S)		North Dakota	
Boutrous, Tophy	5/12(S)		North Dakota	
Ellis, William	38	Barbershop	Syria	USA-1899
Ellis, Lena	34(W)		Syria	
Ellis, Lester	15(S)		Iowa	
Ellis, Sarah	11(D)		North Dakota	
Ellis, Thomas	9(S)		North Dakota	
Ellis, Sadie	6(D)		North Dakota	
Ellis, Floyd	4(S)		North Dakota	
Ellis, Russell	2(S)		North Dakota	
Howard, Sid	44		Assyria	
Nassif, George	29		Syria	
Nassif, Alexandria	26(W)		Syria	
Nassif, Sabie	7(S)		Minnesota	
Nassif, Frederick	5-6/12(S)		Minnesota	
Nassif, Fritz	2-6/12(S)		North Dakota	
Skaff, Farris	35	Agent, Medicine	Syria	USA-1902
Skaff, Mary	28(W)		Syria	
Skaff, George	8(S)		North Dakota	
Skaff, Freda	6-11/12(D)		North Dakota	
Skaff, Sam	4-4/12(S)		North Dakota	
Skaff, Jennie	2-8/12(D)		North Dakota	
Boutrous, Oscar	22	Assistant Mgr., Dry Goods	Illinois	
Boutrous, Butch	19(B)		Iowa	
Boutrous, Shiem	48(M)		Syria	USA-1890
Boutrous, Osewo				
Smiley, Anne	27	Student	North Dakota	
Varge, Joseph S.	48		Turkey	
Nicola, Sam	42	Manager, Hotel	Syria	USA-1905
Nicola, Lottie	30(W)		Syria	
Nicola, Bert	11(S)		North Dakota	
Nicola, Mary	9(D)		North Dakota	
Nicola, Freda	7(D)		North Dakota	
Nicola, John	5(S)		North Dakota	
Nicola, Jymmie	3(S)		North Dakota	
Nicola, Mitchell	6/12(S)		North Dakota	

Name	Age	Occupation	Place of Birth	Date of Arrival
Nicola, Solomon	28	Keeper, Pool Hall	Syria	USA-1905
Nicola, Sophie	25(W)		Syria	
Nicola, Jennie	7(D)		Canada	
Nicola, James	6(S)		Canada	
Nicola, Emeline	4-1/12(D)		North Dakota	
Kirk, Nazen	19(C)	Drayman, Transp.	North Dakota	
Kirk, George	17(C)		North Dakota	

Sterling Twp.

Eele, Hossan A.	42	Farmer	Seria[sic]	USA-1900

Driscoll Twp.

Hamsey, Albert F.	38	Farmer	Assyria	USA-1902
Hamsey, Selma F.	24(W)		North Dakota	
Hamsey, Violet A.	3-6/12(D)		North Dakota	
Hamsey, Phillip A.	1-6/12(S)		North Dakota	
Hamsey, Vernon S.	6/12(S)		North Dakota	

CASS COUNTY—1920 CENSUS

Fargo (City)

Name	Age	Occupation	Place of Birth	Date of Arrival
Assid, Mike	48	Laborer, Street Work	Syria	USA-1895
Assid, Martha	44(W)		Syria	
Assid, Joe	21(S)	Harness Maker	North Dakota	
Assid, James	16(S)		North Dakota	
Assid, John	10(S)		North Dakota	
Assid, William	7(S)		North Dakota	
Assid, Margaret	3-9/12(D)		North Dakota	
Kallil, Albert	28		Syria	
Kallil, Alyal	21(W)		Syria	
Kallil, Cornelius	4-3/12(S)		Minnesota	
Kallil, Allen	3-11/12(S)		Montana	
Kallil, Madeline	7/12(D)		Syria	
Fusis, Moses	23		Syria	
Numa, William A.	29	Owner, Rooming House	Mount Lebanon	
Numa, Rose	22(W)		Mount Lebanon	
Numa, Fred F.	8(S)		Mount Lebanon	
Numa, Theodore	6(S)		North Dakota	
Sage, Ally O.	32	Restaurant Owner	Syria	USA-1907
Sage, Molly	24(W)		Minnesota	(M/F Norway)
Sawaya, Edward	5		Assyria	
Sawaya, Katherine	8		Assyria	
Sawaya, Lewis	5		Assyria	
Sawaya, Victor	10		Assyria	
Sutton, Mike	81 (?)		Syria	
Shallop, Fred	28		Syria	
Shaheen, Tom	41	Owner, Confectionary	Syria	USA-1908
Shaheen, Sarah	37(W)		Canada (M/F Canada)	USA-1908
Shaheen, Albert	20(S)	Garage Mechanic	Canada	USA-1908
Shaheen, Wydia	11(D)		Canada	
Shaheen, Fedow	17(N)		Canada	

Name	Age	Occupation	Place of Birth	Date of Arrival
Hollel, Edward (Roomer)	26	Owner, Pool Hall	Syria	USA-1909
Lyon, Charlie	54	Owner, Hotel	Syria	USA-1892
Lyon, Helen	48(W)		Syria	USA-1892
Lyon, Samuel	26(S)	Clothing Salesman	Minnesota	
Lyon, Rose	24(W)		Syria	
Lyon, Helen	7(D)		North Dakota	
Ferris, Mary	42	Laborer	Syria	USA-1895
Cirrus, Charlie	55(B)	Laborer	Syria	USA-1885
Economou, Anna	26(D)		Syria	USA-1895
Ferris, George	19(S)	Operator, Motion Picture Machine	Indiana	
Ferris, Leslie	18(S)	Bookkeeper/Bank	Minnesota	
Ferris, Rose	16(D)		North Dakota	
Ferris, Sophia	13(D)		North Dakota	
Economoni, Janus	9(GS)		North Dakota	
Economoni, George	33(SIL)	Owner, Pool Hall	Greece	
Balish, Mary	39		Syria	USA-1890
Balish, Olive	22(D)		North Dakota	
Balish, Anna	19(D)		North Dakota	
Balish, Pedarl	16(D)		North Dakota	
Balish, John	13(S)		North Dakota	
Kallel, Albert	28	Commercial Traveler (Peddler)	Syria	USA-1902
Kallel, Alyai	21(W)		Syria	
Kallel, Cornelius	4-3/12(S)		Minnesota	
Kallel, Allen	3-4/10(S)		Montana	
Kallel, Madaline	3/12(D)		North Dakota	
Ferris, Moses	23(BD)	Laborer	Syria	USA-1912
Shibley, Jabir (Roomer)	33	Teacher, Fargo College	Syria	USA-1908
Murhey, Hasson	36	Laborer, Street	Syria	USA-
Murhey, Lizzie	33(W)		Parents: German	
Murhey, Joseph	8(S)		North Dakota	
Murhey, Evlyn	7(D)		North Dakota	
Murhey, Ali	6(S)		North Dakota	
Murhey, Smili	3-4/10(S)		North Dakota	
Murhey, Derhly	Baby(D)		North Dakota	
Alcorday, Dray (Roomer)	32		Syria	
Cash, Alex	38		Syria	
Davis, Alix	25		Syria	

CAVALIER COUNTY—1920 CENSUS

Siarden Twp.

Herbert, Joseph	72	Lodger	Illlinois	M/F Palestine

Hope Twp.

Abas, Alex	24	Dry Goods Merchant	Syria	USA-1914
Ferris, Madene	24		Syria	
Morse, Kassom	27		Syria	

Name	Age	Occupation	Place of Birth	Date of Arrival
DIVIDE COUNTY—1920 CENSUS				
Crosby (City)				
Hassir, Calib K.	29	Proprietor, General Store	Syria	USA-
Hassir, Florence	22(W)		North Dakota	
Parents: Germany				
Hassir, Clifford	2-5/12(S)		Minnesota	
Hassie, Falya	23(BD)	Clerk, Dry Goods	Syria	USA-
Hassie, Anna	25(W)		Minnesota	
Parents: Norway				
Kaddie, Sam (Lodger)	21	General Farm Laborer	Syria	USA-1913
DUNN COUNTY—1920 CENSUS				
Halliday				
Otmen, Eeleax	35	Laborer, RR	Syria	USA-1912
Otmen, Omer	32(C)		Syria	
Durvash, Mahtoad	31	Merchant Store	Turkey	USA-1908
Massot, Massad	40(B)	Merchant Store	Turkey	USA-1906
Otman, Charlie	38	House Carpenter	Syria	USA-1906
EMMONS COUNTY—1920 CENSUS				
Glanavan Twp.				
Abraham, George	47	Farmer	Syria	USA-1894
Abraham, Anna	49(W)		Syria	USA-1895
Abraham, Saddie	13(D)		North Dakota	
Abraham, Katie	12(D)		North Dakota	
Abraham, Gullieus	10(D)		North Dakota	
Abraham, Sebia	8(D)		North Dakota	
Abraham, Edward	6(S)		North Dakota	
Abraham, Philip	4-3/12(S)		North Dakota	
Abraham, Albert	2-3/12(S)		North Dakota	
Williams, Michale	57	Farmer	Syria	USA-1890
Williams, Katherine	43(W)		Syria	USA-1895
Williams, William	23(S)		Minnesota	
Williams, George	9(S)		North Dakota	
Williams, Amelia	5-11/12(D)		North Dakota	
Williams, Grace	3-6/12(D)		North Dakota	
Williams, Lulu	6/12(D)		North Dakota	
Williams, Lila	6/12(D)		North Dakota	
Union School				
Williams, Joseph	52	Farmer	Syria	USA-1896
Williams, Mary	43(W)		Syria	USA-1896
Williams, Anna	23(D)		Syria	
Williams, Bessie	21(D)		South Dakota	
Williams, Edward	20(S)		South Dakota	
Williams, Alice	13(D)		Minnesota	
Williams, Leonard	10(S)		Minnesota	
Williams, Arnold	8(S)		North Dakota	
Williams, Stanford	6(S)		North Dakota	

Name	Age	Occupation	Place of Birth	Date of Arrival
FOSTER COUNTY—1920 CENSUS				
Abess, Joe	32(BD)	Merchandise Peddler	Arabia	USA-1907
GRANT COUNTY—1920 CENSUS				
Vayianes, Joseph K.	39		Turkey	
GRIGGS COUNTY—1920 CENSUS				
Binford				
Abraham, Abe	41	Merchant, Own Store	Syria	USA-1900
Abraham, Agnes	25(W)		Minnesota: Parents Scandinavian	
Abraham, ?	7(S)			
Abraham, Victor	2(S)		Minnesota	
Joseph, Hassan	54(L)	Peddler/Salesman	Syria	USA-1894
Morbey, John	38(L)	Peddler/Salesman	Syria	USA-1905
Morbey, Joseph	47(L)	Peddler/Salesman	Syria	USA-1914
Alley, Mike	42(L)	Peddler/Salesman	Syria	USA-1910
KIDDER COUNTY—1920 CENSUS				
Farmer Twp.				
Solomon, Joseph	35	Farmer	Syria	USA-1900
Pleasant Hill Twp.				
Hamsey, Hamy (Namy)	55	Farmer	Syria	USA-1894
Hamsey, Lothihia	37(W)		Syria	
Hamsey, Ahithihia	12(S)		North Dakota	
Hamsey, Alex	11(S)		North Dakota	
Hamsey, Nels	9(S)		North Dakota	
Hamsey, Jessie	7(D)		North Dakota	
Hamsey, Union	6(S)		North Dakota	
Hamsey, Peter	2-5/12(S)		North Dakota	
Hamsey, Satie	11/12(D)		North Dakota	
Haglain, Harry	28	Laborer, RR	Turkey	USA-1914
Pettibone				
Abes, Hasen	37	Boarder	Asyria	
Haddy, Able	37		Syria/Turkey	
Haddy, Freda	21(W)			
Haddy, Selma	2-10/12(D)		North Dakota	
Kamoni, Ahmed	42		Syria	
Eli, Mohamit	41		Syria/Turkey	
McHENRY COUNTY—1920 CENSUS				
Drake				
Ally, Ahmad	37		Siberia[sic]	
Ally, Sadie	10(D)		North Dakota	
Ally, Mary	8(D)		North Dakota	
Kellel, Joseph	39		Syria	
Kellel, Mary	23(W)		Syria	
Kellel, Abraham	10(S)		North Dakota	
Kellel, Mike	7(S)		North Dakota	
Kellel, John	6(S)		North Dakota	
Kellel, Madeline	3(D)		North Dakota	
Kellel, George	9/12(S)		North Dakota	

Name	Age	Occupation	Place of Birth	Date of Arrival
McINTOSH COUNTY—1920 CENSUS				
Ashley				
Hassen, Joe	32	Pool Hall	Syria	USA-1901
Hassen, Lyda	23(W)		South Dakota	(F/M Russian)
Hassen, Oliver	5(S)		North Dakota	
Hassen, Fotmay	1-9/12(D)		North Dakota	
Hassen, Amenia	3/12(D)		North Dakota	
Casem, Frank	60		Arabia	
Hawatha, Joseph	49		Arabia	
McKENZIE COUNTY—1920 CENSUS				
151-101				
Hiney, Laurence F.	34	Hired Man	Illinois (Speaks Arabic)	F/M Asia
152-101				
Layon, Abraham	46	Farmer	Syria	USA-1890
Layon, Lilby	39(W)		Syria	
Layon, Mary	15(D)		Wisconsin	
Layon, Joe	17(S)		Wisconsin	
Layon, Sophia	15(D)		Wisconsin	
Layon, Isabella	12(D)		Wisconsin	
Layon, George	10(D)		Wisconsin	
Layon, Veavin	5(D)		North Dakota	
Layon, Nicholas	10/12(S)		North Dakota	
Mike, Abraham	42	Farmer	Syria	USA-1885
Mike, Meggie	95(M)		Syria	USA-1885
McLEAN COUNTY—1920 CENSUS				
Rufat, Zilfe A.	23		Turkey/Asia	
MOUNTRAIL COUNTY—1920 CENSUS				
Alger Twp.				
Omar, Sam	38	Farmer	Syria	USA-1902
Omar, Alley	35(B)	Farm Laborer	Syria	USA-1902
Mellem, Hammett	31	Farmer	Syria	
Mellem, Hadge	31(W)		Syria	
Mellem, Mamone	13(D)		Syria	
Mellem, Allick	10(S)		North Dakota	
Mellem, Mary	9(D)		North Dakota	
Mellem, Hamet	7(S)		North Dakota	
Mellem, Selma	3-3/12(D)		North Dakota	
Mellem, Fazel	2-2/12(S)		North Dakota	
Ross Twp.				
Farhart, Bailey (Boaley?)	35	Farmer	Syria	USA-1901
Farhart, Hassen	38		Syria	
Gassem, Ahma	44		Syria	
Gassem, Josefie	25(W)			
Gassem, Gassem	7		Syria	
Gassem, Kamel	5		USA	

Name	Age	Occupation	Place of Birth	Date of Arrival
Yassem, Ahma	44	Laborer, Works Out	Syria	USA-1900
Yassem, Jastia	25(W)		Syria	USA-1914
Yassem, Yassem	7(S)		Syria	
Yassem, Jesse	6(S)		North Dakota	
Yassem, Kamel	5(S)		North Dakota	
Yassem, Neve	3-5/12(S)		North Dakota	
Yassem, Nefil	2-4/12(S)		North Dakota	
Osman, Morris	35	Farmer	Syria	USA-1902
Dean, Thomas	38	Farmer	Syria	USA-1902
Dean, Mable	28(W)		Syria	
Dean, Charley	9/12(S)		North Dakota	
Abdalla, Sam	45	Farmer	Syria	USA-1900
Juma, Allia	43	Farmer	Syria	USA-
Juma, Mary	55	Farm	Syria	USA-1900
Juma, Charley	16(S)	Farm Laborer	North Dakota	

Cottonwood Twp.

Name	Age	Occupation	Place of Birth	Date of Arrival
Osman, Mostafa	38	Farmer	Syria	USA-1903
Osman, Isha	48(W)		Syria	USA-1907
Osman, Albert	10(AS)		North Dakota	
Murrey, Hassen	35	Farmer	Syria	USA-1901

Idaho Twp.

Name	Age	Occupation	Place of Birth	Date of Arrival
Hassin, Albert	28	Farmer	Syria	USA-1911
Hassin, Hammid	49(F)	Farm Laborer	Syria	USA-1899

NELSON COUNTY—1920 CENSUS

Name	Age	Occupation	Place of Birth	Date of Arrival
Hager, Sam	41		Syria	

PEMBINA COUNTY—1920 CENSUS

Advance Twp.

Name	Age	Occupation	Place of Birth	Date of Arrival
Kellel, Sam	36(BD)		Syria	USA-1908

PIERCE COUNTY—1920 CENSUS

Elverum Twp.

Name	Age	Occupation	Place of Birth	Date of Arrival
Shachor, Alick	43	Farmer	Syria	USA-1890
Shachor, Mary	35(W)		Syria	
Shachor, George	17(S)		North Dakota	
Shachor, Harry	15(S)		North Dakota	
Shachor, Erma	12(D)		North Dakota	
Shachor, Lura	10(D)		North Dakota	
Shachor, Rose	8(D)		North Dakota	
Shachor, Theodore	5(S)		North Dakota	
Shachor, Phillip	1/12(S)		North Dakota	

Meyer Twp.

Name	Age	Occupation	Place of Birth	Date of Arrival
Sawaya, Salome	27	Farmer	Syria	USA-1910
Sawaya, Sam	7(S)		North Dakota	
Sawaya, Josephine	5(D)		North Dakota	
Sawaya, Nellie	4-1/12(D)		North Dakota	
Sawaya, Mazzir	1-7/12(S)		North Dakota	
Sawaya, George	26(B)	Farm Laborer	Syria	USA-1910

Name	Age	Occupation	Place of Birth	Date of Arrival
Munyer, Assif	48	Farmer	Syria	USA-1897
Munyer, Maggie	34(W)		Syria	USA-1897
Munyer, Martha	20(D)		North Dakota	
Munyer, Mary	18(D)		North Dakota	
Munyer, Alick	15(S)		North Dakota	
Munyer, Rose	14(D)		North Dakota	
Munyer, George	13(S)		North Dakota	
Munyer, Mike	11(S)		North Dakota	
Munyer, Fred	9(S)		North Dakota	
Munyer, Eddie	8(S)		North Dakota	
Munyer, Sam	6(S)		North Dakota	
Munyer, James	3/12(S)		North Dakota	
Reno Valley Twp.				
Munyer, Frank	38	Farmer	Syria	USA-1899
Munyer, Mable	29(W)		Syria	
Munyer, Victoria	9(D)		North Dakota	
Munyer, Agnes	8(D)		North Dakota	
Munyer, Roy	6(S)		North Dakota	
Munyer, Eddie	4-10/12(S)		North Dakota	
Munyer, Rose	3-9/12(D)		North Dakota	
Munyer, Violet	1-6/12(D)		North Dakota	
Saba, Joe	40	Farmer	Syria	USA-1892
Saba, Ide	21(W)		Syria	
Saba, Josephine	3/12(D)		North Dakota	
Razook, George	21	Farmer	Syria	USA-1909
Razook, Zeta	19(S)		Syria	USA-1909
Razook, Clia	9(S)		North Dakota	
Daan, Abdela (Dann?)	41	Farmer	Syria	USA-1899
Daan, Anna	32(W)		Syria	
Daan, George	15(S)		North Dakota	
Daan, Linda	13(D)		North Dakota	
Daan, Adell	11(D)		North Dakota	
Daan, Michael	10(S)		North Dakota	
Daan, Joe	7(S)		North Dakota	
Daan, Tina (Lizzie ?)	5(D)		North Dakota	
Daan, Jennie	11/12(D)		North Dakota	
T154-R73				
Abraham, Joseph	60	Farmer	Syria	USA-1898
Abraham, Mary	36(W)		Syria	
Abraham, Eva	14(D)		North Dakota	
Abraham, Nelly	13(D)		North Dakota	
Abraham, Jimy	10(S)		North Dakota	
Abraham, Emma	4-8/12(D)		North Dakota	
Abraham, Sylvia	2-6/12(D)		North Dakota	
Abraham, Joseph	1-0/12(S)		North Dakota	
Abraham, Josephine	1-0/12(D)		North Dakota	
Rugby (City)				
Sawaya, Nassif	45	Bowling Alley	Syria	USA-1893
Sawaya, Victor	10(S)		North Dakota	
Sawaya, Katherine	8(D)		North Dakota	

Name	Age	Occupation	Place of Birth	Date of Arrival
Sawaya, Louise	7(D)		North Dakota	
Sawaya, Eddie	6(S)		North Dakota	
Sawaya, George	26(B)		Syria	
Sawaya, Salavna	27(W)		Syria	
Sawaya, Sam	7(S)		North Dakota	
Sawaya, Josephine	5(D)		North Dakota	
Sawaya, Nellie	4-2/12(D)		North Dakota	
Sawaya, Maggie	1-7/12(D)		North Dakota	
David, W. D.	46	General Store	Syria	USA-1893
David, Mary	33(W)		Syria	
David, Jimme	23(S)?		North Dakota	
David, Mitchel	11(S)		North Dakota	
David, Freddie	9(S)		North Dakota	
David, Joseph	7(S)		North Dakota	
David, Rosie	6(D)		North Dakota	
David, John	4-3/12(S)		North Dakota	
David, Victoria	2-8/12(D)		North Dakota	
David, Victor	2/12(S)		North Dakota	
Srur, George	40	RR Section Hand	Syria	USA-1907
Srur, Blanche	30(W)		Syria	
Srur, Alma	9(D)		North Dakota	
Srur, Mary	7(D)		North Dakota	
Srur, Charley	5(S)		North Dakota	
Srur, Jimme	5(S)		North Dakota	
Srur, Hazel	3-8/12(D)		North Dakota	
Srur, Julia	3-8/12(D)		North Dakota	
Srur, Albert	2/12(S)		North Dakota	
Weizer, Metre (Wizer?)	44	Farmer	Syria	USA-1894
Weizer, Dalga	36(W)		Syria	
Weizer, Jama	17(S)		North Dakota	
Weizer, Sophia	14(D)		North Dakota	
Weizer, Mathild	11(D)		North Dakota	
Weizer, George	9(S)		North Dakota	
Weizer, Madeline	7(D)		North Dakota	
Weizer, Joe	4-2/12(S)		North Dakota	
Weizer, Phillip	2-4/12(S)		North Dakota	
Boussad, Joseph	75		Syria	USA-1893
Boussad, Annie	62(W)		Syria	
Boussad, Sarah	19(D)		North Dakota	
Boussad, Charley	15(S)		North Dakota	
Twp. 158-R72				
Fayette, Charles	48	Farmer	Syria	
Fayette, Annie	30(W)		Syria	
Fayette, Eva	15(D)		North Dakota	
Fayette, Fred	13(S)		North Dakota	
Fayette, Mike	20(S)		North Dakota	
Fayette, Helen	8(D)		North Dakota	
Fayette, John	6(S)		North Dakota	
Fayette, Thelma	3-6/12(D)		North Dakota	
Fayette, Joseph	1-2/12(S)		North Dakota	
Fayette, Mary	76(M)	Widow	Syria	USA-1896
Better, Ellis	34		Syria	

Name	Age	Occupation	Place of Birth	Date of Arrival
RAMSEY COUNTY—1920 CENSUS				
Lawton Village				
Anthony, Joseph (Josysa)	42	Retail Merchant, General Store	Assyria	USA-1889
Anthony, Zahai	20(W)		North Dakota	
Anthony, Thomas	13(S)		Minnesota	
Anthony, Mildred	11(D)		Minnesota	
Anthony, Morie	9(S)		Minnesota	
Anthony, Elizabeth	7(D)		North Dakota	
Anthony, Julia	5(D)		North Dakota	
Anthony, Margaret	3-8/12(D)		North Dakota	
Anthony, Hazel	2-6/12(D)		North Dakota	
Church's Ferry (Village)				
Durson, Hassan	38	Labor, RR Section	Turkey	USA-1913
Brocket Village				
Cadry, Abdo W.	41		Aasyria[sic]	
RANSOM COUNTY—1920 CENSUS				
Enderlin				
Farris, William	37	Retail Merchant, Dry Goods	Syria	USA-
Farris, Mable	26(W)		Wyoming	F/M-USA
Farris, Walter M.	7(S)		Nebraska	
McLeod				
Amed, Farhart	47(BD)	Farmer	Asia	USA-1897
RICHLAND COUNTY—1920 CENSUS				
Wahpeton				
Bofamy, Joe		Common Laborer	Syria	
Assad, Mrs. Sadie	48		Damascus	USA-1888
Assad, Osif	26(S)	Electrical Engineer	Minnesota	
Bofamy, Sadie	19(D)		North Dakota	
Bofamy, Fred	33(BIL)	Laborer	Syria	USA-1900
Assad, Mary	13(D)		North Dakota	
Assad, Michael	11(S)		North Dakota	
Bofamy, Jeanette	5/12(GD)		North Dakota	
ROLETTE COUNTY—1920 CENSUS				
Hillside Twp.				
Latiff, John	32	Patient, State Institution	Syria	USA-1909
Alex, Albert	44		Ceria[sic]	
SARGENT COUNTY—1920 CENSUS				
Cayuga				
Bofamy, Joe K.	25		Syria	
Bofamy, Amanda	23(W)		Syria	
Bird, Albert	42		Turkey	

Name	Age	Occupation	Place of Birth	Date of Arrival
SHERIDAN COUNTY—1920 CENSUS				
Highland Twp.				
Nassif, Shaker	62		Syria	USA-1890
Harris Twp.				
Nicola, Salama	38	Farmer	Syria	USA-1897
Nicola, Stella	28(W)		Syria	
Nicola, Barbara	8(D)		North Dakota	
Nicola, Joseph	6(S)		North Dakota	
Nicola, Emily	3-11/12(D)		North Dakota	
Skaff, Abraham	33	Farmer	Sayria[sic]	USA-1905
McClusky (Village)				
Haykel, Alsem M.	38	Agent, Watkins Medicine	Syria	USA-1899
Haykel, Emma	31(W)		Norway	(M/F Norway)
Haykel, James	8(S)		North Dakota	
Haykel, Ahmed	6(S)		North Dakota	
Haykel, Hassen	3-8/12(S)		North Dakota	
Haykel, Abraham	1-3/12(S)		North Dakota	
Kellel, Thomas	30		Syria	
SIOUX COUNTY—1920 CENSUS				
Twp. 129-R88				
Santby, Hamed	44	Farmer	Syria	USA-1914
Abraham, Solomon	50	Farmer	Syria	USA-1914
STARK COUNTY—1920 CENSUS				
Dickinson				
Nicola, Salom	35	Merchant, General Store	Arabia	USA-1912
Nicola, Nellie	29(W)		Arabia	
Nicola, Nick	13(S)		North Dakota	
Nicola, George	9(S)		North Dakota	
Nicola, Mary	6(D)		North Dakota	
Nicola, Mike	3-6/12(S)		North Dakota	
Nicola, Leslie	3-6/12(S)		North Dakota	
Nummer, Sam	24(NE)	Salesman, Dry Goods	Syria	
Ramah, Charles	49		Syria	USA-1899
Ramah, Junir	37(W)		Syria	
Ramah, Sam	7(S)		North Dakota	
Ramah, Chickory	5(S)		North Dakota	
Ramah, Adolph	2(S)		North Dakota	
Massad, George J.	37	Merchant, Junk	Syria	
Massad, Annie	33(W)		Syria	
Massad, Martha	13(D)		North Dakota	
Massad, James	11(S)		North Dakota	
Massad, Lester	8(S)		North Dakota	
Massad, Gemal	6(S)		North Dakota	
Massad, Nasson	4(S)		North Dakota	
Kanan, Charles	49		Syria	

Name	Age	Occupation	Place of Birth	Date of Arrival
STEELE COUNTY—1920 CENSUS				
Westfield Twp.				
Kadra, Aldue	34	Laborer, Grain Farm	Syria	USA-1912
Sharon				
Eli, Hassen	36	Owner, General Store	Syria	USA-1901
Eli, Katherine	26(W)		Minnesota	Parents: American
Eli, Lila	5(D)		Minnesota	
Eli, Joseph	2-6/12(S)		North Dakota	
Eli, Willie	3/12(S)		North Dakota	
Kadry, San	26(C)	Farm Laborer	Syria	USA-1908
Alley, Albert	21(C)	Farm Laborer	Syria	USA-1914
STUTSMAN COUNTY—1920 CENSUS				
139-69				
Amed, Alley	35		Syria	
Abos, Albert	40(BD)		Syria	
Sam, Howard	42	Farmer	Syria	
Sam, Millie	29(W)		Nebraska	F/M Russia
Sam, Alma	8(D)		North Dakota	
Sam, Harry	7(S)		North Dakota	
Sam, Emil	6(S)		North Dakota	
Sam, Ida	4(D)		North Dakota	
Sam, Sam	1-4/12(S)		North Dakota	
Kanan, Amil (Emil)	42	Farmer	Seray[sic]	USA-1883
Kanan, Mary	40(W)		Seray[sic]	USA-1882
Kanan, John	2-6/12(S)		North Dakota	
Jounes, Joseph	51		Syria	
Abdo, Albert	57		Syria	
Alley,Mary	20	Nurse	South Dakota	
TOWNER COUNTY—1920 CENSUS				
Sine, Kassam	24		Syria	
Grainfield Twp.				
Assay, Sam	39	Farmer	Syria	USA-1899
Assay, Martha	29(W)		Syria	USA-1903
Assay, Katherine	14(D)		North Dakota	
Assay, Sophia	12(D)		North Dakota	
Assay, James	10(S)		North Dakota	
Assay, Nicholas	47	Farmer	Syria	USA-1896
Assay, Mary	38(W)		Syria	
Assay, Joseph	20(S)	Farm Laborer, Home Farm	North Dakota	
Assay, John	18(S)	Farm Laborer, Home Farm	North Dakota	
Assay, William	15(S)		North Dakota	
Assay, Agnes	13(D)		North Dakota	
Assay, Rose	9(D)		North Dakota	
Assay, Ella	7(D)		North Dakota	
Assay, Hazel	5(D)		North Dakota	

Name	Age	Occupation	Place of Birth	Date of Arrival
Rock Lake (Village)				
Hager, David	26	Pool Hall Manager	Syria	USA-1906
Hager, Tom	27(HM)	Pool Hall Laborer	Syria	USA-1913
Soloman, Mrs. Rachel	29	Day Laborer	Syria	
Soloman, Abraham	11(S)		North Dakota	
Soloman, Alfred	8(S)		North Dakota	
Soloman, Margaret	6(D)		North Dakota	
Soloman, William	5(S)		North Dakota	
Soloman, Marie	2(D)		North Dakota	

WALSH COUNTY—1920 CENSUS

Name	Age	Occupation	Place of Birth	Date of Arrival
Fairdale (Village)				
Albert, Abraham	64(F)	Salesman, Retail Groceries	Syria	USA-
Albert, Alex	24(S)	Merchant, Retail Goods	Syria	USA-1912
Grafton				
Razook, Amelia	7		North Dakota	M/F Syria
156-59				
Moran, John L.	56	Farmer	Syria	USA-1881
Moran, Annie G.	50		Syria	USA-1904
Absey, Peter	53	Farmer	Syria	USA-1895
Absey, Rose	36(W)		Syria	USA-1898
Absey, Eddie	20(S)	Farm Laborer, Home Farm	North Dakota	
Absey, Jessie S.	15(D)		North Dakota	
Absey, Jimmie R.	13(S)		North Dakota	
Absey, Mable M.	10(D)		North Dakota	
Absey, Alice E.	5(D)		North Dakota	
Abraham, Mostafa	50(HM)	Farm Laborer	Syria	USA-1913
Deraney, Joe H.	24	Farmer	Syria	USA-1912
Deraney, Beedy	25(W)		North Dakota	M/F Syria
Deraney, Arthur	3-1/12(S)		North Dakota	
Deraney, Mary	2-1/12(D)		North Dakota	
Deraney, Jimmie	5/12(S)		North Dakota	
Faiad, Fred	66	Farmer	Syria	USA-1892
Faiad, Annie	60(W)		Syria	USA-1892
Faiad, George	20(S)		North Dakota	
Faiad, Joseph	18(S)		North Dakota	
Freije, Moses	43	Farmer	Syria	USA-1890
Freije, Nasif	58(B)	Farmer	Syria	USA-1885
Freije, Shable N.	22	Farm Laborer	North Dakota	
Freije, Elie	17		North Dakota	

WARD COUNTY—1920 CENSUS

Name	Age	Occupation	Place of Birth	Date of Arrival
Ryder (Village)				
Mellum, Otto	29	Servant, Hotel Cook	Arabia	USA-1908

Name	Age	Occupation	Place of Birth	Date of Arrival
WELLS COUNTY—1920 CENSUS				
Harvey (City)				
West, Avedia	50		Asia Minor	
West, Jessie	40(W)		Canada	
West, Levon F.	20(S)		South Dakota	
West, Natan M.	16(S)		South Dakota	
West, Monica	12(D)		South Dakota	
West, Elliott	7(S)		Minnesota	
West, Marrion	5(S)		South Dakota	
West, Samuel	3-2/12		North Dakota	
West, Jesse	3/12(D)		North Dakota	
Fessenden				
Massad, Nassif	39	Salesman, Watkins	Turkey	USA-1895
Massad, Nellie	35(W)		Turkey	
Massad, Wade	12(S)		North Dakota	
Massad, Lewis	10(S)		North Dakota	
Massad, Mary	8(D)		North Dakota	
Massad, Sophia	6(D)		North Dakota	
Massad, Troy	3(S)		North Dakota	
Massad, Isabella	8/12(D)		North Dakota	
Harvey				
Hapes, Smile	35		Palestine	
Hmomed, Smlon	24		Palestine	
WILLLIAMS COUNTY—1920 CENSUS				
Tyrone Twp.				
Yunoess, Charles	65	Farmer	Syria	USA-1896
Yunoess, Anna	54(W)		Syria	USA-1901
Yunoess, Mike	23(S)		Syria	USA-1901
Yunoess, Fred	15(S)		North Dakota	
Yunoess, Mary	12(D)		North Dakota	
Cow Creek Twp.				
Saab, Joseph S.	43	Farmer	Syria	USA-1893
Saab, Minnie	35(W)		Syria	
Saab, Kammie	19(D)		Iowa	
Saab, Samuel	14-10/12(S)		Syria	
Saab, Rosy	8-4/12(D)		North Dakota	
Saab, Hazel	7-8/12(D)		North Dakota	
Saab, May	5-7/12(D)		North Dakota	
Saab, Della	3-11/12(D)		North Dakota	
Saab, Arthur	1-7/12(S)		North Dakota	
Skaff, Abraham	35	Farmer	Syria	USA-1900
Skaff, Nellie	30(W)		Syria	USA-1895
Skaff, Charles G.	12-3/12(S)		North Dakota	
Skaff, Alfred A.	9-11/12(S)		North Dakota	
Skaff, Mitchell M.	7-10/12(S)		North Dakota	
Skaff, William J.	4-10/12(S)		North Dakota	
Skaff, Helen	2-8/12(D)		North Dakota	
Skaff, Shaker	4/12(S)		North Dakota	
Skaff, Julia	63(M)		Syria	USA-1898
Skaff, Eva	22(S)		Syria	USA-1903

Name	Age	Occupation	Place of Birth	Date of Arrival
Azar, Joseph	39	Farmer	Syria	USA-1898
Azar, Zockia	23(W)		Syria	USA-1909
Azar, Hazel	5-10/12(D)		North Dakota	
Azar, Angeline	3-7/12(D)		North Dakota	
Azar, Helen	1-3/12(D)		North Dakota	
Albert, Charles	38	Farmer	Syria	USA-1899
Albert, Irene	25(W)		Syria	USA-1902
Albert, Donald	2-2/12(S)		North Dakota	
Albert, Winefred	3/12(D)		North Dakota	
Abdo, Abraham	39	Farmer	Syria	USA-1900
Abdo, Sabay	36(W)		Syria	USA-1900
Abdo, Sady	11-0/12(D)		North Dakota	
Abdo, Adeline	5-10/12(D)		North Dakota	
Abdo, Amalie	4-6/12(D)		North Dakota	
Abdo, Rosy	3-3/12(D)		North Dakota	
Abdo, Walt	6/12(S)		North Dakota	
Abdo, Charles	34(B)	Farmer	Syria	USA-1910
Abdo, George	32(B)	Farmer	Syria	USA-1914
Zien, Charles M.	60		Syria	USA-1900
Zien, Esther	50(W)		Syria	USA-1903
Zien, Charles C.	24(S)		Syria	USA-1903
Zien, Jennie	16(D)		North Dakota	
Zien, May	14(D)		Minnesota	
Zien, Sam	8-11/12(S)		North Dakota	

Bull Butte Twp.

Name	Age	Occupation	Place of Birth	Date of Arrival
Abraham, William	22	Farmer	Syria	USA-1908
Abraham, Charley	25(B)	Farmer	Syria	USA-1906
Albert, Joe	33	Farmer	Syria	USA-1905
Albert, Jennie	25(W)		Syria	USA-1905
Albert, George	6(S)		North Dakota	
Albert, Catherine	4-5/12(D)		North Dakota	
Albert, Mary	2-10/12(D)		North Dakota	
Albert, Martha	10/12(D)		North Dakota	
Aly, Sam	32	Farmer	Syria	USA-1908
Kalil, James	39	Farmer	Syria	USA-1899
Kalil, Sophie	20(W)		Syria	USA-1911
Albert, Brien	26(HM)	Farm Laborer	Syria	USA-1912
Barkie, George	45	Farmer	Syria	USA-1904
Barkie, Mary	35(W)		Syria	USA-1906
Barkie, Effie				
Barkie, Aesoph	20(S)		Syria	USA-1906
Barkie, Rose	18(D)		Syria	SA-1906
Barkie, Mike	13(S)		North Dakota	
Barkie, Alfred	7(S)		North Dakota	
Barkie, Wilbert	6(S)		North Dakota	
Barkie, Edward	3-6/12(S)		North Dakota	
Barkie, Joe	1-0/12(S)		North Dakota	
Barkie, Charlie	10/12(S)		North Dakota	

Name	Age	Occupation	Place of Birth	Date of Arrival
Hapip, Frank	40	Farmer	Syria	USA-1898
Hapip, Selma	39(W)		Syria	USA-1898
Hapip, Kati	14(D)		North Dakota	
Hapip, Nave	12(S)		North Dakota	
Hapip, Jim	11(S)		North Dakota	
Hapip, Hamir (Hanie)	8(S)		North Dakota	
Hapip, Olga	6(D)		North Dakota	
Hapip, Mary	5(D)		North Dakota	
Hapip, Fred	3-6/12(S)		North Dakota	
Hapip, Walther	5/12(S)		North Dakota	
Zamata, Joe	40	Traveling Salesman	Syria	USA-1907
Mont Twp.				
Naked, Joseph F.	39	Farmer	Syria	USA-1899
Naked, Susie	28(W)		Syria	USA-1903
Naked, Micke	9(S)		North Dakota	
Naked, Madeline	7(D)		North Dakota	
Naked, Victor	5(S)		North Dakota	
Naked, Philip	1-4/12(S)		North Dakota	
Rehal, Charlie	42		Syria	
Rehal, Rosay	33(W)		Syria	
Rehal, Julia G.	11(D)		North Dakota	
Rehal, Minnie M.	6(D)		North Dakoa	
Rehal, Edna	4-0/12(D)		North Dakota	
Rehal, Roseline R.	1-11/12(D)		North Dakota	
Aboud, Aleck	54	Farmer	Syria	USA-1895
Aboud, Annie	50(W)		Syria	USA-1895
Williston				
Kassis, John	42	Manager, Confectionary	Syria	USA-1904
Kassis, Eva	32(W)		Syria	USA-1904
Kassis, Josephine	12(D)		North Dakota	
Kassis, Fred	10(S)		North Dakota	
Kassis, Isabelle	8(D)		North Dakota	
Kassis, Adele	5(D)		North Dakota	
Kassis, Margaret	2(D)		North Dakota	
Nedoff, Mike	31	Manager, Confectionary	Syria	USA-1902
Nedoff, Sabaya	25(W)		North Dakota	
Boussad, Joe	39	Farm Laborer	Syria	USA-1893
Boussad, Lillie	23(W)		Syria	USA-1899
Boussad, Michtle	6(S)		Canada	
Boussad, Louise	4(D)		Canada	
Boussad, Josephine	3(D)		Canada	
Boussad, Loretta	1-1/12(D)		Canada	
Boussad, Selma	18(SIL)		North Dakota	
Wizer, Mrs. Barbara	39		Syria	USA-1900
Wizer, Sam	21(S)	Laborer	North Dakota	
Wizer, Hazel	16(D)		North Dakota	
Wizer, Olga	12(D)		North Dakota	
Wizer, George	6(S)		North Dakota	
Bahne, Salme J.	54	Studio Photographer	Damascus	USA-1889
Bahne, Sultana	53(W)		Syria	USA-1889
Bahne, Rachel	21(D)	Bookkeeper, Creamery	Nebraska	

Name	Age	Occupation	Place of Birth	Date of Arrival
Bahne, Martha	20(D)	Telephone Operator	Nebraska	
Bahne, Ruth	16(D)		North Dakota	
Lyon, Mrs. Annie	40		Syria	USA-1899
Lyon, Earl	12(S)		North Dakota	
Lyon, Fred	7(S)		North Dakota	
Lyon, Julie	4(D)		North Dakota	
Shikaney, Joe	39	Owner, Confectionary Shop	Syria	USA-1907
Shikaney, Lizzie	33(W)		Syria	USA-1907
Shikaney, Nasser	11(S)		Syria	USA-1907
Shikaney, Isabell	9(D)		North Dakota	
Shikaney, Freda	7(D)		North Dakota	
Shikaney, Julia	5(D)		North Dakota	
Shikaney, Adna	3(D)		North Dakota	
Shikaney, Margaret	1(D)		North Dakota	
Shikany, Ely	40	House Carpenter	Syria	USA-1895
Shikany, Auria	42(W)		Syria	USA-1895
Shikany, Ole	21(S)	Salesman, Dry Goods	North Dakota	
Shikany, Abe	15(S)		North Dakota	
Shikany, Philip	8(S)		North Dakota	
Shikany, Roy	7(S)		North Dakota	
Shikany, Lottie	12(D)		North Dakota	
Zien, Mrs. Debe F.	54		Syria	USA-1908
Zien, John	34(S)		Syria	USA-1900
Bousliman, Assad	51		Syria	USA-1908
Bousliman, Debe	45(W)		Syria	USA-1905
Bousliman, Mary	13(D)		North Dakota	
Bousliman, Robert	25(S)	Farm Laborer	Syria	USA-1905
Bousliman, Abraham	22(S)	Farm Laborer	Syria	USA-1905
Bousliman, Nellie	12(D)		North Dakota	
Bousliman, Marshall	10(S)		North Dakota	
Bousliman, Amelia	8(D)		North Dakota	
Bousliman, Sade	7(D)		North Dakota	
Nedoff, Edward	32	Candy Maker, Confectionary	Syria	USA-1894
Nedoff, Sadie	24(W)		North Dakota	
Nedoff, Joseph	5(S)		North Dakota	
Nedoff, Elizabeth	3(D)		North Dakota	
Nedoff, Mary	2(D)		North Dakota	
Nedoff, Helen	1(D)		North Dakota	
Khoroury, Albert	71[sic]	Grocery Salesman	Syria	USA-1898
Khoroury, Anna	38(W)		Syria	USA-1898
Khoroury, Zera	17(D)		North Dakota	
Khoroury, George	14(S)		North Dakota	
Khoroury, Phillip	9(S)		North Dakota	
Khoroury, Edward	7(S)		North Dakota	
Khoroury, Woodrow	2-6/12(S)		North Dakota	
Kalil, David	39	Merchant, Grocery	Syria	USA-1897
Kalil, Sadie	37(W)		Syria	USA-1896
Kalil, Wilbur	13(S)		North Dakota	
Kalil, Roseline	10(D)		North Dakota	
Kalil, Edward	9(S)		North Dakota	
Kalil, Soloman	7(S)		North Dakota	
Kalil, Adel	3-11/12(D)		North Dakota	

Name	Age	Occupation	Place of Birth	Date of Arrival
Zien, Mrs. Rose (Widow)	28		Syria	USA-1910
Zien, Harvey	8(S)		North Dakota	
Zien, Sadie	7(D)		North Dakota	
Zien, Joseph	5(S)		North Dakota	
Zien, Mike	4(S)		North Dakota	
Zien, Selia	1-8/12(D)		North Dakota	
Munyer, Ele G.	45	Poolroom	Syria	USA-1891
Munyer, Mary	32(W)		Syria	USA-1908
Munyer, George	8(S)		North Dakota	
Munyer, Victor	6(S)		North Dakota	
Munyer, Roy	4(S)		North Dakota	
Munyer, Theodore	2(S)		North Dakota	
Munyer, Edmond	1-2/12(S)		North Dakota	
Scott, Julia	56(BD)		Syria	USA-1898
Scott, Eva	22(BD)		Syria	USA-1913
Farzle, Abraham	47	Pool Hall	Syria	USA-1892
Farzle, Martha	43(W)		Syria	USA-1892
Farzle, Victor	17(S)		Minnesota	
Farzle, Freda	15(D)		Minnesota	
Farzle, Rose	13(D)		Minnesota	
Farzle, George	11(S)		North Dakota	
Farzle, Helen	5(D)		North Dakota	
Joseph, Charles J.	35	Dry Goods Merchant	Syria	USA-1900
Joseph, Margaret H.	23(W)		Minnesota	
Joseph, Jamel L.	3(S)		Utah	
Joseph, Willie E.	8/12(S)		North Dakota	
Bohamra, Abe	75(BD)		Syria	USA-1892
Bohamra, Sadie	60(BD)		Syria	USA-1890
Esta, Joseph	46	Owner, Pool Hall	Syria	USA-1889
Esta, Elizia	47(W)		Syria	USA-1889
Esta, Abraham	18(S)		North Dakota	
Barkie, Rose	17	Servant	Syria	USA-1906
Bousliman, Charley	34 (36?)	Manager, Pool Hall	Syria	USA-1903
Bousliman, Elizabeth	31(W)		Syria	USA-1903
Bousliman, Josephine	12(D)		North Dakota	
Bousliman, Vivian	10(D)		North Dakota	
Bousliman, Lewis	6(S)		North Dakota	
Bousliman, Anglin	4(D)		North Dakota	
Bousliman, George	1(S)		North Dakota	
Aklan, Albert	31		Syria	
Albert, Joseph	48	Laborer	Syria	
Albert, Brien	26		Syria	
George, Sam	34		Syria	
Wizer, Mabel	18		Syria	
Zamata, Joe	40		Syria	

POLK COUNTY (MINNESOTA)—1920 CENSUS

Crookston City

Name	Age	Occupation	Place of Birth	Date of Arrival
Salem, Barbara	34	Labor/RR	Syria	USA-1913
Salem, Norma	26(W)		Syria	USA-1913
Salem, Merail	8(D)		Syria	USA-1913

Name	Age	Occupation	Place of Birth	Date of Arrival
Salem, Mary	5(D)		Minnesota	
Salem, Mike	3-11/12(S)		Minnesota	
Salem, Telma	10/12(D)		Minnesota	
Salem, Thomas	38	Laborer/Steam RR	Syria	USA-1906
Salem, Latiflie	55(M)	Washwoman/RR Off	Syria	USA-1910
Salem, Millie	20(D)	Laundress/		
Laundry	Syria	USA-1910		
Joseph, Eva	46		Syria	USA-1910
Thomas, Joseph	63	Flagman/RR	Syria	USA-1897
Thomas, Eva	57(W)		Syria	USA-1906
Thomas, Anthony	29(W)	Section Laborer/RR	Syria	USA-1905
Thomas, George	23(S)	Locomotive Fireman	Syria	USA-1908
Carey, John	35	Section Laborer/RR	Syria	USA-1910
Carey, Sultana	30(W)		Syria	USA-1910
Carey, Soddie	4-9/12(D)		Minnesota	
Hager, Ahmed	55	Peddler/Dry Goods	Syria	USA-1914
Hager, Mary	35(W)	Commercial Wash	Syria	USA-1908
Hager, Allie	26(S)	Peddler, On Road	Syria	USA-1908
Issac, Moran	42	Laborer, Roundhouse	Syria	USA-1899
Issac, Bedore	46(W)		Syria	USA-1899
Issac, Thomas	24(S)	Laborer/Section RR	Syria	USA-1910
Issac, Michael	25(S)	Laborer/RR	North Dakota	
Issac, Mary M.	18(D)		North Dakota	
Issac, Peter	12(S)		North Dakota	
Abas, Hussan	49	Owner/Dry Goods	Syria	USA-1889
Abas, Mahada	28(W)		Syria	USA-1902
Abas, Morris	8(S)		Minnesota	
Abas, Alice	6(D)		Minnesota	
Abas, Nasiyfe	4-11/12(S)		Minnesota	
Abas, Haseyse	2-2/10(S)		Minnesota	
Heider, Comeral	52	Salesman/Dry Goods	Syria	USA-1902
Heider, Haufut	45(W)		Syria	USA-1902
Noah, Thomas	55	Merchant, General Store	Assyria	USA-1891
Noah, Mary	48(W)		Assyria	USA-
Noah, Gabral	18(S)	Delivery Clerk, Grocery	Minnesota	
Noah, Martha	17(D)	Waitress, Restaurant	Minnesota	
Mike, Thomas	35	Laborer/Steam RR	Assyria	USA-1901
Mike, Amelia	30(W)		Assyria	
Mike, Moran	10(S)		Minnesota	
Mike, Hassin	7(S)		Minnesota	
Mike, Bertha	68(M)		Assyria	USA-
Mike, Eva	25(S)		Assyria	USA-
Ammon, Anthony	21	Laborer/Steam RR	Assyria	USA-1913
Ammon, Amelia	43(M)		Assyria	USA-1913
Noah, Martha	63(GM)		Assyria	USA-1913
Joseph, Charley	25	Laborer/Steam RR	Assyria	USA-1913
Joseph, Eva	20(W)	Dishwasher, Restaurant	Assyria	USA-1918

Name	Age	Occupation	Place of Birth	Date of Arrival
Gaberal, Rose	51	Peddler	Assyria	USA-1906
Amelia, Salem	29(D)		Assyria	USA-1906
Amelia, George	12(GS)		Minnesota	
Euging, Mary	25(L)		Assyria	USA-
Haddy, David	47	Farming	Assyria	USA-1896
Haddy, Julia	34		Assyria	USA-
Haddy, Charles	16(S)		North Dakota	
Haddy, Lillian	14(D)		North Dakota	
Haddy, Michall	12(S)		North Dakota	
Noah, Michael	30	Salesman, Groceries	Syria	USA-1906
Noah, Christina	29(W)		Syria	USA-1902
Noah, Veronica	6(D)		Minnesota	
Noah, Lucy	4(D)		Minnesota	
Noah, Margaret	2(D)		Minnesota	
Noah, Eva	1(D)		Minnesota	
Tanus, Mary A.	27	Laborer	Syria	USA-
George, Peter	51	Laborer/RR	Syria	USA-1900
George, Peter W.	23(S)	Laborer/RR	Syria	USA-1913
Issac, Jacob	35	Laborer/RR	Syria	USA-1909
Issac, Rose J.	30(W)		Syria	USA-1909
Issac, Anna L.	10(D)		Minnesota	
Issac, Sadie	8(D)		Minnesota	
Issac, Lulu	7(D)		Minnesota	
Issac, John	5(S)		Minnesota	
Issac, Alma	3-5/10(D)		Minnesota	
Romanos, Mike	34	Laborer/RR	Syria	USA-1909
Romanos, Mary	34(W)		Syria	USA-1909
Romanos, Thomas M.	7(W)		Minnesota	
Romanos, Marcy	5(D)		Minnesota	
Romanos, George M.	3-6/12(S)		Minnesota	
Romonas, Moran	5/12(S)		Minnesota	
Ramonos, Joe	25	Laborer/RR	Syria	USA-1912
Ramonas, Hazel	63(M)		Syria	USA-1908
Ramonas, Fouse	28(S)		Syria	USA-1908
John, Peter	48	Laborer/RR	Syria	USA-1911
John, Berthea	38(W)		Syria	USA-1911
John, Alice	15(D)		Syria	USA-1911
John, James	6(S)		Minnesota	
John, Latifa	5(D)		Minnesota	
John, Elizabeth	2-2/12(D)		Minnesota	
John, George	2-2/12(S)		Minnesota	
Harris, George	36	Manager/Store	Syria	USA-1900
Harris, Ellan	28(W)	Clerk/Store	Minnesota	
M-F/Sweden				
Harris, Said	23(S)	Commercial Waiter	Syria	USA-

Appendix B

Naturalization Records
Taken from lists compiled by the
State of North Dakota Historical Society

Syria

Name	Country	Date	Papers	County
Assal, Abdallah	Syria	January 18, 1910	2nd	Cass
Abas, Albert	Syria	April 17, 1917	1st	Stutsman
Abas, Alec	Syria	May 23, 1928	2nd	Towner
Abas, Alex	Syria	August 15, 1921	1st	Rolette
Abas, Sam	Syria	September 20, 1924	2nd	Cass
Abdalla, George	Syria	December 17, 1910	1st	Williams
Abdalla, George	Syria	May 19, 1917	2nd	Pierce
Abdallah, Ali	Syria	March 10, 1902	1st	Bottineau
Abdallah, Amid	Syria	October 02, 1916	2nd	Mountrail
Abdallah, Hamod	Syria	March 10, 1902	1st	Bottineau
Abdallah, Michael	Syria	April 15, 1903	1st	Wells
Abdallah, Pakree	Syria	May 09, 1903	1st	Ward
Abdella, Albert	Syria	May 19, 1903	1st	Ramsey
Abdellah, Hamid	Syria	February 06, 1905	1st	Ward
Abdellah, Hamid	Syria	May 13, 1902	1st	McHenry
Abdo, Abraham	Syria	October 07, 1910	2nd	Williams
Abdo, Albert	Syria	April 30, 1917	1st	Stutsman
Abdo, Charley	Syria	September 14, 1910	1st	Williams
Abdolah, Isaac	Syria	May 01, 1903	1st	Wells
Abdulla, Gebran	Syria	August 18, 1948	2nd	Williams
Abdullah, Alle	Syria	January 18, 1906	1st	Ward
Abedahl, Side	Syria	April 14, 1902	1st	Ward
Abedahl, Side	Syria	May 13, 1907	2nd	Ward
Aboud, Abraham	Syria	July 26, 1909	2nd	Williams
Aboud, Ann	Syria	September 22, 1908	1st	Williams
Aboud, Manasses	Syria	June 13, 1906	1st	Williams
Aboud, Mike	Syria	March 10, 1913	1st	Williams
Aboud, Namy	Syria	July 03, 1907	1st	Williams
Abourezk, Alex M.	Syria	May 25, 1903	1st	Burleigh
Abourezk, Henry M.	Syria	May 25, 1903	1st	Burleigh
Abourezk, Paul	Syria	November 14, 1910	2nd	Morton
Abraham, Albert	Syria	October 06, 1910	2nd	McIntosh
Abraham, Albert	Syria	December 21, 1904	1st	McIntosh
Abraham, George	Syria	June 30, 1906	1st	Emmons
Abraham, George	Syria	October 04, 1910	2nd	Emmons
Abraham, James	Syria	April 12, 1904	1st	Williams
Abraham, James	Syria	October 25, 1920	1st	Burke

Name	Country	Date	Papers	County
Abraham, James	Syria	September 27, 1923	2nd	Burke
Abraham, Mohamid Allie	Syria	August 21, 1907	1st	Willliams
Abraham, Sahid	Syria	November 02, 1904	1st	McIntosh
Abraham, Salma	Syria	November 02, 1904	1st	McIntosh
Abrass, Elias	Syria	November 21, 1904	1st	Williams
Abrass, William	Syria	November 18, 1904	1st	Williams
Abriham, Achmidt	Syria	April 09, 1907	1st	McIntosh
Acey, Hsain	Syria	August 01, 1911	1st	McIntosh
Adray, Abdalla	Syria	January 18, 1906	1st	Ward
Adray, Abdalla	Syria	May 13, 1907	2nd	Ward
Adray, Abdul Ramen	Syria	August 10, 1908	1st	Ward
Adrey, Negab	Syria	January 02, 1907	1st	Ward
Agamay, Nassar	Syria	April 10, 1916	1st	Cass
Ahmad, Abad	Syria	January 25, 1908	1st	McIntosh
Ahmed, Ally	Syria	April 19, 1912	1st	Stutsman
Ahmed, Ally	Syria	October 08,1919	1st	Stutsman
Ahmed, Ally	Syria	December 03, 1923	2nd	Stutsman
Albert, Abraham	Syria	April 27, 1903	1st	McIntosh
Albert, Alex	Syria	December 13, 1920	1st	Cavalier
Albert, Alex	Syria	May 10, 1923	2nd	Cavalier
Albert, Ali	Syria	July 16, 1904	1st	McIntosh
Albert, Allick	Syria	November 01, 1904	2nd	Rolette
Albert, Bryan	Syria	August 18, 1948	2nd	Williams
Albert, Gebran	Syria	June 19, 1913	1st	Williams
Albert, George	Syria	December 02, 1907	1st	McHenry
Albert, George	Syria	December 29, 1915	1st	Rolette
Albert, Joe	Syria	April 23, 1943	2nd	Williams
Albert, Joseph	Syria	August 14, 1942	1st	Williams
Albert, Joseph	Syria	September 21, 1909	1st	Williams
Albert, Joseph	Syria	July 17, 1940	1st	Williams
Albert, Joseph	Syria	August 20, 1945	2nd	Williams
Albert, Joseph	Syria	November 01, 1904	2nd	Rolette
Alcodrey, Abdo	Syria	August 27, 1912	1st	Cass
Alec, Albert	Syria	October 31, 1904	1st	McIntosh
Alex, Abdo	Syria	April 15, 1943	1st	Walsh
Alex, Abdo	Syria	May 27, 1947	2nd	Walsh
Alex Sein	Syria	June 19, 1919	1st	Cavalier
Alex, Sini	Syria	May 22, 1925	2nd	Cavalier
Alick, Joseph	Syria	November 13, 1915	1st	Rolette
Alick, Sam	Syria	November 01, 1904	2nd	Rolette
Alle, Siad	Syria	February 06, 1905	1st	Ward
Alleck, George	Syria	February 09, 1906	1st	McIntosh
Alley, Albert	Syria	February 21,1920	1st	Steele
Alley, Albert	Syria	September 25, 1925	2nd	Steele
Alley, George	Syria	July 08, 1919	1st	Steele
Alley, George	Syria	May 24, 1923	2nd	Steele
Alley, Hasen	Asyria	September 14, 1936	2nd	Barnes
Alley, Mell	Syria	May 23, 1924	2nd	Steele
Alley, Mohmad	Syria	July 22, 1925	1st	Cavalier
Alley, Mohomed	Syria	May 18, 1928	2nd	Cavalier

Name	Country	Date	Papers	County
Allick, Asmael	Syria	April 05, 1916	1st	Rolette
Allick, Joseph	Syria	July 08, 1907	1st	McHenry
Allie, Abedel	Syria	October 20, 1902	1st	Ward
Allie, Annis	Syria	April 09, 1904	1st	Ward
Allie, Kadreiy	Syria	July 13, 1910	1st	Stutsman
Ally, Ahmad	Syria	May 13, 1942	2nd	McHenry
Ally, Charley	Syria	July 06, 1926	1st	Griggs
Aly, Sam	Syria	September 18, 1912	1st	Williams
Aly, Sam	Syria	October 03, 1916	2nd	Williams
Ameen, Ahmed	Syria	July 29, 1907	1st	Dickey
Amein, George	Syria	January 14, 1908	2nd	Kidder
Aomer, Hessen	Syria	March 24, 1903	1st	Ward
Apwood, Helen	Syria	April 14, 1904	1st	Ward
Apwood, John	Syria	April 14, 1904	1st	Ward
Apwood, John	Syria	July 26, 1909	2nd	Williams
Apwood, Sarah	Syria	April 14, 1904	1st	Ward
Arjain, Allie	Syria	September 08, 1919	1st	Ward
Arrooney, Maggie	Syria	August 26, 1907	1st	Williams
Asi, Joseph J.	Syria	March 22, 1894	1st	Richland
Assad, George	Syria	November 01, 1900	2nd	Richland
Assal, Abdallah	Syria	May 09, 1903	1st	Ward
Assat, Joe	Syria	August 29, 1904	1st	McIntosh
Assye, Nicholas	Syria	May 22, 1905	2nd	Towner
Assye, Nikas	Syria	April 15, 1898	1st	Towner
Assye, Samuel	Syria	September 04, 1899	1st	Towner
Assye, Samuel	Syria	May 24, 1905	2nd	Towner
Awen, Charley Abraham	Syria	September 17, 1921	2nd	Towner
Azar, Maggie	Syria	August 01, 1904	1st	Williams
Azar, Maggie	Syria	September 08, 1909	2nd	Williams
Azar, Nick	Syria	September 20, 1939	1st	Williams
Azar, Nick	Syria	August 24, 1942	2nd	Williams
Bahy, Sam	Syria	January 07, 1905	1st	McIntosh
Bajan, Abdellah	Syria	October 09,1917	2nd	Burke
Balish, Mary	Syria	September 20, 1924	2nd	Cass
Barky, George	Syria	November 06, 1903	1st	Ward
Barky, George	Syria	March 07, 1911	2nd	Williams
Barry, Albert	Syria	May 21, 1906	1st	Williams
Benogn, Ally	Syria	January 10, 1906	1st	Ward
Bird, Albert	Syria	June 01, 1927	1st	Sargent
Bird, Albert	Syria	June 02, 1931	2nd	Sargent
Bofamy, George	Syria	November 28, 1913	1st	Richland
Bofamy, Joseph	Syria	March 04, 1940	1st	Richland
Bofamy, Joseph	Syria	May 18, 1942	2nd	Richland
Bohamra, Abbdla	Syria	November 02, 1903	1st	Williams
Bomrod, Mathy	Syria	October 05, 1937	1st	Rolette
Bomrod, Mathy	Syria	October 05, 1940	2nd	Rolette
Bomrod, Mohamed Alley	Syria	May 18, 1928	2nd	Cavalier
Boomrid, Albert	Syria	May 13, 1929	2nd	Walsh
Boomrid, Albert	Syria	September 05, 1923	2nd	Pembina
Bounejiem, Thomas	Syria	October 07, 1910	2nd	Williams

Name	Country	Date	Papers	County
Bousliman, Asad	Syria	March 20, 1905	2nd	Williams
Bousliman, Assad	Syria	September 09, 1904	1st	Williams
Bousliman, Joseph	Syria	April 01, 1907	1st	Williams
Bousliman, Robert	Syria	October 31, 1907	1st	Williams
Bousliman, Shaphika M.	Syria	March 29, 1906	1st	Williams
Bouslman, Mary	Syria	October 19, 1903	1st	Williams
Boutrous, Attas	Syria	July 08, 1904	1st	McLean
Brahim, Charley	Syria	December 21, 1903	1st	Wells
Bukuy, Mostof	Syria	February 03, 1911	1st	McIntosh
Bumrad, Albert	Syria	May 06, 1904	1st	McIntosh
Bushami, Ali Forhart	Syria	June 11, 1915	2nd	Mountrail
Bushami, Ally Forhart	Syria	June 01, 1917	1st	Mountrail
Bwofiesill, Izez	Syria	July 15, 1899	1st	Benson
Cadry, Abdo N.	Syria	June 20, 1911	1st	Cavalier
Cadry, Abdo Najab	Syria	March 31, 1914	2nd	Cavalier
Cadry, Mickal	Syria	March 30, 1900	1st	McIntosh
Cadry, Sahid	Syria	March 30, 1903	1st	McIntosh
Calel, Ally	Syria	December 15, 1906	1st	Ward
Calid, Mike	Syria	July 18, 1904	1st	McIntosh
Cashey, Hassen A.	Syria	January 21, 1918	1st	Steele
Cashey, Hassen A.	Syria	May 20, 1921	2nd	Steele
Dalier, Nicolas	Syria	December 02, 1901	1st	Burleigh
Darosg, Hasian	Syria	September 20, 1901	1st	Ward
Davis, Alex	Syria	March 08, 1919	1st	Cass
Davis, Alex	Syria	May 24, 1924	2nd	Cass
Dean, Alick	Syria	April 25, 1903	1st	Foster
Dell, Albert Abraham	Syria	October 09, 1907	1st	McIntosh
Deraney, Joseph N.	Syria	September 04, 1943	2nd	Grand Forks
Dishorn, Siod	Syria	July 02, 1906	1st	Ward
Eady, Sam	Syria	November 06, 1903	1st	Ward
Eady, Sam	Syria	March 22, 1909	2nd	Williams
Eattol, William	Syria	April 10, 1903	1st	Williams
Eattol, William	Syria	October 01, 1908	2nd	Williams
Eele, Hasian	Syria	June 16, 1902	1st	Burleigh
Eele, Hasien	Syria	August 10, 1907	2nd	Burleigh
Eklen, Albert	Syria	July 16, 1917	1st	Ward
Eli, Mohmond	Syria	June 13, 1910	2nd	Stutsman
Fadel, Kaly S.	Syria	June 23, 1898	1st	Pierce
Fadel, Kaly S.	Syria	November 03, 1900	2nd	Pierce
Farah, Aineu N.	Syria	June 11, 1912	1st	Stark
Farah, Roy	Syria	August 29, 1938	2nd	Williams
Farah, Saad	Syria	October 01, 1908	2nd	Williams
Farhart, Abdul	Syria	March 27, 1908	1st	Williams
Farhart, Ahmed	Syria	July 02, 1918	1st	Mountrail
Farhat, Rachide	Syria	October 03, 1919	2nd	Mountrail
Farhit, Richeed	Syria	January 15, 1915	1st	Mountrail
Faries, Allix	Syria	October 01, 1915	1st	Griggs
Faroah, Asof J.	Syria	June 14, 1904	1st	Williams
Farough, Deeby	Syria	October 01, 1908	2nd	Williams
Farra, Katherine	Syria	October 01, 1908	2nd	Williams

Name	Country	Date	Papers	County
Farreg, Hassen Murray	Syria	August 24, 1920	1st	Mountrail
Farreg, Hassen Murrey	Syria	May 28, 1923	2nd	Mountrail
Farris, Hansen Murrey	Syria	March 19, 1907	1st	McIntosh
Farrow, Seiber	Syria	November 05, 1894	1st	Eddy
Ferres, Asad Richard	Syria	May 13, 1908	1st	Williams
Ferris, Albert	Syria	November 01, 1904	2nd	Rolette
Ferris, George	Syria	May 22, 1919	1st	Grand Forks
Ferris, George	Syria	March 28, 1919	1st	Cass
Ferris, Maa Deen Bou	Syria	May 23, 1931	2nd	Towner
Ferris, Sallie	Syria	December 13, 1920	1st	Rolette
Ferris, Sallie	Syria	November 02, 1936	1st	Rolette
Ferris, Sallie	Syria	May 11, 1942	2nd	Rolette
Ferris, Whadean B.	Syria	July 26, 1926	1st	Towner
Firo, Rahmy	Syria	May 28, 1904	1st	Williams
Firo, Rahmy	Syria	May 29, 1909	2nd	Williams
Firoah, Asof George	Syria	October 07, 1910	2nd	Williams
Firoah, Bertha	Syria	April 18, 1903	1st	Williams
Firoah, George	Syria	April 18, 1903	1st	Williams
Firoah, John	Syria	April 18, 1903	1st	Williams
Firoah, Joseph	Syria	April 16, 1903	1st	Williams
Fish, Foyat	Syria	September 01, 1902`	1st	Ward
Forage, Albert	Syria	June 21, 1909	1st	Logan
Forhal, Hassim	Syria	May 13, 1907	2nd	Ward
Forhite, Joseph	Syria	October 12, 1906	2nd	Ward
Forhivt, Ally	Syria	May 02, 1908	1st	Williams
Forzly, Abraham G.	Syria	April 30, 1906	1st	Willliams
Foshal, Hassim	Syria	April 19, 1902	1st	Ward
Fouad, Farge	Syria	July 03, 1902	2nd	Walsh
Fouad, Forge	Syria	June 16, 1897	1st	Walsh
Frage, Albert	Syria	July 19, 1909	1st	Kidder
Freije, Moses	Syria	June 16, 1897	1st	Walsh
Frein, Richard	Syria	December 17, 1909	1st	Walsh
Garder, Aley	Syria	March 24, 1903	1st	Ward
Gassom, Mohamid Allie	Syria	August 21, 1907	1st	Williams
Gennary, Alex	Syria	October 03, 1919	2nd	Mountrail
George, Andrew	Syria	March 18, 1904	1st	Emmons
George, Edward B.	Syria	December 16, 1931	1st	Williams
George, Edward B.	Syria	August 29, 1938	2nd	Williams
George, Moses	Syria	September 12, 1913	2nd	Morton
George, Nicholas	Syria	June 27, 1906	1st	Ward
George, Ole	Syria	July 21, 1904	1st	McIntosh
Grawan, Habab	Syria	May 18,1916	2nd	McKenzie
Grawan, Habib	Syria	July 08, 1911	1st	Williams
Habib, Jacob	Syria	March 22, 1894	1st	Richland
Habib, Salma	Syria	October 01, 1908	2nd	Williams
Hach, Alex	Syria	May 09,1924	2nd	Cavalier
Hach, Hanidy Anka	Syria	December 10, 1941	2nd	Cavalier
Hadad, Abraham E.	Syria	September 07, 1903	1st	Richland
Hadad, Albert F.	Syria	September 07, 1903	1st	Richland
Haddid, James	Syria	June 05, 1900	1st	Ransom

Name	Country	Date	Papers	County
Hadid, Salmon	Syria	December 01, 1909	1st	Walsh
Hagar, David	Syria	June 03, 1920	2nd	Towner
Hagemy, Colel	Syria	October 06, 1910	2nd	McIntosh
Hager, Alex	Syria	September 23, 1924	2nd	Nelson
Hager, Alex	Syria	September 27, 1921	2nd	Nelson
Hager, David	Syria	February 07, 1916	1st	Towner
Haggar, Albert	Syria	April 04, 1903	1st	McIntosh
Haggar, Assaf	Syria	April 04, 1903	1st	McIntosh
Haggar, Bcharlie	Syria	October 24, 1903	1st	Williams
Haggar, Jim	Syria	November 07, 1911	1st	McIntosh
Haggar, Joseph	Syria	October 23, 1911	1st	McIntosh
Haggar, Joseph	Syria	April 04, 1903	1st	McIntosh
Haggar, Martha	Syria	October 24, 1903	1st	Williams
Haggar, Salamon	Syria	September 07, 1903	1st	McIntosh
Haggar, Sam	Syria	May 29, 1903	1st	McIntosh
Hajjar, Assad Abdallah	Syria	September 16, 1932	2nd	Burke
Hamedan, Abdul Cram	Syria	February 06, 1942	1st	Mountrail
Hamedan, Abdul Cram	Syria	August 23, 1944	2nd	Mountrail
Hamid, Moses	Syria	April 19, 1902	1st	Ward
Hamid, Moses	Syria	October 12, 1906	2nd	Ward
Hammod, Mohamed	Syria	November 02, 1904	1st	McIntosh
Hamway, Abraham	Syria	February 22, 1908	1st	McIntosh
Hamway, Alex	Syria	June 10,1904	1st	McIntosh
Hamway, Sahid	Syria	January 27, 1905	1st	McIntosh
Hanmed, Albert	Syria	July 15, 1910	1st	Kidder
Harman, Sam	Syria	May 19, 1903	1st	Ramsey
Hasen, Alik Zender	Syria	October 06, 1910	2nd	McIntosh
Hasen, Shirley Lyla	Syria	June 23, 1949	2nd	Rolette
Hash, Hammond	Syria	June 27, 1902	1st	Towner
Hash, Alex	Syria	December 17,1903	1st	McIntosh
Hash, Mohammed L.	Syria	August 20, 1906	1st	Richland
Hasheesh, Lottie	Syria	February 23, 1909	1st	Willliams
Hasn, Alick Zander	Syria	September 30, 1908	2nd	McIntosh
Hassan, Homed Hamond	Syria	May 12, 1913	1st	Grand Forks
Hassan, Rymn	Syria	December 02, 1909	1st	Mountrail
Hassen, Albert	Syria	September 18, 1919	1st	Mountrail
Hassen, Albert	Syria	July 09, 1940	1st	Mountrail
Hassen, Albert	Syria	August 25, 1943	2nd	Mountrail
Hassen, Albert R. B.	Syria	January 10, 1905	1st	McIntosh
Hassen, Amel	Syria	December 04, 1907	1st	McHenry
Hassen, Cassem Mok	Syria	August 25, 1943	2nd	Mountrail
Hassen, Jal	Syria	April 07, 1914	2nd	McIntosh
Hassen, Jal	Syria	April 07, 1914	2nd	McIntosh
Hassen, Raymond	Syria	October 03, 1919	2nd	Mountrail
Hassie, Calib	Syria	September 13, 1921	2nd	Divide
Hassie, Faiz Ashod	Syria	May 26, 1923	2nd	Cass
Hassie, Neal	Syria	April 20, 1914	1st	Burleigh
Hassiem, Emiel	Syria	March 14, 1929	1st	Rolette
Hassien, Amel	Syria	December 29, 1915	1st	Rolette
Hassien, Emiel	Syria	September 11, 1924	2nd	Rolette

Name	Country	Date	Papers	County
Hassin, Hamid	Syria	April 19, 1902	1st	Ward
Hatch, Albert	Syria	February 04, 1905	1st	McIntosh
Hatch, Sam	Syria	August 10, 1905	1st	McIntosh
Hatoom, Sam	Syria	April 17, 1902	1st	Pierce
Hatoon, Alex	Syria	August 15, 1903	1st	Ramsey
Hay, Joe	Syria	September 02, 1909	1st	Williams
Haykel, Aisem Mohamed	Syria	March 14, 1911	2nd	Sheridan
Hazemy, Calel	Syria	April 09, 1907	1st	McIntosh
Hech, Alex	Syria	May 08, 1920	1st	Cavalier
Hellick, Gassam	Syria	May 23, 1907	1st	McIntosh
Hepip, Frank	Syria	March 22, 1909	2nd	Williams
Hessen, Joe	Syria	September 16, 1911	1st	McIntosh
Hessie, Kamel	Syria	June 29, 1905	2nd	Burleigh
Hessie, Kemel	Syria	June 18, 1902	1st	Burleigh
Hiawatha, Joe	Syria	October 06, 1910	2nd	McIntosh
Hiawatha, Joe	Syria	January 07, 1905	1st	McIntosh
Hikel, Isim	Syria	April 23, 1903	1st	Wells
Hodge, Solomon	Syria	September 20, 1921	2nd	Ransom
Holt, Ell	Syria	February 11, 1905	1st	McIntosh
Homsey, Anisa	Syria	April 18, 1903	1st	Williams
Homsey, Ased	Syria	February 11, 1910	2nd	Kidder
Housey, Albert	Syria	June 01, 1908	2nd	Kidder
Housey, Mary	Syria	June 01, 1908	2nd	Kidder
Howard, Edward	Syria	April 30, 1904	1st	Logan
Howard, Edward	Syria	April 24, 1911	2nd	Logan
Howard, Sied	Syria	February 01, 1919	1st	Burleigh
Howard, Sied	Syria	June 16, 1911	1st	Stark
Howard, Sied	Syria	December 05, 1916	2nd	Stark
Hussein, Mahmond	Syria	September 13, 1937	2nd	Barnes
Ish, Alay	Syria	February 20, 1905	1st	Ward
Jaha, Saien Hassen	Syria	October 01, 1921	1st	Mountrail
Jaha, Saien Hassen	Syria	September 29, 1924	2nd	Mountrail
Joe, John	Syria	July 15, 1904	1st	McIntosh
Joha, Allah Hassin	Syria	June 05, 1903	1st	Ward
John, Allie Reseuk	Syria	October 20, 1902	1st	Ward
Johnson, Frank	Syria	July 21, 1904	1st	McIntosh
Jones, Albert	Syria	May 16, 1904	1st	McIntosh
Jones, Albert	Syria	March 19, 1909	2nd	McIntosh
Joseph, Albert	Syria	April 12, 1935	1st	Cass
Joseph, Albert	Syria	May 10, 1938	2nd	Cass
Joseph, Alex	Syria	April 22, 1903	1st	Ward
Joseph, Alex	Syria	June 06, 1903	1st	Ward
Joseph, Alle	Syria	June 30, 1903	1st	Ward
Joseph, Hassan	Syria	April 19, 1902	1st	McHenry
Joseph, Hasson	Syria	June 05, 1907	2nd	McHenry
Juhr, Allie Risuk	Syria	May 13, 1907	2nd	Ward
Juhr, Amud Asse	Syria	October 20, 1902	1st	Ward
Juhr, Jaja Allie	Syria	October 20, 1902	1st	Ward
Juhr, Jaja Allie	Syria	June 20, 1908	2nd	Ward
Juma, Ally Calel	Syria	July 20, 1914	1st	Mountrail

Name	Country	Date	Papers	County
Juma, Hassyn Alla	Syria	February 05, 1910	1st	Stutsman
Juma, Hassyn Alla	Syria	June 15, 1914	2nd	Stutsman
Juma, Salem Caled	Syria	September 27, 1920	2nd	Mountrail
Juma, Selim Caled	Syria	August 22, 1908	1st	Ward
Juma, Silem Caled	Syria	May 21, 1914	2nd	Mountrail
Junis, Albert	Syria	July 23, 1904	1st	McIntosh
Jurima, Hassen	Syria	April 05, 1907	2nd	Ward
Kacem, Albert	Syria	December 21, 1904	1st	McIntosh
Kacem, Frank	Syria	December 21, 1903	1st	McIntosh
Kadry, Abdo M.	Syria	January 27, 1921	1st	Steele
Kadry, Abdo M.	Syria	September 21, 1923	2nd	Steele
Kadry, Alli	Syria	July 18, 1904	1st	McIntosh
Kadry, Sam	Syria	April 20, 1914	1st	Burleigh
Kadry, Seid	Syria	September 19, 1924	2nd	Steele
Kadry, Sid	Syria	March 03, 1920	1st	Steele
Kaled, Hassen B.	Syria	November 05, 1921	1st	Steele
Kall, David	Syria	April 16, 1903	1st	Williams
Kallial, Alex Albert	Syria	May 10, 1923	2nd	Cavalier
Kalliel, Najla	Syria	May 13, 1936	2nd	Cavalier
Kamoni, Ahorndt	Syria	January 13, 1909	2nd	Kidder
Kanan, Eman	Syria	July 09, 1908	2nd	Stutsman
Kanan, Masaad	Syria	October 14, 1903	1st	Stutsman
Kanan, Masod	Syria	July 09, 1908	2nd	Stutsman
Kassis, Eli Joseph	Syria	July 19, 1909	1st	Williams
Kassis, John	Syria	September 22,1908	1st	Williams
Kassis, Regina	Syria	July 22, 1903	1st	Williams
Kassis, Regina	Syria	October 01, 1908	2nd	Williams
Katb, John Smille	Syria	September 30, 1924	2nd	Wells
Kellel, Joseph	Syria	April 16, 1902	1st	Ward
Kellel, Joseph	Syria	December 11, 1907	2nd	McLean
Kellel, Thomas	Syria	July 14, 1938	1st	Sheridan
Kellel, Thomas	Syria	September 18, 1941	2nd	Sheridan
Kellel, Tom	Syria	November 07, 1905	1st	McLean
Kellod, James	Syria	November 25, 1921	1st	Benson
Keney, Albert	Syria	May 09, 1939	2nd	Pembina
Kirk, Mike	Syria	April 10, 1908	1st	Pierce
Kory, Lillie	Syria	July 29, 1907	1st	McIntosh
Kouri, Thomas	Syria	March 13, 1906	1st	Williams
Kourivian, Zarouhe	Syria	September 16,1940	2nd	Stutsman
Liean, Richard	Syria	October 01, 1907	1st	Williams
Lyon, Hasaba	Syria	April 17, 1903	1st	Williams
Lyon, Nickolas	Syria	May 17, 1907	1st	Williams
Lyon, Salma	Syria	April 11, 1903	1st	Pierce
Mabarak, Elias	Syria	May 25, 1917	1st	Williams
Machola, Deep	Syria	April 05, 1909	2nd	Kidder
MacKay, Sada	Syria	April 18, 1903	1st	Williams
Mahmod, Massod	Syria	September 18, 1916	2nd	Dunn
Maloff, Tekman	Syria	May 14, 1903	1st	Pierce
Malouf, James A.	Syria	July 22, 1910	1st	Williams
Mamod, Esad	Syria	June 16, 1902	1st	Burleigh

Name	Country	Date	Papers	County
Mamod, Esad	Syria	August 10, 1907	2nd	Burleigh
Marby, Kamil M. H.	Syria	November 18, 1924	1st	Griggs
Marby, Kamil M. H.	Syria	September 12, 1939	2nd	Griggs
Mary, Kamil M. H.	Syria	March 29, 1935	1st	Griggs
Masse, Abdo	Syria	March 25, 1911	1st	Williams
Mehamed, Mahfad	Syria	December 01, 1914	2nd	Stark
Melhm, Otto	Syria	May 27,1907	1st	Ward
Mellem, Hammett	Syria	March 24, 1917	1st	Mountrail
Merril, Hassin	Syria	April 19, 1902	1st	Ward
Mike, Abraham	Syria	November 16, 1910	1st	Williams
Mike, Abraham	Syria	May 22, 1914	2nd	Williams
Milham, Domat	Syria	August 20, 1906	1st	Emmons
Millem, Hamett	Syria	May 29, 1907	1st	Ward
Millem, Hamett	Syria	October 03, 1919	2nd	Mountrail
Minder, Sali	Syria	May 12, 1913	1st	Grand Forks
Modem, Sahel	Syria	August 10, 1907	2nd	Burleigh
Mohued, Muhfod	Syria	January 04, 1912	1st	Stark
Morse, Kasim	Syria	November 26, 1918	1st	Cavalier
Morse, Kasin	Syria	October 02, 1922	2nd	Cavalier
Mospa, Abdil	Syria	April 19, 1902	1st	Ward
Mostaf, Isha	Syria	May 29, 1907	1st	Ward
Mostafa, Aisha	Syria	October 17, 1913	2nd	Mountrail
Moussi, George	Syria	March 21, 1894	1st	Richland
Mred, Joseph	Syria	April 12, 1935	1st	Cass
Mred, Joseph	Syria	May 10, 1938	2nd	Cass
Mrid, Ally J.	Syria	December 00, 0000	2nd	LaMoure
Munyer, Mayre	Syria	December 20, 1907	1st	Williams
Murrey, Hansen	Syria	July 08, 1914	2nd	Kidder
Muste, Mohamid A.	Syria	October 12, 1906	2nd	Ward
Myren, Aanen R.	Syria	July 10, 1911	1st	McLean
Naked, Joseph	Syria	January 06, 1905	1st	Williams
Naked, Joseph	Syria	June 24, 1910	2nd	Williams
Nassif, Caram	Syria	December 21, 1905	1st	McLean
Nassif, Rustum	Syria	June 16, 1906	1st	McLean
Nassif, Shaker	Syria	February 09, 1910	1st	Sheridan
Nassif, Shaker	Syria	March 11, 1913	2nd	Sheridan
Naymur, Joseph	Syria	June 11, 1924	1st	Walsh
Nedoff, Edward	Syria	August 26, 1940	2nd	Williams
Nedoff, Mike	Syria	November 01, 1909	1st	Williams
Nehmey, Thomas	Syria	May 02, 1903	1st	Williams
Neimy, Despina	Syria	July 20, 1903	1st	Pierce
Nicholas, Mary Hajj	Syria	December 08, 1913	2nd	Stutsman
Nicola, Salem	Syria	May 05, 1906	1st	McLean
Nicola, Salem	Syria	October 17, 1911	2nd	Sheridan
Nicola, Salma	Syria	December 10, 1907	1st	McLean
Nicola, Salma	Syria	May 19, 1903	1st	Wells
Nicola, Salma	Syria	February 09, 1910	2nd	Sheridan
Nicola, Salma	Syria	December 09, 1907	2nd	McLean
Nicola, Satamon	Syria	December 31, 1915	1st	Stark
Nicola, Solomon	Syria	June 26, 1924	1st	Burleigh

Name	Country	Date	Papers	County
O'Sine, Mohamrad B.	Syria	July 23, 1913	1st	Towner
Ogill, Shdid	Syria	July 09, 1908	2nd	Stutsman
Ohmar, Ally	Syria	June 20, 1908	1st	Ward
Ojile, Joseph	Syria	November 14, 1905	1st	Stutsman
Ojile, Joseph	Syria	June 12, 1911	2nd	Stutsman
Omar, Allay	Syria	March 13, 1924	1st	Mountrail
Omar, Allay	Syria	August 23, 1944	2nd	Mountrail
Omar, Alley	Syria	January 19,1909	1st	Ward
Omar, Emil	Syria	May 11, 1907	1st	McIntosh
Omar, Gasman	Syria	October 17, 1905	1st	Ward
Omar, Sam	Syria	December 17, 1906	1st	Ward
Omar, Sam	Syria	March 31, 1919	1st	Mountrail
Omar, Sam	Syria	September 16, 1921	2nd	Mountrail
Omer, Abdo	Syria	June 10, 1913	1st	Towner
Omer, Machmod	Syria	June 12, 1908	1st	McIntosh
Ostman, Monstaf	Syria	January 16, 1905	1st	McIntosh
Osman, Mosa	Syria	October 11, 1921	1st	Mountrail
Osman, Mosa	Syria	May 26, 1924	2nd	Mountrail
Osman, Mostafa	Syria	December 24, 1919	1st	Mountrail
Osman, Nostafa	Syria	May 28,1923	2nd	Mountrail
Ostman, Amid	Syria	April 22, 1903	1st	Ward
Otman, Hassen	Syria	May 16,1917	2nd	Dunn
Otman, Hassen	Syria	June 29, 1911	1st	McIntosh
Ottman, Sam	Syria	December 23, 1920	1st	Griggs
Owan, William Abraham	Syria	May 23, 1936	1st	Williams
Owan, William Abraham	Syria	August 28, 1939	2nd	Williams
Pazie, Mahamoud J.	Syria	September 07, 1909	1st	Richland
Peter, Joe	Syria	March 26, 1923	1st	Stark
Rahall, Anis	Syria	February 20, 1934	1st	Eddy
Rahall, Anis	Syria	September 22,1936	2nd	Eddy
Rashid, Fred J.	Syria	October 25, 1909	1st	Adams
Rashid, Mary	Syria	December 05, 1911	1st	Adams
Rashid, Mike M.	Syria	October 25, 1909	1st	Adams
Rashid, Samuel F.	Syria	August 25, 1911	1st	Adams
Rashid, Shaffick S.	Syria	October 25, 1909	1st	Adams
Rassake, Mohemmed	Syria	September 30, 1908	1st	Ward
Rehal, Charlie	Syria	January 03, 1911	1st	Williams
Rehal, Charlie	Syria	May 22, 1914	2nd	Williams
Reith, Asath	Syria	March 11, 1910	2nd	McIntosh
Remden, Machet	Syria	May 18, 1912	1st	Stark
Remden, Machet	Syria	June 05, 1915	2nd	Billings
Reney, Hassen	Syria	July 03, 1930	1st	Burke
Reney, Hassen	Syria	September 14, 1934	2nd	Burke
Rezonk, Coleal	Syria	August 27, 1907	1st	Williams
Rokker, Anis	Syria	April 15, 1905	1st	Ward
Roumie, Serafin	Syria	July 20, 1903	1st	Williams
Ruscen, Ashmid O.	Syria	June 06, 1902	1st	Ward
Saad, Elias	Syria	October 26, 1894	1st	Eddy
Saba, Mary	Syria	October 19, 1903	1st	Williams
Saba, Mika	Syria	May 09, 1904	1st	Wells

Name	Country	Date	Papers	County
Saba, Mike	Syria	September 27, 1923	1st	Burleigh
Saba, Richard John	Syria	October 03, 1907	1st	Williams
Saba, Saidie	Syria	August 22, 1942	2nd	Burleigh
Sadden, Mhamed	Syria	February 15, 1902	1st	Ward
Sadden, Mhamed	Syria	April 05, 1907	2nd	Ward
Saddy, Allek	Syria	November 05, 1906	1st	Pierce
Sage, Albert Oman	Syria	May 28, 1925	2nd	Cass
Saign Michael	Syria	September 13, 1937	2nd	Barnes
Saign, Michael	Syria	November 15, 1933	1st	Barnes
Saim, Alle	Syria	December 31, 1908	2nd	Ward
Sain, Alex	Syria	January 13, 1908	1st	McIntosh
Saine, Kassam	Syria	December 13, 1915	1st	Rolette
Sajg, Balis	Syria	December 31, 1909	1st	Williams
Sajg, Rose	Syria	July 30, 1910	1st	Williams
Sakeen, Albert	Syria	April 27, 1903	1st	McIntosh
Salamon, Albert	Syria	January 16,1904	1st	McIntosh
Salebay, Nasseph	Syria	August 03, 1914	1st	Williams
Salem, Charles	Syria	February 18, 1902	1st	Ward
Saly, Joe	Syria	January 13, 1905	1st	McIntosh
Sam, Howard	Syria	January 04, 1909	2nd	Stutsman
Santabye, Hamod	Syria	September 15, 1925	1st	Sioux
Santabye, Hamod	Syria	June 03, 1922	1st	Sioux
Santabye, Solomon	Syria	January 07, 1927	1st	Sioux
Santabye, Solomon	Syria	September 16, 1930	2nd	Sioux
Saouya, Aefefoe Rahal	Syria	April 13, 1903	1st	Williams
Saowya, Rosa Rahal	Syria	August 01, 1904	1st	Williams
Sardin, Sam	Syria	May 23, 1907	1st	Ward
Sarien, Abas	Syria	December 00, 0000	2nd	Steele
Saty, Charley	Syria	April 12, 1906	1st	Williams
Saur, Howard	Syria	August 19, 1903	1st	Stutsman
Sawaya, Charles	Syria	February 25, 1907	1st	Williams
Sawaya, George J.	Syria	May 17, 1924	2nd	Pierce
Saykally, James H.	Syria	April 20, 1910	1st	Williams
Schicany, Affie	Syria	May 17, 1904	1st	Pierce
Seamin, Joseph	Syria	May 15, 1905	1st	McIntosh
Seioin, Ally	Syria	July 15, 1904	1st	McIntosh
Seleh, Richard	Syria	September 07, 1909	1st	Richland
Selem, Albert	Syria	February 15, 1902	1st	Ward
Selem, Albert	Syria	April 05, 1907	2nd	Ward
Selem, Charles	Syria	April 05, 1907	2nd	Ward
Sem, Hemd	Syria	May 29, 1907	1st	Ward
Shahn, Salomon	Syria	May 19, 1913	1st	Towner
Shakany, Salame	Syria	July 23, 1906	1st	Williams
Shakany, Salma	Syria	March 02, 1906	1st	Williams
Shallop, Fred	Syria	October 26, 1915	1st	Pierce
Shickany, Nassim	Syria	November 17, 1905	1st	Williams
Shickony, Abraham	Syria	April 09, 1903	1st	Williams
Shihany, Ed	Syria	June 12, 1916	1st	Williams
Shikany, Joseph Tamer	Syria	April 28, 1920	1st	Willliams
Shikany, Maggie	Syria	September 10, 1906	1st	Williams

Name	Country	Date	Papers	County
Shikany, Mary	Syria	March 19, 1910	1st	Williams
Shody, Mohamed	Syria	June 02, 1906	1st	Ward
Siam, Alle	Syria	May 14, 1903	1st	Ward
Sian, Boshaura	Syria	April 01, 1903	1st	Ward
Sian, Said	Syria	July 13, 1910	1st	Stutsman
Side, Abraham	Syria	December 12, 1903	1st	Dickey
Side, Achmid Hammod	Syria	October 15, 1910	1st	McIntosh
Side, Achmid Hammod	Syria	April 03, 1913	2nd	McIntosh
Sien, Apdallh	Syria	December 02, 1905	1st	Ward
Sign, Homan	Syria	April 16, 1902	1st	Ward
Skaff, Abraham	Syria	October 01, 1907	1st	McLean
Skaff, Abraham Saleem	Syria	March 11, 1915	1st	Sheridan
Skaff, Abraham Saleem	Syria	November 23, 1917	2nd	Sheridan
Skaff, Abraham Saleem	Syria	March 11, 1913	2nd	Sheridan
Skaff, Farris Saleem	Syria	February 09, 1910	2nd	Sheridan
Skaff, Julia A.	Syria	May 05, 1906	1st	Williams
Skaff, Mary	Syria	February 08, 1909	1st	Williams
Slebay, Mary	Syria	November 04, 1903	1st	Williams
Slebay, Mary	Syria	March 22, 1909	2nd	Williams
Smille, John K.	Syria	June 02, 1920	1st	Wells
Smille, John Katb	Syria	September 30, 1924	2nd	Wells
Solomon, Amen	Syria	January 31, 1913	1st	Towner
Solomon, Ed	Syria	October 24, 1905	1st	Williams
Solomon, Joseph	Syria	September 23, 1902	1st	Rolette
Solomon, Joseph	Syria	October 28, 1905	1st	Ward
Solomon, Joseph	Syria	May 24, 1905	2nd	Towner
Srur, George	Syria	June 14, 1941	1st	Pierce
Srur, George	Syria	March 06,1945	2nd	Pierce
Swiden, Rashad	Syria	May 19, 1920	2nd	Sargent
Swiden, Ashed	Syria	May 24, 1915	1st	Sargent
Tannus, Mary	Syria	May 16, 1906	1st	Williams
Tanouss, Abdallah	Syria	April 06, 1898	1st	Towner
Tanouss, Abdallah	Syria	May 27, 1903	2nd	Towner
Teneres, Mohmoud	Syria	September 22, 1901	1st	Stutsman
Thah, Albert	Syria	April 22, 1903	1st	Ward
Tieb, Georg	Syria	December 17, 1903	1st	McIntosh
Toby, Maggie	Syria	April 10, 1903	1st	Williams
Toha, Omar K.	Syria	July 23, 1913	1st	Towner
Unice, Joseph	Syria	April 25, 1903	1st	Foster
Unice, Joseph	Syria	December 13, 1909	2nd	Stutsman
Unis, Esad	Syria	June 16, 1902	1st	Burleigh
Unis, Esad	Syria	August 10, 1907	2nd	Burleigh
Unise, Charles	Syria	June 13, 1913	2nd	Morton
Urvanawich, Frank	Syria	May 02, 1910	1st	Stutsman
Warzook, Abrah	Syria	January 25, 1908	2nd	Pierce
Wase, Sam	Syria	July 18, 1904	1st	McIntosh
Williams, Annie	Syria	March 18, 1904	1st	Emmons
Yeph, Joseph	Syria	April 20, 1914	1st	Burleigh
Yons, Charley	Syria	April 02, 1906	1st	Williams
Youness, Charley	Syria	June 24, 1910	2nd	Williams

Name	Country	Date	Papers	County
Youness, Joseph	Syria	December 09, 1905	1st	Williams
Yuens, Rosay	Syria	September 24, 1906	1st	Williams
Yunoess, Joseph A.	Syria	April 20, 1903	1st	Ward
Yuoness, Joseph C.	Syria	April 20, 1903	1st	Ward
Yuoness, Joseph C.	Syria	October 01, 1908	2nd	Williams
Zamata, Joseph	Syria	March 04, 1910	1st	Pierce
Zamata, Joseph	Syria	October 02, 1914	1st	Williams
Zamata, Joseph	Syria	October 02, 1914	2nd	Williams
Zamata, Joseph	Syria	June 09, 1917	2nd	Williams
Zammiatta, Charley	Syria	December 17, 1910	2nd	Williams
Zarh, Mohammed	Syria	June 15, 1903	1st	Ramsey
Zarh, Syde	Syria	June 10, 1903	1st	Ramsey
Zear, Ed	Syria	February 11, 1905	1st	McIntosh
Zeden, George	Syria	May 12, 1913	1st	Grand Forks
Zeden, Joseph	Syria	May 12, 1913	1st	Grand Forks
Zeden, Sali	Syria	May 12, 1912	1st	Grand Forks
Zeden, Smial	Syria	May 12, 1913	1st	Grand Forks
Zeer, Mohammed	Syria	July 22, 1907	2nd	Pierce
Zein, John	Syria	July 12, 1907	1st	Williams
Zein, John	Syria	September 09, 1927	1st	Williams
Zein, John	Syria	March 21, 1936	1st	Williams
Zein, John	Syria	August 29, 1938	2nd	Williams
Zein, Joseph E.	Syria	August 04, 1914	1st	Williams
Zein, Lottia	Syria	April 13, 1903	1st	Ward
Zien, Cary	Syria	July 09, 1906	1st	Williams
Zien, Charlie M.	Syria	December 19, 1910	2nd	Willliams
Zien, Joe	Syria	April 13, 1911	1st	Williams
Zien, Mamie A.	Syria	January 29, 1913	1st	Williams
Zihn, Jennie	Syria	April 05, 1910	1st	Willliams
Zitoone, Jos. M.	Syria	November 29, 1902	1st	Burleigh
Zittoone, Norman	Syria	December 02, 1902	1st	Burleigh

Turkey

Name	Country	Date	Papers	County
Abdala, Mahmoud	Turkey	March 09, 1903	1st	Pierce
Abdella, Masess	Turkey	March 24, 1903	1st	Richland
Abdella, Moses	Turkey	July 13, 1909	2nd	Sheridan
Abes, Hasan	Turkey	March 17, 1903	1st	Richland
Abood, Nicholas	Turkey	May 03, 1907	1st	Williams
Abood, Nicholas	Turkey	May 19, 1918	2nd	Williams
Abourezk, Carl	Turkey	April 04, 1896	2nd	Cass
Abourezk, George	Turkey	April 04, 1896	2nd	Cass
Abourezk, Mike	Turkey	April 04, 1896	2nd	Cass
Abourezk, Zachary	Turkey	April 04, 1896	2nd	Cass
Abraham, Joseph	Turkey	July 21, 1902	1st	Pierce
Abraham, Katherine	Turkey	September 16, 1940	1st	Stutsman
Abrahano, Albert	Turkey	February 26,1903	1st	Wells
Absey, Joseph	Turkey	July 17, 1897	1st	Walsh
Absey, Joseph	Turkey	July 03, 1902	2nd	Walsh
Absey, Peter	Turkey	July 17, 1897	1st	Walsh

Name	Country	Date	Papers	County
Absey, Peter	Turkey	July 03, 1902	2nd	Walsh
Aghamey, Moses	Turkey	November 30, 1901	1st	Towner
Aivazian, Hrant	Turkey	December 02, 1912	1st	Cass
Akidakis, John	Turkey	April 11, 1924	1st	LaMoure
Albit, Alli	Turkey	November 01, 1901	1st	Pierce
Alexander, Frank	Turkey	September 25, 1916	1st	Ransom
Ali, Mahomed	Turkey	September 19, 1927	2nd	Grand Forks
Ali, Mohmad	Turkey	February 03, 1923	1st	Grand Forks
Alley, Abraham	Turkey	December 07, 1901	1st	Ward
Alley, Abraham	Turkey	February 25, 1905	2nd	Bottineau
Alley, Abraham	Turkey	February 25, 1905	2nd	Bottineau
Alli, Sien	Turkey	January 09, 1902	1st	Cass
Allia, Mohamit	Turkey	August 16, 1911	1st	Kidder
Ally, Ahmad	Turkey	March 17, 1903	1st	Richland
Almed, Jesse	Turkey	November 14, 1906	1st	Logan
Altounian, Sogomon	Turkey	September 15, 1937	2nd	Cass
Altounian, Soyomon	Turkey	May 12, 1931	1st	Cass
Aly, Mahmod	Turkey	March 17, 1903	1st	Richland
Amid, Abdallah	Turkey	June 10, 1913	1st	Mountrail
Apanian, Anthony	Turkey	September 21, 1921	1st	Bottineau
Apanian, Anthony	Turkey	May 15, 1924	2nd	Bottineau
Apanian, Hagoh	Turkey	September 02, 1916	1st	Nelson
Apkarian, Arshag	Turkey	February 16, 1926	1st	Stutsman
Apkarian, Arshag	Turkey	September 22, 1930	2nd	Stutsman
Apkarian, Nouritza	Turkey	June 27, 1949	2nd	Stutsman
Arakian, Dick	Turkey	April 27, 1914	1st	Benson
Ardekian, Mike	Turkey	May 10, 1920	1st	Ramsey
Asadoorian, Avedis M.	Turkey	December 02, 1918	2nd	Morton
Asadoorian, Toras	Turkey	November 12, 1925	1st	Morton
Asadoorian, Toras	Turkey	September 30, 1930	2nd	Morton
Asdourian, Mugurdich H.	Turkey	November 02, 1931	1st	Cass
Asdourian, Mugurdich H.	Turkey	September 18, 1935	2nd	Cass
Assad, Rasheed	Turkey	November 03, 1900	2nd	Richland
Asseff, Wadie Shaheen	Turkey	June 12, 1919	1st	Cass
Avakian, Tom	Turkey	July 11, 1922	1st	Stutsman
Avakian, Tom	Turkey	September 27, 1926	2nd	Stutsman
Awen, Charley Abraham	Turkey	January 19, 1914	1st	Williams
Azadian, Sam	Turkey	September 15, 1937	2nd	Cass
Azadian, Soyomon	Turkey	May 12, 1931	1st	Cass
Azar, Nicholas	Turkey	April 17, 1907	1st	Williams
Azarian, James	Turkey	April 23, 1938	1st	Williams
Azarian, James	Turkey	August 28, 1939	2nd	Williams
Baba, Joe	Turkey	June 13, 1905	1st	Ramsey
Baba, Joseph	Turkey	October 27, 1903	1st	Pierce
Baba, Joseph	Turkey	February 02, 1906	2nd	Pierce
Bahne, Salem	Turkey	February 02, 1906	2nd	Pierce
Balish, Mary	Turkey	December 00, 0000	2nd	Pierce
Bashian, Hagop	Turkey	August 23, 1915	1st	Golden Valley
Belch, Joseph	Turkey	November 04, 1899	1st	Pierce
Belish, Joseph	Turkey	June 12, 1901	1st	Pierce

Name	Country	Date	Papers	County
Blumhagen, Christoph	Turkey	September 27, 1886	1st	Benson
Blumhager, Christoph	Turkey	April 05, 1892	2nd	Foster
Bofamy, Fred	Turkey	November 21, 1918	1st	Richland
Bofamy, Fred	Turkey	May 08, 1922	2nd	Richland
Bonfiasll, Frasll	Turkey	July 03, 1902	1st	Pierce
Bonshahla, Mary	Turkey	May 02, 1902	1st	Pierce
Bossin, Davis	Turkey	July 10, 1897	1st	Cass
Bossin, Davis	Turkey	November 03, 1902	2nd	Pierce
Boumejim, Tom	Turkey	October 20, 1902	1st	Pierce
Bounejim, Tom	Turkey	April 24, 1903	1st	Ward
Bourestom, James	Turkey	April 17, 1907	1st	Willliams
Boureston, James	Turkey	October 20, 1902	1st	Pierce
Bousliman, Joseph	Turkey	October 20, 1902	1st	Pierce
Bousliman, Naseef	Turkey	August 12, 1905	1st	Williams
Bousliman, Naseef	Turkey	June 12, 1915	2nd	Williams
Boussad, Abraham	Turkey	April 19, 1897	1st	Pierce
Boussad, Abraham	Turkey	November 03, 1900	2nd	Pierce
Boussad, Hannah	Turkey	May 07, 1906	1st	Pierce
Boussad, James	Turkey	November 29,1901	2nd	Pierce
Boussad, Joseph	Turkey	April 19, 1897	1st	Pierce
Boussad, Joseph	Turkey	June 16, 1906	2nd	Pierce
Boussad, Joseph	Turkey	November 26, 1901	2nd	Pierce
Boussad, Mageeb	Turkey	August 30, 1899	1st	Pierce
Boussad, Mary	Turkey	July 26, 1898	1st	Pierce
Boussad, Mary	Turkey	February 08, 1905	2nd	Pierce
Boussad, Nassif	Turkey	November 27, 1901	2nd	Pierce
Boussad, Nassif	Turkey	June 18, 1898	1st	Pierce
Boussad, Richan	Turkey	November 03, 1902	2nd	Pierce
Boyajian, Krikor	Turkey	July 29, 1911	1st	Williams
Bozen, Petro	Turkey	February 08, 1921	1st	Stutsman
Bozen, Petro	Turkey	September 22, 1927	2nd	Stutsman
Broodo, Jack	Turkey	October 25, 1905	1st	Towner
Cadry, Herman	Turkey	May 20,1912	1st	Cavalier
Carakehian, Garabet	Turkey	November 26, 1919	1st	Ramsey
Carian, George	Turkey	May 12, 1924	2nd	Ramsey
Cash, Alex	Turkey	October 01, 1913	1st	Cass
Cash, Alex	Turkey	April 24, 1917	2nd	Cass
Christ, John George	Turkey	November 10, 1915	2nd	McIntosh
Christ, John George	Turkey	March 24, 1915	1st	McIntosh
Christ, John George	Turkey	May 08, 1912	1st	McIntosh
Christ, John George	Turkey	December 18, 1916	1st	McIntosh
Constantina, Andrew A.	Turkey	April 01, 1918	1st	Wells
Couchigian, George	Turkey	September 03, 1938	2nd	Ward
Daan, Abdela	Turkey	August 15, 1899	1st	Pierce
Daan, Katie	Turkey	March 03, 1902	1st	Pierce
Dardarian, Sam	Turkey	September 16, 1943	1st	Cass
Daruni, Sam	Turkey	November 17, 1920	1st	Burke
Darwish, Abdolader	Turkey	March 09, 1903	1st	Pierce
David, Albert	Turkey	July 01, 1902	1st	Pierce
David, Salima	Turkey	December 00, 0000	2nd	Pierce

Name	Country	Date	Papers	County
David, Tanous	Turkey	November 19, 1901	1st	Pierce
David, Tanous	Turkey	February 02, 1906	2nd	Pierce
Dowalebee, Mary	Turkey	May 14, 1900	1st	Pierce
Dowalebee, Mary	Turkey	August 17,1906	2nd	McHenry
Dulion, Aspen	Turkey	April 04, 1898	2nd	Cass
Egaa, Constantine	Turkey	September 14, 1916	1st	Cass
Eli, Hassen	Turkey	June 22, 1905	1st	Stutsman
Eli, Mohmond	Turkey	July 03, 1905	1st	Stutsman
Eli, Willie	Turkey	December 04, 1906	1st	Stutsman
Eli, Willie	Turkey	January 09, 1912	2nd	Kidder
Eli, Willie	Turkey	January 15, 1913	2nd	Kidder
Elis, Jeles K.	Turkey	March 24, 1903	1st	Richland
Elly, Charley	Turkey	July 15, 1905	1st	Ward
Emon, George	Turkey	October 07, 1922	1st	Benson
Ermie, Joseph	Turkey	May 05, 1917	1st	Benson
Essect, Mahmad	Turkey	May 22, 1915	1st	Foster
Esta, Filemena	Turkey	March 03, 1902	1st	Pierce
Esta, Helen	Turkey	June 21, 1898	1st	Pierce
Esta, Helen	Turkey	June 18, 1903	2nd	Pierce
Esta, Joseph	Turkey	March 29, 1898	2nd	Cass
Faiad, Charley	Turkey	March 29, 1898	2nd	Cass
Farbat, Alfred	Turkey	August 13, 1903	1st	Ward
Farhart, Bo Aley	Turkey	July 05, 1918	1st	Mountrail
Farhart, Bo Aley	Turkey	May 04, 1922	2nd	Mountrail
Farhart, Bo Aley	Turkey	May 21, 1914	2nd	Mountrail
Farhart, Jisam	Turkey	August 25, 1910	1st	Williams
Farhat, Bo Aleg	Turkey	September 24, 1908	1st	Ward
Farhat, Jisam	Turkey	May 21, 1914	2nd	Mountrail
Farra, Katherine	Turkey	April 16, 1903	1st	Ward
Farrell, Seiber	Turkey	November 16, 1903	2nd	Benson
Farris, William	Turkey	September 20, 1921	2nd	Ransom
Ferris, Asmil	Turkey	May 28, 1906	1st	McHenry
Ferris, Mike A.	Turkey	March 28, 1902	1st	Pierce
Ferris, Mike Asid	Turkey	April 02, 1906	2nd	McHenry
Feyatt, Charley	Turkey	June 12, 1901	1st	Pierce
Feyiad, Mary	Turkey	July 05, 1901	1st	Pierce
Feyiad, Mary	Turkey	April 16, 1907	2nd	Pierce
Forheat, Kalle	Turkey	March 17, 1903	1st	Richland
Forsley, Mary	Turkey	May 01, 1902	1st	Pierce
Fortomorof, Alexo Vane	Turkey	June 24, 1911	1st	Foster
Fren, William	Turkey	July 17,1897	1st	Walsh
Fren, William	Turkey	July 03, 1902	2nd	Walsh
Frieje, Moses	Turkey	April 08, 1902	2nd	Walsh
Frien, Abraham	Turkey	April 08, 1902	2nd	Walsh
Gagoran, George	Turkey	June 05, 1918	1st	Kidder
Geawan, Michael	Turkey	May 18, 1916	2nd	McKenzie
Gekeff, Louis	Turkey	October 01, 1924	2nd	McKenzie
George, Nellie	Turkey	April 24, 1907	1st	Williams
George, Peter	Turkey	March 02, 1918	1st	Kidder
George, Peter	Turkey	December 00, 0000	1st	Kidder

Name	Country	Date	Papers	County
George, Salima	Turkey	May 25, 1903	1st	Pierce
George, Steve	Turkey	May 31, 1916	2nd	McIntosh
George, Vanne	Turkey	June 09, 1939	1st	McKenzie
George, Vannie	Turkey	August 26, 1941	2nd	McKenzie
Georgeff, Dines	Turkey	June 14, 1915	2nd	McKenzie
Ghazian, Ghazar	Turkey	April 05, 1924	1st	Burleigh
Gorra, Lizzie	Turkey	September 18, 1906	1st	Williams
Gossom, Mohamid Allie	Turkey	August 05, 1905	2nd	Mountrail
Gostigan, Mardiros	Turkey	July 29, 1911	1st	Williams
Haarsh, Carl	Turkey	November 27, 1905	1st	Richland
Hadad, Jacob	Turkey	August 25, 1902	1st	Pierce
Haddad, Jacob	Turkey	March 31, 1900	2nd	Cass
Haddie, Daywood	Turkey	February 02, 1906	2nd	Pierce
Haddie, Sam	Turkey	February 02, 1906	2nd	Pierce
Haddy, George	Turkey	June 15, 1903	1st	Pierce
Hadey, Abdel	Turkey	April 13, 1909	1st	Cass
Hadey, Abdel	Turkey	December 08, 1913	2nd	Stutsman
Hadey, Abdel	Turkey	December 00, 0000	2nd	Stutsman
Hagar, Mary	Turkey	December 01, 1902	1st	Ramsey
Hagger, Charles	Turkey	October 27, 1902	1st	Towner
Hagger, Charles	Turkey	April 05, 1910	2nd	Towner
Haisch, Sam	Turkey	December 09, 1904	1st	Wells
Hajian, Harry	Turkey	October 01, 1932	2nd	Burleigh
Hallaway, Joseph	Turkey	June 16, 1902	1st	Pierce
Hallaway, Joseph	Turkey	September 06, 1910	2nd	Pierce
Haloway, George	Turkey	June 10, 1899	1st	Pierce
Hapip, Dep	Turkey	August 25, 1902	2nd	Pierce
Harootonnian, Mouses	Turkey	September 11, 1914	1st	Grand Forks
Haschi, Allah	Turkey	October 25, 1902	1st	Pierce
Haschi, Hammod	Turkey	October 25, 1902	1st	Pierce
Haschi, Hassan	Turkey	October 25, 1902	1st	Pierce
Hash, Ali	Turkey	August 18, 1906	1st	Foster
Hassein, Sayid Abou	Turkey	June 05, 1900	1st	Pierce
Hassin, Hamid	Turkey	February 23, 1911	2nd	Mountrail
Hassin, Salem	Turkey	May 20, 1910	2nd	Mountrail
Haverstraw, Julian	Turkey	May 16, 1904	2nd	Pierce
Heddie, Daywood	Turkey	March 07, 1902	1st	Pierce
Heddie, Sam	Turkey	April 02 1902	1st	Pierce
Helet, Alay	Turkey	March 21, 1902	1st	Pierce
Helmy, Moohamed	Turkey	June 23, 1917	1st	Cass
Hepip, Dep	Turkey	May 04, 1900	1st	Pierce
Hepip, Frank	Turkey	February 04, 1902	1st	Pierce
Heringer, August	Turkey	July 07, 1892	1st	Foster
Hesen, Mahmoud	Turkey	March 21, 1902	1st	Pierce
Hessen ,Emil	Turkey	May 26, 1932	2nd	Bottineau
Hodge, Solomon	Turkey	February 03, 1909	2nd	Cass
Hodge, Solomon	Turkey	September 13, 1909	2nd	Pierce
Hodge, Solomon	Turkey	September 10, 1913	1st	Cass
Hodge, Solomon	Turkey	March 09, 1914	2nd	Cass
Holoway, George	Turkey	May 16, 1904	2nd	Pierce

Name	Country	Date	Papers	County
Holt, Alex	Turkey	June 13, 1906	1st	Ramsey
Howard, Cyde	Turkey	October 28, 1906	1st	Logan
Howard, Side	Turkey	February 09, 1922	1st	McIntosh
Iserma, Sadie	Turkey	April 03, 1899	1st	Towner
Jamgochian, Takvor	Turkey	October 22, 1925	2nd	Stutsman
Janenney, Hassen Merly	Turkey	February 25, 1905	2nd	Bottineau
Janenney, Hassen Mirhy	Turkey	February 25, 1905	2nd	Bottineau
John, Annie George	Turkey	October 09, 1897	1st	Richland
Joseph, Aleck	Turkey	October 10, 1902	1st	Pierce
Joseph, Charley	Turkey	October 25, 1902	1st	Pierce
Joseph, Hamid	Turkey	October 10, 1902	1st	Pierce
Joseph, Mohamed	Turkey	November 13, 1906	1st	Stutsman
Jovanoff, Nicola	Turkey	April 14, 1916	1st	Pembina
Juma, Hassyn Alla	Turkey	September 10, 1913	2nd	Cass
Kadrie, George	Turkey	October 01, 1913	1st	Cass
Kadrie, George	Turkey	June 13, 1916	2nd	Cass
Kadry, Alli	Turkey	April 22, 1913	2nd	Cass
Kaiaian, Zakaria	Turkey	April 28, 1934	1st	Nelson
Kaiaian, Zakaria	Turkey	September 18, 1936	2nd	Nelson
Kalk, Gottlieb	Turkey	June 30, 1896	1st	Ramsey
Kalk, Gottlieb	Turkey	January 22, 1902	2nd	Wells
Kallas, James	Turkey	August 23, 1915	1st	Barnes
Kallel, Edward	Turkey	May 27, 1918	1st	Cass
Kallel, Edward	Turkey	May 20, 1922	2nd	Cass
Kaloustian, Hagop	Turkey	October 05, 1950	1st	Stutsman
Kaloustian, Hagop	Turkey	June 16, 1952	2nd	Stutsman
Kamoni, Ahamidt	Turkey	March 17, 1903	1st	Richland
Kamoni, Ahamidt	Turkey	May 08, 1903	1st	Burleigh
Kamoni, Ali	Turkey	March 17, 1903	1st	Richland
Kamoni, Ali	Turkey	March 28, 1905	2nd	Richland
Kanan, Shaker S.	Turkey	November 07, 1904	2nd	Stutsman
Kargosian, Rauken	Turkey	December 03, 1923	2nd	Stutsman
Karry, Alexander	Turkey	January 06, 1905	2nd	Ramsey
Kary, Alexander	Turkey	May 06, 1899	1st	Pierce
Kassis, Afaffee E.	Turkey	August 26, 1904	1st	Williams
Kassis, Assid	Turkey	June 01, 1898	1st	Pierce
Kassis, Assid	Turkey	December	2nd	Pierce
Kassis, John	Turkey	May 20, 1897	1st	Pierce
Kassis, John	Turkey	July 03, 1902	2nd	Pierce
Kateeb, Kallel	Turkey	May 22, 1920	2nd	Cass
Katz, Herman	Turkey	March 29, 1898	2nd	Cass
Kazala, Joseph	Turkey	September 03, 1902	1st	Pierce
Kazala, William	Turkey	September 03, 1902	1st	Pierce
Kazian, Charles	Turkey	August 03, 1936	1st	Burleigh
Kazian, Charles	Turkey	May 16, 1939	2nd	Burleigh
Kazola, William	Turkey	October 31, 1904	2nd	Pierce
Kenner, Masad	Turkey	November 07, 1904	2nd	Stutsman
Kenner, Richard	Turkey	November 07, 1904	2nd	Stutsman
Kgazzm, Mohamad Alle	Turkey	June 06, 1913	2nd	Mountrail
Killel, Albert	Turkey	April 24, 1917	2nd	Cass

Name	Country	Date	Papers	County
Killel, Widey	Turkey	August 12, 1916	1st	Cass
Kirk, Frank L.	Turkey	June 23, 1923	1st	Traill
Kirk, Frank Lazarus	Turkey	April 21, 1927	2nd	Traill
Kirk, Frank Lazarus	Turkey	September 28, 1925	2nd	Traill
Kirk, Richard B.	Turkey	November 29, 1901	2nd	Pierce
Kourajian, Hagek	Turkey	March 02, 1938	1st	Stutsman
Kourajian, Hagek	Turkey	August 17, 1942	2nd	Stutsman
Kouray, Albert	Turkey	April 02, 1902	1st	Pierce
Kouray, Albert	Turkey	April 02, 1906	2nd	McHenry
Kouray, Charley	Turkey	April 02, 1902	1st	Pierce
Kourney, Charles	Turkey	April 02, 1906	2nd	McHenry
Lambroff, George	Turkey	August 15, 1911	1st	Mountrail
Layon, Aspur	Turkey	November 29, 1901	2nd	Cass
Layon, Nicola	Turkey	March 27, 1902	1st	Ramsey
Lotiff, Joseph	Turkey	October 09, 1897	1st	Richland
Lowis, John	Turkey	May 04, 1910	1st	Grand Forks
Lyon, Calley	Turkey	December 12, 1902	1st	Ramsey
Lyon, Fahed	Turkey	April 02, 1902	1st	Pierce
Lyon, Fahed	Turkey	November 11, 1904	2nd	Cass
Lyon, Kalil M.	Turkey	May 20, 1922	2nd	Cass
Lyon, Kalil Mike	Turkey	March 17, 1919	1st	Cass
Lyon, Nicholas	Turkey	April 02, 1906	2nd	McHenry
Lyons, Abraham	Turkey	June 11, 1917	2nd	McKenzie
Lyons, Mike	Turkey	April 01, 1910	1st	Williams
Mackay, Sada	Turkey	October 01, 1908	2nd	Williams
Maik, John	Turkey	September 13, 1897	1st	Grand Forks
Maloff, Rosa	Turkey	February 26, 1900	1st	Towner
Maloof, Abraham	Turkey	August 12, 1905	1st	Williams
Maloof, Mair	Turkey	May 22, 1900	1st	Pierce
Maloof, Rahill	Turkey	November 09, 1901	1st	Pierce
Maloof, Said	Turkey	May 31, 1900	1st	Pierce
Maloof, Said	Turkey	July 11, 1906	2nd	McHenry
Maloof, Zamarrod	Turkey	July 22, 1907	2nd	Pierce
Maloof, Zamorrod	Turkey	July 08, 1901	1st	Pierce
Marat, Joseph	Turkey	November 07, 1904	2nd	Stutsman
Mardihiam, Alexan	Turkey	September 29, 1923	1st	Kidder
Margulies, Aaron	Turkey	February 09, 1915	2nd	Hettinger
Margulies, Idel	Turkey	February 10, 1914	2nd	Hettinger
Marmaras, Harry	Turkey	March 29, 1911	1st	Grand Forks
Marmaras, Harry	Turkey	October 05, 1916	2nd	Grand Forks
Marmaras, Nick	Turkey	August 14, 1912	1st	Grand Forks
Marron, Lotof John	Turkey	April 08, 1902	2nd	Walsh
Massad, George	Turkey	October 18, 1902	1st	Pierce
Massad, George	Turkey	March 14, 1911	2nd	Sheridan
Massahd, James	Turkey	April 24, 1903	1st	Ward
Maumanar, Mausstafa	Turkey	September 17, 1907	2nd	Stutsman
Mauradian, Marderos	Turkey	August 09, 1917	1st	Benson
Mauridian, George	Turkey	September 29, 1924	2nd	Stutsman
Maxoud, Bessie	Turkey	May 02, 1902	1st	Pierce
May, Lizzie	Turkey	July 07, 1898	1st	Foster

Name	Country	Date	Papers	County
Maydeen, Said	Turkey	March 09, 1903	1st	Pierce
Medlom, Masoov	Turkey	September 11, 1911	1st	Kidder
Medlom, Massod	Turkey	May 16, 1917	2nd	Dunn
Medlom, Massod	Turkey	December 00, 0000	2nd	Dunn
Meerzo, Abdo Dahoot	Turkey	October 08, 1915	1st	Grand Forks
Mehwood, Ebdol	Turkey	October 09, 1909	1st	Morton
Meksetian, Mekset	Turkey	May 02, 1922	1st	Williams
Meksetian, Mekset	Turkey	September 17, 1926	2nd	Williams
Melikian, Art	Turkey	October 22, 1925	2nd	Stutsman
Melikian, Arten	Turkey	June 09, 1922	1st	Burleigh
Melikian, Marguerite K.	Turkey	September 16, 1940	2nd	Stutsman
Menasian, Setrag	Turkey	September 16, 1943	1st	Cass
Merhiy, Houssyn	Turkey	December 24, 1909	1st	Cass
Millem, Hammett	Turkey	October 01, 1914	2nd	Mountrail
Minasian, Hagof M.	Turkey	November 08, 1924	1st	Nelson
Minasian, Hagop	Turkey	September 21, 1928	2nd	Nelson
Mograbe, Abdel R.	Turkey	February 28, 1910	1st	Kidder
Mohammed Bofamy	Turkey	September 11, 1911	1st	Kidder
Monssi, George	Turkey	November 05, 1894	2nd	Richland
Moshas, James	Turkey	July 17, 1919	1st	Wells
Moshas, James	Turkey	January 22, 1924	2nd	Wells
Mounnarar, Mousstafa M.	Turkey	June 24, 1905	1st	Stutsman
Mrid, Ally J.	Turkey	April 10, 1903	1st	Stutsman
Mrid, Ally J.	Turkey	December 20, 1918	1st	LaMoure
Mrid, Ally J.	Turkey	February 13, 1917	2nd	LaMoure
Mrid, Homet J.	Turkey	April 10, 1903	1st	Stutsman
Mseek, Abraham	Turkey	June 16, 1903	2nd	Walsh
Mseek, Mike	Turkey	June 16, 1903	2nd	Walsh
Mungar, Frank	Turkey	March 29, 1898	2nd	Cass
Munger, Mike	Turkey	July 24, 1902	1st	Ramsey
Munyer, Assif	Turkey	October 03, 1898	1st	Pierce
Munyer, Frand	Turkey	October 03, 1898	1st	Pierce
Mussallem, Sam	Turkey	February 26, 1900	1st	Towner
Nackola, Deap	Turkey	March 24, 1903	1st	Richland
Nackola, Salom	Turkey	March 24, 1903	1st	Richland
Nackola, Salom	Turkey	July 13, 1909	2nd	Sheridan
Namara, Dubes	Turkey	April 06, 1896	2nd	Cass
Namara, Mike	Turkey	April 04, 1896	2nd	Cass
Nami, Joseph	Turkey	May 16, 1904	2nd	Pierce
Neima, Mary	Turkey	April 25, 1917	1st	Cass
Neima, William Abraham	Turkey	November 07, 1913	1st	Cass
Neima, William Abraham	Turkey	January 08, 1918	2nd	Cass
Nemar, Salem	Turkey	November 14, 1899	1st	Pierce
Nicola, Solomon	Turkey	January 03, 1910	1st	Cass
Numar, Debis	Turkey	September 27, 1898	1st	Pierce
Numar, Mike	Turkey	September 27, 1898	1st	Pierce
Offor, Chrest	Turkey	March 21, 1919	1st	Cass
Ogill, Shdid	Turkey	May 02, 1903	1st	Stutsman
Okert, Karl	Turkey	July 19,1899	2nd	Stutsman
Olly, Mike	Turkey	October 25, 1902	1st	Pierce

Name	Country	Date	Papers	County
Omar, George	Turkey	June 07, 1906	1st	McHenry
Omar, George	Turkey	June 18, 1913	2nd	Rolette
Osman, Morris	Turkey	June 18, 1905	1st	Ward
Osman, Morris	Turkey	October 01, 1914	2nd	Mountrail
Othman, Ames	Turkey	July 07, 1913	1st	McIntosh
Papadopolos, Athanasis	Turkey	August 27,1926	1st	Ward
Papahatzis, Constantin	Turkey	August 29, 1944	2nd	Stark
Papazian, Miguirditch	Turkey	September 23, 1931	2nd	Cass
Papazian, Setrak	Turkey	July 10, 1911	1st	Williams
Pappas, Tom	Turkey	August 27, 1926	1st	Ward
Paristuin, Joe	Turkey	April 04, 1898	2nd	Cass
Pengelley, Doreen E.	Turkey	August 09, 1943	1st	Williams
Piedt, Jacob	Turkey	November 10, 1886	1st	Eddy
Piedt, Jacob	Turkey	November 01, 1894	2nd	Wells
Pitt, Fredrerica	Turkey	April 20, 1886	1st	Wells
Popoff, Theodore V.	Turkey	May 21, 1920	1st	LaMoure
Popoff, Theodore V.	Turkey	May 19, 1924	2nd	LaMoure
Popoff, V. P.	Turkey	December 00, 0000	2nd	LaMoure
Radetzke, Samuel	Turkey	July 01, 1896	1st	Ramsey
Saeg, Said	Turkey	May 31, 1907	1st	Logan
Rahal, Jeam	Turkey	March 08, 1906	1st	Williams
Rashid, Mamie	Turkey	July 10, 1912	1st	Adams
Razook, Abraham	Turkey	March 11, 1901	1st	Pierce
Rehal, Shebel	Turkey	November 10, 1904	1st	Williams
Remij, Aboul	Turkey	August 14, 1905	1st	Stutsman
Reney, Hassen	Turkey	March 05, 1921	1st	Burke
Renny, Abdul	Turkey	January 09, 1912	2nd	Kidder
Reunen, Richard	Turkey	June 21, 1902	1st	Stutsman
Roll, Jacob	Turkey	November 01, 1894	2nd	Wells
Romball, Walter F.	Turkey	May 16, 1900	2nd	Towner
Roseau, Mary	Turkey	November 08, 1897	1st	Pierce
Roseau, Mary	Turkey	June 16, 1903	2nd	Pierce
Roseau, Natali	Turkey	January 07, 1899	1st	Pierce
Noseau, Natalia	Turkey	June 16, 1903	2nd	Pierce
Rotenberg, Jonus	Turkey	September 03, 1888	1st	Ramsey
Ruff, Wilhelm	Turkey	July 14, 1897	2nd	Stutsman
Ruff, Wulhelm	Turkey	June 10, 1892	1st	Wells
Rumball, Walter F.	Turkey	June 13, 1893	1st	Rolette
Saad, Elias	Turkey	September 07, 1900	2nd	Eddy
Saba, Annie	Turkey	October 21, 1901	1st	Pierce
Saba, Joseph G.	Turkey	August 17, 1906	2nd	McHenry
Saba, Joseph G.	Turkey	August 16, 1901	1st	Pierce
Sabb, George	Turkey	November 14, 1899	1st	Pierce
Sabb, Joseph M.	Turkey	November 14, 1899	1st	Pierce
Sabb, Moses	Turkey	November 14, 1899	1st	Pierce
Safady, Nosser	Turkey	November 07, 1902	1st	Pierce
Sahaly, Wm.	Turkey	October 25, 1902	1st	Pierce
Said, Albert	Turkey	October 13, 1902	1st	Pierce
Sallemen, Tom	Turkey	December 09, 1913	1st	Williams
Sarkisian, Casper	Turkey	June 18, 1917	1st	Ramsey

Name	Country	Date	Papers	County
Satuff, Peter	Turkey	July 06, 1914	1st	Ramsey
Savaides, Youvan Sava	Turkey	January 02, 1917	2nd	Barnes
Sawaya, Abraham	Turkey	October 18, 1902	1st	Pierce
Sawaya, Kaley	Turkey	October 08, 1898	1st	Pierce
Sawaya, Mike	Turkey	February 26, 1906	1st	Pierce
Sawaya, Mike	Turkey	July 02, 1910	2nd	Pierce
Sawaya, Nassif	Turkey	December 08,1897	1st	Pierce
Sawaya, Nassif	Turkey	January 26, 1903	2nd	Ramsey
Sawaya, Risk	Turkey	November 03, 1900	2nd	Pierce
Sawaya, Rosa	Turkey	August 17, 1898	1st	Pierce
Sawaya, Zaheya	Turkey	May 21, 1901	1st	Pierce
Sawayo, Kalil	Turkey	January 26, 1903	2nd	Ramsey
Schicaney, Joseph T.	Turkey	March 01, 1900	1st	Pierce
Sebold, Peter	Turkey	November 03, 1884	1st	Foster
Seibold, Fred M.	Turkey	October 31, 1900	2nd	Wells
Seibolt, Peter	Turkey	November 08, 1889	2nd	Stutsman
Selbhashan, Meron	Turkey	May 18, 1917	1st	Ward
Semack, Samuel	Turkey	October 28,1908	1st	Cass
Shaben, Hassen	Turkey	March 21, 1902	1st	Pierce
Shabine, Mistofa	Turkey	January 30, 1902	1st	Wells
Shaddy, Hassan	Turkey	January 09, 1902	1st	Cass
Shaddy, Mahmoud	Turkey	March 21, 1902	1st	Pierce
Shaddy, Said	Turkey	March 21, 1902	1st	Pierce
Shaheen, Nassh	Turkey	April 27, 1917	1st	Cass
Shaheen, Toufic	Turkey	June 30, 1915	1st	Cass
Shaheen, Toufic	Turkey	November 04, 1919	2nd	Cass
Shaine, Mometood	Turkey	November 17, 1920	1st	Burke
Shakany, Elias N.	Turkey	November 03, 1902	2nd	Pierce
Shalla, Tom Mike	Turkey	October 16, 1922	1st	Benson
Shama, A.	Turkey	November 03, 1900	2nd	Pierce
Shama, Frada	Turkey	April 13, 1901	1st	Pierce
Shama, Frada	Turkey	January 24, 1906	2nd	Pierce
Shcaker, Alex G.	Turkey	February 06, 1905	2nd	Pierce
Shcakor, Alex	Turkey	June 12, 1899	1st	Pierce
Sheronick, Hamid	Turkey	March 22, 1902	1st	Pierce
Shicany, Elias N.	Turkey	April 18, 1898	1st	Pierce
Shicany, John	Turkey	July 03, 1902	2nd	Pierce
Shicany, Joseph	Turkey	October 13, 1898	1st	Pierce
Shicany, Joseph T.	Turkey	December 00, 0000	2nd	Pierce
Shicany, Ole	Turkey	December 00, 0000	2nd	Pierce
Shickany, Nassim	Turkey	December 18, 1902	1st	Pierce
Shicuny, Nicola	Turkey	June 28, 1897	1st	Pierce
Shwany, Mary	Turkey	September 28, 1898	1st	Pierce
Shwary, Mary	Turkey	June 16, 1903	2nd	Pierce
Shwery, Naiman	Turkey	April 28, 1902	1st	Pierce
Skaaf, Joseph	Turkey	August 25, 1902	2nd	Pierce
Smiley, Assis	Turkey	October 21, 1907	2nd	Pierce
Sofady, Nasser	Turkey	May 16, 1904	2nd	Pierce
Srour, Nicolas	Turkey	November 11, 1903	1st	Ramsey
Srour, Nicolas	Turkey	July 05, 1902	1st	Pierce

Name	Country	Date	Papers	County
Taleb, Mastafa	Turkey	March 21, 1902	1st	Pierce
Tamer, Patros	Turkey	September 11, 1911	1st	Cass
Tans, Ebraham J.	Turkey	November 03, 1894	2nd	Richland
Tarpinian, Aghavnie	Turkey	September 16, 1940	2nd	Stutsman
Tarpinian, Garabed	Turkey	April 16, 1923	1st	Stutsman
Tennis, Joseph	Turkey	November 20, 1897	1st	Towner
Thomas, Deep	Turkey	May 15, 1897	1st	Towner
Thomas, Derp	Turkey	May 27, 1903	2nd	Towner
Townas, Joseph	Turkey	October 29, 1900	2nd	Towner
Tsoumpariotis, Nicholas	Turkey	November 10, 1917	2nd	Grand Forks
Tsoumpariotis, Nick	Turkey	July 14, 1912	1st	Grand Forks
Turk, Chas	Turkey	April 04, 1898	2nd	Cass
Vartamian, Sam	Turkey	February 23, 1917	1st	Richland
Wazer, Elias	Turkey	July 07, 1902	2nd	Pierce
Wazer, Metre	Turkey	June 16, 1903	2nd	Pierce
Wazer, Metree	Turkey	July 05, 1897	1st	Pierce
Wendland, Fridrich	Turkey	November 25, 1882	1st	Stutsman
Windland, Jacob	Turkey	December 26, 1882	1st	Stutsman
Womis, Edieb	Turkey	June 22, 1903	1st	Burleigh
Yeramian, Arshalonis	Turkey	February 27, 1926	1st	Stutsman
Yonas, Sam	Turkey	June 16, 1906	2nd	Pierce
Yonas, Silo	Turkey	November 08, 1900	1st	Pierce
Yonas, Tanous	Turkey	April 28, 1902	1st	Pierce
Yonesse, Kallel	Turkey	October 13, 1898	1st	Pierce
Younas, Joseph	Turkey	June 26, 1902	1st	Pierce
Younes, Joseph	Turkey	May 22, 1914	2nd	Williams
Zakes, Gust	Turkey	November 15, 1939	1st	Adams
Zakes, Gust	Turkey	August 29, 1944	2nd	Stark
Zammiatta, Charley	Turkey	November 08, 1905	1st	Ward
Zeer, Mohammer	Turkey	November 25, 1902	1st	Pierce
Zien, Lottia	Turkey	October 01, 1908	2nd	Williams
Zihn, Mary	Turkey	April 24, 1902	1st	Pierce
Zine, Eddie	Turkey	March 21, 1911	1st	Williams
Zine, Fred C.	Turkey	April 24, 1909	1st	Williams
Ziton, Nicholas	Turkey	September 03, 1906	1st	Emmons
Zyady, John	Turkey	June 19, 1900	1st	Pierce

Arabia

Name	Country	Date	Papers	County
Abdoud, Tom	Arabia	April 14, 1909	1st	Williams
Albert, Joseph	Arabia	March 26, 1909	1st	Williams
BuToumay, Sarkers	Arabia	March 17, 1896	1st	Richland
Dann, Thomas	Arabia	June 30, 1902	1st	Ramsey
Farris, Mhadeen B.	Arabia	July 07, 1919	1st	Pembina
Foshiti, Joseph	Arabia	April 14, 1902	1st	Ward
Jurima, Hassen	Arabia	April 14, 1902	1st	Ward
Musti, Albert	Arabia	April 14, 1902	1st	Ward
Rahmen, Abdul	Arabia	April 19, 1902	1st	Ward
Smili, Esses	Arabia	November 01, 1902	1st	Burleigh

Name	Country	Date	Papers	County
Sofy, Michael J.	Arabia	March 17, 1896	1st	Richland
Tallib, Amot	Arabia	November 01, 1902	1st	Burleigh
Toumay, Sakes Bu	Arabia	March 17, 1896	1st	Richland
Vangstad, Edward	Arabia	April 14, 1902	1st	Ward
Willem, Joseph	Arabia	June 14, 1902	1st	Burleigh

Egypt

Aggie, Soman Aid	Egypt	September 20, 1924	2nd	Cass
Hannoun, Aziz	Egypt	May 24, 1907	1st	Williams
Rye, Alexander	Egypt	March 13, 1916	1st	Burleigh

Persia

Alamschak, Paulus	Persia	June 02, 1892	1st	Stutsman
Pera, Augustin	Persia	November 22, 1920	1st	Mountrail
Pera, Augustin	Persia	May 26, 1924	2nd	Mountrail

Lebanon

Ayash, John Joseph	Lebanon	September 29, 1947	2nd	Ward
Nedoff, Edward	Lebanon	June 26, 1937	1st	Williams

Palestine

Eli, Hassen	Palestine	July 07, 1908	2nd	Stutsman

Appendix C

Land Acquisition Records (B.L.M.)

Listed below are Syrian-Lebanese individuals who received title for their land at the completion of their homestead, "tree claim," or preemption requirements. As mentioned in the Introduction this information comes from the Internet through the courtesy of Joe Zsedeny and Joy Fisher. The following address is given as an example of a search of Bureau of Land Management (BLM) records for Pierce County, N.D.: ftp://ftp.rootsweb.com/pub/usgenweb/nd/pierce/land/pier-ab.txt

Note that dates entered below are the times of completion, not the original moment of filing. Completion could be anywhere from two to as many as ten years (and even longer) after the filing took place. Those who filed and for some reason (abandonment? relinquishment?) never "proved up" are not on this list. Their numbers are often considerable: sometimes 30 percent? 40 percent? This compilation of names, therefore, does not represent the total number of individuals who were present on land at one time or another in any given county.

Additional Note: The list probably contains numerous misspellings: indistinct handwriting? clerks' errors? difficulties in converting Arabic names into English-sounding letter-symbols?

No country of origin is indicated in the land office books. This list has been extracted by the authors from a North Dakota all-national group compilation by the "sound of the name" and geographic location method. This procedure has its obvious problems. Some entries may sound "Arabic" and are not. Some Arabic names are so Anglicized that they are unrecognizable. Yet the information presented below presents a general picture of the times and places of Lebanese settlement and that in itself has value.

Name	Township	Section	Acreage	Date of Acquisition
ADAMS COUNTY				
Bussamas, John C.	T129-R95	23	40	6/16/1910
Bussammas, John C.	T129-R95	24	40	6/16/1910
Rashid, Peter	T129-95	34	80	12/1/1909
BENSON COUNTY				
Abraham, Henry	T152-R65	36	40	8/19/1920
Sams, Joseph H.	T155-R70	6	40	3/12/1901
Sams, Joseph H.	T155-R70	6	40.16	3/23/1901
Sams, Joseph H.	T155-R70	6	38	3/23/1901
Sams, Joseph H.	T155-R70	6	37.93	3/23/1901
Sawaya, Mike	T155-R71	19	160	3/1/1909
BOTTINEAU COUNTY				
Ally, Abraham	T159-R81	15	160	12/30/1904
BOWMAN COUNTY				
Hedeen, Adolph Peter	T130-R104	35	160	5/20/1912
Hedeen, Adolph Peter	T130-R104	35	160	2/12/1916
Hedeen, Adolph Peter	T130-R104	35	160	2/12/1916
Hedeen, Adolph Peter	T130-R104	35	160	2/12/1916
BURLEIGH COUNTY				
Dbysh, Martin	T138-R81	13	25.05	1/11/1919
Dbysh, Martin	T138-R81	13	31.70	1/11/1919
Dykowna, Alle	T144-R78	34	120	3/6/1911
CASS COUNTY				
Agasadeba, Joseph	T139-R52	14	160	10/10/1876
Smylie, Thomas A.	T138-R53	4	80	10/4/1884
Smylie, Thomas A.	T138-R53	4	39.69	10/4/1884
Smylie, Thomas A.	T138-R53	4	39.81	10/4/1884
Smylie, William M.	T139-R53	34	160	6/30/1882
CAVALIER COUNTY				
Abraham, Albert	T161-R63	4	40	9/5/1903
Abraham, Albert	T161-R63	4	39.77	9/5/1903
Fagg, Jabez W.	T161-R60	19	80	12/7/1897
Fagg, Jabez W.	T161-R60	19	40.56	12/7/1897
Fagg, Jabez W.	T161-R60	19	40.52	12/7/1897
Massoz, Joseph	T161-R60	34	160	5/25/1900
Mostad, Nicolay A.	T163-R58	22	80	5/8/1901
Mostad, Nicolay A.	T163-R58	27	80	5/8/1901
DICKEY COUNTY				
Ameen, Ahmed	T129-R66	34	160	1/28/1910
Eassom, George W.	T131-R64	27	160	10/16/1889
Side, Abraham	T129-R66	29	160	7/26/1909

Name	Township	Section	Acreage	Date of Acquisition
DUNN COUNTY				
Sage, Alex	T147-R93	4	320	4/12/1922
Sage, Alex	T147-R93	5	40	4/12/1922
Sage, Alex	T147-R93	4	320	4/12/1922
Sage, Alex	T147-R93	5	40	7/3/1918
Sage, Alex	T147-R93	5	40	4/15/1921
Sage, Sylvan Sybert	T147-R95	1	80	8/29/1924
Sage, Sylvan Sybert	T147-R95	1	80	8/29/1924
Sage, Sylvan Sybert	T147-R95	1	38.85	8/29/1924
Sage, Sylvan Sybert	T147-R95	1	1.15	8/29/1924
Sage, Sylvan Sybert	T147-R95	1	38.85	8/29/1924
Sage, Sylvan Sybert	T147-R95	1	1.15	8/29/1924
Sage, Sylvan Sybert	T148-R95	36	80	8/29/1924
EDDY COUNTY				
Sadd, Elias	T149-R66	35	80	3/23/1901
EMMONS COUNTY				
Abia, John C.	T129-R77	10	160	5/10/1893
Aboling, John	T131-R78	34	80	5/20/1909
Aboling, John	T131-R76	20	80	5/27/1907
Abraham, Annie	T129-R77	33	120	2/11/1910
Abraham, Annie	T129-R77	34	40	2/11/1910
Abraham, George	T130-R78	13	80	5/27/1913
Abraham, George	T130-R78	24	80	9/6/1957
Adsit, Charlie W.	T130-R77	20	160	12/1/1904
George, Peter	T129-R77	33	120	9/17/1907
George, Peter	T129-R77	34	40	9/17/1907
Hammitt, Henry	T130-R79	23	160	6/29/1891
GRAND FORKS COUNTY				
Mahood, Stephen	T150-R56	13	160	10/24/1891
GRANT COUNTY				
Abourzk, Paul	T137-R89	30	160	7/13/1911
GRIGGS COUNTY				
Sebbey, Christian T.	T144-R61	24	160	12/12/1891
KIDDER COUNTY				
Eli, Hassen	T138-R70	24	160	5/16/1912
Eli, Mahmond	T138-R70	24	160	12/13/1910
Eli, Willie	T138-R70	14	160	1/7/1914
Hamsey, Albert	T139-R74	30	160	4/20/1909
Hamsey, Ased	T139-R74	32	160	9/26/1910
Hamsey, Namy	T139-R74	30	80	4/20/1909
Hamsey, Namy	T139-R74	30	38.74	4/20/1909
Hamsey, Namy	T139-R74	30	38.81	4/20/1909

Name	Township	Section	Acreage	Date of Acquisition
Hasel, Joe	T142-R71	2	21.40	9/20/1922
Hasel, Joseph	T143-R70	26	160	12/17/1912
Hash, Ali	T142-R70	12	80	10/21/1909
Sam, Howard	T139-R70	12	24.71	3/14/1916
Sam, Howard	T139-R70	12	15.29	9/26/1984
LAMOURE COUNTY				
Bassen, Henry	T136-R60	34	160	6/27/1889
Bassen, John P.	T136-R60	32	160	6/27/1894
McHENRY COUNTY				
Abdillah, Hamid	T159-R79	23	40	7/18/1905
Abraham, Albert	T155-R77	19	80	8/15/1958
Abraham, Albert	T155-R77	19	35.24	4/15/1977
Abraham, Albert	T155-R77	19	35.28	4/15/1977
Albert, Allick	T157-R76	26	80	2/11/1910
Albert, Frank	T151-R75	5	80	12/31/1904
Albert, Frank	T151-R75	5	40.11	12/31/1904
Albert, Frank	T151-R75	5	40.17	12/31/1904
Albert, George	T155-R77	19	80	10/14/1909
Albert, George	T155-R77	19	35.32`	10/14/1909
Albert, George	T155-R77	19	35.36	10/14/1909
Allick, Joseph	T155-R77	18	160	12/1/1909
Allick, Sam	T155-R78	24	160	9/18/1907
Ferris, Albert	T155-R78	23	160	10/26/1908
Ferris, Asmil	T155-R77	20	160	2/13/1908
Handy, Abdallo	T155-R75	7	120	6/16/1904
Handy, Abdallo	T155-R75	7	33.50	6/16/1904
Handy, Lloyd	T157-R79	23	160	8/23/1907
Handy, Nathan D.	T157-R78	18	160	4/5/1907
Hassen, Amel	T155-R78	12	160	12/1/1909
Hassien, Sayid A.	T157-R76	23	120	7/18/1903
Omar, George	T155-R77	19	160	10/14/1909
Shibley, Lyle D.	T155-R79	25	160	1/2/1908
McINTOSH COUNTY				
Abraham, Achmidt	T131-R68	31	80	4/21/1910
Abraham, Achmidt	T131-R68	31	43.66	4/21/1910
Abraham, Achmidt	T131-R68	31	43.89	4/21/1910
Abraham, Albert	T131-R69	24	120	1/28/1909
Abraham, Albert	T131-R69	24	20	1/28/1909
Abraham, Albert	T131-R69	24	20	1/28/1909
Abraham, Said	T131-R67	32	80	1/8/1912
Abraham, Said	T131-R67	33	80	1/8/1912

Name	Township	Section	Acreage	Date of Acquisition
Albert, Abraham	T130-R67	17	80	2/4/1905
Albert, Abraham	T130-R67	18	80	2/4/1905
Alec, Albert	T129-R67	31	80	9/10/1908
Alec, Albert	T129-R67	32	80	9/10/1908
Alleck, George	T131-R69	23	80	2/4/1909
Alleck, George	T131-R69	24	80	2/4/1909
Bahy, Sam	T131-R67	29	80	12/19/1907
Bahy, Sam	T131-R67	30	80	12/19/1907
Cadry, Mickal	T129-R67	9	10.5	2/4/1904
Cadry, Mickal	T129-R67	9	29.5	10/8/1965
Cadry, Mickal	T129-R67	9	36.6	10/8/1965
Cadry, Mickal	T129-R67	9	3.4	10/8/1965
Cadry, Mickal	T129-R67	9	10.7	10/8/1965
Cadry, Mickal	T129-R67	9	29.9	10/8/1965
Cadry, Sahid	T130-R67	21	160	3/11/1905
Fay, George H.	T129-R69	7	80	12/21/1889
Fay, George H.	T129-R69	7	39.96	12/21/1889
Fay, George H.	T129-R69	7	39.97	12/21/1889
Fay, Saleme	T131-R67	28	160	1/25/1909
Haggar, Assaf	T130-R67	33	80	2/4/1905
Haggar, Joseph	T130-R67	17	160	2/4/1905
Haggar, Salamon	T130-R67	5	37.70	5/12/1905
Haggar, Salamon	T131-R67	32	120	5/12/1905
Hamway, Abraham	T131-R67	29	160	8/8/1910
Hamway, Alex	T130-R67	5	37.36	9/21/1908
Hamway, Alex	T131-R67	32	160	9/21/1908
Hamway, Sahid	T129-R67	26	120	8/20/1907
Hasz, David	T131-R68	6	40	12/1/1909
Hasz, David	T131-R68	6	39.61	12/1/1909
Hasz, David	T131-R68	6	39.77	12/1/1909
Hasz, David	T131-R68	6	39.15	12/1/1909
Hazemy, Caleb	T131-R68	20	160	1/17/1910
Hiawatha, Joe	T131-R68	30	120	4/16/1909
Hiawatha, Joe	T131-R68	30	42.38	4/16/1909
Kacem, Albert	T131-R69	23	80	9/21/1908
Kacem, Albert	T131-R69	26	80	9/21/1908
Kacem, Frank	T131-R68	18	41.37	9/10/1908
Kacem, Frank	T131-R68	19	40	9/10/1908
Kacem, Frank	T131-R68	19	41.56	9/10/1908
Kacem, Frank	T131-R68	19	41.77	9/10/1908
Kaddy, Alli	T130-R68	10	40	9/21/1908
Kaddy, Alli	T130-R68	11	40	9/21/1908
Kaddy, Alli	T130-R68	14	80	9/21/1908
Meyries, Abraham	T130-R68	23	80	8/1/1904
Meyries, Abraham	T130-R68	23	24.50	8/1/1904
Meyries, Abraham	T130-R68	23	28.80	8/1/1904

Name	Township	Section	Acreage	Date of Acquisition
Omar, Emil	T131-R68	21	160	6/27/1910
Omer, Machmod	T131-R68	15	160	6/27/1910
Osman, Monstaf	T131-R68	21	160	9/21/1908
Sain, Alex	T131-R68	30	80	2/3/1910
Sakeen, Albert	T130-R68	9	40	2/4/1905
Sakeen, Albert	T130-R68	10	120	2/4/1905
McKENZIE COUNTY				
Bousliman, Aasad	T152-R101	21	160	1/14/1919
Bousliman, Aasad	T152-R101	28	160	1/14/1919
Fallon, Allie	T151-R101	28	40	4/5/1916
Fallon, Allie	T151-R101	29	120	4/5/1916
Fallon, John H.	T151-R101	29	80	12/6/1912
Fallon, John H.	T151-R101	30	80	12/6/1912
Fallon, Laura E.	T151-R101	29	160	12/5/1914
Farris, Fauze Nassif	T152-R101	32	160	6/6/1912
Grawan, Habib	T150-R102	17	320	11/11/1916
Grawan, Habib	T150-R102	17	320	8/1/1936
Mike, Abraham	T152-R101	32	40	11/7/1914
Mike, Abraham	T152-R101	33	160	11/7/1914
Mike, Abraham	T152-R101	28	40	6/2/1920
Sem, Haaken	T149-R100	3	120	9/23/1912
Sem, Haaken	T149-R100	3	40.46	9/23/1912
McLEAN COUNTY				
Abdallah, Michael	T149-R80	14	160	10/14/1909
Babiak, Jawdoha	T145-R79	28	160	5/27/1909
Hallem, Ed	T150-R86	30	80	12/13/1909
Hallem, Ed	T150-R86	30	37.56	12/13/1909
Hallem, Ed	T150-R86	30	37.64	12/13/1909
Haslam, Anna J.R.	T150-R82	30	160	3/9/1908
Hatoom, Alex	T149-R79	25	160	9/10/1908
Zarh, Mohammed	T149-R79	25	160	12/18/1908
Zarh, Syde	T149-R79	25	160	8/7/1906
MERCER COUNTY				
Sage, Alex	T147-R89	35	5	4/12/1922
Sage, Alex	T147-R89	35	35	4/12/1922
Sage, Alexander	T146-R88	8	40	4/12/1922
Sage, Gertrude	T147-R90	14	160	8/29/1924
Sage, Gertrude	T147-R90	14	40	8/29/1924
Sage, Gertrude	T147-R90	14	37.25	8/29/1924
Sage, Gertrude	T147-R90	14	2.75	8/29/1924
Sage, Gertrude	T147-R90	23	40	8/29/1924
Sage, Gertrude	T147-R90	23	40	8/29/1924

Name	Township	Section	Acreage	Date of Acquisition
MORTON COUNTY				
Dbysh, Martin	T138-R81	12	40	1/11/1919
Hassan, Isaac M.	T136-R84	34	160	1/24/1910
MOUNTRAIL COUNTY				
Aabia, Asmund	T156-R89	6	80	11/16/1908
Aaby, Asmund	T156-R89	8	80	3/27/1911
Abdalla, Alle	T156-R92	28	80	5/23/1906
Abdalla, Alle	T156-R92	33	80	5/23/1906
Abdallah, Amid	T157-R92	12	240	7/9/1917
Abdallah, Hamid	T156-R92	4	120	8/19/1907
Abedahl, Side	T156-R92	34	160	4/9/1908
Adray, Abdalla	T156-R92	34	160	5/23/1906
Adray, Abdul Ramen	T155-R91	29	160	3/27/1911
Adray, Urgab	T156-R92	34	160	2/15/1909
Afseth, Theodore	T157-R92	1	80	8/19/1907
Afseth, Theodore	T157-R92	1	40	8/19/1907
Afseth, Theodore	T157-R92	1	40	8/19/1907
Alle, Annis	T155-R92	18	160	8/19/1907
Alle, Siad	T156-R92	14	160	8/19/1907
Caled, Ally	T156-R92	35	160	1/28/1909
Farhart, Abdul	T153-R93	8	40	5/2/1910
Farhart, Abdul	T153-R93	8	20	5/2/1910
Farhart, Abdul	T153-R93	8	20	5/2/1910
Farhart, Abdul	T153-R93	8	20	5/2/1910
Farhart, Abdul	T153-R93	8	20	5/2/1910
Farhart, Abdul	T153-R93	8	6.75	5/2/1910
Farhart, Abdul	T153-R93	8	33.25	5/2/1910
Farhart, Ahmed	T155-R92	8	80	8/13/1908
Farhart, Ahmed	T156-R92	28	80	8/19/1907
Farhart, Hasen	T156-R92	33	160	6/23/1910
Farhart, Jisam	T154-R94	13	120	7/12/1915
Farhart, Jisam	T154-R94	14	40	7/12/1915
Farhart, Jisam	T154-R94	13	40	11/30/1915
Farhart, Bo Aley	T156-R92	4	160	5/29/1911
Farhite, Joseph	T156-R92	22	160	5/23/1906
Forhiot, Ally	T153-R93	2	120	3/27/1911
Forhiot, Ally	T153-R93	2	39.42	3/27/1911
Forhit, Hassen	T156-R92	24	160	4/9/1908
Gannany, Ally	T157-R90	22	160	
Hamid, Moses	T156-R92	13	160	5/23/1906
Hassen, Hamid	T156-R92	13	160	5/23/1906
Hassen, Rymn	T157-R92	24	160	6/11/1912

Name	Township	Section	Acreage	Date of Acquisition
Hassien, Salem	T157-R92	14	240	4/30/1921
Ish, Alay	T155-R92	20	160	2/17/1908
Jobe, Booten	T151-R91	3	80	
Jobe, Booten	T151-R91	3	80	
Joseph, Allie (heirs of)	T156-R93	28	160	10/23/1907
Joseph, Allie (heirs of)	T156-R93	28	160	9/6/1957
Jossart, Moses	T152-R91	12	80	3/15/1916
Jossart, Moses	T152-R91	12	30.78	3/15/1916
Jossart, Moses	T152-R91	12	30.80	3/15/1916
Jossart, Moses	T152-R91	12	30.83	3/15/1916
Juha, Allie Resenk	T155-R92	6	80	5/21/1908
Juha, Allie Resenk	T155-R92	7	80	5/21/1908
Juha, Amid Asse	T156-R92	35	160	9/21/1908
Juha, Juja Allie	T156-R92	35	160	9/21/1908
Juma, Hassyn Alla	T157-R92	27	40	8/1/1934
Juma, Ramed	T157-R92	25	40	7/18/49
Juma, Selim Calid	T157-R92	20	80	1/23/1914
Jumma, Hassen	T156-R92	23	160	1/6/1908
Mosfa, Abdil	T156-R92	27	160	12/16/1907
Mostaf, Isha	T156-R91	6	60.51	4/1/1909
Mostaf, Isha	T157-R92	24	40	9/23/1914
Mostaf, Isha	T157-R92	25	40	9/23/1914
Mostafa, Mhamed	T156-R92	22	160	4/11/1907
Ohmar, Ally	T156-R92	3	40	4/7/1910
Ohmar, Ally	T157-R92	25	40	1/23/1914
Ohmar, Ally	T157-R92	26	80	1/23/1914
Omar, Abdullah	T156-R92	33	120	6/19/1911
Omar, Alley	T155-R92	8	160	4/10/1911
Omar, Gasman	T156-R92	26	160	2/5/1906
Omar, Sam	T155-R92	5	80	8/13/1907
Omar, Sam	T155-R92	8	80	8/13/1907
Osman, Ahmed	T156-R92	29	160	6/26/1906
Osman, Morris	T156-R92	4	160	9/6/1907
Rahmen, Abdul	T156-R92	23	160	9/26/1906
Rezouk, Coleal	T155-R93	14	160	4/7/1910
Robbins, Asahel S.	T154-R93	27	80	6/25/1913
Robbins, Asahel S.	T154-R93	27	39.06	6/25/1913
Robbins, Asahel S.	T154-R93	27	0.94	6/25/1913
Robbins, Asahel S.	T154-R93	27	36.23	
Salaba, Frank J.	T155-R93	2	40	12/1/1909
Salaba, Frank J.	T155-R93	11	40	12/1/1909
Salaba, Frank J.	T155-R93	12	80	12/1/1909

Name	Township	Section	Acreage	Date of Acquisition
Saby, Malenius	T155-R94	7	160	9/14/1916
Sadden, Mhamed	T156-R92	27	160	5/21/1908
Selem, Albert	T156-R92	27	160	3/26/1908
Selem, Omar	T156-R92	27	160	3/26/1908
Shady, Mohamed	T155-R92	7	40	6/18/1908
Shady, Mohamed	T155-R92	7	36.65	6/18/1908
Sian, Alle	T156-R92	15	160	6/26/1906
Sian, Boshama	T156-R92	13	160	9/24/1907
Sien, Addallh	T155-R92	6	40	3/28/1910
Sien, Addallh	T155-R92	6	36.58	3/28/1910
Sien, Addallh	T155-R92	7	40	3/28/910
Sien, Addallh	T155-R92	7	36.61	3/28/1910
PEMBINA COUNTY				
Ady, George	T159-R53	22	160	10/15/1884
Gamash, Peter	T161-R57	7	160	2/13/1891
PIERCE COUNTY				
Abraham, Joseph	T154-R73	25	80	12/1/1904
Abraham, Joseph	T154-R73	25	80	6/29/1907
Albit, Alli	T157-R74	34	40	5/7/1904
Awad, Rahil	T155-R72	33	80	5/7/1904
Baba, Joseph	T154-R72	17	40	6/6/1907
Baba, Joseph	T154-R73	18	120	10/2/1905
Bahne, Saleem	T153-R73	1	80	7/2/1904
Bahne, Saleem	T153-R73	1	40.01	7/2/1904
Bahne, Saleem	T153-R73	1	40.03	7/2/1904
Balesh, Joseph	T158-R72	10	80	5/7/1904
Balesh, Joseph	T158-R72	15	80	5/7/1904
Bonfiasll, Fiasll	T154-R73	31	80	12/1/1904
Bonfiasll, Fiasll	T154-R73	31	37.66	12/1/1904
Bonfiasll, Fiasll	T154-R73	31	37.86	12/1/1904
Bossin, Davis	T155-R72	3	80	9/16/1904
Bossin, Davis	T155-R72	3	39.76	9/16/1904
Bossin, Davis	T155-R72	3	39.86	9/16/1904
Bourstum, Abraham	T155-R72	35	160	10/10/1902
Boussad, Abraham	T156-R72	32	160	8/27/1901
Boussad, Joseph	T156-R72	32	160	3/19/1904
Boussad, Joseph	T155-R72	2	80	5/7/1904
Boussad, Joseph	T155-R72	2	40.03	5/7/1904
Boussad, Joseph	T155-R72	2	39.91	5/7/1904
Boussad, Mary	T156-R72	33	160	9/5/1905
Boussad, Najeeb	T156-R72	28	120	5/2/1903
Boussad, Najeeb	T156-R72	21	40	9/15/1904
Boussad, Nassef	T156-72	28	160	10/10/1904

Name	Township	Section	Acreage	Date of Acquisition
Boussad, Richard	T156-R72	32	160	3/1/1904
Dann, Abdella	T154-R72	12	160	8/12/1902
David, Albert	T154-R72	23	80	3/27/1905
David, Alex	T154-R72	14	160	5/14/1906
David, Atlas	T154-R72	2	160	8/18/1902
David, Salima (heirs of)	T154-R72	20	80	6/10/1909
David, Tanous	T154-R72	14	40	10/28/1904
David, Tanous	T154-R72	15	40	10/28/1904
David, Tanous	T154-R72	11	40	5/25/1908
Dean, Seba A.	T151-R74	11	40	1/13/1910
Dean, Seba A.	T151-R74	12	80	1/13/1910
Dowalabee, Mary	T155-R72	5	120	8/18/1902
Dowalabee, Mary	T155-R72	5	40	4/11/1907
Emslie, Allie	T155-R72	2	39.79	5/2/1905
Emslie, Allie	T155-R72	35	120	5/2/1905
Emslie, Ruth A.	T155-R72	2	40	11/10/1903
Emslie, Ruth A.	T155-R72	2	39.67	11/10/1903
Emslie, Ruth A.	T155-R72	2	40	11/10/1903
Emslie, Ruth A.	T155-R72	2	39.66	11/10/1903
Esta, Filimena	T155-R72	4	40	
Esta, Helen	T155-R72	4	40.04	
Esta, Helen	T155-R72	4	40.12	
Esta, Helen	T155-R72	33	80	
Esta, Phillemina (heirs of)	T155-R72	28	40	
Esto, Joseph	T156-R72	21	160	
Fadel, Kaly S.	T157-R71	10	40	7/2/1904
Fadel, Kaly S.	T157-R71	10	22.20	7/2/1904
Fadel, Kaly S.	T157-R71	10	21.50	7/2/1904
Fadel, Kaly S.	T157-R71	10	41.70	7/2/1904
Fadel, Kaly S.	T157-R71	10	39.30	7/1/1904
Ferris, Benjamin A.	T158-R74	22	80	5/23/1893
Ferris, Benjamin A.	T158-R74	22	36.30	5/23/1893
Ferris, Benjamin A.	T158-R74	22	27.80	5/23/1893
Ferris, Henry	T158-R74	32	160	5/23/1893
Ferris, Mike Assid	T154-R73	28	160	5/4/1905
Feyatt, Charley	T158-R72	10	80	12/1/1904
Feyatt, Charley	T158-R72	11	80	12/1/1904
Feyiad, Mary	T158-R72	14	80	1/21/1909
Feyiad, Mary	T158-R72	15	80	1/21/1909
Haasen, Kittil O.	T157-R69	14	160	4/6/1897
Haman, Adam	T155-R74	17	80	
Haman, Adam	T155-R74	8	40	
Haman, Adam	T155-R74	17	140	
Hash, Mohammed L.	T152-R73	7	80	3/1/1909
Hash, Mohammed L.	T152-R73	7	29.36	3/1/1909
Hash, Mohammed L.	T152-R73	7	29.49	3/1/1909

Name	Township	Section	Acreage	Date of Acquisition
Hassien, Sayid A.	T156-R74	2	40	3/16/1906
Hatoom, Sam	T154-R72	5	120	8/3/1904
Hatoom, Sam	T154-R72	1	40	5/5/1905
Heddie, Daywood	T154-R73	26	160	8/3/1904
Heddie, Sam	T154-R73	26	120	12/30/1904
Heddie, Sam	T154-R73	27	40	12/30/1904
Hepip, Dep	T155-R72	19	120	2/4/1905
Hepip, Dep	T155-R72	19	36.86	2/4/1905
Hepip, Frank	T156-R72	21	40	5/21/1904
Hepip, Frank	T156-R72	22	80	5/21/1904
Hesen, Mahmond	T153-R74	20	80	12/30/1904
Hesen, Mahmond	T153-R74	29	80	12/30/1904
Hyyssen, Carl H.	T153-R72	1	80	10/19/1911
Hyyssen, Carl H.	T153-R72	12	80	10/19/1911
Kaftan, Michael	T151-R74	12	160	3/30/1904
Kassis, Abraham	T156-R72	29	160	7/1/1903
Kassis, Assid	T155-R72	1	120	7/2/1904
Kassis, Assid	T155-R72	1	37.40	7/2/1904
Kassis, Charley	T155-R72	4	80	5/15/1903
Kassis, Charley	T155-R72	4	40.20	5/15/1903
Kassis, Charley	T155-R72	4	40.28	5/15/1903
Kassis, John	T156-R72	29	160	3/19/1904
Kazala, Joseph	T158-R72	11	40	12/12/1904
Kazala, William	T158-R72	25	40	2/4/1905
Kazala, William	T158-R72	26	80	2/4/1905
Kirk, Richard	T155-R72	5	160	
Kouray, Albert	T156-R72	26	40	10/19/1911
Kouray, Albert	T154-R73	27	120	2/4/1905
Kouray, Charley	T154-R73	28	160	8/23/1904
Maloaf, Said	T154-R72	1	60	12/16/1906
Maloof, Zamorrod	T154-R72	2	40	4/27/1908
Maloof, Zamorrod	T154-R72	11	80	4/27/1908
Maloof, Zamorrod	T154-R72	12	40	4/27/1908
Maset, Joseph	T153-R74	4	80	7/20/1911
Maset, Joseph	T153-R74	9	80	7/20/1911
Munyer, Assef	T155-R72	3	40	12/31/1904
Munyer, Assef	T155-R72	3	39.96	12/31/1904
Munyer, Assef	T155-R72	34	80	12/31/1904
Munyer, Mike	T154-R73	6	39.22	
Munyer, Mike	T154-R73	25	80	
Munyer, Frank	T156-R72	34	160	12/1/1904
Razook, Abraham	T155-R72	13	160	7/22/1903
Roseau, Mary	T155-R72	10	160	8/10/1906

Name	Township	Section	Acreage	Date of Acquisition
Roseau, Natalia	T155-R72	10	160	12/31/1904
Saba, Joseph G.	T155-R72	24	160	8/21/1907
Saba, Wolf	T155-R72	22	160	12/1/1904
Sabia, Kabal	T155-R72	9	160	4/8/1904
Salem, Ole K.	T156-R74	22	120	3/30/1904
Salem, Ole K.	T156-R74	23	40	3/30/1904
Sali, Jacob	T152-R72	15	120	2/18/1903
Sawaya, Abraham (heirs of)	T154-R74	7	160	5/5/1905
Sawaya, Afefy	T156-R72	28	80	11/24/1903
Sawaya, Afefy	T156-R72	33	80	11/24/1903
Sawaya, Kaly	T156-R72	21	40	3/30/1905
Sawaya, Kaly	T156-R72	22	80	3/30/1905
Sawaya, Kaly	T156-R72	28	40	3/30/1905
Sawaya, Nassif	T156-R72	27	80	4/8/1904
Sawaya, Nassif	T156-R72	28	80	4/8/1904
Shaben, Hassan	T153-R74	27	160	6/16/1904
Shaddy, Hassan	T152-R74	20	40	10/10/1904
Shaddy, Hassan	T152-R74	21	80	10/10/1904
Shama, Frada	T157-R72	17	80	2/6/1908
Shama, Frada	T157-R72	18	80	2/6/1908
Shawa, Abdalla	T157-R72	7	160	2/4/1905
Shcakor, Alex G.	T154-R72	1	40	9/5/1905
Shcakor, Alex G.	T154-R72	12	120	9/5/1905
Shedin, Charles	T153-R73	5	160	10/26/1908
Shicany, John	T156-R72	33	160	10/16/1903
Shicany, Joseph Tomar	T155-R72	11	160	10/16/1902
Shicany, Nicola	T156-R72	33	160	10/16/1903
Skeff, Joseph	T155-R72	35	160	2/13/1905
Skeff, Nezmi	T155-R72	34	40	2/18/1903
Skeff, Nezmi	T155-R72	35	120	2/18/1903
Slama, Joseph M.	T152-R74	29	120	4/5/1907
Slama, Joseph M.	T152-R74	32	40	4/5/1907
Srour, Nicolas	T154-R73	18	80	12/6/1905
Srour, Nicolas	T154-R73	18	36.03	12/6/1905
Srour, Nicolas	T154-R73	18	36.10	12/6/1905
Swery, Naman	T155-R72	13	80	
Swery, Norman	T155-R72	4	40	
Taleb, Mestafa	T153-R74	27	160	10/10/1904
Tannous, Abram B.	T155-R72	10	160	12/30/1905
Tasa, Thomas B.	T152-R74	30	120	
Tasa, Thomas B.	T152-R74	30	35.24	

Name	Township	Section	Acreage	Date of Acquisition
Turk, Charles	T156-R72	35	160	8/8/1901
Wazer, Elias	T155-R72	10	160	
Wazer, Metree	T155-R72	10	160	
Yenas, Tanous	T154-R73	20	80	4/1/1905
Yenas, Tanous	T154-R73	29	80	4/1/1905
Yoness, Kallel	T155-R72	14	160	3/29/1902
Youness, Joseph	T154-R73	28	80	4/1/1905
Younesse, Silo	T155-R72	32	120	5/7/1904
Zeer, Mohammed	T152-R74	5	80	4/17/1905
Zeer, Mohammed	T152-R74	5	47.89	4/17/1905
Zeer, Mohammed	T152-R74	5	47.76	4/17/1905
Zid, Frank	T152-R74	32	80	8/3/1904
Zid, Frank	T152-R74	34	80	8/3/1904
Zook, Samuel Y.	T158-R70	8	160	
Zyady, John	T155-R72	34	80	8/18/1902
Zyady, John	T155-R72	2	80	7/2/1904
RAMSEY COUNTY				
Mahood, James A.	T154-R62	26	160	12/28/1888
Mahood, William R.	T154-R62	35	160	6/21/1889
Mahood, William R.	T154-R62	35	160	3/10/1890
RENVILLE COUNTY				
Abraham, Charles	T161-R85	2	80	4/11/1907
Abraham, Charles	T161-R85	2	39.91	4/11/1907
Abraham, Charles	T161-R85	2	39.94	4/11/1907
Ahmann, Henry	T159-R85	24	80	4/16/1909
Shibley, Frank	T158-R86	6	80	10/28/1903
Shibley, Frank	T158-R86	6	39.75	10/28/1903
Shibley, Frank	T158-R86	6	39.82	10/28/1903
RICHLAND COUNTY				
Dewaha, Eugene	T132-R52	14	160	9/20/1884
Gabriel, Joseph	T132-R49	22	160	3/31/1884
Gassen, Henry	T130-R52	33	160	10/10/1889
Gassen, Henry J.	T130-R52	33	160	11/15/1886
Kissam, Charles A.	T130-R49	10	160	6/30/1882
ROLETTE COUNTY				
Abraham, Albert	T162-R70	30	80	7/22/1958
Albert, Frank	T160-R72	23	160	6/17/1903
SARGENT COUNTY				
Afdem, Charles	T132-R54	22	160	11/7/1888

Name	Township	Section	Acreage	Date of Acquisition
SHERIDAN COUNTY				
Abdella, Moses	T148-R76	35	160	4/28/1910
Abdellah, Issac	T148-R76	26	80	6/11/1908
Abdellah, Issac	T148-R76	35	40	6/11/1908
Abes, Hasan	T149-R76	19	120	6/9/1905
Abes, Hasan	T149-R76	30	40	6/9/1905
Ally, Ahmad	T149-R76	27	120	8/8/1905
Ally, Ahmad	T149-R76	14	40	12/28/1908
Aly, Mahmod	T149-R76	28	160	4/5/1905
Boutrous, Attas	T148-R76	7	35.59	5/4/1908
Boutrous, Attas	T148-R77	12	120	5/4/1908
Hikel, Aisem	T148-R76	18	160	6/25/1908
Kellel, Joseph	T147-R76	1	80	6/25/1908
Kellel, Joseph	T147-R76	1	40.59	6/25/1908
Kellel, Joseph	T147-R76	2	40	6/25/1908
Kellel, Tom	T148-R77	12	160	10/28/1909
Mahloff, Andreas	T144-R75	22	160	6/25/1908
Masad, Nassif	T147-R76	2	80	4/27/1912
Masad, Nassif	T147-R76	11	80	4/27/1912
Massad, George	T147-R76	10	160	9/17/1908
Melham, Salem	T147-R76	2	80	2/24/1908
Melham, Salem	T147-R76	2	40.64	2/24/1908
Melham, Salem	T147-R76	2	40.64	2/24/1908
Momment, Abraham	T149-R77	5	80	1/17/1910
Momment, Abraham	T149-R77	5	40.42	1/17/1910
Momment, Abraham	T149-R77	5	40.39	1/17/1910
Nackola, Solon	T147-R76	2	40	4/2/1908
Nackola, Solon	T147-R76	2	40.59	4/2/1908
Nackola, Solon	T147-R76	2	40.56	4/2/1908
Nackola, Solon	T147-R76	35	40	4/2/1908
Nassif, Coram	T148-R75	20	80	12/26/1907
Nassif, George	T147-R76	24	160	6/25/1908
Nassif, Rustum	T147-R76	15	80	3/30/1908
Nassif, Shaker	T149-R76	19	40	6/4/1908
Nassif, Shaker	T149-R76	19	39.50	6/4/1908
Nassif, Shaker	T149-R76	19	39.58	6/4/1908
Nassif, Shaker	T149-R76	19	39.67	6/4/1908
Netzlof, Michael	T147-R78	14	160	4/18/1910
Nicola, Salem	T148-R77	1	40	6/20/1912
Nicola, Salem	T148-R77	2	80	6/20/1912
Nicola, Salem	T148-R77	12	40	6/20/1912
Nicola, Salma	T148-R76	6	21.40	9/10/1908
Nicola, Salma	T148-R76	6	21.48	9/10/1908
Nicola, Salma	T148-R76	6	17.93	9/10/1908

Name	Township	Section	Acreage	Date of Acquisition
Nicola, Salma	T148-R76	6	33.58	9/10/1908
Nicola, Salma	T148-R76	6	34.02	9/10/1908
Nicola, Salma	T148-R77	1	40	9/10/1908
Nicola, Salom	T148-R76	7	80	4/20/1909
Nicola, Salom	T148-R76	7	34.81	4/20/1909
Nicola, Salom	T148-R76	7	35.07	4/20/1909
Nicola, Salom	T148-R76	7	35.33	3/10/1910
Nicola, Salom	T148-R76	7	35.33	11/1/1909
Nicola, Salom	T148-R76	7	35.33	3/10/1910
Nicola, Salom	T148-R77	12	40	5/17/1909
Nuckola, Salom	T147-R76	2	40	5/14/1909
Skaff, Abraham S.	T148-R77	11	40	3/22/1919
Skaff, Abraham Sleem	T148-R77	6	22.87	5/12/1910
Skaff, Abraham Sleem	T148-R77	6	23	5/12/1910
Skaff, Abraham Sleem	T148-R77	6	23.12	5/12/1910
Skaff, Abraham Sleem	T148-R77	6	20.12	5/12/1910
Skaff, Abraham Sleem	T148-R77	6	34.82	5/12/1910
Skaff, Farris S.	T148-R77	1	160	10/28/1909

STUTSMAN COUNTY

Name	Township	Section	Acreage	Date of Acquisition
Ahmed, Ally	T138-R68	28	40	3/29/1924
Aman, John F.	T137-R67	26	160	3/12/1906
Hadey, Abdel	T138-R68	10	160	3/17/1917
Hadey, Abdel	T138-R68	10	160	3/17/1917
Hadey, Abdel	T138-R68	10	160	9/23/1914
Juma, Hassyn Alla	T138-R68	12	40	4/17/1915
Juma, Hassyn Alla	T138-R68	12	40	9/6/1957
Kanan, Masood	T138-R68	2	160	4/27/1911
Kanan, Shaker S.	T138-R68	2	80	3/23/1908
Kanan, Shaker S.	T138-R68	2	39.53	3/23/1908
Kanan, Shaker S.	T138-R68	2	39.58	3/23/1908
Mounnaur, Mousstafa Mahmond	T138-R69	18	80	4/6/1908
Mounnaur, Mousstafa Mahmond	T138-R69	18	40.23	4/6/1908
Mounnaur, Mousstafa Mahmond	T138-R69	18	40.63	4/6/1908
Sam, Howard	T139-R69	6	40	10/25/1909
Sam, Howard	T139-R69	6	40	10/25/1909
Sam, Howard	T139-R69	6	16.8	10/25/1909
Sam, Howard	T139-R69	6	31.8	10/25/1909

TOWNER COUNTY

Name	Township	Section	Acreage	Date of Acquisition
Aghemy, Sadie	T161-R67	25	160	10/29/1906
Assyc, Nikas	T160-R67	18	40	12/30/1901
Assyc, Nikas	T160-R67	18	34.49	12/30/1901
Assyc, Samuel	T160-R67	18	34.49	6/24/1903
Assye, Nikos	T160-R68	11	160	10/28/1904
Hamari, Isaac	T162-R68	12	160	11/15/1904
Hamari, Meer	T162-R67	10	160	2/13/1905

Name	Township	Section	Acreage	Date of Acquisition
Tannis, Joseph	T160-R67	7	80	2/13/1905
Tannis, Joseph	T160-R67	7	34.49	2/13/1905
Tannis, Joseph	T160-R67	7	34.88	2/13/1905
Tanous, Abdallah	T161-R67	22	160	12/19/1907

WALSH COUNTY

Name	Township	Section	Acreage	Date of Acquisition
Absey, Joseph	T156-R59	15	160	5/15/1903
Absey, Peter	T156-R59	15	160	5/15/1903
Freije, Moses	T156-R56	6	160	4/20/1903
Harazim, Frank	T156-R59	27	160	2/13/1905
Hareish, Vencels	T156-R59	25	160	10/24/1891
Mahood, John	T156-R54	26	160	2/18/1888
Mahood, Stephen	T156-R54	26	160	4/10/1886
Marron, Latof John	T156-R59	19	160	3/13/1905
Mseeh, Abraham	T156-R59	22	80	7/2/1904
Mseeh, Abraham	T156-R59	23	80	7/2/1904
Mseeh, Mike	T156-R59	23	160	7/2/1904
Najman, Jakob	T156-R59	27	80	5/26/1905
Najman, Jakob	T156-R59	28	80	5/26/1905

WARD COUNTY

Name	Township	Section	Acreage	Date of Acquisition
Hakon, Maxim	T151-R82	5	160	6/30/1905
Hakon, Zimory	T151-R82	4	160	8/22/1907
Halama, Dimidre	T152-R82	22	160	9/19/1906
Kazima, Kerman	T151-R82	9	160	11/18/1907
Kazinia, Mecha	T152-R82	32	160	3/18/1905

WELLS COUNTY

Name	Township	Section	Acreage	Date of Acquisition
Haadem, Lage L.	T150-R70	14	160	8/8/1901

WILLIAMS COUNTY

Name	Township	Section	Acreage	Date of Acquisition
Abdo, Abraham	T156-R102	20	160	8/24/1911
Abood, Alexander	T155-R102	4	160	7/26/1910
Aboud, Abraham	T156-R103	26	160	6/13/1910
Aboud, Manasses	T156-R103	26	160	9/21/1908
Aboud, Namy	T156-R103	22	80	6/16/1910
Aboud, Nicholas	T156-R103	23	160	11/15/1909
Abourezk, Alex M.	T155-R102	5	80	3/30/1908
Abourezk, Alex M.	T155-R102	5	40.82	3/30/1908
Abourezk, Alex M.	T155-R102	5	40.93	3/30/1908
Abrass, Elias	T156-R102	19	80	6/26/1906
Abrass, Elias	T156-R102	19	34.44	6/26/1906
Abrass, Elias	T156-R102	19	34.57	6/26/1906

Name	Township	Section	Acreage	Date of Acquisition
Abrass, William	T156-R102	19	80	6/26/1906
Abrass, William	T156-R102	19	34.19	6/26/1906
Abrass, William	T156-R102	19	34.32	6/26/1906
Aly, Sam	T156-R102	18	34.02	5/27/1918
Aly, Sam	T156-R102	18	34.05	5/27/1918
Aien, Albert	T158-R97	12	80	9/28/1911
Aien, Albert	T158-R97	13	80	9/28/1911
Argo, Peter G.	T155-R98	24	160	
Asad, Rashad	T154-R101	17	160	4/14/1906
Assey, Martha	T156-R103	24	160	5/7/1908
Atol, Abraham	T156-R102	28	160	11/5/1908
Azar, Maggie	T155-R102	10	160	
Azar, Nicols	T155-R102	3	41.01	
Azar, Nicols	T155-R102	4	40.97	
Barkey, George	T156-R103	23	160	
Bohamra, Joseph	T156-R102	34	160	2/5/1906
Bouhamra, Abdalla	T156-R102	35	160	5/2/1908
Bourstom, Sabh	T156-R102	32	160	11/27/1905
Bousliman, Lizzie	T155-R102	4	40	9/10/1908
Bousliman, Lizzie	T155-R102	5	120	9/10/1908
Bousliman, Naseef	T156-R103	12	160	9/24/1907
Bousliman, Robert	T156-R102	6	33.56	9/7/1909
Bousliman, Robert	T156-R102	6	33.59	9/7/1909
Bousliman, Robert	T156-R103	1	80	9/7/1909
Bousliman, Sophika M.	T156-R102	31	160	3/30/1908
Bouslman, Mary	T156-R102	33	160	2/5/1906
David, Deeb	T155-R102	3	160	2/11/1910
David, George Deeb	T156-R102	32	160	2/24/1908
David, Mike	T156-R102	21	160	4/2/1908
Eattol, Charles	T156-R102	28	160	5/2/1908
Eattol, William	T156-R102	27	160	5/27/1909
Farah, Saad	T156-R103	12	160	5/27/1909
Farough, Deeby	T156-R103	12	160	6/10/1909
Farra, Katherine	T156-R102	21	160	5/27/1909
Ferres, Asar Richard	T156-R102	30	160	4/7/1910
Firoah, Asof G.	T155-R102	8	80	6/5/1911
Firoah, Asof G.	T155-R102	9	80	6/5/1911
Firoah, Rahmy	T154-R100	23	80	6/5/1911
Firoah, Rahmy	T154-R100	24	80	6/5/1911
Forzly, Abraham	T156-R102	7	33.65	11/9/1908
Forzly, Abraham	T156-R102	7	33.75	11/9/1908
Forzly, Abraham	T156-R102	7	33.85	11/9/1908
Forzly, Abraham	T156-R102	7	33.95	11/9/1908

Name	Township	Section	Acreage	Date of Acquisition
Gazal, Owad	T156-R102	21	160	6/19/1911
Habib, Salma	T156-R103	12	160	2/3/1910
Hajem, Torten	T158-R95	12	160	4/7/1910
Harob, Sam	T156-R104	25	160	
Jermanus, Thomas	T156-R102	17	160	
Kalil, David	T156-R103	24	160	4/1/1909
Kassis, Afaffae E.	T155-R102	9	160	5/2/1908
Kassis, John	T155-R102	8	40	6/24/1909
Kassis, John	T155-R102	9	80	
Kassis, Maggie	T154-R103	1	160	7/30/1908
Kassis, Regina	T154-R103	1	80	8/5/1909
Kassis, Regina	T154-R103	1	39.99	8/5/1909
Kassis, Regina	T154-R103	1	39.97	8/5/1909
Lyon, Farris	T156-R103	15	160	
Mackay, Sada	T155-R102	4	160	
Massahd, James	T156-R103	24	160	4/1/1909
Massahd, Mamie A.	T154-R102	1	80	11/11/1916
Massahd, Mamie A.	T154-R102	1	40.02	11/11/1916
Massahd, Mamie A.	T154-R102	1	40.08	11/11/1916
Masse, Abdo (heirs of)	T156-R101	19	160	11/30/1915
Massee, Abbie	T155-R101	31	80	10/10/1904
Massee, Abbie	T155-R101	32	80	10/10/1904
Massee, Clarissa A.	T154-R99	31	80	6/11/1908
Massee, Clarissa A.	T154-R99	31	37.45	6/11/1908
Massee, Clarissa A.	T154-R99	31	37.55	6/11/1908
Munyer, Asof	T156-R103	15	160	5/2/1908
Munyer, Elias	T156-R103	22	160	11/9/1908
Munyer, Jabour	T156-R103	26	160	6/18/1908
Munyer, Mayre	T156-R103	15	160	6/18/1908
Naked, Joseph	T155-R102	8	160	5/18/1911
Rehal, Charlie	T156-R101	18	34.16	1/4/1915
Rehal, Charlie	T156-R101	19	40	1/4/1915
Rehal, Charlie	T156-R101	19	34.10	1/4/1915
Rehal, Charlie	T156-R101	19	34.07	1/4/1915
Rehal, Rosay	T156-R102	24	160	6/19/1911
Saowya, Rosa (Rehal) (heirs of)	T155-R102	10	160	6/12/1911
Saowya, Rosa (Rehal) (heirs of)	T155-R102	10	160	6/12/1911
Saowya, Rosa (Rehal) (heirs of)	T155-R102	10	160	12/24/1910
Shakany, Aefefoe Rahal	T155-R102	8	160	10/9/1906
Shakany, Elias	T155-R102	9	40	5/6/1912
Shakany, Elias	T155-R102	10	120	5/6/1912
Shickany, Nassim	T155-R102	10	160	5/4/1906

Name	Township	Section	Acreage	Date of Acquisition
Shakany, Salame	T155-R102	15	160	8/10/1908
Skaff, Abraham C.	T154-R99	30	80	3/18/1909
Skaff, Abraham C.	T154-R99	30	37.32	3/18/1909
Skaff, Abraham C.	T154-R99	30	37.38	3/18/1909
Skaff, Julia A.	T156-R102	6	160	6/3/1908
Skaff, Mary	T156-R102	7	160	6/8/1911
Tannous, Mary	T155-R102	13	80	5/2/1908
Tannous, Mary	T155-R102	24	80	5/2/1908
Toby, Joseph M.	T156-R102	11	160	4/19/1909
Toby, Maggie	T156-R102	28	160	2/5/1906
Youness, Charley	T156-R101	19	80	12/27/1912
Youness, Charley	T156-R101	19	34.05	12/27/1912
Youness, Charley	T156-R101	19	34.05	12/27/1912
Youness, Joseph A.	T156-R102	33	80	1/4/1915
Youness, Joseph C.	T156-R101	17	40	6/3/1916
Youness, Joseph C.	T156-R102	22	160	6/14/1909
Zamata, Joseph	T156-R104	10	80	
Zamata, Joseph	T156-R104	10	36.94	
Zamata, Joseph	T156-R104	10	36.73	
Zamata, Joseph	T156-R104	15	80	
Zamata, Joseph	T156-R104	15	36.49	
Zamata, Joseph	T156-R104	15	36.27	
Zein, Assena M.	T156-R102	28	160	3/18/1909
Zein, Charlie A.	T156-R102	27	160	3/11/1909
Zein, Charlie M.	T156-R102	17	160	8/5/1912
Zein, John	T156-R103	13	160	10/2/1911
Zein, Lottie	T156-R102	27	160	6/10/1909
Zein, Toma	T156-R102	32	40	6/3/1909
Zein, Toma	T156-R102	29	160	3/30/1908
Zien, Cary	T156-R102	29	80	3/30/1908
Zine, Fred A.	T156-R102	13	160	

* Naturalization records (Appendix B) and Veterans lists (Appendix D) often have non-Arabic people under the heading "Turkey." The Ottoman Empire extended, at the turn of the century, into areas which are now part of Romania, Greece, Bulgaria, and Armenia. Immigrant petitioners whose names end in "ian" are Armenian; names ending in "off" or "ov" are usually Bulgarian. Greek names are sometimes obvious: Papadopolos, Tsoumpariotis. Germans from the Dobrudja (modern Romania) are usually evident: Gottlieb Kalk, Christoph Blumhagen, Fred Seibold.

Appendix D

North Dakota Veterans of World War I

The following men of "Syrian," "Arabian," or "Turkish" origin either enlisted or were drafted into the United States Armed Services during the First World War. The names and accompanying information are found in the four-volume set: Official Roster of North Dakota Soldiers, Sailors and Marines, World War 1917-1918, published under the direction of G. Angus Frazer, Adjutant General of North Dakota (Bismarck, 1931). An occasional individual may have been overlooked, but, for the most part, the compilation is complete. It is possible that an Armenian or Dubrudja German might be on this list.

ABAS, SAM (Vol. I, pg. 11)

Army number 4,544,717, Registrant, Cass County, born Arabia, July 6, 1897, naturalized citizen, occupation, laborer, inducted at Fargo on Nov. 5, 1918; sent to North Dakota Agricultural College; served in Student's Army Training Corps, to discharge. Discharged at Fargo, No. Dak. on Dec. 9, 1918, as a private.

ABDALLA, ALEX (Vol. I, pg. 12)

Army number: 2,147,893, Registrant, Ransom County, born Crbet Roaha, Syria, 1888, declarant citizen, occupation, merchant; inducted at Lisbon on March 29, 1918; sent to Camp Dodge, Iowa, served in Company H, 2nd Battalion, 163rd Depot Brigade, to April 20, 1918; Company 10, Provisional Battalion, 138th Infantry, to May 1, 1918; Company 48, 12th Battalion, 153rd Depot Brigade, to June 10, 1918; Company D. 12th Battalion, U.S. Guards, Fort Niagara Falls, N.Y. to July 4, 1918; Company B, Development Battalion No. 1, Camp Upton, N.Y., to Sept. 12, 1918; Company V, Development Battalion No. 6, Camp Upton, N.Y., to Oct. 8, 1918; Ordance Department, Aberdeen Proving Grounds, Aberdeen, Md. to discharge. Discharged at Camp Dodge, Iowa, on Feb. 15, 1919, as a private.

ABDALLA, GEORGE (Vol. I, pg. 12)

Army number: 2,858,358, registrant, Pierce County, born Mashta, Syria, Dec. 10, 1889, naturalized citizen, occupation, farmer; inducted at Rugby on April 29, 1918; sent to Camp Dodge, Iowa; served in 163rd Depot Brigade, to April 30, 1918; Battery D, 338th Field Artillery, to May 15, 1918; 90th Division, Camp Travis, to May 23, 1918; Company L, 358th Infantry; to death;

overseas from June 20, 1918, to death. Engagements: Offensive: St. Mihiel. Defensive sectors: Puvenelle and Villers-en-Have (Lorraine). *Killed in action on Sept. 26, 1918; buried, Grave 14, Row 18, Block D, St. Mihiel American Cemetery, Thiaucourt, Meurthe-et-Moselle, France.*

ALBERT, GEORGE (Vol. I, pg. 26)
    Army number, 4,038,129; registrant, Rolette County; born, Inarab, Syria, July 10, 1892; naturalized citizen; occupation, farmer; inducted at Rolla on July 22, 1918; sent to Camp Custer, Mich.; served in 11th Company, 3rd Battalion, 160th Depot Brigade, to Aug. 31, 1918; Company D, 77th Infantry, to Oct. 21, 1918; Company C, 42nd Machine Gun Battalion, to discharge. Discharged at Camp Dodge, Iowa, on Feb. 7, 1919, as a Private.

ALCODRAY, ABDO ALJALELL (Vol. I, pg. 29)
    Army number, 3,681,331, registrant, Cass County, born El Rafud, Syria, April 17, 1888; declarant citizen, occupation, bookkeeper; inducted at Fargo on June 28, 1918; sent to Camp Dodge, Iowa; served in 163rd Depot Brigade, to July 19, 1918; Company F, 313th Ammunition Train, to discharge; overseas from Aug. 15, 1918 to May 28, 1919. Engagement: Defensive sector: Center (Alsace). Discharged at Camp Dodge, Iowa, on June 12, 1919, as a private.

ALICK, JOSEPH (Vol. I, pg. 33)
    Army number 2,704,087, registrant, Towner County, born, Tranap, Syria, July 10, 1886; declarant citizen; occupation, laborer; inducted at Cando on June 23, 1918; sent to Camp Dodge, Iowa; served in Company C, 352nd Infantry, to discharge. Grade: Private 1st class, March 13, 1919; overseas from Aug. 16, 1918, to June 3, 1919. Engagement: Defensive sector: Center (Alsace). Discharged at Camp Dodge, Iowa, on June 13, 1919, as a private 1st class.

ALLICK, ASMAEL (Vol. I, pg. 37)
    Army number 4,037,023; registrant, Rolette County, born, Beirut, Syria, July 25, 1893; naturalized citizen; occupation, farmer; inducted at Rolla on July 22, 1918; sent to Camp Custer, Michigan; served in 11th Company, 3rd Battalion, 160th Depot Brigade, to Aug. 31, 1918; Company D, 77th Infantry, to discharge. Discharged at Camp Dodge, Iowa, on Feb. 7, 1919, as a private.

APOSTOS, SAM (Vol. I, pg. 105)
    Army number 3,300.397, registrant, Burke County, born, Smyrna, Turkey, Oct. 1889; citizenship, alien; occupation, laborer; inducted at Bowbells on May 31, 1918, sent to Camp Funston, Kans.; served in 2nd Company, 164th Depot Brigade, to June 25, 1918; Company B, 351st Infantry, to discharge. Discharged on Jan. 14, 1919, as a private.

ASSAD, OSSIFF (Vol. I, pg. 123)

Army number 177,769; registrant, Richland County, born, St. Paul, Minn., Jan. 9, 1894, of Syrian parents; occupation, student; enlisted at Spokane, Wash., on Sept. 14, 1917; sent to Fort George Wright, Wash.; served in Truck Company No. 1, 23rd Engineers, to discharge; overseas from Jan. 24, 1918, to July 9, 1919. Engagements: Offensive: St. Mihiel, Defensive sector: Lorraine. Discharged at Camp Lewis, Wash., on July 22, 1919, as a private. *Drowned June 12, 1921, in Red River, at Fargo, No. Dak. Buried at Wahpeton, N. Dak.*

BARKIE, CHARLIE (Vol. I, pg. 172)

Army number 3,082,888; not a registrant; born, Marseilles, France, Oct. 5, 1899; naturalized citizen, occupation, waiter; enlisted at Jamestown on June 21, 1918; sent to Jefferson Barracks, Mo, served in 5th Company, Coast Artillery Corps, Fort H. G. Wright, N.Y., to Sept. 12, 1918; Battery A, 38th Artillery, Coast Artillery Corps, to Oct. 11, 1918; Battery B, 45th Artillery, Coast Artillery Corps, to discharge; overseas from Oct. 21, 1918 to Feb. 1, 1919. Discharged at Camp Dodge, Iowa, on Feb. 19, 1919, as a private.

BEJAN, ABDELLAH A. (Vol. I, pg. 220)

Army number 4,035,657; registrant, Burke County; born, Betroney, Syria, July 5, 1892; naturalized citizen; occupation, merchant; inducted at Bowbells on July 22, 1918; sent to Camp Custer, Mich.; served in 45th Company, 12th Battalion, 160th Depot Brigade, to Nov. 9, 1918; Company C, 41st Machine Gun Battalion, to discharge. Discharged at Camp Dodge, Iowa, on Feb. 7, 1919, as a private.

BOUSLIMAN, ROBERT (Vol. I, pg. 355)

Army number 2,143,523, registrant, Williams County, born Zahley, Syria, July 15, 1898, naturalized citizen; occupation, clerk; inducted at Williston on Sept. 5, 1917; sent to Camp Dodge, Iowa; served in Battery A, 338th Field Artillery, to discharge. Grades: corporal, Feb. 19, 1918; private, Oct. 1, 1918; private 1st Class, Dec. 1, 1918; overseas from Aug., 18, 1918 to Jan. 5, 1919. Discharged at Camp Dodge, Iowa, on Jan. 16, 1919, as a private 1st class.

BOUTROUS, OSCAR TOM (Vol. I, pg. 355)

Navy number 1,126,690; not a registrant; born, Peoria, Ill., April 23, 1897, of Turkish parents; occupation, clerk; enlisted in the Navy at Sioux City, Iowa, on July 24, 1918; served at Naval Training Station, Great Lakes, Ill., to Nov. 11, 1918. Grade: Apprentice seaman, 110 days. Released from active duty at Great Lakes, Ill., on Feb. 19, 1919, as an Apprentice seaman.

CHRIST, JOHN GEORGE (Vol. 5, pg. 544)

Army number 509,276; registrant, McIntosh County; born, Sorovitch, Turkey, June 29, 1889; naturalized citizen; occupation, locomotive fireman; inducted at Ashley on May 9, 1918; sent to Fort Logan, Colo.; served in

Company B, 24th Machine Gun Battalion, to Nov., 18, 1918; 132nd Ordnance Depot Company, Camp Fremont, Calif., to Feb. 5, 1919; 116th Ordnance Depot Company, Camp Fremont, Calif., to discharge. Grades: Private 1st Class, June 1, 1918; Corporal, June 22, 1918; Sergeant, Oct. 20, 1918. Discharged at Camp Lewis, Wash., on March 6, 1919, as a Sergeant.

DALLAS, MIKE (Vol. I, pg. 669)
    Army number 4,036,623; registrant, Ward County; born, Rothostes, Turkey, March 20, 1886; naturalized citizen; occupation, laborer; inducted at Minot on July 22, 1918; sent to Camp Custer, Mich.; served in 160th Depot Brigade, to (date not given); Company D, Development Battalion, to discharge. Discharged at Camp Beauregard, La., on Dec. 6, 1918, as a Private.

EKLEN, ALBERT (Vol. I, pg. 808)
    Army number 46,166; registrant, McKenzie County; born, Palestine, Assyria, Feb. 18, 1888; naturalized citizen; occupation, hotel keeper; enlisted in Company E, 1st Infantry, North Dakota National Guard, at Minot, on July 15, 1917; served in Company D, 1st Infantry, North Dakota National Guard (Company D, 164th Infantry), to Jan. 9, 1918; Company B, 18th Infantry, to discharge. Grade: Private 1st Class, Sept. 1, 1918; overseas from Dec. 15, 1917, to Sept. 3, 1919. Engagements: Offensives: Aisne-Marne; St. Mihiel; Meuse-Argonne. Defensive: Montdidier-Noyon. Defensive Sectors: Ansauville and Saizerais (Lorraine); Cantigny (Picardy). Discharged at Camp Dodge, Iowa, on Sept. 24, 1919, as a Private 1st Class. Cited in General Orders No. 5, Headquarters, 1st Infantry Brigade, AEF; Selters, Germany, June 1, 1919, for gallant conduct and self-sacrificing spirit displayed during the battles of Montdidier-Noyon defensive; Aisne-Marne, St. Mihiel and Meuse-Argonne offensives. Entitled to wear a silver star.

FARHART, JISAM (Vol. I, pg. 885)
    Army number 2,054,931; registrant, Mountrail County, born, Rafeti, Syria, July 4, 1888, naturalized citizen; occupation, farmer; inducted at Stanley on May 29, 1918; sent to Camp Custer, Mich.; served in 160th Depot Brigade, to June 23, 1918; Auxiliary Remount Depot No. 320 to Aug. 2, 1918, 160th Depot Brigade, to Sept. 3, 1918; Company C, 3rd Battalion, U.S. Guards, to discharge. Discharged on Dec. 30, 1918, as a private.

FEY, JOHN ALLY (Vol. I, pg. 903)
    Army number 718,235; not a registrant, under age; born, Power, N. Dak., Dec. 22, 1897, of American parents; occupation, farmer; enlisted at Fargo on Jan. 18, 1918; sent to Jefferson Barracks, Mo.; served in Battery B, 2nd Trench Mortar Battalion, Coast Artillery Corps (2nd Battalion, Trench Artillery), to discharge; overseas from May 29, 1918, to April 20, 1919. Engagement: Defensive Sector: Lorraine. Discharged at Camp Dodge, Iowa, on May 7, 1919, as a Private.

GABRIEL, WOLF (Vol. II, pg. 1005)

Army number 2,110,225; registrant, Sargent County, born, Kenway, Syria, Dec. 14, 1894; naturalized citizen; occupation, laborer; inducted at Forman on Sept. 19, 1917; sent to Camp Dodge, Iowa; served in Company L, 352nd Infantry, to Nov. 28, 1917; Company I, 348th Infantry, to June 1, 1918; 162nd Depot Brigade, to Nov. 4, 1918; Camp Pike October Automatic Replacement Draft, to discharge. Discharged at Camp Dodge, Iowa, on Dec. 7, 1918, as a private.

GENNANY, ALEXANDER (Vol. II, pg. 1033)

Army number 2,560,266; registrant, Mountrail County; born, Syria, 1889; naturalized citizen; occupation, farmer; inducted at Stanley on March 28, 1918; sent to Camp Dodge, Iowa; served in 163rd Depot Brigade, to April 19, 1918; Medical Department, Base Hospital No. 165, to discharge. Grade: Private 1st Class, Nov. 1, 1918. Discharged at Camp Dodge, Iowa, on Dec. 23, 1918, as a Private 1st Class.

GWAWAN, MICHAEL (Vol. II, pg. 1155((also GERAWAN, p. 1035)

Army number 4,038,088; registrant (place not given); born, Michagra, Syria, Aug. 13, 1888; citizenship (not given); occupation (not given); inducted at Williston on July 22, 1918; sent to Camp Custer, Mich.; served in 160th Depot Brigade, to Aug. 18, 1918. Battery A, 41st Field Artillery, to discharge. Grade: Private 1st Class, Dec. 1, 1918. Discharged on March 26, 1919, as a Private 1st Class.

HASSEN, RAYMOND (Vol. II, pg. 1268)

Army number 2,560,265, registrant, Mountrail County, born, Rofid, Syria, June 18, 1887, naturalized citizen; occupation, farmer; inducted at Stanley on March 29, 1918; sent to Camp Dodge, Iowa; served in Company B, 139th Infantry, to discharge (casual in hospital from June 6, 1918 to discharge); overseas from May 2, 1918 to Dec. 2, 1918. Discharged at Camp Dodge, Iowa, on Jan. 11, 1919, as a private.

JUMA, HASSYN ALLA (Vol. II, pg. 1613)

Army number 4,038,429; registrant, Cass County, born Rfid (Syria), Arabia, July 2, 1889, naturalized citizen, occupation, farmer, inducted at Fargo on July 23, 1918, sent to Camp Custer, Mich.; served 160th Depot Brigade to discharge. Discharged at Camp Custer, Mich. on March 6, 1919, as a private.

JUMA, SALEM CALED (Vol. II, pg. 1613)

Army number 2,704,775; registrant, Mountrail County, born, Beyna, Syria, June 21, 1888, declarant citizen; occupation, farmer, inducted at Stanley on June 24, 1918; sent to Camp Dodge, Iowa; served in Company A, 352nd

Infantry, to July 27, 1918; 163rd Depot Brigade, to Nov. 18, 1918, Auxiliary Remount Depot No. 322, to discharge. Discharged at Camp Dodge, Iowa, on March 8, 1919, as a private.

KALAD, ALBERT O. (Vol. II, pg. 1619)

Army number 46,884, registrant, Pembina County, born Midamy, Arabia, Aug. 7, 1892; citizenship, alien, occupation, farmer, enlisted Company C, North Dakota National Guard, at Cavalier, on June 11, 1917; called into federal service, World War, on July 15, 1917, served in Company C, 1st Infantry, North Dakota National Guard (Company C, 164th Infantry) to Jan. 9, 1918, Company G, 18th Infantry, to June 10, 1918; *Machine Gun Company, 18th Infantry, to death; overseas from Dec. 15, 1917, to death.* Engagements: Defensive: Montdidier-Noyon. Offensives: Aisne-Marne; St. Mihiel, Meuse-Argonne. Defensive sectors: Ansauville and Saizerais (Lorraine), Cantigny (Picardy). *Killed in action on Oct. 4, 1918; buried in France; remains returned to U.S. on Aug. 1, 1921, and consigned to Sam Omar, 317 N. Broadway, Crookston, Minn. (Place of burial not given.)* Cited in General Orders No. 5, Headquarters, 1st Infantry Brigade, A.E.F., Selters, Germany, June 2, 1919. The Brigade Commander cites the following named officers and enlisted men for gallant conduct and self-sacrificing spirit displayed during the battles of Aisne-Marne, St. Mihiel and Meuse-Argonne. The success of these engagements was due to the efforts and spirit of the officers and enlisted men engaged: … Private Albert O. Kalad … cited in General Orders No. 1, Headquarters, 1st Division, Camp Zachary Taylor, Ky., Jan. 2, 1920, for gallantry in action and especially meritorious services. *Entitled to wear a silver star.*

KALLEL, WIDEY (Vol. II, pg. 1621)

Army number 4,066,165; registrant, Valley County, Mont.; born, Sheba, Syria, May 10, 1895; naturalized citizen; occupation, laborer; inducted at Moorhead, Minn., on July 23, 1918; sent to Camp Wadsworth, S.C.; served in Company C, 56th Pioneer Infantry, to Aug. 11, 1918; Company L, 54th Pioneer Infantry, to discharge; overseas from Aug. 30, 1918, to July 10, 1919. Engagement: Offensive: Meuse-Argonne. Discharged at Fort D. A. Russell, Wyo., on July 22, 1919, as a Private.

KAPRELIAN, SOLOMON (Vol. II, pg. 1627)

Army number 168,441; not a registrant; under age; born, Erzeroom, Turkey, Sept. 1898; citizenship (not given); occupation (not given); enlisted in the Reserve Corps at Minneapolis, Minn. on June 19, 1917; served in Company D, 17th Engineers, to discharge. Grade: Private 1st Class, April 17, 1918; overseas from July 28, 1917, to March 25, 1919. Discharged on April 9, 1919, as a Private 1st Class.

KASSIS, ELI JOSEPH (Vol. II, pg. 1631)

Army number 3,142,623; registrant, Williams county; born Zahish, Syria, July 15, 1888; naturalized citizen; occupation, confectioner; inducted at Casper, Wyo. on June 28, 1918; sent to Camp Lewis, Wash.; served in 166th Depot Brigade, to July 16, 1918; Company B, 145th Machine Gun Battalion, to Oct. 23, 1918; Company E, 9th Infantry, to discharge; overseas from Aug. 7, 1918, to Aug. 1, 1919. Engagement: Offensive: Meuse-Argonne. Discharged at Camp Dodge, Iowa, on Aug. 14, 1919, as a Private.

KOPARIAN, VAHAN (Vol. II, pg. 1730)

Army number 2,140,560; registrant, Cass county; born Akrak, Turkey, Oct.,, 1892; declarant citizen; occupation, blacksmith; inducted at Fargo, on Jan. 9, 1918; sent to Camp Dodge, Iowa; served in Company B, 352nd Infantry, to March 24, 1918; Company C. 39th Engineers, to April 21, 1918; Battery F, 306th Field Artillery, to Nov., 14, 1918; Battery E, 17th Field Artillery; to June 20, 1919; Headquarters Company, 12th Field Artillery, to discharge; overseas from April 24, 1918, to Aug. 6, 1919. Engagements: Offensives: Olse-Alsne; Meuse-Argonne. Defensive Sectors: Baccarat and Forci-d' Argonne (Lorraine). Vesle (Champagne). Discharged at Camp Dodge, Iowa, on August 14, 1919, as a Private.

MABARAK, ELIAS (Vol. III, pg. 1972)

Army number 54,241, not a registrant, enlisted prior, born Zahlie, Syria, March 1898, citizenship (not given), occupation (not given), enlisted in Company E, 1st Infantry, North Dakota National Guard at Williston on May 25, 1917; called into federal service, World War, on July 15, 1917; served in Company E, 1st Infantry, North Dakota National Guard (Company E, 164th Infantry) to Jan. 18, 1918, Company H, 26th Infantry, *to death, overseas from Dec. 15, 1917, to death,* wounded slightly, June 18, 1918. Engagements: Defensive: Montdidier-Noyon. Offensive: Aisne-Marne. Defensive sectors: Ansauville (Lorraine); Cantigny (Picardy). *Killed in action on July 20, 1918, grave unlocated.* Cited in General Orders No. 1, Headquarters, 1st Division, Camp Zachary Taylor, Ky., Jan. 2, 1920 for gallantry in action and especially meritorious services. *Entitled to wear a silver star.*

MAVROMATIS, GEORGE (Vol. III, pg. 2116)

Army number 2,162,965; registrant (place not given), born, Adalia, Asia Minor, June, 1893; citizenship (not given); occupation (not given); inducted at Milwaukee, Wis., on April 2, 1918; sent to Camp Dodge, Iowa; served in 163rd Depot Brigade, to Nov. 9, 1918; Company K, 2nd Infantry, to discharge. Discharged on April 29, 1919, as a Private.

MEDLOM, MASSOD (Vol. III, pg. 2124

Army number 2,142,790; registrant, Dunn county; born, Batrom, Syria, May 16, 1887; naturalized citizen; occupation, salesman; inducted at Manning on Sept. 5, 1917; sent to Camp Dodge, Iowa; served in Battery E, 338th Field Artillery, to April 1, 1918; Company I, 326th Infantry, to discharge. Grades: Private 1st Class, Sept. 12, 1918; Corporal, Feb. 15, 1919; overseas from April 29, 1918, to May 29, 1919. Engagements: Offensives: St. Mihiel; Meuse-Argonne. Defensive Sectors: Lucey and Marbache (Lorraine). Discharged at Camp Dodge, Iowa, on June 8, 1919, as a Corporal.

MEERZO, ABDO DAHOOT (Vol. III, pg. 2125)
Army number 4,040,315; registrant, Grand Forks county, born, Damascus, Turkey, April 19, 1894, declarant citizen; occupation, bellboy; inducted at Grand Forks on July 22, 1918; sent to Camp Custer, Mich.; served in 160th Depot Brigade, to Sept. 14, 1918; 355th Reserve Labor Battalion to (date not given), 448th Reserve Labor Battalion, to discharge. *Discharged on Nov. 19, 1918, as a private, by reason of being an alien enemy.*

MEHELES, JAMES (Vol., III, pg. 2126)
Army number 52,560; registrant (not given); born, Smyrna, Turkey, 1893; citizenship (not given); occupation (not given); enlisted in Company B, 2nd Infantry, North Dakota National Guard, at New Rockford, on Sept. 25, 1917; served in Company B, 2nd Infantry, North Dakota National Guard, to Oct. 10, 1917; Company H. 164th Infantry, to Jan. 18, 1918; Company A, 26th Infantry, to death; overseas from Dec. 15, 1917, to death; wounded, degree undetermined, July 19, 1918. Engagements: Defensive: Montdidier-Noyon. Offensives: Alsne-Marne; St. Mihiel; Meuse-Argonne. Defensive Sectors: Ansauville (Lorraine); Cantigny (Picardy). Killed in action on Oct. 5, 1918; buried in Grave 23, Row 5, Block C, Meuse-Argonne American Cemetery, Romagne-sous-Montifancon, Meuse, France. Cited in General Orders No. 1, Headquarters, 1st Division, Camp Zachary Taylor, Ky., Jan. 1, 1920, for gallantry in action and especially meritorious services. *Entitled to wear a silver star.*

MOSTFA, MOHAMMED (Vol. III, pg. 2235)
Army number 2,049,470; registrant, Mountrail County, born, Damascus, Syria, June 17, 1890; declarant citizen, occupation, laborer, inducted at Highland Park, Mich., on April 29, 1918, sent to Camp Custer, Mich.; served in 160th Depot Brigade, to Sept. 27, 1918; 64th Depot Brigade, to discharge. *Discharged on Nov. 29, 1918, as a private, by reason of being an alien enemy.*

MOURADIAN, MARDEROS (Vol. III, pg. 2236)
Army number 2,113,956; registrant, Benson county; born Akrak, Turkey, Jan. 10, 1890; naturalized citizen; occupation, laborer; inducted at Minnewaukan on Sept. 18, 1917, sent to Camp Dodge, Iowa; served in Battery A, 338th Field Artillery, to Nov. 30, 1917; Battery C, 335th Field Artillery, to June 4, 1918; Air Service Corps, to discharge. Grade: Corporal, Dec. 1, 1918; overseas from Sept. 22, 1918, to April 21, 1919. Discharged at Camp Dodge, Iowa, on May 10, 1919, as a Corporal.

MOURIDAN, GEORGE (Vol. III, pg. 2236)

Army number 3,234,617; registrant, Burleigh county; born Kotue, Turkey, Dec. 15, 1890; declarant citizen; occupation, laborer; inducted at Bismarck on March 28, 1918; sent to Camp Dodge, Iowa; served in 163rd Depot Brigade, to (date not given); Company No. 11, 3rd Battalion, 163rd Depot Brigade, to discharge. Discharged at Camp Dodge, Iowa, on July 8, 1918, as a Private. Surgeon's Certificate of Disability, 50%.

MUNYER, JOSEPH G. (Vol. III, pg. 2248)

Army number 3,680,3l3; registrant, Williams County, born, Zaly, Syria, Sept. 19, 1891, declarant citizen; occupation, storekeeper, inducted at Williston on June 25, 1918, sent to Camp Dodge, Iowa, served in Company A, 352nd Infantry, to discharge; overseas: from Aug. 16, 1918, to June 3, 1918. Engagements: Defensive sector: Center (Alsace). Discharged at Camp Dodge, Iowa, on June 13, 1919, as a private.

NARSASION, OHANNAS (Vol. III, pg. 2270)

Army number 4,822,127; registrant, Ramsey county; born, Akrak, Turkey, Sept. 27, 1894; declarant citizen; occupation, laborer; inducted at Minnewaukan on Sept. 19, 1918; sent to Camp Dodge, Iowa; served in 163rd Depot Brigade, to discharge. Discharged at Camp Dodge, Iowa, on Dec. 7, 1918, as a Private. Surgeon's Certificate of Disability.

NASTOFF, SVETCO (Vol. III, pg. 2272)

Army number 2,094,07l; registrant, Williams County, born, Turkey, March 25, 1890; declarant citizen; occupation, merchant, inducted at Chicago, Ill. on Mar. 29, 1918, sent to Camp Grant, Ill., served in 161st Depot Brigade, to Sept. 16, 1918; Motor Ambulance Company No. 437 to (date not given); Motor Ambulance Company No. 62 to discharge. *Discharged on Dec. 9, 1918, as a private, by reason of being a subject of Turkey.*

NEDHOFF, MIKE (Vol. III, pg. 2275)

Army number 2,560,350, registrant, Williams County, born Zahly, Syria, Dec. 22, 1888, naturalized citizen, occupation, clerk, inducted at Williston on March 29, 1918, sent to Camp Dodge, Iowa, served in 163rd Depot Brigade, to April 22, 1918; Personnel Office, 139th Infantry, to April 19, 1919; Company G, 139th Infantry, to discharge; overseas from May 3, 1918, to April 24, 1919. Engagements: Meuse-Argonne. Defensive sectors: Gerardmer (Alsace); Grange-le-Comte (Lorraine). Discharged at Camp Dodge, Iowa, on May 2, 1919, as a private.

OMAR, GEORGE (Vol. III, pg. 2436)

Army number 944,730; registrant (not given); born, Paris, France, March,

1893; citizenship (not given); occupation (not given); enlisted at Fort Snelling, Minn., on Oct. 1, 1917; served in Company E, 40th Infantry, to discharge. Grade: Private 1st Class, July 1, 1918. Discharged on Jan. 21, 1919, as Private 1st Class.

OMER, ABDO (Vol. III, pg. 2437)
Army number 2,081,577; registrant, Rolette County, born Essyria, Turkey, June 24, 1894, naturalized citizen, occupation, farmer, inducted at Crookston, Minn. on June 24, 1918, sent to Camp Grant, Ill., served in 9th Company, 1st Training Regiment, 161st Depot Brigade, to July 15, 1918. Battery C, 331st Field Artillery, to Aug. 16, 1918; Company D, 1st Development Battalion, Camp Grant, Ill., to discharge. Discharged at Camp Grant, Ill. on Dec. 18, 1918, as a private.

OTMAN, HASSAN DARWASH (Vol. III, pg. 2457)
Army number 2,140,857; registrant, Dunn County; born, Bartronia, Syria, Aug. 23, 1887; naturalized citizen, occupation, pool hall owner, inducted at Sioux City, Iowa, on April 11, 1918; sent to Camp Dodge, Iowa; served in Company H, 138th Infantry, to discharge; overseas from May 2, 1918 to April 28, 1919. Engagements: Offensive: Meuse-Argonne. Defensive sectors: Gerardmer (Alsace); Grange-le-Comte (Lorraine). Discharged at Camp Dodge, Iowa, on May 12, 1919, as a private.

OTMEN, OMER (Vol. III, pg. 2457)
Army number 2,857,839; registrant, McIntosh County, born, Burton, Syria, June 5, 1888, naturalized citizen, occupation, farmer, inducted at Ashley on April 29, 1918; sent to Camp Dodge, Iowa, served in Company I, 350th Infantry, to May 16, 1918; Company K, 360th Infantry, to discharge; overseas from July 6, 1918, to June 7, 1919. Engagements: Offensive: St. Mihiel; Meuse-Argonne. Defensive sectors: Villers-en-Haye and Puvenelle (Lorraine). Discharged at Camp Dodge, Iowa, on June 14, 1919, as a private.

OTTMAN, ALEXANDER (Vol. III, pg. 2458)
Army number 2,559,659; registrant, Oliver county; born, Damascus, Syria, March 31, 1888; naturalized citizen; occupation, laborer; inducted at Bismarck on March 29, 1918; sent to Camp Dodge, Iowa; served in 163rd Depot Brigade, to June 24, 1918; Company D, 360th Infantry, to July 23, 1918; 163rd Depot Brigade, to Nov. 8, 1918; 59th Depot Brigade, to discharge. Discharged at Camp Cody, N. Mex., on Dec. 10, 1918, as a private.

PANOSIAN, GEORGE (Vol. III, pg. 2476)
Army number 3,684,885; registrant, Ramsey county; born, Sevgen, Turkey, May 5, 1895; declarant citizen; occupation, laborer; inducted at Devils Lake on Aug. 13, 1918; sent to Camp Dodge, Iowa; served in 163rd Depot Brigade to

Nov. 8, 1918; 59th Depot Brigade, to discharge. Discharged at Camp Cody, N. Mex., on Dec. 10, 1918, as a Private.

SAWAYA, GEORGE RICK (Vol. IV, pg. 2835)

Army number 46,227, registrant, Haven, Mont., born, St. Paul, Minn., Feb. 19, 1892, of Syrian parents, occupation, cook, enlisted in Company D, 1st Infantry, North Dakota National Guard, for Mexican border duty and served there until discharge; discharged from federal service at Fort Snelling, Minn. on Feb. 14, 1917, and resumed national Guard status; called into federal service, World War, on July 15, 1917; served in Company D, 1st Infantry; North Dakota National Guard (Company D, 164th Infantry), to Jan. 9, 1918; Company B, 18th Infantry, to discharge. Grades: Private 1st class, Aug. 1, 1917; corporation, Sept. 18, 1917; private, Nov. 1, 1917, cook, June 18, 1918, private, Sept. 1, 1918; overseas from Dec. 15, 1917, to discharge; wounded slightly, Sept. 12, 1918. Engagements: Defensive: Montdidier-Noyon. Offensives: Aisne-Marne; St. Mihiel, Meuse-Argonne. Defensive sectors: Ansauville and Saizerais (Lorraine); Cantigny (Picardy). Discharged at Siershohn, Germany, July 1, 1919, as a cook.

SAWAYA, OLE R (Vol. IV, pg. 2835)

Army number 54,290, not a registrant, underage, born, Rugby, N. Dak., April 18, 1898, of Syrian parents, occupation, harnessmaker; enlisted in Company D, 1st Infantry, North Dakota National Guard, at Minot, on Aug. 1, 1917; served in Company D, 1st Infantry, North Dakota National Guard, to Aug. 20, 1917; Company L, 1st Infantry, North Dakota National Guard (Company L, 164th Infantry), to Jan. 12, 1918, Company H, 26th Infantry, to discharge; overseas from Dec. 15, 1917, to Aug. 13, 1919. Engagements: Aisne-Marne, St. Mihiel, Meuse-Argonne. Defensive: Montdidier-Noyon. Defensive sectors: Ansauville and Saizerais (Lorraine); Contigny (Picardy). Discharged at Camp Robert E. Lee, Va, on Aug. 17, 1919, as a private.

SELBASHAN, MERON (Vol. IV, p. 2910)

Army number, none; not a registrant; enlisted prior; born Turkey, July, 1894; citizenship (not given); occupation (not given); enlisted at Jefferson Barracks, Mo., on May 22, 1917; served in Company H,. 34th Infantry, to discharge. Discharged on Oct. 6, 1917, as a Private.

SHAHEEN, NASSB (Vol. IV, pg. 2927)

Army number 52,590, not a registrant, enlisted prior, born, Syria, Sept. 1892, citizenship (not given); occupation (not given), enlisted in Company H, 1st Infantry, North Dakota National Guard at Fargo, on May 1, 1917, served in Company H. 1st Infantry, North Dakota National Guard (Company H, 164th Infantry), to Jan. 18, 1918; *Company A, 26th Infantry, to death overseas from Dec. 15 1917, to death.* Engagements: Defensive sectors: Ansauville (Lorraine); Cantigny (Picardy). *Killed in action on May 28, 1918; buried, Grave 5, Row 7, Block D, Somme American Cemetery, Bony, Aisne, France.*

SHALLOP, FRED (Vol. IV, pg. 2927)

Army number 2,559,312, registrant, Pierce County, born, Zahler, Syria, march 15, 1891, naturalized citizen, occupation, farmer; inducted at Rugby on March 29, 1918, sent to Camp Dodge, Iowa; served in Machine Gun Company, 139th Infantry, to Nov. 12, 1918, Company G, 139th Infantry, to discharge; overseas from May 2, 1918, to Feb. 9, 1919. Engagements: Offensive: Meuse-Argonne. Defensive sector: Gerardmer (Alsace). Discharged at Fort Snelling, Minn. on June 4, 1919, as a private.

SHIKANY, SHAKER A (Vol. IV, pg. 2942)

Army number 3,142,631, registrant, Williams County, born, Zahlic, Syria, Oct. 16, 1895; naturalized citizen; occupation, clerk; inducted at Watrona County, Wyo. on June 25, 1918, sent to Camp Lewis, Wash., served in 166th Depot Brigade, to Nov. 7, 1918; Machine Gun Training Center, Central officers Training School, Camp Hancock, Ga, to discharge. Grade: corporal, Aug. 7, 1918. Discharged on Dec. 5, 1918, as a corporal.

SHIKANY, WALTER J (Vol. IV, pg. 2942)

Army number 86,312, not a registrant, enlisted prior; born, Rugby, N. Dak. Oct. 1897, of (nationality of parents not given); occupation (not given), enlisted in Company E, 1st Infantry, North Dakota National Guard, at Williston on May 2, 1917; called into federal service, World War, on July 15, 1917; served in Company E, 1st Infantry, North Dakota National Guard (Company E, 164th infantry) to Feb. 14, 1918; 116th Ammunition Train, to Feb. 21, 1918; Headquarters Troop, 1st Army Corps, to May 20, 1918; Headquarters, 102nd Infantry to discharge. Grades: corporal, Aug. 6, 1918; sergeant, Oct. 7, 1918, overseas from Dec. 15, 1917, to April 7, 1919, *wounded slightly, June 14, 1918.* Engagements: Offensives: St. Mihiel, Meuse-Argonne. Defensive sectors: Toul-Baucq, Rupt and Troyan (Lorraine). Discharged on April 25, 1919, as a sergeant. *Surgeons certificate of disability, 10%.*

SINE, KASSAM (Vol. IV, pg. 2968)

Army number 2,162,976; registrant, Cavalier county; born, Tenearah, Syria, June 15, 1895; naturalized citizen; occupation, laborer; inducted at Crookston, Minn., on April 12, 1918; sent to Camp Dodge, Iowa; served in 51st Engineers to June 8, 1918; Company C, 5th Engineers Training Regiment, Camp Humphreys, Va., to Sept. 5, 1918; Provost Guard Company Camp,. Humphreys, Va., to discharge. Discharged at Camp Grant, Ill., on March 25, 1919, as a Private.

TANOUS, THOMAS JOSEPH (Vol. IV, pg. 3187)

Army number 2,759,136, registrant, Adams County; born, Grafton, N. Dak., Sept. 23, 1895, of Syrian parents; occupation, clerk; inducted at Hettinger on July 30, 1918; sent to Syracuse, N.Y., served in chemical warfare service, to discharge. Grade: sergeant 1st class, April 7, 1919; overseas from Sept. 20, 1918, to May 10, 1919. Discharged at Camp Dodge, Iowa, on May 20, 1919, as a sergeant 1st class.

THEOPHILL, GEORGE (Vol. IV, pg. 3205)

Army number 4,705,524; registrant, Bowman county; born, Smyrna, Turkey, march 25, 1891; citizen, alien; occupation, laborer; inducted at Bowman on Aug. 28, 1918; served in Company M, 1st Infantry, to discharge. Discharged on Dec. 9, 1918, as a Private.

THOMAS, MOSES (Vol. IV, pg. 3211)

Army number 2,703,604; registrant, Sioux county; born, Bihwyta, Syria, May 5, 1889; naturalized citizen; occupation, farmer; inducted at Fort Yates on June 23, 1918; sent to Camp Dodge, Iowa; served in Company C, 37th Battalion, US Guards, to discharge. Discharged at Camp Dodge, Iowa, on Jan. 9, 1919, as a Private.

WILSON, ASAD EXPERIENCE (Vol. IV, pg. 3486)

Army number 3,455,413, registrant, Mountrail County; born, Verndale, Minn., June 21, 1895, of American parents; occupation, farmer; inducted at Stanley on Sept. 1, 1918, sent to University of North Dakota; served in Training Detachment, to Oct. 28, 1918; 144th Engineers, to discharge. Discharged at Camp Dodge, Iowa, on Dec. 21, 1918, as a private. Previous military record: North Dakota National Guard, from June 2, 1916, to Feb. 25, 1917, including Mexican border duty.

SEHIRE, ALEX (Vol. IV, pg. 3554)

Army number 2,162,815; registrant, Cass County, born, Damascus, Syria, April 3, 1887; declarant citizen, occupation, laborer, inducted at Fargo, on Dec. 1, 1917; sent to Camp Dodge, Iowa; served in Company L, 352nd Infantry, to March 24, 1918, 395th Engineers, to April 16, 1918; 302nd Trench Motor Battery, to discharge; overseas: from April 25, 1917, to Feb. 12, 1919. Engagements: Offensive: Oisne-Aisne. Defensive sectors: Baccarat (Lorraine); Vesle (Champagne). Discharged at Camp Dodge, Iowa, on March 25, 1919, as a private.

Appendix E

Section I

Name Changes

It was a common practice among new arrivals in the United States to undergo a change from Old Country names to ones that were perceived to be "American." Many families will remind their neighbors that some previous generation of officials—immigration or school—were at fault, perhaps simplifying spellings or even arbitrarily giving the newcomer a new name that was considered more appropriate.

Other influences were also at work. Many individuals whose origins go back to recent immigrant groups can name families who adopted an advantageous "Anglo" name for business purposes. Sometimes the name change may have been brought about to "hide" from outer-group prejudice or from a disreputable Old Country past.

First and last name changes occurred with regularity in the North Dakota Syrian world. That fact is obvious (see the sequences in the Census and Naturalization lists in this Appendix). Yet most Syrian descendants said that North Dakota name changes did not represent an attempt to "hide," rather it was a matter of simplicity. Arabic names did not fall easily from the tongue of German and Scandinavian people, no matter how much good will might be present among the neighbors: George is easier to pronounce than Guirguis; James is easier to remember than Najeeb.

The small town and countryside tendency to impose nicknames on friends and relatives also comes into play. As seen throughout this volume, Tannous became Thomas, Mohammed often became Mike, Shahedeh became Charley.

It frequently happened that early-day Lebanese assigned the first name of the immigrant father to the ensuing American generations as a family surname: the Nicholas family of the Cando, North Dakota area takes its name from Nicholas Ausey, the original settler. The descendants of the Attiyeh family of Ain Arab have in America a variety of names, all tracing from the first name of an Old Country immigrant: Nicola, Nassif, Kellel, Saba, Masad.

Listed below is a sampling of name changes that were evident in the Lebanese North Dakota experience:

Lebanese/Syrian Name	American Name
Yusefibn Ibrahim	Joe Abraham
Ameen Nasseef Fallah	Ameen Nassif
Housein Hassen Jaha	Sam George
Ali Hasen Debaji	Alex Hasen
Mohammad el Sabiyeh	Charley Alley
Anees Tanous	Ernest Thomas
Boutrous Attiyeh	Attas Boutrous
Dibi Niqoula Awad	David Nicola
Hassen al Shaman	Hassen Mohamad
Maroun Hajjar	J. M. Haggar
Gantous Tawfiq	Tony Ghantous
Farah Farouz	Sam Farah
Elias Shawan	James Ellis
Tanous Bounjaim	Thomas George
Mostofa Babecah	Albert Mostafa
Fatima Fayad	Annie Fayette
Atteah Naseeb	Sam Ateah
Nassif Attiyeh	George Nassif
Abdallah Boshara	Joe Albert
Shalhoub Abdnoor	Sam Abdner
Shalhoub Faiz	Nick Shahean
Ibrahim Mousa	Mike Abraham
David Daoud	Dave Hamed
Saman Musa	Simon Moses
Butrous Hadded	Peter Smith
Lateif Shoophio	Sophia Lateif
Subbi Farah	Sam Farah
Naif al Khouri	Jack Khoury
Casseb Abdo	Annie Casseb
Malooly Azar	Esau Maboly
Ali Hadji	Alley Elias
Jabour Alcodray	Ed Jabour
Abdouch Abdnour	Abe Abdnor
Saleem Ayoub	Sam Salem
Effi Mikhail	Sam Mitchell
Assad Tannous	Abe Thomas
Abdullah Faiz	Fred Albert
Saide Haj	Solomon Hodge
Abdullah Najjar	Albert Najar
Kalifa Jumail	Sam Kalifa
Abdoulah Saad	Al Abdullah

Gebron Khounaisser	Phil Gebron
Rafik Mussellan	George Rafik
Isaac Bouhahoub	Jacob Isaac
Latifa Bouhahoub	Latifa Jacob
Najwah Qadisa	Jane Alley
Bashir Aliyah	Tony Bashir

No set of rules can compress all the happenings of the past. Name changes came about in fascinating ways. Here are just a few of the "not so ordinary" family name experieces:

Shahadeh Yusef Jaibot was the Old Country name. Immigration people in New York called the gentleman Charlie Joseph. That name continued through the rest of his life.

Newly arrived, Ibrahim Sheban became "Jim Kallod," a name that was on a peddler's cart when he bought it in Sioux City, Iowa.

In Walsh County, Nassif Freijie arrived at the turn of the century. Norwegian farmers couldn't remember Nassif—they called him Nels. Nassif then began to call himself Nels.

In the Stanley area, Amed Jaha became known as "Brownie George." He accepted the phrase and is still remembered by that American nickname.

Hassen Ali el Kadrey, of Glenfield, got off the boat in New York Harbor. By the time he left the Immigration Offices he was Hassen Eli.

Section II

Name Patterns

Anglicized names: from Arabic but still Islamic. (A Lebanese Christian would rarely give one of the following names to their child.)*

Men's Ideal Names	Women's Names
Muhammad	Fatima
Ahmad	Zeinab
Yahya	Lila
Harun	Isha
Mustapha	Azziza
Haim	Najla
Rodwan	Safaa
Jalal	Amira

Khalil
Kenal
Abdo
Abdullah
Hassan
Hussein
Ikhsan
Sharif
Ghassan
Janal
Ali
Nazeah (others)
Omar
Othmar
Abu Bakr

Ailia
Khadija
Sousan
Svad
Emira
Zehra
Emney

*This list is presented through the courtesy of David Omar
of Cedar Rapids, Iowa.

Section III

Early Lebanese names clearly separate Lebanese and Anglicized
versions.*

Christian Men		Christian Women	
Arabic	**English Version**	**Arabic**	**English Version**
Azar	Arthur	Budrah	Budra
Antonius	Anthony	Morta	Martha
Boulus	Paul	Moran	Mary
Boutrus	Peter	Sorah	Sarah
Dauod	David	Warda	Rose
Elia	Eli		
Gibrail	Gabriel		

* Courtesy: George and Sara Gubash, St. Paul, Minnesota.

Appendix F

Sample of WPA Interview

(A Photographic Reproduction)

```
County:        Williams
Name of Field
Worker:        Roy R. Perman
Address:       Williston, N. Dak.

Name of Informant (Person
interviewed:   Dave Knlil
Place of inter-
view:          724 Fourth Avenue West
Address:       Williston, N. Dak.
```

I was born in Tarbal, Syria, on July 4th, 1880, in what you'd call a village here. We had a good home and lived in the village. My people all farmers; we would all put in crops together, a kind of community farm, and we had to take the stock inevery day to village. Turks would raid our farms and steal everything they could take. So we had to take everything home with us at night. There was schools and churches but I did not go to church very often, and only went to school very little. Did not learn much in old country.

I worked on farm all time, wages very low, nothing like here. Everything was cheap there and one dollar would buy a pile of stuff. Groceries and clothing awful cheap. Government taxes were all we paid and the government would take ten per cent of crops for taxes. No crop, no taxes. I think it good way. One hundred bushel crop, ten bushel tax. We use horses and cattle for farming, but did a lot of it by hand. No labor organizations.

We had lots of dances but they were in the homes. Went from house to house, one house one time, another house another time. No dance halls like here. Sure did have good times. Everybody happy. When there was a wedding we celebrated for a week, if they could afford it - depended on how much money they had. Everybody drinking liquor, all kinds, mostly arrac, and everything to eat.

The Turks got so mean stealing everything and caused so much trouble, I wanted to leave there. Heard of the United States and there were Syrians in Boston, Massachusetts, and in New York that I knew, so I had money enough of my own to pay my fare. So got on boat at Beyrouth, Syria, and went to France. Seven days from Syria to France. I paid for a first-class ticket from France to New York. That was November, 1899. They put us on an old German freighter boat. Sure was dirty. Did not like it after paying first-class fare. We had lots of storms and bad weather;took us twenty-four days from France to New York. Did not have a good time on boat. Got in New York, along December some time. It looked pretty good, but I got lonesome and did not know what to do; wanted to go back right away. I got a job in factory while in New York and

(1)

then went to Massachusetts and got a job in brickyard in Boston.-
piece work. Had an awful rough trip in boat to Boston from New
York. Boat went up and down and up and down all the time, worse
as when I come across ocean. Made fifteen dollars a week, worked
there until I saved one thousand dollars. Think it was in 1902
of 3, I went to Duluth and started a small store. Did not run this
store very long until I went broke - too much credit. Owed the
wholesale house for goods and told him he had to give me job so I
could pay him what I owed. He gave me job; I still could not talk
hardly any English although I learned some when I was in store. I
couldn't read and when I was unloading box-cars I would see picture
of tomatoes on box and then would try and spell it out - did not
make mistake. Lucky, I guess. I studied nights after work and that
is how I learned English.

I have worked in factory, brick-yard, wholesale-house, run
stores and farmed since I came here to this country. I heard of
homesteads in North Dakota and there was some Syrians had homesteaded here before, so left Duluth and filed on land in 1903,
northwest of Williston. Went back to Duluth and worked a while.
I had a letter written to land office here at Williston and they
told me land was still here, so I came here and went out on homestead in 1904, I think so. Broke up all my homestead with horses
and proved up, raised quite a few horses and cattle and had good
crop.

In 1908 I moved in to Williston and started a small store.
I had good neighbors on homestead and lots of 'em. Had good time,
plenty to eat and wear; got along fine. Lots of dances and parties
too. After 1908 I didn't farm myself, but rented farm and bought
another section of land by homestead. Rented farm until 1925 or
1926 when my son who stays at home and through high school started
to farm with me, that is he looks after it and works it. I haven't
used horses but tractor since my son and I started to farm this time.
We have been farming from seven hundred to one thousand acres, but
since 1928 have been spending money. No crop, no price, drouth and
grasshoppers, always something wrong. In 1937 best prospects for
crop ever had, wheat five feet high all headed out. In two days,
nothing; grasshoppers took most of it, only got 2400 bushel off all
the land. Best income was wheat and cattle when conditions were
good. I spent all the money I had, borrowed money at the bank, and
lost it all since the drouth started.

I never complied with the A A A but am very sorry now that I
didn't. I would have been three thousand dollars better off in the
last two years. I think it good thing. Children has always had
enough to eat and wear and depression has not hurt their schooling
any. I think the dams are a good thing and like to see them build
more. The irrigation is fine on the bottom land if they can get a
price and market for their crops. I have never received any grants
or had any W P A work. Do not know much about F S A but do not see

how people could get along without government aid of some kind.
Wouldn't be much business if they didn't have it in this part of
North Dakota, no gardens, no crops, nothing. I don't see how I'm
going to even pay taxes, wouldn't know how to better conditions.

Wife was born in Syria. The children are Wilbur, age 31, farms
and works in pool-room winter time; Rosalie, age 29, works in office
in Montgomery Ward's store; Edward, age 28, lives in California,
office work; Sam, age 26, stays at home, works State Highway Department part time; Adele, age 24, at home; Leona, age 20, California going to school; Marian, age twelve, at home going to school;
and Charles, he's age ten and at home going to school. They all went
through high school but Adele. We talked Syrian at home till the
children went to school; Edward and Wilbur can talk Syrian, but the
others don't know anything but English. I take the Al Hada, a Syrian
paper published in New York, and the Williston Herald and Farmers
Press. We still prepare some of our foods like we did in Syria.

I don't know whether America should have entered the first war
or not. I lost $175.00 in the Williams County State Bank; got ten
per cent back, one payment. I think this war in Europe is awful,
and it wouldn't surprise me if the United States didn't get into it
yet. I hope they don't. There is no comparison between this country
and Syria, at least when I come over anyway. Turks grabbing everything. I would still come over to this country if I had it to do over
again. It will come back some time and I'll hit it yet farming.

- - -

Appendix G

Interviews: Federal Writers Projects for North Dakota

(Works Project Administration)

Mike Abdallah, Ross, ND, December 1939

Side Abdallah, Ross, ND, 1939 (?)

Joseph Abraham, Williston, ND, August 1940

Annie Aboud, Williston, ND, December 1939

Joe Albert, Williston, ND, February 16, 19, 1l, 1940

Joseph Azar, Bismarck, ND, August 10,11, 14, 1939

George Bittus, Bismarck, ND, April 18,1939

Attas Boutrous, Bismarck, ND, July 28,1939

Boaley Farhart, Ross, ND, October 31, November 1, 3, 1939

Mary Farris, Williston, ND, January 15, 1940

Joe Hiawatha, Rock Lake, ND, October 4, 1936

Mrs. Charles Juma, Ross, ND, 1939 (?)

Hassyn Alla Juma, Ross, ND, October 12, 1939

Dave Kalil, Williston, ND, January 1940

Mrs. David Kalil, Williston, ND, August 8, 19, 1940

John Kassis,Williston, ND, January 1940

Mrs. Libbie Layon,Williston, ND, March 26, 1940

Abe Mikel, Williston, ND, January 1940

Jabour John Munyer, Williston, ND, February 1940

Joseph Munyer, Williston, ND, February 2, 1940

Louie Nassif, Bismarck, ND, August 16-18, 1939

Thomas Nassif, Bismarck, ND, August 1, 3, 1939

Edward Nedoff, Williston, ND, January 1940

Samuel Nicola, (?), July 25-26, 1939

Mrs. George Nicola, Bismarck, ND, July 21, 1939

Allay Omar, Ross, ND, 1939 (?)

Sam Omar, Ross, ND, October 3, 1939

Kassam Rameden, Lignite, ND, October 23, 26, 27, 1939

George Saba, Bismarck, ND, July 24-25, 1939

Mrs. Mary Saliba, Bismarck, ND, August 4, 1939

Joe Salmon, Bismarck, ND, August 23, 1939

Joe Seeb, Williston, ND, April 1, 1940

Deeby Sine, Williston, ND, December 1939

Mrs. Joe Tanous, Bismarck, 1939

Mrs. Barbara Wizer, Williston, ND, February 1940

TOTAL: 35 interviews

Donors

The publication of this book was assisted by the generosity of heritage-minded men and women who responded to an appeal for financial support. The authors gratefully list their names below.

Donors

Attas Boutrous

Anonymous

Phil and Mary Deraney

Dan Kalil - Kalil Farms

Nathan and Briana Nassif

Mary Nassif

John and Mary Noah

Donors	In Memory Of
Betty Absey	Bob Absey
Darlain Atol	Raymond Atol, Husband
Shirley L. Foien	Abdo Kadry
Robert and Diane A. Fritel	James Abram Shalala
Irene Kadry	Abdo Kadry
Deborah Absey Kauffman	Ed Absey
Thomas and Loretta Kennedy	Joe Nicholas
Ronald and Frieda Ayad Hasen	Parents
Gene and Connie Nicholas	Nicholas Family Members
Isabel Owan	George Owan
Vemon Owan, V.O. Inc.	Owan Family Members
Charles and Rose Owan	Owan Family Members
Maureen R. Lee-Robinson	Charles and Rose Owan, *"You inspired the generations that followed"*
Floyd and Hazel Starr	Mary and Nicholas Ausey

Index